# DIMENSIONS
# OF PERSONALITY

# DIMENSIONS
# OF PERSONALITY

by H. J. EYSENCK, Ph.D. (London)

DIRECTOR, PSYCHOLOGICAL DEPARTMENT, INSTITUTE OF PSYCHIATRY.
SENIOR PSYCHOLOGIST, THE MAUDSLEY HOSPITAL

*A Record of Research carried out
in collaboration with*

*H. T. HIMMELWEIT, M.A. (Cantab.), Ph.D. (London)*
*W. LINFORD REES, M.D., B.Sc., M.R.C.P., D.P.M.*

*and with the help of*

*M. DESAI, Ph.D., W. D. FURNEAUX, A.I.P.*
*H. HALSTEAD, M.A., O. MARUM, D.Phil.,*
*M. McKINLAY, M.A., Ed.B., A. PETRIE, B.Sc.,*
*P. M. YAP, B.A., M.B.*

*With a Foreword by*
*PROFESSOR AUBREY LEWIS, M.D., F.R.C.P.*

LONDON
ROUTLEDGE & KEGAN PAUL LIMITED
BROADWAY HOUSE: 68–74 CARTER LANE, E.C.4

*First published* 1947
*Second impression* 1948

TO

# MARGARET

WHO HELPED

THIS BOOK IS PRODUCED IN COMPLETE
CONFORMITY WITH THE AUTHORIZED
ECONOMY STANDARDS

PRINTED IN GREAT BRITAIN BY
LUND HUMPHRIES'
LONDON · BRADFORD

# TABLE OF CONTENTS

# CONTENTS

# FOREWORD

PERSONALITY is so cardinal a matter in psychiatry, that any ambiguity in the concept or uncertainty about how to describe and measure the qualities it stands for, must weaken the whole structure of psychiatry, theoretical and clinical. This is nowhere more insistently brought to the attention of the psychiatrist than in a wartime neurosis centre where so many of the patients come with symptoms that are, very plainly, traits writ large. Dr. Eysenck and his collaborators have turned to fruitful purpose the opportunities such a place affords for studying some of the main dimensions of personality.

Psychiatrists, concerned to understand their patient rather than to measure him, are disposed to look askance at methods which could seem to them atomistic, aridly statistical, and untrue to the dynamic influences which mould and determine human individuality. It is, however, precisely in its methods that the research described in this book may be found to contribute most to the psychology of personality, and consequently to the theory and ultimately to the practice, of psychiatry. These methods are neither atomistic nor static, but aim at the analysis, by reliable statistical techniques, of experimental and clinical data, so that measurement may be possible and a sight obtained of the promised land where mental organisation will be as well understood as the physical organisation of human beings now is.

It would be wrong to judge the value of such research as this, by seeing how readily its results can be applied to clinical practice: but Dr. Eysenck has shown in this book that they can be, and it has become very plain to those associated with the studies that the collaboration between psychologist and psychiatrist implicit in them works, even on a short view, to the manifest profit of both fields of knowledge.

AUBREY LEWIS.
*Professor of Psychiatry,*
*University of London.*

# INTRODUCTION

THE work here presented is the result of a concentrated and co-operative effort to discover the main dimensions of personality, and to define them operationally, i.e. by means of strictly experimental, quantitative procedures. More than three dozen separate researches were carried out on altogether some 10,000 normal and neurotic subjects by a research team of psychologists and psychiatrists. Such success as we may have achieved is in large measure due to their unselfish help and co-operative attitude; for such faults as remain, the author must take full responsibility.

A number of the studies here reviewed have already appeared in print, and are referred to in the appropriate place. This fact has made it possible to avoid the minute description of many experimental and statistical details of the experiments, which the interested reader can find in the various research papers and articles, and to stress rather the broad lines of the picture which emerges from our work. In spite of this fact, it has not been possible to eliminate all technical and statistical discussion from these pages; the reader whose interest lies mainly in the results and not in the methods will find little difficulty in omitting the offending pages.

Little novelty is claimed for most of the experimental procedures adopted, or the theories advanced. In my view, the time has come when the preliminary surveys of isolated traits, and the exploratory studies of small groups, must give way to work planned on an altogether larger scale; while small-scale exploratory studies will, of course, always retain their value in opening up new fields, such exploration must ultimately lead to consolidation if its full fruits are to be reaped. Similarly, while the large number of theories which has emerged in the past few decades has done much to stimulate interest in the scientific study of temperament and personality, these theories have been so divorced in the main from operational definition and experimental control that simplification and ruthless discarding appeared more necessary than an attempt to add to the confusion.

No claim is made that we have been able to do more than advance a very small distance toward the goal which we set ourselves. The more obvious objections to, and criticisms of our methods and results, are discussed in the body of the book; in spite of them, we believe that essentially our main conclusions are valid. In this belief we are encouraged particularly by the amount of agreement which became obvious, as our work advanced, between our results and those of other investigators. Such unanimity among students working with subjects normal and neurotic, young and old, male and female, student and non-academic, is truly encouraging to those who believe that it is possible to build up a strictly empirical science of personality.

One special feature of our work has been the close collaboration between psychologists and psychiatrists. I firmly believe that the exploration of personality would have reached a more advanced state if such collaboration had been the rule rather than the exception, and that both disciplines would have benefited by working together on the many problems which they have in common. It is my hope that this book will be read by both psychologists and psychiatrists, and for this reason I have at times explained at length for the psychological reader matters which will be obvious to the psychiatrist, and for the psychiatrist matters which the psychologist will take for granted. The necessity of having to resort to such an expedient illustrates the great gulf still existing between the two disciplines.

In concluding this Introduction, I am glad of the opportunity to thank all those whose efforts made this work possible. The Rockefeller Foundation, by their generous grants to the Hospital,[1] afforded a firm basis for our work. The Hospital authorities, particularly Dr. W. S. Maclay, O.B.E., and Dr. A. B. Stokes, did everything in their power to further our efforts. The psychiatrists employed at the Hospital helped us in every conceivable way, never grudging the time for selecting patients to our specifications. The Assistant Matron, Miss Goodyear, gave invaluable help in dealing with the voluminous hospital records, and in arranging for group tests. Mr. J. C. Raven allowed us to use his standardization data for the Matrices Test, and to reproduce in this book parts of his Matrices Test and of the Mill Hill Vocabulary Test. Dr. M. Jones and Dr. D. Richter kindly consented to an inclusion

---

[1] The work described in this book was carried out at the Mill Hill Emergency Hospital, which, together with Sutton Emergency Hospital, was the war-time transformation of the Maudsley Hospital.

of an account of their work on effort response and choline esterase secretion in this book.

Many authorities outside Mill Hill Emergency Hospital contributed to the success of our work, whether by permitting us to test normal groups, or by furnishing us with test material otherwise unobtainable. I am particularly indebted to the Army authorities, mainly to Lt.-Col. E. Trist and to Chief Commander E. Mercer; to the Kodak Research Dept.; and to the G. E. C. works.

Dr. P. E. Vernon read through the whole book, and his comments and criticisms were of great value.

Permission to reproduce Figures and Tables was kindly granted by the *British Journal of Psychology*, the *British Journal of Medical Psychology*, the *Journal of General Psychology*, the *Journal of Mental Science*, the *Journal of Experimental Psychology*, and the *Psychological Bulletin*.

Lastly, I wish to make grateful acknowledgment of the heavy debt I owe to two of my teachers. I am indebted to Professor Sir Cyril Burt for the inspiration of his teaching and his writings, and for having taught me that statistics is an invaluable servant, but a bad master. I am equally indebted to Professor A. Lewis for showing me how a severely critical attitude of mind can be combined with the enthusiasm so indispensable in research work.

H. J. EYSENCK.

Psychological Department,
The Maudsley Hospital.

# CHAPTER ONE

# METHODS AND DEFINITIONS

## 1. INTRODUCTION

WRITING in 1943, Henderson and Gillespie pointed out that "if it is doubtful what we measure with 'intelligence' tests, it is still more uncertain what we would try to measure if we tackled 'emotions' in a similar way". An effort is made in this book to discover the main dimensions along which such "measurement of the emotions" can take place, and to provide experimental evidence of the feasibility of such measurement.

In planning the series of researches which are summarized here, we have tried to combine two fields of psychological work which in the past have unfortunately been kept separate to a large extent. On the one hand, there exist large numbers of factorial studies of personality questionnaires and ratings; on the other, there are many experimental studies of isolated segments of behaviour. Little attempt has been made to fit these experimental determinations of a person's persistence, suggestibility, sense of humour, level of aspiration, perseveration, personal tempo, rigidity, or irritability into a consistent conceptual scheme, a scheme which can be elaborated, in the present state of our knowledge, only by factorial studies of the type mentioned.

In effecting such a combination of two rather distinct fields of research, we may hope to overcome restrictions and difficulties associated with either of these fields separately. The main drawback of the statistical treatment of questionnaires and ratings has always been the stigma of subjectivity which inevitably adheres to procedures which involve the attribution of personality qualities to oneself or to others on the basis of uncontrolled observation. The main drawback of the experimental approach has always been the fact that such work is almost inevitably restricted to such a small segment of personality that the results became subject to the charge of "atomism" (Allport, 1937). The combination of the two approaches here suggested reduces the dangers of subjectivity by closely associating ratings with experimental checks on their validity, and equally reduces the dangers of atomism by fitting each experimental result into the pattern of the whole personality. Such, at least, was the underlying theory on which the present series of researches was planned; how far we have been able to translate this theory into effect it must be left to the reader to decide.

## 2. THE EXPERIMENTAL POPULATION

In view of the fact that experimental data, strictly speaking, are valid only for the population from which the samples tested were originally drawn, a short description of the type of case referred to Mill Hill Emergency Hospital may not be out of order. These patients are admitted to the hospital on a psychiatrist's recommendation, and present a mainly neurotic symptomatology of a rather monotonous character. Few examples of psychotics, mental defectives, or the physically ill are encountered; those admitted usually show some admixture of neurotic symptoms. The symptoms encountered in the majority of patients have been described by Slater (1943) as follows:

"In general the 'neurosis' exhibited was not so much an illness as a simple failure to adapt to army routine and discipline, in part an incapacity to adapt, and a response to this incapacity. Whether ill or not, the commonest symptoms were those of anxiety, hysteria, depression, hypochondriasis, etc., and tended to be shown by members of all diagnostic groups. The causes of breakdown were of the same uniform character: separation from home and family, home worries, a life of relative hardship, army discipline, the pressure of tasks physically, intellectually or temperamentally beyond them. Only in a minority of patients were the more violent stresses of war the main precipitating factor. . . .

"The monotonous character of precipitating cause and clinical picture was mirrored by a monotonous uniformity of the underlying personality. There were few who did not show to some degree a psychic asthenia, a feebleness of will and purpose, coupled with tendencies to worry, pessimism and moodiness or hysterical traits. This was indeed the fundamental disability, and indications had been shown in childhood and adult life. When one considers the large number of men who have had to be invalided for such conditions as these, one is impressed with the size of the problem."

A more detailed picture of the hospital population may be gained by reference to the "Item Sheet" prepared for each patient. On this sheet, the psychiatrist in charge recorded certain data regarding the patient's family history, personal history, personality, his symptoms, aetiology, diagnosis and treatment, disposal, and various social data. The data in most cases were recorded dichotomously, and transferred to punched cards, for statistical analysis. A selection of items used is given below, together with percentage occurrence of the particular item for 5,300 male and 2,000 female service patients separately. Each item is set out in full below; when reference to any item in the Item Sheet is made in the text, such reference will be in an abbreviated form, sufficient to make possible consultation of the full text by reference back to this section. Some of the items are reworded slightly, in order to make them intelligible to the reader not familiar with the official military terminology. In certain cases, where the percentages might have been expected to add up to 100, overlapping of symptoms, multiple diagnosis and similar causes account for the fact that totals may not give that figure.

### ITEM SHEET

| Social Data | | | | | | | M% | F% |
|---|---|---|---|---|---|---|---|---|
| Service occupation—skilled | . | . | . | . | . | . | 26 | 47 |
| unskilled | . | . | . | . | . | . | 74 | 53 |
| | | | | | | | | |
| Duration of service—less than 1 year | . | . | : | . | . | 14 | 24 |
| 1 to 3 years | . | . | . | . | . | 49 | 63 |
| more than 3 years | . | . | . | . | 37 | 13 |
| | | | | | | | | |
| Rank—N.C.O. | . | . | . | . | . | . | . | 14 | 15 |
| otherwise | . | . | . | . | . | . | . | 86 | 85 |
| | | | | | | | | |
| Discharged from the service | . | . | . | . | . | . | 54 | 50 |

ITEM SHEET—*continued.*

*Social Data—continued*           M%  F%

| | M% | F% |
|---|---|---|
| Modal civilian occupation—unskilled . . . . | 40 | 48 |
| semi-skilled . . . . | 35 | 31 |
| skilled . . . . . | 20 | 13 |
| admin. or profess. . . . | 5 | 0 |
| Unemployment—none . . . . . . . | 61 | 59 |
| little . . . . . . . | 21 | 17 |
| much . . . . . . . | 18 | 16 |
| Work-history—degraded or unduly frequent changes of occupation . . . . . . | 7 | 4 |

*Family History*

| | M% | F% |
|---|---|---|
| Abnormality in parents or siblings— | | |
| none . . . . . . . . . | 39 | 45 |
| psychosis . . . . . . . . . | 6 | 4 |
| epilepsy . . . . . . . . . | 2 | 1 |
| mental deficiency . . . . . . . . | 1 | 1 |
| neurosis or psychopathic personality: pronounced . . | 34 | 30 |
| slight . . | 18 | 20 |
| Father or brothers rejected or discharged from Services on medical grounds . . . . . . . . | 13 | 9 |
| Patient's symptoms described as resembling those of parents or siblings . . . . . . . . . | 24 | 15 |

*Personal History*

| | M% | F% |
|---|---|---|
| Upbringing by both parents until age of 10 . . . | 90 | 84 |
| Home atmosphere during childhood and adolescence satisfactory . . . . . . . . . | 71 | 70 |
| Education—elementary poor (St. 5 or under) . . . | 23 | 8 |
| elementary good . . . . . . | 62 | 59 |
| secondary or central . . . . . | 12 | 31 |
| higher . . . . . . . . | 3 | 2 |
| Civil state—married . . . . . . | 64 | 20 |
| engaged . . . . . . . . | 3 | 18 |
| single . . . . . . . . | 29 | 53 |
| widower or separated . . . . . | 1 | 3 |
| complicated . . . . . . . | 3 | 6 |
| Sexual activity apparently—normal or unknown . . . | 76 | 56 |
| inhibited or unwanted . . | 13 | 25 |
| subject of worry . . . | 10 | 18 |
| perverse . . . . . | 1 | 2 |
| Hobbies and interests—broad . . . . . . | 24 | 37 |
| Alcohol—teetotal or abstemious . . . . . | 48 | 74 |
| moderate . . . . . . . | 48 | 24 |
| excessive . . . . . . . . | 4 | 2 |

*Personal History—continued.*

|  | M% | F% |
|---|---|---|
| Past physical health—good . . . . . . | 55 | 66 |
| medium . . . . . . | 41 | 28 |
| bad . . . . . . | 5 | 6 |
| Epilepsy . . . . . . . . . | 1 | 0 |
| Head injury—mild, not part of present illness . . . | 7 | 2 |
| severe, not part of present illness . . . | 2 | 0 |
| mild or severe, part of present illness . . | 7 | 3 |
| Previous organic disease of nervous system, other than head injury or epilepsy . . . . . . . . | 2 | 3 |
| Other physical disease relevant to present symptoms . . | 10 | 7 |
| Mental health before present illness— | | |
| normal . . . . . . . . . . | 35 | 33 |
| symptoms in childhood . . . . . . | 46 | 46 |
| symptoms and behaviour in adult life indicating clear predisposition . . . . . . . | 41 | 39 |
| definite illness . . . . . . . . | 10 | 16 |

*Personality*

|  | M% | F% |
|---|---|---|
| Unstable, ill-adjusted . . . . . . . | 56 | 57 |
| Weak, dependent, timorous—somewhat . . . . | 38 | 38 |
| very . . . . . | 16 | 16 |
| Delinquent . . . . . . . . . | 6 | 3 |
| Drive and energy—inert without initiative . . . . | 27 | 20 |
| average go . . . . | 67 | 73 |
| conspicuous energy . . . . | 6 | 7 |
| Rebellious or aggressive—somewhat . . . . . | 15 | 22 |
| very . . . . . . | 3 | 5 |
| Touchy or suspicious—somewhat . . . . . | 25 | 32 |
| very . . . . . . | 3 | 5 |
| Cyclothymic or consistently depressive or hypomanic— | | |
| somewhat . . . . . . . . . | 31 | 24 |
| very. . . . . . . . . . | 3 | 6 |
| Schizoid, seclusive—somewhat . . . . . . | 32 | 23 |
| very . . . . . . . | 6 | 6 |
| Hysterical, seeking limelight, exaggerating—somewhat . | 18 | 25 |
| very . . . | 6 | 7 |
| Anxious, highly strung—somewhat . . . . . | 53 | 55 |
| very . . . . . . | 10 | 14 |

B

| Personality—*continued.* | M% | F% |
|---|---|---|
| Hypochondriacal—somewhat | 25 | 19 |
|        very | 3 | 4 |
| "Obsessional," meticulous—somewhat | 18 | 25 |
|        very | 2 | 4 |

*History of present illness*

| | M% | F% |
|---|---|---|
| Duration of illness since onset—less than 1 month | 1 | 3 |
|      1 to 3 months | 5 | 16 |
|      3 to 6 months | 10 | 23 |
|      6 to 12 months | 16 | 24 |
|      more than 1 year | 67 | 33 |
| Onset of illness—sudden | 18 | 26 |
|      prodromata and then acute | 6 | 13 |
|      gradual | 77 | 66 |
| Exposure to enemy attack at any time in this war— | | |
|      slight or none | 60 | 70 |
|      medium | 20 | 24 |
|      severe | 20 | 6 |

*Symptoms and findings*

| | M% | F% |
|---|---|---|
| Somatic anxiety (palpitations, dyspnoea, precordial discomfort, sweat, flushing, diarrhoea) | 46 | 28 |
| Headache—mild | 43 | 44 |
|      severe | 16 | 13 |
| Fatigue, lassitude, effort intolerance | 51 | 54 |
| Dyspepsia, vomiting | 14 | 12 |
| Fainting, fits | 13 | 14 |
| Pain—not of demonstrable organic origin and excluding headache | 25 | 16 |
| Tremor | 27 | 17 |
| Stammer | 8 | 3 |
| Enuresis | 4 | 2 |
| Sexual anomalies (impotence, ejac. praecox, masturbation worries, homosexuality, other) | 13 | 11 |
| Anxiety—mild | 40 | 38 |
|      moderate | 33 | 36 |
|      severe | 8 | 6 |
| Depression—mild | 38 | 45 |
|      moderate | 21 | 26 |
|      severe | 4 | 3 |

## ITEM SHEET—*continued.*

| Symptons and findings—continued | M% | F% |
|---|---|---|
| Suicidal—thoughts | 10 | 10 |
| attempts | 1 | 3 |
| Paranoid | 6 | 5 |
| Elation | 1 | 1 |
| Irritability | 33 | 37 |
| Apathy, retardation | 18 | 21 |
| Hypochondriacal—mild | 22 | 20 |
| moderate | 11 | 10 |
| severe | 2 | 2 |
| Depersonalization | 1 | 2 |
| Hysterical attitude to symptoms | 36 | 43 |
| Hysterical conversion symptoms—motor | 9 | 10 |
| sensory | 17 | 13 |
| special senses | 2 | 1 |
| visceral and other | 8 | 11 |
| none | 70 | 69 |
| Dissociative-dysmnesic hysterical symptoms | 7 | 6 |
| Obsessive-compulsive symptoms | 5 | 5 |
| Delusions | 1 | 2 |
| Hallucinations | 1 | 1 |
| Schizophrenic symptoms—mild | 2 | 2 |
| severe | 0 | 1 |
| Muscular tone and posture—good | 36 | 38 |
| average | 52 | 52 |
| poor | 12 | 10 |
| Loss of weight—more than ½ stone | 14 | 7 |
| Definite physical signs of organic disease of nervous system | 2 | 1 |
| Definite physical or other organic disease, not trivial | 8 | 5 |
| Intellectual impairment, deterioration, dementia— | | |
| mild | 2 | 1 |
| moderate | 0 | 0 |
| severe | 0 | 0 |

ITEM SHEET—*continued.*

| *Aetiology* | M% | F% |
|---|---|---|
| Physical causes—precipitating | 17 | 17 |
|     unimportant | 72 | 73 |
|     important | 10 | 8 |
|     dominant | 2 | 2 |
| Psychological causes—precipitating | 13 | 4 |
|     unimportant | 5 | 5 |
|     important | 42 | 25 |
|     dominant | 53 | 68 |
| Among chief psychological causes— | | |
|   stress of bombardment or exposure | 20 | 5 |
|   stress of wartime separation and regimentation | 58 | 52 |
|   stress of unsuitable work | 28 | 24 |
|   stress of domestic problems | 27 | 40 |

| *Diagnosis* | | |
|---|---|---|
| Anxiety—acute severe | 7 | 5 |
|     acute mild | 16 | 16 |
|     chronic | 36 | 23 |
| Hysteria—conversion type | 21 | 24 |
|     dysmnesic type | 4 | 4 |
| Psychopathic personality—with antisocial trends | | |
|     with sex abnormality | 11 | 12 |
|     with emotional instability | | |
| Depressive, or other affective, state—reactive in the main | 18 | 24 |
|     mainly endogenous | 3 | 4 |
| Obsessional state | 2 | 2 |
| Mental deficiency | 1 | 0 |
| Organic mental syndrome | 1 | 1 |
| Physical disease not included under organic mental syndrome | 5 | 4 |

| *Treatment* | | |
|---|---|---|
| Systematic psychological— | | |
|   hypnosis and/or intravenous barbiturate | 8 | 5 |
|   discussion and re-education | 93 | 83 |
|   analytical type of procedure | 1 | 1 |
| Systematic physical—insulin | 3 | 3 |
|     continuous narcosis | 1 | 1 |
|     other | 12 | 5 |

These figures must not be taken as correct in any absolute sense. Quite clearly, individual psychiatrists will differ in the standards behind their ratings; also, it is inevitable that the interpretation of the terms used (anxiety, reactive depression etc.), will vary from psychiatrist to psychiatrist. Efforts were made to establish certain usages through staff conferences, but it is impossible to measure the success of the meetings in ensuring agreement. Analysis of the percentages in the various categories by successive 200 admissions shows little change through the years, except on such items as "duration of service"; this finding may reflect the maintenance of a roughly similar standard of rating, and a fair similarity in the populations rated. In Figure 1 are given percentages for successive groups of 200 male patients of the incidence of five selected items; these may serve to illustrate the relative stability of the human material entering the hospital.

A comparison of the male and the female groups studied reveals little difference between them with respect to the type of disorder manifested. It would appear, however, that on

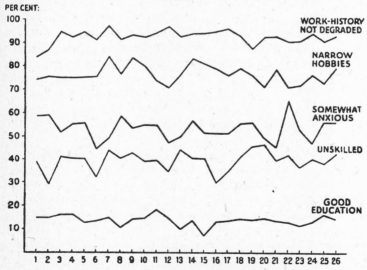

FIG. 1. INCIDENCE OF 5 ITEMS IN 26 SUCCESSIVE SAMPLES OF 200 NEUROTICS.

the whole the women suffer from less serious disorders, and are quite generally a group characterized by better personality, better heredity, and better background, than are the men. This is shown by the fact that more of them have skilled service occupation, that they show less abnormality in parents or sibs, a smaller percentage of their relatives is rejected from the Services on medical grounds, their education is considerably better, they have broad hobbies and interests more frequently, they drink less, their past physical health is rated as better, the history of their present illness is shorter, the onset more sudden, and autonomic disorders much less frequent. They also show less loss of weight, and the incidence of organic diseases of various kinds, of head injuries, and of epilepsy is smaller. In addition, it will be shown later that both with respect to intelligence and to vocabulary the women are superior to the men. These considerations lead us to believe that in this hospital the women referred for neurotic disorders are better human material than are the men referred for the same reason; experimental evidence for this belief will be given later. The reason for the sex-difference is probably to be found in the selection process which precedes entry into the A.T.S. and the other female services; no similar selection process screens out the less intelligent and the less stable male army recruits. In addition, a much larger percentage of women entered the services voluntarily as compared to the men; presumably, it is the better type of girl who puts herself at the service of her country without waiting to be conscripted.

## 3. THEORIES OF TEMPERAMENT

The individual hypotheses and theories which we have investigated will be described in the appropriate place; there is one theory, however, which demands at least a short description here because it is more fundamental than the others, and because it lies, as it were, at the root of most of our work. This is the famous dichotomic type theory of temperament which has given rise to so much speculation and to so many efforts at experimental validation that it is perhaps the most universally known psychological theory in the field of personality study, as well as the most widely accepted.

In its modern form, this theory may perhaps be said to stem from Kraepelin (1899), who contrasted the *manic depressive*

*The error of dichotomous theories on level of high order abstractions* psychoses on the one hand with the *dementia praecox* types on the other, thus establishing a fundamental dichotomy in the field of the functional psychoses. Bleuler's (1924) modification in changing the *dementia praecox* concept to the more inclusive one of *schizophrenia* did nothing to weaken the fundamental dichotomy, and Kretschmer's (1926) work, which extended the dichotomy to the near-psychotic and the normal as well, and which argued in favour of a close correlation between body-build and temperament, considerably widened the field covered by this theory. As regards the psychoses at least, the fundamental distinction between *schizophrenic* and *manic-depressive* illness is widely accepted among psychiatrists of all persuasions.

Janet (1894, 1903) established a similar dichotomy in the field of the neuroses, where he distinguished between *hysteria* on the one hand, and *psychasthenia* on the other. Jung (1909, 1923), who had at first advanced the concept of introversion to account for the personality of the schizophrene, accepted Janet's view and made the hysteric and the psychasthenic the prototypes of his extraverted and his introverted personality types respectively. Inevitably, this led him to postulate an "essential relationship" between *psychasthenia* and *schizophrenia*, thus linking up the psychotic typology with the neurotic. McDougall (1926) took over the Jungian dichotomy, and maintained that "there are . . . two great categories of disorder under one or other of which we may attempt to place many of the cases, though without confidence in respect to many of them. . . . These two categories are the dissociative or the hysteric class, on the one hand; the neurasthenic or anxiety class, on the other. The liability to disorder of one or other of these two great types seems to be a matter mainly of innate constitution; persons of the extravert temperament seem more liable, under strain, to disorders of the hysteric or dissociative type; those of introvert . . . temperament to disorders of the neurasthenic type."

While the terms "*psychasthenic*" and "*neurasthenic*" are now obsolescent, the theories associated with them are very far from being so. Attempts have been made ever since the original conceptions were advanced to find psychological correlates of the two main temperamental types. Thus for instance Janet (1894) and Babinski (1918), as well as later writers, believed in a close relationship between hysteria and suggestibility; Scholl

(1927) and Lindberg (1938) believed that the cyclothyme was colour-reactive, while the schizothyme was form-reactive; Spearman (1927) believed that the introvert was perseverative, while the extravert was non-perseverative; Jaensch (1926, 1930) believed that the two types were distinguished by special types of eidetic imagery; and so on. Few of these views have stood the test, but nevertheless they still influence psychological thinking to a considerable extent.

The relation between the various views already mentioned, as well as some others which appeared important, are presented in the form of a synoptic table below. It is not maintained that all the traits, disorders, and attitudes presented on one side of the dividing line correlate together positively, while correlating negatively with the traits, disorders, and attitudes on the other side of the line. Nor is it maintained that any one person has ever held a theory maintaining that such a relation existed. Implicitly, many investigators do hold a belief which is roughly represented by this table, and the influence this belief has had on psychological thought is very great. As MacKinnon (1944), who presents a Table in many ways similar to our own, has pointed out, "types are crude pictures of personality. That is why they are so easily drawn, why they invariably overlap, and why such a scheme of interrelationships as pictured in Table 1 is so easily developed and yet so difficult to prove or disprove, for only that which is precisely stated can be definitely tested. To be sure, many of the relationships assumed to exist among the dichotomous typologies have been investigated both clinically and experimentally, but with little success so far. For the most part these studies have been made by partisan investigators; the details of experimental procedure have not been clear; the bases of selection of subjects, extremely important in studies of this sort, have not been specified; and the statistical treatment of results demanded by the very nature of these investigations has been lacking. The problem of the relationships among the various dichotomous typologies remains a problem."

As representative of the difficulties which arise, we may take the following passage from Henderson and Gillespie's (1943) textbook: "In schizophrenia it is found that in a strikingly large percentage the personality that existed before the disease occurred or was recognised was of the so-called 'shut-in' type. . . . This

| PSYCHOTIC TYPES | | | AUTHOR |
|---|---|---|---|
| Manic-depressive | vs. | Dementia Praecox | Kraepelin (1899) |
| Syntonic | vs. | Schizophrenic | Bleuler (1924) |

| NEUROTIC TYPES | | | |
|---|---|---|---|
| Hysteric | vs. | Psychasthenic | Janet (1894) |
| Hysteric | vs. | Neurasthenic | McDougall (1926) |

| PERSONALITY TYPES | | | |
|---|---|---|---|
| Extraverted | vs. | Introverted | Jung (1923) |
| Objective | vs. | Subjective | Binet (1900) |
| Sthenic | vs. | Asthenic | Burt (1937) |
| Cyclothymic | vs. | Schizothymic | Kretschmer (1926) |
| Extratensive | vs. | Introvertive | Rorschach (1942) |
| Surgent | vs. | Desurgent | Cattell (1933) |
| Inhibitory | vs. | Excitatory | Pavlov (1941) |
| Explosive | vs. | Obstructive | James (1890) |
| Shallow-broad | vs. | Deep-narrow | Gross (1902) |
| Syntropic | vs. | Idiotropic | Wertheimer et al. (1926) |
| B–Type | vs. | T–Type | Jaensch (1926) |
| Adient | vs. | Avoidant | Holt (1931) |
| Viscerotonic | vs. | Cerebrotonic | Sheldon (1942) |
| Manic | vs. | Melancholic | Heymans et al. (1908) |

| PERSONALITY TRAITS | | | |
|---|---|---|---|
| Suggestibility | vs. | Non-suggestibility | Babinski (1918) |
| Short secondary function | vs. | Long secondary function | Gross (1902) |
| Fluency | vs. | Lack of fluency | Cattell (1933) |
| Dissociation | vs. | Anxiety | McDougall (1926) |
| Plastic eidetic imagery | vs. | Rigid eidetic imagery | Jaensch (1926) |
| Colour-attitude | vs. | Form-attitude | Scholl (1927) |
| Non-perseveration | vs. | Perseveration | Spearman (1927) |
| Slow oscillation | vs. | Quick oscillation | McDougall (1926) |
| Synthetic ability | vs. | Abstractive ability | Kretschmer (1926) |
| Careless | vs. | Careful | Downey (1923) |
| Slow personal tempo | vs. | Quick personal tempo | Kretschmer (1926) |
| Lacking in persistence | vs. | Persistent | Downey (1923) |
| Ascendent | vs. | Submissive | Allport (1928) |
| Sociable | vs. | Unsociable | Guilford (1936) |
| Emotionally demonstrative | vs. | Non-demonstrative | Guilford (1936) |

| CONSTITUTIONAL TYPES | | | |
|---|---|---|---|
| Digestive | vs. | Respiratory-cerebral | Rostan (1828) |
| Sympatheticotonic | vs. | Vagotonic | Eppinger (1917) |
| Megalosplanchnic | vs. | Microsplanchnic | Viola (1933) |
| Pyknic | vs. | Leptosomatic | Kretschmer (1926) |
| Endomorph | vs. | Ectomorph | Sheldon (1940) |

Synoptic table showing sample of current dichotomous typologies, arranged according to psychotic type, neurotic type, personality type, personality trait, and constitutional type. A more detailed table of constitutional types is given later in the book.

is identical with an extreme degree of introversion (Jung) and with
the 'schizoid' personality of Kretschmer. The type of personality
that is prone to manic-depressive illness is the so-called syntonic
(Bleuler) or cycloid (Kretschmer) or cyclothymic personality.
This type represents an extreme degree of extraversion and is
characterized by its affective lability and responsiveness." As
Bowlby (1940) points out, "a moment's reflection will show the
serious confusion in these passages. It is probably true that the
shut-in personality is identical with what Jung means by an
extreme degree of introversion, but it is certainly not the same
as the 'schizoid' personality types of Kretschmer. For instance,
in addition to the seclusive schizoids there are the hysterical
schizoids . . . who are the reverse of being shut-in." Kretschmer
(1934) himself maintains that "there is no doubt whatever that
there are many 'nervous' and 'hysterical' individuals . . . who
are biologically nothing other than schizoids". The existence of
these "hysterical schizoids" shows plainly the difficulty of identifying the schizoid with the introvert, seeing that the hysteric is the
prototype of the extravert. Bowlby (1940) concludes: "Whatever
the similarity . . . of these rival classifications, it is evident that
they are not identical and nothing but confusion can result from
the facile equation of their terms."

What is true of the typologies of Jung and Kretschmer is also
true of the other classifications given on page 13. In spite of
obvious similarities, there are also profound differences between
any two of them, and much confusion of thought has resulted
from a glossing over of these differences. It seems clear that only
a rigorously objective investigation, dealing with operationally
defined concepts throughout, can hope to reduce the almost
entirely theoretical and clinical views represented in our table to
something like order and simplicity. The possibility must also
be faced, of course, that under objective enquiry nothing at all
may remain of this vast theoretical structure, and that specificity
instead of generality may play a predominant part in the affective
and conative adjustments of human beings.

## 4. GENERALITY VERSUS SPECIFICITY

From some points of view, indeed, the main result of our
investigations may be judged to be the light which they throw

on the vexed question of specificity versus generality of personality traits. It has been argued in some quarters that personality is nothing more than a mere aggregation of stimulus-response elements, possessing no enduring structure whatever (Guthrie, 1944). "According to this theory there are no broad, general traits of personality, no general and consistent forms of conduct which, if they existed, would make for consistency of behaviour and stability of personality, but only independent and specific stimulus-response bonds or habits" (MacKinnon, 1944). This theory, which grew out of James's revolt against faculty psychology, and out of the experimental studies of Thorndike (1913) into "transfer of training", found its main experimental support in the work of the Character Education Inquiry, directed by Hartshorne and May (1928, 29, 30).

The theory, and the experiments supporting it, have been strongly criticized by the proponents of the theory of generality or non-specificity (Allport, 1937). They maintain that generality rather than specificity predominates in the organization of personality, and attempt to account for the consistency of behaviour by postulating "broad, generalized, complex, overlapping, but relatively stable and enduring dispositions to action as the important and genuine components of personality" (MacKinnon, 1944). Experimental investigations such as those of Braun (1927), Olson (1929), Pear (1931), Cantril (1932), Allport and Vernon (1933), Trawick (1940), Eysenck (1944) and many others have shown that a certain amount of generality is undoubtedly present in the organization of behaviour-patterns and of attitudes.

In fact, the question of "Generality or specificity?" seems to be wrongly put; we should ask, rather, "How general and how specific?" Both specificity and generality of behaviour, attitudes and sentiments have been shown experimentally to exist; the question remains of just how specific each action is, and how far it is predictable from knowing the tendency to perform a quite different action. Thus, in a study into the structuring of political and social attitudes of various "unorthodox" groups, it was found that the variance contributed by the communal factors amounted to about 50%; in other words, for the groups studied the influence of generality and specificity was approximately equal (Eysenck, 1944). Similarly, in a study of philosophical beliefs the communal factors were shown to account for over 60% of the variance, demonstrating the importance of both generality and specificity (Eysenck, 1944). A hierarchical view of personality structure, akin both to Burt's (1940) statistical conception of "factors" and to McDougall's theory of sentiments (1923), would appear to account for the known facts better than any other; a view of this kind will be presented later on.

Ultimately, any view of personality must be based on experimental results treated by statistical methods. The mutually complementary nature of experiment and statistics has not always been recognized sufficiently, and may be stressed here in connection with our view of the nature of statistical factors. As will be seen, the statistical tool on which we have relied in the main is factorial analysis, and in view of the very strong opinions which have been held on the nature of factors, and on the proper method of analysis, a few words may be useful in indicating our own position.

Historically, factor analysis is merely an extension of the underlying logical postulate of all correlation procedures, viz. Mill's so-called "method of concomitant variation". The aim of factor analysis is to discover the smallest number of independent factors or variables which will adequately describe and classify mental abilities and temperamental traits; it attempts to give the most parsimonious account of the experimental findings in so far as these are interdependent. In doing so, it gives rise to four different types of factors: (1) General factors, which are common to all the tests or traits used in the investigation; (2) Group factors, common to certain of the tests or traits only, but absent in others; (3) Specific factors, which are peculiar to a single test or trait whenever it occurs; and (4) Error factors, which are present only on one occasion, and absent on all others. These four types of factors, as Burt (1940) has shown, correspond closely to the categories of the scholastic logicians: Genus, Species, Proprium, and Accidens.

The status of these factors once they have been isolated has given rise to much argument. Thurstone (1935) and Holzinger (1937), for instance, regard factors as primary or fundamental abilities; similarly, Spearman (1927) regards them as fundamental functions of the mind. If factor analysis is to be applied to the study of personality as well as to the study of abilities, this definition has to be broadened somewhat, and it would become necessary to think of factors as elementary or unitary traits of personality (Kelley, 1935), or as the fundamental dimensions of the mind (Guilford, 1940). On the other hand, Anastasi (1938), Allport (1937) and Thomson (1939) consider that factors are statistical artefacts, having no "reality" of any kind.

Our own position is very similar to that of Burt (1940), who regards factors as principles of classification. "Rigorously speaking, factors cannot be regarded as substances or as parts of a substance, or even as causal attributes inhering in a substance. They are not separate 'organs' or isolated 'properties' of the mind; they are not 'primary abilities', 'unitary traits', 'mental powers or energies'. They are principles of classification described by selective operators. The operand on which these operators operate is not 'the mind', but the sum total of the relations between minds and their environment."

There is, however, one way in which we would venture to modify and extend this view. If there are "unitary" or "primary" abilities, or fundamental dimensions of the mind, factor analysis alone is not sufficient to reveal them (and to prove them to be such. If a factorial study of temperament showed the existence of one fundamental factor of introversion-extraversion, we would have to regard this demonstration merely as evidence that a classification along these lines would be expedient. If later on introversion could be shown to be due to demonstrable Mendelian factors, inherited in predictable ways, then our factor would surely deserve a higher status scientifically than a mere principle of classification; it could rightly be regarded as a fundamental dimension of the mind. It is on this interdependence of factor analysis and experiment, based on the results of such analysis, that we have laid particular stress in this book.

The nature of factors can perhaps best be understood by reference to the difference between *denotative* and *connotative* concepts (Northrop, 1939). The characteristics of a denotative concept are given by abstraction, and its meaning can always be demonstrated by pointing to something, or by apprehending something, that is given or presented with immediacy. Thus we may consider the green of the grass and abstract from it the concept "green".

In contradistinction, a connotative concept is designated by the basic assumptions and postulates of the scientific theory in which it occurs. An electron, for instance, is not observed; it is defined by the postulates of electron theory. These unobserved concepts may be defined in any desired way as long as their properties are specified unambiguously in the terms of the general theory, and as long as logical deductions can be made from them, and verified or checked in terms of directly observable facts.

The relation of these two types of concepts to factor theory may be made explicit by a historical parallel. Newton, in the *Scholium* at the beginning of his Principia, points out that sensed time and sensed space are not to be confused with "true or mathematical" time or space; it is the former type of concept (denotative) which is experienced in everyday activity, while he is concerned with the latter type of concept (connotative) in his book. Anyone who confuses the two, he goes on to say, is guilty of vulgar ignorance.

Now clearly a statistical factor is a connotative concept, not a denotative one; yet much criticism of factorial work has been based on a misunderstanding of this position. The intelligence and suggestibility, the sense of humour and persistence which are observed and talked about by the man in the street are denotative concepts; stripped by experimental and factorial studies of popular misconceptions closely bound up with them, and of emotional elements inevitably mixed with them, they become *connotative* concepts. Certainly, Spearman's "g" bears some relation to the popular concept of "intelligence", just as Newton's or even Einstein's concept of space bears some relation to popular notions. But in spite of these similarities, the origin and meaning of the respective denotative and connotative concepts are sufficiently diverse to make it necessary to distinguish between them with great care.

When, therefore, we find factors in our work which bear certain resemblances to such denotative concepts as "neuroticism" or "introversion", it should be borne in mind that these terms are not used in their ordinary, denotative meaning, but that they are connotative concepts, designated by the basic assumptions and postulates of factorial theory.

These assumptions and postulates have been stated so well

by Burt (1940), Thompson (1939), Thurstone (1935), Holzinger (1941) and others that there is no need to restate them here. Certain points at issue within the general framework of factor analysis, such as the problem of rotation and primary structure, will be discussed in the appropriate place.

## 5. ARRANGEMENT OF MATERIAL

Our general view of factor analysis has determined the way in which this book has been set out. In Chapter 2 is reported a factorial study of the intercorrelations of 39 personality traits in 700 patients at this Hospital, as rated in each case by the psychiatrist in charge. This study revealed two major factors, general traits, dimensions, or principles of classification. In the first place, patients were seen to vary with respect to *general neuroticism*, and in the second place they were seen to vary with respect to *introversion-extraversion.*

In Chapter 3, factorial studies are reported of body measurements of various groups of patients, which also gave rise to two factors: (1) A general factor of body size, and (2) a factor of body build, differentiating the patients whose growth was preponderantly in length from those whose growth was preponderantly in breadth. This factor of body build, which is similar in many ways to the traditional pyknic-asthenic dichotomy, was quantified in the form of an Index, which was shown to be normally distributed, and to differentiate significantly between introverts and extraverts. Other investigations into constitutional factors are also reported in this chapter; these are mainly concerned with the greater lability of the autonomic nervous system of the introverts.

In the fourth chapter, intelligence test records and vocabulary scores of several thousand neurotics and normals are analysed in an attempt to find differentiating marks between neurotics and normals, and between extraverts and introverts. Particular attention was paid to actual scores, reliabilities, effects of incentives, scatter, form of distribution, and vocabulary/intelligence ratios; several special experimental investigations were carried out in an effort to gain information on these various points. Studies are also reported of various aspects of the "efficiency" with which neurotics and normals can bring their abilities to bear on concrete problems, and of the attitudes shown towards the work.

In subsequent chapters, various personality traits are taken up in turn, and investigations described in which attempts were made to find batteries of tests which would significantly differentiate (1) the neurotic from the non-neurotic, and (2) the introvert from the extravert. In other words, having derived our principles of classification from a factorial study, we then proceed to give operational definitions of the resultant factors. The traits examined were determined by two considerations: (1) They should be likely on theoretical grounds to differentiate between the various groups measured, and (2) their measurement should be practicable in the circumstances in which the investigation was conducted. The latter condition did much to circumscribe the possible field, and while we do not wish to escape the responsibility of having chosen the traits which were studied, our choice was necessarily limited due to wartime difficulties and shortage of apparatus.

The traits finally chosen were taken as far as possible from different sectors and fields; thus the motor sector, the sensory sector, the perceptual sector, and the conceptual sector, are all fairly equally represented. The fields covered, as shown in the Table of Contents, may appear a trifle heterogeneous; this heterogeneity is, however, intentional. In the terminology of Gross (1902), our approach is shallow-broad, rather than deep-narrow; if our factors are really *personality* factors, they should be expected to cover all the diverse features of personality.

While we have thus used a great variety of tests, we do not claim to have treated each of the traits they are supposedly measuring equally extensively. Within the limits set by external circumstances, that would indeed have been quite impossible. The number of investigations devoted to each particular trait, and the number of subjects tested with each particular test, were determined by various considerations which may be set out in brief.

The first consideration which influenced us in deciding how much time and work to devote to a particular test and/or trait was the agreement of our preliminary results with clinical expectation. Thus while clinical expectation led us to believe that hysterics would be more suggestible than other neurotics, our preliminary studies showed that this was not so; similarly, while previous experimenters had found no reason to believe that neurotics are more suggestible than normals, our preliminary results showed a close correlation between suggestibility and neuroticism. Consequently, we found it necessary to go into the whole complex of questions bound up with suggestibility very thoroughly, and to test some 2,000 normal and neurotic subjects before we were satisfied that our conclusions were really beyond cavil. On the other hand, our preliminary trials of persistence tests agreed so closely with expectation that only about 400 tests in all were carried out.

Another important consideration was the following. Some traits had received what we considered to be adequate experimental and statistical treatment in the past, and their unitary nature had been established to our satisfaction. Under those conditions, we did not hesitate to make use of the results reported by others, without going to the trouble of repeating the original investigations. In the case of suggestibility tests, however, no satisfactory factorial studies had been reported, and we found it essential to carry out such a study on a dozen tests of this trait before we could decide even on the proper test to use in our major investigation.

Accordingly it will be seen that our account of the personality correlates of suggestibility is at least ten times as long as our account of persistence; while this introduces a kind of lopsidedness into the make-up of this book, we could see no way of avoiding this difficulty. Similar considerations apply to other fields; thus sense of humour required more discussion than perseveration, and level of aspiration or speed/accuracy more than irritability or sensory acuity.

In the last chapter, a summary of the results of our work is presented, and certain theoretical implications are discussed. As far as possible, we have kept theoretical considerations out of the main part of the book, and have confined ourselves to factual reports of experimental results. In one or two places however, it seemed necessary to anticipate criticisms of certain interpretations made, and terms used, in the course of the argument, by entering into immediate theoretical discussion.

C

## 6. CONCEPTS AND DEFINITIONS

While we are concerned in this book with experimental material rather than with theory, it is clear that a certain theoretical background is implied in the set-up of the experiments, and in the conclusions which we have drawn from them. We consider it appropriate, therefore, that the underlying theoretical considerations which have guided our approach should be made explicit, and that the terms we have used should be rigidly defined. In doing so we have not aimed at originality, nor do we believe that the way in which we have used terms and concepts is necessarily the best way in which they can be used, or should be used in the future. We have found the scheme outlined below useful in ordering our thinking, and include it here mainly to save the interested reader from having to discover our premisses by arguing back from our methods and our findings. As far as possible, we have endeavoured to keep our definitions "operational"; indeed, only by adopting some variety of "operationism" would it appear possible to rescue the psychology of personality from the many romantic pitfalls into which it has shown itself all too eager to fall (Symposium on Operationism, 1945).

The leading term in the title of this book is "personality", and unfortunately it is particularly in relation to this term that agreement as to meaning is almost wholly absent. Allport (1937), whose book on the subject contains perhaps the best summary of the literature, distinguishes fifty meanings; similarly, Roback (1931) stresses the wide differences in usage of this and other terms in the field of temperament. Quite generally, however, definitions of personality may be grouped according to whether they stress superficial, observable, objective appearances (*persona* or mask definitions), or whether they stress rather underlying inner, subjective essentials (*anima* or substance definitions). Watson's (1924) famous definition of personality as "the end product of our habit systems" may stand as an example of the first type of definition, Allport's (1937) view that it is "the dynamic organization within the individual of those psycho-physical systems that determine his unique adjustments to his environment" as an example of the latter type of definition.

Definitions which lay stress on the outward, observable appearance are usually associated with a behaviouristic, nomothetic approach, while definitions stressing the inner, subjective organization are usually associated with an analytical, idiographic approach. To some extent, these differences in approach are nationally conditioned; the nomothetic approach is predominantly American, the idiographic approach German (Maller, 1933; Vernon, 1933).

While seemingly antagonistic, these two different methods of approaching the fundamental problem of psychology are in reality complementary. There is after all no scientific way of investigating the inner, subjective organization of a person's fundamental needs and drives except by studying "the sum of activities that can be discovered by actual observation over a long enough time to give reliable information" (Watson, 1924). And there is no way of accounting for observed consistencies and characteristic tendencies except by assuming some kind of inner organization, embracing "every phase of human character: intellect, temperament, skill, morality, and every attitude that has been built up in the course of one's life" (Warren and Carmichael, 1930).

A definition which includes both views and comes perhaps nearest to a general consensus of psychological thought at the present time is Warren's view of personality as "the integrated organization of all the cognitive, affective, conative, and physical characteristics of an individual as it manifests itself in focal distinctness to others" (1934). It is in this sense that the term has been used throughout this book.

Temperament has frequently been used synonymously with personality, but in the interests of economy and clarity the term has partly shed its protean character and is used by many writers to cover "the general affective nature of an individual as determined by his inheritance and life history" (Warren, 1934). Allport and Vernon (1930) have distinguished three main aspects under which temperament has been viewed in the past: the emotional, the physiological, and kinetic. Many writers have considered temperament to be defined largely by the habitual emotional reactivity of an individual (Wundt, 1903; Allport, 1924); others have emphasized physiological and bio-chemical factors (Cobb, 1927; Hoskins, 1933; McDougall, 1923); yet others have stressed the motor responses character-istic of the individual (Downey, 1923; Bloor, 1928; Allport and

Vernon, 1933). These three aspects are happily combined in Allport's (1937) definition, which will constitute the basis of our own usage of the term: "Temperament refers to the characteristic phenomena of an individual's emotional nature, including his susceptibility to emotional stimulation, his customary strength and speed of response, the quality of his prevailing mood, and all peculiarities of fluctuation and intensity in mood." We have not been able to accept the final part of Allport's definition, " . . . these phenomena being regarded as dependent upon constitutional make-up, and therefore largely hereditary in origin" because of lack of evidence on this point; the theories of social learning associated with the Yale Institute of Human Relations may on *a priori* grounds be as capable of giving a satisfactory account of the presence of such observed differences between individuals as an hereditary view, and in the absence of very strong evidence in either direction we considered it premature to express in a definition an opinion as to their origin.

The next term to be discussed, character, has been defined in two different and unrelated ways, one definition stressing the moral or ethical aspect of personality, the other stressing the conative aspect (Allport and Vernon, 1930). The former type of definition, although more usual in non-technical writing, is of little use in psychology because of its evaluative nature, and the second type, introduced into psychology mainly through the writings of McDougall (1923, 1926), seems more promising. In this sense, Warren's (1934) definition of character as a "system of directed conative tendencies" seems to cover the ground satisfactorily. In this way of looking at character, "the emphasis is upon the force of activity rather than upon its direction, upon the quality of behaviour in terms of strength, persistence, readiness, rapidity, etc., rather than upon its value as right or wrong, good or bad, wise or foolish, etc." (Filter, 1922).

Character, as thus defined, is clearly closely related to the concept of "will", as studied by James, Ach, Michotte, Aveling, and others; it may be regarded as "an enduring psychophysical disposition to inhibit instinctive impulses in accordance with a regulative principle" (Roback, 1931). As such, it will be seen to have many points in common with Freud's (1920) ego and super-ego, with Webb's "w" factor (1915), with McDougall self-regarding sentiment (1923), with Luria's "functional barrier"

(1932), and with the concepts of "conscience" and "will-power" of popular terminology. This identity is brought out very clearly in McDougall's view that character is that in man which "gives, or rather is, the ground of consistency, firmness, self-control, power of self-direction or autonomy" (1933).

Intelligence is another concept notoriously difficult to define; in the main, definitions can be subsumed under three headings, derived respectively from clinical studies, animal experimentation, and educational measurement (Cattell, 1943). "The respective representative definition issuing from these fields are; (1) the capacity to think abstractly, (2) the ability to learn, and (3) the capacity to adapt means to ends." Perhaps Burt's (1924) definition of intelligence as "innate, all-round mental ability" comes closest to a generally acceptable usage. It is well-known that the existence of a general factor of this kind has for long been denied by some critics of Spearman's (1927) fundamental work, notably Thurstone (1935, 1938); recent demonstrations, however, that in Thurstone's own correlational studies a general factor plays an important part (Spearman, 1939; Eysenck, 1939), and the admission on Thurstone's (1942) part that the group factors to which his own analysis gives rise can themselves be analysed into what he calls a "second order general factor" have between them led to a close rapprochement between factorists of all views.

Combining the definitions we have presented so far, we may say that personality is the sum-total of the actual or potential behaviour-patterns of the organism, as determined by heredity and environment; it originates and develops through the functional interaction of the four main sectors into which these behaviour-patterns are organized: the cognitive sector (intelligence), the conative sector (character), the affective sector (temperament) and the somatic sector (constitution).

In the description of personality, two further terms are often invoked which may require brief definition. These are *type* and *trait*. Many authors consider that a theory invoking "traits" must inevitably be opposed to a theory invoking "types", on the grounds that trait theory presupposes a normal distribution of the characteristic measured, while type theory presupposes a bimodal distribution. "Type theory tends to classify people into sharply divided groups, while trait theory assumes a continuous gradation with most people near the average" (Stagner, 1937). Thus type theory would call all people either introvert or extravert, while trait theory would find that most people tended to be ambivert (Conklin, 1927).

There are several assumptions in this very common view which are at least doubtful. Thus few of the writers who have used the concept of "type" have used it so as to imply the existence of sharply divided groups; more frequently, they have presented their types as hypothetical pure cases, to which people might approximate more or less closely. Lewin (1935) has argued in favour of basing scientific laws upon pure cases rather than upon averages of observations contaminated by errors and inaccuracies, and this view is certainly a tenable one, although fundamentally it may be asked how one is to arrive at the pure case, except on the basis of such observations.

Even when writers have actually thought of the distribution of their types as approaching a bimodal rather than a normal curve, arguments on either side based on the actual distribution of raw scores on a rating-scale or on single tests seem to lack an appreciation of the complexity of the problems raised. Most "proofs" of the nature of the distribution of any variable, such as intelligence, are circular, and show nothing but the possibility of arranging a series of problems in such a way that raw scores derived from the answers of a random group shall give a normal distribution (Thorndike, 1926). It would be possible to arrange a series of problems in such a way that a bimodal, a multimodal, a skewed normal, or a rectangular distribution of raw scores appeared. Thus the fact that many questionnaires seem to give normal distributions when analysed may be due to the fact that the trait measured is actually normally distributed; it may also be due, however, to the fact that questions pertaining to different and unrelated "type" dichotomies are included in the questionnaire, to the fact that a "halo" factor swamps any real temperamental differences, to the fact that specific and error factors play a decisive part, or to a combination of these influences.

What is true of questionnaires and ratings is even more true of raw scores derived from experiments; the fact that the raw scores derived from suggestibility tests are usually found to give U-shaped distributions, thus apparently arguing in favour of a type theory, and against a trait theory, really tells us nothing about the distribution of the underlying trait (cf. chapter 5). This question will be dealt with in detail later, but we may anticipate the conclusion derived from a study of nearly two thousand experimental records of suggestibility tests, that the U-shaped distribution usually found in these tests is compatible statistically with a normal distribution of the underlying trait.

These considerations make us chary of accepting a view which would differentiate between traits and types on the basis of unimodal or bimodal distribution of scores. Neymann and Kohlstedt's (1929) demonstration that their introvert-extravert questionnaire, which was derived from a study of 100 schizophrenics and 100 manic-depressives, gave a bimodal distribution of scores when applied to normal subjects, cannot be accepted as proving the truth of "type" theory any more than the demonstration of Root and Root, using the same questionnaire on 1,000 college students, that the distribution of scores was unimodal and almost perfectly normal can be accepted as proving the truth of "trait" theory (quoted by Stagner, 1937). Both demonstrations are equally at fault in assuming a one-to-one correspondence between raw scores on a test and strength of the trait assumed to underlie the scores.

A view which attempts to reconcile type and trait theory has been presented by Murphy and Jensen (1932). These writers maintain that true types of personality consist of *necessary interconnections* between traits, rather than of mere classifications on a trait scale. This view has been criticized by Stagner (1937) on the grounds that writers on type theory conceive of the connections between traits not as being *necessary*, but rather as being *habitual*. He quotes Jung, who says: "When the orientation to the object and to objective facts is so predominant that the most frequent and essential decisions and actions are determined, not by subjective values but by objective relations, one speaks of an extraverted attitude. *When this is habitual, one speaks of an extraverted type*" (Jung, 1923, our italics). Stagner concludes, "it seems more correct to speak of introversion-extraversion as a trait continuum describing habitual forms of behaviour, rather than as definite types with necessary connections between responses" (p. 213).

Our own definitions of "type" and "trait" bear some

resemblance to the view of Murphy and Jensen, except that instead of *necessary connections* we will speak rather of *observed connections*. We shall speak of "Types" as *observed constellations or syndromes of traits*, and of "Traits" as *observed constellations of individual action-tendencies*. Thus we make the distinction between types and traits not in terms of their distribution, but in terms of their *relative inclusiveness as determined experimentally*.

## 7. A Theory of Personality

This view is presented graphically in Figure 2. It will be seen that we are here dealing with four levels of behaviour-organization. At the lowest level, we have specific responses, $S.R._1$, $S.R._2$, $S.R._3$, ...... $S.R._n$. These are acts, such as responses to an experimental test or to experiences of everyday life, which are observed once, and may or may not be characteristic of the individual.

At the second level, we have what are called habitual responses, $H.R._1$, $H.R._2$, $H.R._3$, ...... $H.R._n$. These are specific responses which tend to recur under similar circumstances; i.e. if the test is repeated, a similar response is given, or if the life-situation recurs, the individual reacts in a similar fashion. This is the lowest level of organization; roughly speaking, the amount of organization present here can be measured in terms of reliability coefficients, i.e. in terms of the probability that on repetition of a situation behaviour will be consistent.

At the third level, we have organizations of habitual acts into traits $T_1$, $T_2$, $T_3$, ...... $T_n$. These traits, accuracy, irritability, persistence, rigidity, etc., are theoretical constructs, based on observed intercorrelations of a number of different habitual responses; in the language of the factor analyst, they may be conceived of as group factors.

At the fourth level, we have organization of traits into a general type; in our example, the *introvert*. This organization also is based on observed correlations, this time on correlations between the various traits which between them make up the concept of the type under discussion. Thus in our example, persistence, rigidity, suggestibility, irritability and various other traits would form a constellation of traits intercorrelating among

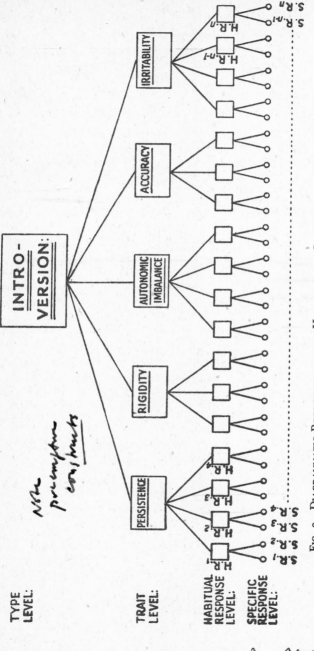

FIG. 2. DIAGRAMMATIC REPRESENTATION OF HIERARCHICAL ORGANISATION OF PERSONALITY.

themselves, thus giving rise to a higher-order construct, the type. It will be noted that our four levels of personality organization correspond closely to the four types of factor distinguished in our discussion of factorial methods: error factors, specific factors, group factors, and general factors. An "habitual response" is merely a "specific response" divested of its error component, and made into a specific factor; a "trait" is a system of "specific responses" divested of its error and specific variance; a "type" is a system of "specific responses" which has lost its error, specific, and group factor variance.

Two consequences follow from this analysis. In the first place, as the field covered by each term grows, so the predictability of each "specific response" falls. It is much easier, and more rewarding, to predict a "specific response" from knowledge of a person's "habitual response" than from knowing his "trait" score, or from knowing his "type". If we wished to predict a person's score on the body-sway test of suggestibility, for instance, we should do well to give him the actual test, and make the result the basis of our prediction for future behaviour. As the test-retest correlation in this case is over ·9, we can be fairly sure that our prediction will come true within a narrow margin of error.

If we cannot do that, then knowing his performance on other suggestibility tests, such as the Chevreul Pendulum, the Arm Levitation, or the Press-release test, would give us a predictive score with somewhat less certainty than if we knew his "habitual response". But as this trait is a comparatively well-defined one in terms of "habitual response" intercorrelations, our prediction would still be of some value. To take a practical example, we found that it was possible to predict hypnotizability with considerable accuracy from knowing a person's score on two other suggestibility tests.

If we were deprived even of this knowledge, and were told only a person's general type, then our prediction, while still better than chance, would be rather inaccurate, and would not inspire much confidence. Thus as we go up in the scale of generality, our ability to predict specific acts decreases; if our ability to predict is to be increased we must confine ourselves more and more closely to the actual "habitual response" in question.

The other consequence of the identification of our four levels of personality organization with the four types of factor is clearly implicit in Burt's discussion of the differences between these types of factor. He points out that "the differences throughout are principally differences of degree; the 'general factor' is simply the 'group factor' that has the most widespread occurrence; and the 'specific factors' are simply the 'group factors' that are most narrowly limited in their operation. . . . Thus the distinctions between general, group-, and specific factors are formal rather than material, relative rather than fixed. . . . By itself no factor can be styled general, group, or specific; such designations have reference solely to the particular set of tests and traits that have been correlated."

These admissions may appear to lower considerably the value of the type of analysis proposed. If predictability decreases as generality grows, then what is the value of discovering such general factors, the reader may ask; or he may enquire what is the purpose of analysing tables of correlations into factors which have no absolute but only relative value. The first type of criticism is made explicitly by Thomson (1939), who doubts the usefulness of factor analysis because a better prediction of individual behaviour can usually be obtained by direct regression equations, the second is made implicitly by Thurstone (1935), who seeks for "invariance".

In reply it may be pointed out that the investigation of the structure of the mind is in itself of scientific interest, regardless of the predictive powers, narrowly conceived, which such an analysis may bring. If a hierarchical structure such as we have outlined above succeeds in giving a more or less accurate picture of the kind of organization which obtains in the mind, then we are justified in using the methods outlined, and treating the problem of prediction as a secondary one, for whose solution other methods may be more appropriate. On the other hand, we do not claim that the factorial method can give us a definitive, final answer to all our questions. It is only as a first approach, as an approximation, that we regard our data and our theories; no more than heuristic value is claimed for them. As Burt (1940) has pointed out, "if factor analysis tells the truth and nothing but the truth, we need not condemn it for failing to tell the whole truth".

## 8. SUMMARY

In the present chapter, the main terms used in the course of the book (personality, temperament, character, type, trait, etc.), have been defined, and the methodology used described. Also given was a detailed description of the experimental population.

In particular, attention was drawn to the many questions raised by the famous theory of temperamental types (introversion-extraversion, schizophrenia-cyclothymia, etc.), associated with the names of Jung, Kretschmer, McDougall, Jaensch and other writers, and the relation of these theories to experimental research was discussed.

More generally, a theory of personality organization was proposed which was based on Burt's views of factorial analysis and the nature of statistical factors, and on the hierarchical theories of sentiment-formation of McDougall. The view proposed, which attempts to reconcile the two main points of view in personality research (belief in specificity and belief in generality), stresses the actual amount of organization present, thus turning a qualitative difference of viewpoint into a quantitative problem for research.

# CHAPTER TWO

## ASSESSMENTS AND RATINGS

1. A Factorial Analysis of Personality  2. Neuroticism
3. Theories of Neuroticism       4. Introversion-Extraversion
5. Theories of Introversion  6. Questionnaire Study of Neuroticism
7. Questionnaire Study of Persistence and Irritability  8. Summary

### 1. A Factorial Analysis of Personality

THE results of the first investigation to be reported underlie most of our subsequent work. Thirty-nine items were selected from the item-sheet on the basis of their general psychological interest; these items covered the social history of the patient, his personality, and his symptoms fairly adequately. The actual items selected are given in Table 1. Our experimental population originally consisted of 1,000 male service patients; in order to reduce the complexity of the factors operating, however, the following groups of cases were excluded: cases of epilepsy, cases where head injury formed part of the present illness, cases with previous organic illness of the Central Nervous System, or with present sign of such illness, cases with organic mental syndromes, and cases where physical illness was an important factor. Thus our experimental group was finally reduced to 700 patients suffering from the mainly reactive types of mental illness. No attempt was made to equate the numbers of patients diagnosed as hysterics, anxiety states, depressions, psychopaths, etc.; apart from the patients excluded on the above-mentioned grounds, our group represents successive admissions completely unselected.

Correlations were calculated for this group between the 39 items, and the resulting table factor-analyzed. The full table of 741 intercorrelations has been given elsewhere (Eysenck, 1944); the results of the factor analysis are shown in Table 1. It will be seen that a first, general factor accounts for 14% of the variance, while a second, bipolar factor accounts for an additional 12%. A third, bipolar factor, accounting for 8%, and a fourth, bipolar factor, accounting for 6%, make up the communality to 40%

33

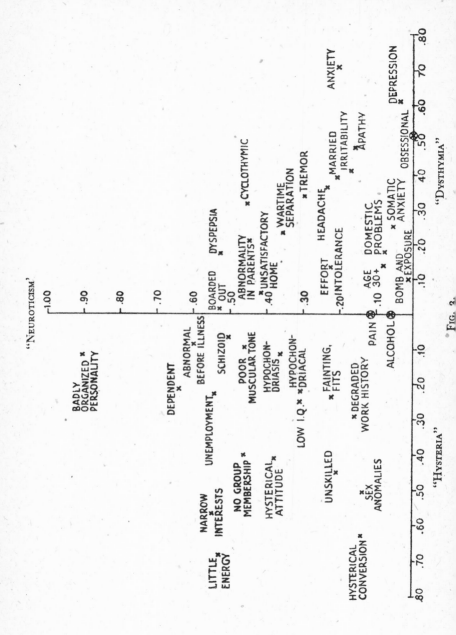

Fig. 2

altogether, leaving us with a uniqueness of 60%. A diagrammatic representation of the first two factors is given in Figure 3; this figure will assist the reader to understand the nature of the two factors involved.

TABLE ONE

| Variable. | Factor saturations. | | | | |
|---|---|---|---|---|---|
| | 1. | 2. | 3. | 4. | $h^2$. |
| 1. Age above 30 | ·08 | ·14 | −·27 | −·22 | ·15 |
| 2. Unskilled | ·22 | −·45 | ·12 | −·48 | ·49 |
| 3. Unemployment | ·55 | −·23 | −·12 | −·36 | ·49 |
| 4. Degraded work-history | ·16 | −·29 | ·16 | −·29 | ·22 |
| 5. Abnormality in parents | ·47 | ·21 | ·35 | ·31 | ·48 |
| 6. Unsatisfactory home | ·43 | ·06 | ·45 | ·00 | ·38 |
| 7. Married | ·21 | ·39 | −·12 | −·19 | ·24 |
| 8. No group membership | ·46 | −·40 | −·16 | −·32 | ·50 |
| 9. Narrow interests | ·55 | −·57 | ·04 | −·10 | ·63 |
| 10. Alcohol | ·07 | ·00 | ·17 | −·36 | ·16 |
| 11. Abnormal before illness | ·61 | −·09 | ·24 | ·33 | ·56 |
| 12. Badly organized personality | ·92 | −·12 | ·35 | ·15 | 1·00 |
| 13. Dependent | ·65 | −·22 | ·06 | ·24 | ·53 |
| 14. Little energy | ·53 | −·69 | ·06 | −·24 | ·82 |
| 15. Cyclothymic | ·46 | ·31 | ·00 | ·37 | ·45 |
| 16. Schizoid | ·52 | −·07 | ·26 | ·29 | ·42 |
| 17. Hypochondriacal personality | ·31 | −·22 | −·41 | ·07 | ·32 |
| 18. Obsessional | ·00 | ·51 | ·07 | ·25 | ·32 |
| 19. Somatic anxiety | ·05 | ·25 | −·37 | ·12 | ·21 |
| 20. Effort intolerance | ·23 | ·13 | −·63 | ·26 | ·54 |
| 21. Dyspepsia | ·54 | ·17 | −·36 | −·01 | ·45 |
| 22. Fainting, fits | ·23 | −·23 | −·42 | ·23 | ·33 |
| 23. Pain | ·12 | ·00 | −·39 | ·03 | ·16 |
| 24. Tremor | ·30 | ·34 | ·17 | ·10 | ·25 |
| 25. Sex anomalies | ·14 | −·50 | ·54 | −·01 | ·56 |
| 26. Irritability | ·18 | ·41 | ·13 | −·10 | ·23 |
| 27. Apathy | ·18 | ·48 | −·02 | −·46 | ·47 |
| 28. Hysterical attitude | ·38 | −·41 | ·11 | −·04 | ·32 |
| 29. Poor muscular tone | ·47 | −·09 | −·17 | ·45 | ·46 |
| 30. Headaches | ·24 | ·36 | −·15 | −·06 | ·21 |
| 31. Anxiety | ·21 | ·72 | ·14 | −·09 | ·59 |
| 32. Depression | ·04 | ·61 | ·02 | −·23 | ·42 |
| 33. Hypochondriasis | ·36 | −·11 | −·79 | ·24 | ·82 |
| 34. Hysterical conversion | ·14 | −·63 | ·08 | ·11 | ·44 |
| 35. Bomb and exposure | ·02 | ·10 | ·03 | −·04 | ·01 |
| 36. Wartime separation | ·36 | ·23 | ·39 | ·23 | ·38 |
| 37. Domestic problems | ·08 | ·17 | ·17 | −·19 | ·11 |
| 38. Low intelligence | ·32 | −·25 | ·08 | −·13 | ·19 |
| 39. Boarded out of army | ·54 | ·02 | ·25 | ·05 | ·35 |
| Variance | ·14 | ·12 | ·08 | ·06 | ·40 |

The first factor is characterized by the items: Badly organized personality, dependent, abnormal before illness, boarded out, narrow interests, little energy, abnormality in parents, schizoid, dyspepsia, poor muscular tone, unsatisfactory home, no group membership, and cyclothymic; clearly this factor delineates a general lack of personality integration, lack of adaptability, and lack of general drive which might justifiably be called "neuroticism".

The second factor contrasts two groups of symptoms and personality traits. The first group contains the following items: anxiety, depression, obsessional tendencies, apathy, irritability, headache, tremor, somatic anxiety, married state, cyclothymic, and wartime separation; the second group contains hysterical conversion, sex anomalies, little energy, narrow interests, hysterical attitude, no group membership, unemployed, low intelligence, hypochondriasis, and degraded work history. Clearly we have here a contrast between the affective, dysthymic, or inhibited group of traits and symptoms on the one hand, and the hysterical or asocial group on the other.

The third factor is characterized, on the one hand, by items such as hypochondriasis, effort intolerance, dyspepsia, fainting fits, pain, hypochondriacal personality, somatic anxiety, etc., i.e. by items stressing preoccupation with the body; on the other hand by sex anomalies, wartime separation, unsatisfactory home, abnormality in parents, and badly organized personality, i.e. by items of a more psychological type. We may label this factor "hypchondriasis"; it seems of little fundamental importance.

The fourth factor is characterized, on the one hand, by items such as unskilled, apathy, alcohol, unemployed, no group membership, little energy, degraded work history; and, on the other hand, by items such as poor muscular tone, cyclothymic, abnormality in parents, schizoid, abnormal before illness, obsessional, effort intolerance, badly organized personality, and hypochondriasis. Possibly this factor distinguishes between the stupid, drunken, shiftless social misfit on the one hand, and the "psychological conflict" group on the other. Not too much faith is felt in the interpretation of this factor.

We are left, then, with the following two main factors, or principles of classification: (1) A general "neuroticism" factor, and (2) the dichotomous division between hysteria and dysthymia.[1] These two factors or dimensions are assumed to vary independently from one another, and it behoves us to consider their relation to the general background of psychological theory, and experimental work on normal subjects.

## 2. NEUROTICISM

Regarding the general factor of neuroticism, we can find adumbrations of it in such theoretical concepts as McDougall's "self-regarding sentiment" (1926), Janet's view of "misère psychologique" (1903), Hollingworth's concept of "redintegration" (1931), Pavlov's theory of "strength of nervous functioning" (1941), Luria's view of a "functional barrier" (1932), and the many similar concepts elaborated by psychologists and psychiatrists. The Slaters' concept of "neurotic constitution" (1944) would appear to come closest to our own findings.

Much collateral evidence for the existence of a factor such as the one posited here can be gathered from the experimental literature. As Cattell has pointed out (1945), such evidence may be of four kinds:

1. Behaviour ratings;
2. Questionnaires;
3. Objective tests;
4. Clinical syndromes.

In the main, however, past psychological work has restricted itself to behaviour ratings and questionnaires, and only comparatively rarely have factorial studies been carried out on objective tests, or with regard to clinical syndromes.

It is not intended here to give a review of the whole literature of factorial study of personality, which has by now achieved the respectable total of some 350 factors; such a review is available elsewhere (Cattell, 1945). We are more concerned with elucidating certain points of principle regarding factorial methods used, and with tracing the direct historical antecedents, in the factorial field, of our two main factors.

[1] The term "Dysthymia" is used throughout this book to characterize the syndrome of anxiety, reactive depression, and obsessional tendencies found in our analysis. It was considered necessary to introduce a new term for this syndrome as none of the existing terms were found adequate.

D

In an important set of papers, Guilford (1934, 1936, 1939) has published the results of a number of factor analyses carried out on questionnaire responses of large numbers of students. These analyses, in which he succeeded in isolating various group factors, such as "social introversion", "emotional introversion", "masculinity", "nervousness", "general drive", and so on, failed entirely to disclose any general factor of "neuroticism" or of "introversion", and this demonstration of relative specificity has been accepted by many writers as disposing of the claims of those who maintain that more general factors exist.

However, this conclusion does not follow from the evidence. In the first place, Guilford, by using statistical methods of rotation which are designed to eliminate any general factor which may be present, and to spread its variance among the group factors, has shown only that if we so desire we can eliminate the general factor statistically; it does not follow that such elimination would be useful, or more "correct" than its retention.

In the second place, Guilford's success in eliminating the general factor is a very partial success indeed. While admittedly the "first-order factors" give no evidence of a general factor, Guilford himself has shown that these factors themselves are intercorrelated, thus giving rise to a second-order general factor. Thus essentially Guilford's results are not different from those of writers who extract the general factor first, and then analyse the residual matrix for group factors; the factors which emerge from these two types of analyses are fundamentally identical.

This conclusion emerges even more clearly when we factor analyze Guilford's tables by means of a procedure which enables us to apportion the amount of variance due to general and group factors respectively. Thanks to Professor Guilford's kindness in sending us unpublished tables, and discussing the whole problem by letter, we were in a position to carry out such re-analyses of all his tables. Taking only the main research, on Personality Factors S, E, and M (sociability, emotionality, and masculinity), the analysis, undertaken in conformity with Burt's group-factor method, showed a general factor, accounting for 10% of the variance, and three group factors, accounting for 14% of the variance together. The general factor was characterized most strongly by the following items: Does not adapt readily to new conditions, likes to read about things rather than experience them, limits acquaintances to a select few, gets rattled easily, does not like people to watch him, keeps quiet in company, does not take the lead in group activities, does not like to work with others, does not like public speaking, does not like to sell things, is slow and deliberate in movement, keeps in the background on social occasions, and does not enjoy getting acquainted. This factor in many ways resembles our general "neuroticism" factor.[1]

The three group factors which appear after the general factor has been eliminated correspond closely to Guilford's Personality Factors S, E, and M. Analyses of Guilford's subsequent tables, dealing with other Personality Factors, of Mosier's (1937) table, and of the tables of correlations published by a number of other writers, essentially reinforce the conclusions drawn from the analysis just discussed: we find first of all a general factor, resembling Neuroticism, which accounts for 10% to 15% of the variance, and after this factor has been eliminated group factors make their appearance which are very similar to those isolated by the author who originally published the table.

While it is thus possible to demonstrate that the two main procedures for treating correlation tables, viz. the Thurstonian rotation (Primary Structure) method, and the Burtian Iterative Summation method, give results which are in good agreement regarding the nature of the factors isolated, there are certain difficulties in identifying factors reached by the use of one method with factors reached by the use of the other. This is particularly true of the general factor, which is extracted first in Burt's analysis, and only at the very end, or not at all, in Thurstone's analysis.

Nevertheless, it is often possible to reanalyze published tables, either directly or by re-rotation, and thus a general-factor analysis can be made of data originally analyzed by means of a primary-structure analysis.[2] When in the following pages comparison is made between our results and those of others, it is

---

[1] It may be objected to this interpretation that the factor also contains many "introverted" items. This objection is discussed in Appendix A, where experimental data are brought forward in support of the method of analysis adopted here, and of our interpretation.

[2] This statement can, of course, be inverted Thus Cattell (1945) has made a "primary structure" analysis of the table of inter-correlations given by the writer in his paper (1944); the resulting factors appear to bear a close resemblance to those extracted by means of our "general factor" analysis.

to these reworked tables and factors that reference is made, not to the original factoring. (This qualification, of course, does not apply to the work of those who, like Webb (1914), Burt (1915), and Oates (1929), used general-factor methods.)

Turning now to the actual studies, we find that pride of place must go to Webb's pioneering work in 1914. He was the first to use Spearman's recently developed factorial methods on correlations between a variety of ratings carried out on 200 students and 120 children. He showed that such traits as perseverance in the face of obstacles, kindness, trustworthiness, conscientiousness, excellence of character, and strength of will tended to go together; to this syndrome of traits, which would seem to characterize the opposite pole of our "neuroticism" factor, he gave the appellation "w" (Will).

This study is somewhat tainted with the subjectivity inevitably associated with ratings; other workers have provided evidence not dependent on subjective factors of any kind. Brogden (1940) confirmed the existence of the "w" factor by a factor-analysis of the intercorrelations between a series of experimental tests; he showed that it was highly correlated with "resistance to suggestion". A similar conclusion is reported by Cracknell (1939), who tested 103 10-year old school children and reported significant correlations between positive personality traits and resistance to suggestion, as tested by the Chevreul Pendulum test, the Heat Illusion test, and other tests of suggestibility.

Other authors who furnish evidence for the existence of a general factor of neuroticism, or lack of integration, from analyses of the intercorrelations between various tests are Line and Griffin (1935) and Oates (1929). Maller's factor "c", or readiness to forgo an immediate gain for the sake of a remote but greater gain, must also be mentioned here; his evidence came from the analysis of the intercorrelations of tests of honesty, co-operation, inhibition and persistence, carried out on some 700 pupils (Maller, 1934). Attention should also be drawn to the important work of Culpin and Smith (1930) on the "nervous temperament"; their experimental results are in many ways similar to our own, and have suggested various methods of approach to us.

Even in the field of animal studies, the existence of a factor of this kind is suggested by Pavlov's work on conditioning. Allusion has already been made to his concept of "strength of nervous functioning" (1941); he considers that "primary and chief significance attaches to the factor of the *strength* of the neurones which determines the basic division of types of higher nervous activity into strong and weak. . . . The formation of a reflex to strong stimuli serves as a kind of sign of the 'boldness' of the animal, or, what is the same thing, the working capacity of its nerve cells" (Frolov, 1937). Krasnogorski has duplicated this type of analysis on children (1931), and Rosenthal has attempted to apply it to the problems of human typology (1931), as has Bruce (1941).

Broadly speaking, then, we believe that the first, general factor isolated in our analysis corresponds closely to Webb's "w" and Maller's "c" factors. It further corresponds to similar factors of emotional instability or neurotic tendency isolated by Hart (1943), Perry (1934), Kelley and Krey (1934), Studman (1935), Flanagan (1935), McCloy (1936), Howie (1945), Chi (1937), Rexroad (1937), Vernon (1938), Reyburn and Taylor (1939), and Gibb (1942). It would appear that this factor might justifiably be labelled "neuroticism", and indeed several of the authors quoted have used this term in attempts to designate the factor.

### 3. THEORIES OF NEUROTICISM

There are certain dangers, however, inherent in the use of psychiatric terms of this kind, and some discussion and clarification of the issues involved would appear necessary. This is all the more essential because (1) there is much controversy in psychiatric circles regarding the nature of neurosis, and mention at least must be made of the position we consider our factor to occupy with regard to the various issues raised, and (2) recent attempts have been made to define and isolate the concept of "neurotic constitution" (Slater, 1943, 1944) which is similar in many ways to our own factor, but which must be carefully differentiated from it in order to avoid confusion.

Roughly speaking, there appear to be two main views regarding the nature of "neuroticism". The traditional, German, view of neurosis, which is still perhaps more or less the orthodox view, is presented by Henderson and Gillespie (1943). According to this view, the neuroses, as compared with the psychoses, represent entirely different modes of reaction; "the distinctions between psychoneuroses in general and psychoses are symptomatic, psychopathological and therapeutic. . . . Considered biologically, that is, regarded as types of reaction to environment, the psycho-neuroses are distinctive in several ways. A psychosis involves a change in the whole personality of the subject in whom it appears, while in the psychoneuroses it is only a part of the personality that is affected. . . . Furthermore, in a psychosis reality is changed qualitatively and comes to be regarded in a way very different from the normal, and the patient behaves accordingly; in the psychoneuroses reality remains unchanged qualitatively, although its value may be quantitatively altered (diminished)."

This conception of qualitative differences between neuroses and psychoses has given rise to much dispute in the realm of the affective disorders. Ross (1937), who is one of the main exponents of the doctrine that such qualitative differences exist, has advanced the view that a special neurotic syndrome is manifested by "those patients whose chief symptom is either frank mental anxiety or its somatic manifestations, of which palpitations, sweating, flushing and tremor are the chief"; this view is supported by Rogerson (1940), who concludes his survey of the conflicting theories in this field by maintaining that "it may properly be said that the affective neuroses can be distinguished from the affective psychoses". Yellowlees (1930), Crichton-Miller (1930), and other writers have taken up a similar position.

On the other hand, Lewis (1934) maintains that "one cannot set up the symptom anxiety as an independent type of reaction", and accordingly includes anxiety reactions as a sub-group of the affective disorders. Curran (1937), who took two groups of cases, suffering from anxiety and depression, the one supposedly neurotic, the other psychotic, compared various features of the two groups and came to the conclusion that no list of criteria for differential diagnosis could be found. His results thus showed quantitative rather than qualitative differences. Bowlby (1940) also puts forward a "gradation" theory in support of this general view.

The difference in point of view of these writers may perhaps be clarified by comparing the concept of "neuroticism" with the modern view of mental defect. According to this view, "the genetic background of intellectual defect is multifactorial, when the special clinical types are excluded" (Penrose, 1944). Superimposed on this "multifactorial background", which gives rise to the well-known type of curve of distribution commonly found in examinations using modern intelligence tests, are a number of cases due to specific agents, e.g. phenylpyruvic amentia, amaurotic idiocy, cretinism, mongolism, hydrocephalus, microcephalus, and so forth. Thus a number of defectives are, as E. O. Lewis has pointed out, biological variants; they are simply those members of the population who occupy the lower end of the normal curve of distribution of intelligence. Alongside these are set those defectives whose condition is actually pathological, and whose presence accounts for the "hump" found in the normal distribution towards the lower end.

As Roberts (1939) has pointed out, "general intelligence . . . is a graded character and displays continuous variation from one extreme to the other. . . . Over the great bulk of the range there is no discontinuity. . . . A frequency curve is found to conform to the normal form. But at the extreme end . . . we find variations which are no longer continuous, and the curve is no longer normal. . . . At the very lowest levels, we find not merely the very backward; we find gross deviations, the idiots, and the imbeciles. . . . This portion of the curve is far from normal, for such individuals are far too numerous. The distinction, on the basis of measurement only is not absolute . . . (but) it is fundamental genetically. . . . We have, on the one hand, multifactor inheritance, on the other hand, the transmission of single genes; on the one hand, the genes of individually small effect, on the other, the gene whose bearer is sharply distinguished from the rest of his fellows. . . ."

In a similar manner, it might be argued, do we find a curve of distribution, of multifactorial origin, determining the personal adjustment level of the various members of the population; superimposed on this possibly normal curve there are the pathological variants—psychotics and, in the opinion of some writers, also the so-called neurotics.

Thus the discussion between the two opposing schools may be reduced to the simple question of whether or not certain types of abnormality are to be included in the "normal" distribution, as mere extreme cases occurring towards the lower end, or whether these types constitute pathological variants, superimposed on that curve. We cannot pretend to offer any evidence on this point, and indeed for our purpose there is relatively little need for taking sides on the issue.

The trait of "neuroticism", with which we shall be concerned in this book, is clearly similar in conception to the general trait of "intelligence"; pathological variants may or may not be present in the population on which our results are based, but it is only in so far as these variants find a position on the general scale of "neuroticism" that they would concern us. This view accords with that of a research worker concerned, say, with the elaboration of an intelligence test which would help him in diagnosing mental deficiency; for his purpose, the pathological variant is on the same footing as is the person representing the extremely low end of the normal distribution, and for his primary purpose the distinction is of purely academic interest.

By saying this we do not mean to deny that such distinctions are important, and indeed have great value, in other connections; we are merely concerned with pointing out that regardless of which view is taken of the nature of "neurosis", our results will retain their validity, although in certain points their interpretation might be affected. Evidence will be presented later to show that the view here advocated, viz. that in our tests we have been concerned with the "normal variant", rather than with the "pathological variant", is indeed the correct one; this is done in the main by showing that tests which measure degree of neuroticism in our neurotic group, also measure this trait as between a neurotic and a normal group, or within a normal group.

It is regrettable that the terminology which custom forces us to use tends to make the distinctions drawn above less vivid than they ought to be. Thus if we assume that the neurotic proper constitutes a "pathological variant", similar to the psychotic, then it is indeed unfortunate in the extreme that the general trait should be called "neuroticism". The only way out of this difficulty (apart from a renaming procedure which would only add to the profusion of new terms in psychology and psychiatry) would be for the word "neurotic" to be used exclusively for the person who occupies the low end of the distribution of "general adaptedness" or "personality organization", or whatever we conceive to constitute the essence of this trait. The pathological variant, then, would be called "psychotic".

This view, it may perhaps be claimed, has a certain heuristic value, although the difficulties besetting it cannot be ignored. In the first place, it is doubtful if any clearly-marked distinction can be drawn between the "normal" and the "pathological" variant; where should a mild depression, or a schizoid personality be put? In the second place, our experiments were done exclusively on non-psychotic patients, and consequently the position of a mildly psychotic individual on our scale cannot be determined, and is at best guess-work. These objections indicate the provisional nature of the scheme proposed, and point out certain deficiencies which further research must attempt to make good; whether such further research would force us to alter the whole scheme drastically it is impossible to say.

We shall attempt to clarify further our use of the term "neuroticism" by a critical discussion of a number of theories which have been held in the past, or are held at present, regarding the neuroses. As the Slater brothers (1944) have pointed out, there are three main classes of theories which have been advanced in this field. The first of the classes embraces theories which regard neurotic phenomena as types of response to which all human beings are equally liable; severity of neurosis, and type of neurosis, would then be solely or largely due to environmental effects. This theory may be called the *environmental stress* theory.

The second class of theories regards neuroticism as being of a unitary kind, and dependent on genetic factors. The genetic basis of the disorder might lie (a) in a single abnormal gene, whose variations in expression could be accounted for by environmental differences and by differences in the genotypic milieu, or it might lie (b) in a large number of separate genes of small but similar effect. This type of theory might be called the *hereditary predisposition* kind, occurring in a *unifactorial* and in a *multifactorial* form.

The third type of theory assumes more than one genetic factor, with dissimilar effects, to account for the neurotic constitution. These genetic factors may be conceived (a) to be specific to a particular type of neurosis, or else they may be thought of as (b) overlapping in their effects, and producing predispositions to more than one type of neurosis. This type of theory may be called the *multiple causation* kind, occurring in a *specific* or in an *overlapping* form.

All these theories agree that environmental stress plays some part in the production of the neurosis; the first question to be answered, therefore, is whether such stress alone is sufficient to account for the phenomena observed. Symonds (1943) has shown that "the incidence of neurosis in different tactical duties varies directly with the amount of hazard encountered, as measured by the casualty rates", a demonstration which strongly argues in favour of the "environmental stress" theory; he also showed, however, that predisposition played an important part in the breakdown of 2,200 neurotic casualties studied by him. From his data, Slater (1944) calculated that the correlation between degree of predisposition and degree of stress in these breakdown cases was negative ($r = -.0.26 \pm .02$). Thus the greater the degree of predisposition, the less stress was needed to provoke a neurotic reaction; this finding argues against the pure form of the environmental stress theory.

Against this theory may also be quoted the various studies of the personality differences and similarities in uniovular and binovular twins (Lange, 1929; Kranz, 1936; Stumpfl, 1936; Newman et al., 1937), as well as a number of studies in the familial incidence of neurosis and psychopathy quoted by the Slaters (1944). Thus we agree with Slater that this theory in its pure form must be rejected.

The Slaters also reject the hereditary predisposition theory in its unifactorial form. They point out that a theory of this kind has found some support as regards such psychiatric conditions as phenylpyruvic amentia, juvenile amaurotic idiocy, gargoylism, oxycephaly, epiloia, Huntington's chorea, cerebral dysrhythmia and epilepsy, manic-depressive psychoses, and schizophrenia; "in all these conditions findings are made which are believed to be specific for the condition in question, and it is worth remarking that similar investigations of neurosis and psychopathy have not resulted in comparable findings. On the basis of the theory, transitional forms between the normal and abnormal may occur, but will either be relatively infrequent, or will be capable of resolution with more refined examination into

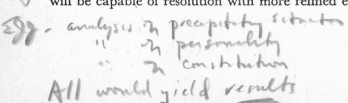

*E.g.? - analyses of precipitating situation*
*    " of personality*
*    " of constitution*
*All would yield results*

character-bearers and normals. Where this is only doubtful, as, for instance, in manic-depressive psychosis, some doubt is thrown on the postulation of a single gene. If a single abnormal gene were postulated as the basis of neurosis, necessary consequences would be that neurotics would be relatively homogeneous, and would show some highly discriminant characteristic which would differentiate them with fair certainty from the average population. . . . No single discriminant characteristic has so far been discovered."

The Slaters also reject the multifactorial form of the hereditary predisposition theory. They point out that "a necessary consequence of the unitary theory is the homogeneity of selected samples. . . . If the neurotic predisposition is a unitary trait, variations in characteristics which differentiate neurotics from normals will be smaller among neurotics, who form a selected sample, than among an unselected normal population. The presence or absence of homogeneity among neurotic subjects is, therefore, a matter of crucial importance; if it fails to hold . . . the theory breaks down."

Proof for the relative heterogeneity of neurotics is sought from two sources, and it is here that we must join issue with the Slaters. The first point they adduce is that such heterogeneity is a commonplace of clinical experience; anxiety states differ from hysterics, and so forth. This form of proof appears fallacious to us, as it rests on a false statistical premise. A factor may be unitary, but that does not necessitate the absence of any subsidiary group factors. Intelligence is considered a unitary factor, but in addition a number of group factors, such as verbal ability, visuo-spatial ability, arithmetical ability and so forth are recognized. Similarly, there is no reason why there should not be important group-factors subsidiary to a unitary general factor of neuroticism. Lack of homogeneity cannot be proved by an argument of this kind.

The Slaters' second method of proof is open to a different objection. They have shown that when certain tests (such as intelligence tests, tests of reaction time, and others) are given to neurotics, two observations can be made. (A): There is evidence of heterogeneity among the neurotics because *certain syndromes differ significantly from other syndromes*. This finding is fully borne out by our own researches, but cannot be regarded as affecting the issue because of the reasons given in the last paragraph.

(B): They have shown that with respect to certain tests neurotics are more heterogeneous (show larger S.D.'s) than do comparable normal groups. This finding also does not appear to have any real bearing on the issue. Clearly, the relative homogeneity of a group depends entirely on the way that group has been selected. If we measure trait A in the whole population, then the S.D. of that trait would differ from the S.D. of the same trait measured in a selected sub-population in ways predictable if we knew the principle of selection. If, for instance, the sub-population included a much larger proportion of cases from one extreme of the normal distribution than did the whole population, while also including rather a smaller proportion of cases from various other points of the normal distribution, then it is quite conceivable (depending on the exact number of cases from each point of the distribution included) that the S.D. of the sub-population would be considerably larger than the S.D. of the original population.

Now, this seems to be the actual position with respect to the selection of service neurotics. A hospital such as the one from which the Slaters took their experimental population includes a much larger number of extreme cases of trait A (neuroticism) than does the normal population; it also includes, however, a fair number of people who would fall on intermediate portions of the curve. Indeed, some so-called "neurotic" inmates of such a hospital show very little evidence of the "neurotic constitution", and would presumably be situated rather towards the "normal" end of the distribution. Consequently, unless much more is known about the actual distribution of the trait "neuroticism" in the hospital population, as compared with the total population, the argument is at best inconclusive.

To this negative type of disproof may be added a more positive type of proof in favour of the unitary factor theory. If a number of tests could be found which vary directly with "degree of neuroticism", and which were relatively unaffected by such personality-differences as exist within the neurotic group, then the position of those who advocate a unitary kind of theory would be considerably strengthened. Several such tests have been found, and are described in the following chapters. Consequently, we are unable to follow the Slaters in their dismissal of the unitary theory of predisposition, in its multifactorial form.

The Slaters advocate a theory of the overlapping multiple causation kind (1943, 1944). We do not consider that such evidence as is available makes it possible to decide between their theory and the multifactorial hereditary predisposition theory which we should prefer. Only direct genetic experimentation can give us the necessary evidence on this point, and it is hoped that the elaboration of a series of tests of "neuroticism" presented in this book will make this kind of experiment possible. Until such further evidence is forthcoming, we shall consider neuroticism in the manner indicated, admitting the possibility that our data might have to be reinterpreted in terms of a multiple causation theory.

In view of all the difficulties and doubts raised by the attempt to identify a statistical factor with a psychiatric concept, it would no doubt be preferable in some ways to employ a more neutral kind of label.[1] Thus in a similar situation, Spearman decided that the term "intelligence" had too many different connotations to be useful in designating the statistical factor which he had isolated, and accordingly named this factor "g". Other writers followed suit, and now we have a whole factorial alphabet, from Burt's "e" and Garnett's "c" to Webb's "w" and Spearman's "o". If, therefore, we consider it wise to label our factor in a manner which does not prejudice further research into its psychological nature by assuming identity with better-understood concepts, we may have recourse to the terminology used in characterizing the item most closely correlated with the factor, viz. "Badly organized personality". We may then denote our factor "P", for personality organization, referring to the less stable, less well organized, or more neutral part of the distribution as "P–", and to the more stable, better organized, or less neurotic part of the distribution as "P + ".

[1] The necessity of changing our stock of psychiatric and psychological terms, with their multitudinous connotations and their emotional significance, into operationally defined symbols, has been well put by a well-known historian of science: "It is only after centuries of apparently sterile but necessary quarrels and after the final establishment of the experimental method and attitude that we have slowly learned to consider words as symbols, which, as far as scientific purposes are concerned, would be usefully replaced by arbitrary signs having no signification but the one explicitly defined. The distinction between names and things is now so deeply rooted in the mind of scientifically trained men that they would find it difficult to understand how they could ever be confused, if they did not detect examples of such confusion almost every day in their own environment" (Sarton, 1927).

Although the method of labelling statistical factors in this fashion has certain advantages, in practice it has not been found possible to adhere strictly to the letter-terminology. Thus Spearman has not been able to omit the concept of "intelligence" completely, and for the most part the two different appellations of the same factor have continued to exist side by side. Similarly, in this book use is made both of the term "neuroticism" and of the letter "P"; convenience alone has determined in each case which term should be used.

The distribution of "P" in the hospital population may be of interest. Taking the eight items most highly saturated with the general factor, weights were assigned to them according to the Cowdry-Kelley weighting formula (Guilford, 1936). Each of 1,000 male and 1,000 female patients (unselected) was then given a score on the basis of the items scored positively on the Item Sheet, each item being multiplied by the weight it had received. Both sexes show very similar distributions, with means of 4·89 and 4·85 for the men and the women respectively. Both distributions closely resemble a normal distribution curve.

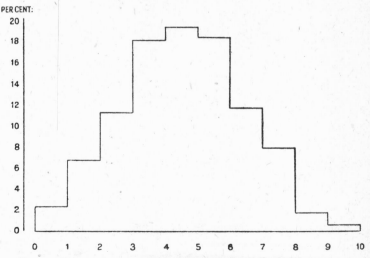

FIG. 4. DISTRIBUTION OF "NEUROTICISM" FOR 1,000 MALE AND 1,000 FEMALE NEUROTICS.

In Figure 4 is shown the distribution of the combined scores for males and females. The mean is 4·87, with a S.D. of 2·25.

The fact that the distribution is so close to a normal curve is, perhaps, rather surprising. If we assume that "P" is distributed normally in the total population, then it might have been thought that only one end of this distribution would be found in a psychoneurotic hospital. For if we cut off one end of a normal distribution, the persons making up that end should form a group showing a J-shaped distribution rather than a normal one. The explanation presumably is to be sought in the fact that neurotic breakdown must be traced to a combination of two factors: (1) the constitutional and (2) the environmental. A person's constitution may render him liable to breakdown at the slightest provocation; on the other hand, a person of first-class constitution may finally break down when the stress is too great (Slater, 1944). Consequently the population of a hospital such as the one under discussion here is made up not only of the "P–" end of the normal population, but also of "P +" personalities who have experienced very great stress. When we add to this factor the large error variance inevitably associated with ratings of any kind, which presumably would tend to create the impression of normality in the distribution, our results seem to be capable of adequate explanation.

### 4. Introversion-Extraversion

We may now turn to the nature and distribution of our second, bipolar factor. This discussion may, perhaps, best be opened by a quotation. Jung believes that "medical experience has taught us that there are two large groups of functional nervous disorders —the one embraces all those forms of disease which are designated hysteria, the other all those forms which the French school has designated psychasthenia. . . . The hysteric belongs to the type of Extraversion, the psychasthenic to the type of Introversion".

Our findings would certainly seem to support the view that neurotics can be classified along an axis stretching from the "pure hysteric" to the opposite pole characterized by many of the traits which make up Jung's picture of "psychasthenia" (dysthymia); thus far we are in agreement with Jung. Are we justified in assuming further (1) that these disorders form two separate classes, relatively separate one from the other, and

(2) that persons liable to fall into these classes belong to the extraverted and introverted types respectively? A review of the evidence available may throw light on these questions.

One great difficulty immediately threatens to make any identification between hysteric tendency and extraversion, and dysthymia and introversion, quite impossible. This difficulty lies in the fact that American investigators using a variety of questionnaires have shown conclusively that questionnaires of "introversion" measure essentially the same personality qualities as questionnaires of "neuroticism" (Bernreuter, 1934). Factorial studies of these questionnaires usually reveal a general factor which, as Vernon points out, "does in part correspond to a genuine maladjusted-psychoneurotic-introverted tendency" (1938). But if introversion is thus to be identified with neuroticism, how can we explain that in our own study these two factors are quite independent?

The answer to this problem is given in an excellent study by Collier and Emch (1938), who show that most questionnaire-constructors have used Freud's conception of "introversion", rather than Jung's. Freud identifies "introversion" with incipient neuroticism; he writes: "An introvert is not yet a neurotic, but he finds himself in a labile condition; he must develop symptoms at the next dislocation of forces, if he does not find other outlets for his pent-up libido" (1920). Jung on the other hand considers that "it is a mistake to believe that introversion is more or less the same as neurosis. As concepts, the two have not the slightest connection with each other" (1923). Thus the conceptual identification of introversion and neuroticism, so common in much recent work, rests on a misapprehension of Jung's work, and does not invalidate our findings.

Another difficulty also would appear to be due to faulty understanding of Jung's point of view. Tests of "Introversion" usually contain a large number of questions regarding sociability; in fact, extraversion and sociability are completely identified in the minds of many writers. Close study of Jung's writings discloses that "sociability" is not one of the outstanding marks of the extravert; the view that there is a close connection between the two appears due to Freyd (1924), who maintained that the extravert is "an individual in whom exists a diminution of the thought processes in relation to directly observable social behaviour with an accompanying tendency to make social contacts". This view does not fit in too well with descriptions of the hysteric as given by clinical observers. Thus Henderson and Gillespie (1943), for instance, show that "the personality in hysteria is frequently an unusual one, apart from the tendency to dissociation. The hysterical patient is often emotional, shy and reserved, even a little 'peculiar'. There has been described an 'hysterical personality'. This consists of lifelong theatricality of behaviour and a desire to impress and gain sympathy, a contrast between actual shallowness of the feelings and the intensity of the expression of them, a contrary contrast of external shyness and intense erotic interest, a lack of persistence of emotion and of effort, and much compensatory day-dreaming." This quotation, which represents the hysteric as "shy and reserved", must throw grave doubt on the propriety of using sociability as the main criterion of extraversion, as is done by most questionnaire-authors of recent years.

The main burden of our argument is that lack of "sociability" must be regarded as an index of neuroticism, not as a sign of introversion. This conclusion is in opposition to most modern psychological theorizing in this field, and runs counter to almost all recent practice in constructing questionnaires of introversion, so that a separate proof in favour of our contention appears desirable. It is provided in an unpublished report by Dr. Russell Fraser and other members of this hospital, on "The Incidence of Neurosis among Factory Workers". The authors of this report examined 3,083 unselected adult workers in 13 light or medium engineering factories employing over 30,000 workers. The sample was chosen at random from the whole staff between the ages of 21 and 60. Men and women were equally represented. Each individual was examined twice; he was given intelligence and other tests, had his blood analyzed, was examined physically and psychiatrically, and finally had an interview with the social worker. Work records, records of absenteeism, and other objective data were also available on each worker.

A special analysis was undertaken of the incidence of neurosis, and of the circumstances most usually associated with neurosis. It was found that 10% of the workers studied suffered from definite disabling neurotic illness, and that a further 20% suffered from minor forms of neurosis, during the course of the six months covered by the study. As regards the second point, Dr. Fraser found that "a decrease in social contacts was the circumstance most commonly associated with neurosis. Those whose leisure was usually spent alone or only with their immediate family, suffered more than average neurosis. Those with diminished recreation and leisure interests also, but less strikingly, suffered more from neurosis. . . . It is evident that the circumstances outside the factory which were associated with a high incidence of neurosis, are characterized by unsatisfactory human relationships. The more obviously unsatisfactory the human relationships, the closer the association."

To give an illustration of the kind of data on which this conclusion is based, we may quote some figures on the incidence of neurosis in groups of men and women showing respectively: (a) many social contacts; (b) average or more; (c) less than average, and (d) definitely below average social contacts. The results are given in the Table below, where N = number of workers in each group.

TABLE SHOWING INCIDENCE OF NEUROSIS IN GROUPS DIFFERING IN "SOCIABILITY"

| | Neurosis.: | | N=. | |
| Group. | Men. | Women. | Men. | Women. |
|---|---|---|---|---|
| (a) Many social contacts . | 24·2% | 32·0% | 296 | 194 |
| (b) Average or more . | 23·9% | 32·4% | 626 | 451 |
| (c) Less than average . | 32·0% | 34·0% | 375 | 462 |
| (d) Definitely below average | 45·1% | 43·4% | 149 | 341 |
| Total group . | 28·3% | 36·0% | 1446 | 1448 |

In this Table, minor and major neuroses have been taken together under the heading: "Neurosis". Taking only definite neuroses, percentages increase from group (a) to group (d) for men and women respectively in the following manner: 5·8%, 7·2%, 8·7%, 19·3% and 8·6%, 12·9%, 10·2%, 18·2%. When it is realized that the differences brought out in these figures are heavily attenuated by varying standards of "neuroticism" and "sociability", it becomes clear that these two personality traits show a considerable correlation. We may, therefore, claim that this study powerfully reinforces our argument in favour of dropping "absence of sociability" as a part of the "introvert" syndrome, and of including it rather in the "neurotic" syndrome.

The possibility cannot, of course, be ruled out that in addition to being correlated with neuroticism, lack of sociability may show slightly more affinity with dysthymia than with hysteria, or *vice versa*. In the absence of any experimental work on this point, the question must be left open.

We must dismiss, for the reason given, most of the questionnaire studies so plentiful in the literature (in 1942, Super was able to review 147 such studies carried out with one particular questionnaire alone!). An exception is the work of Vernon (1938), who used the Boyd questionnaire and factor-analysed the intercorrelations between the questions. He found one factor, presumably similar to our "P +" factor, which showed high saturations with freedom from instability, ready action, carefulness, freedom from emotional thinking, and strong self-control. He also found two further factors, presumably similar to the "dysthymia" and the "hysteria" pole of our second factor respectively. These factors were characterized by "depression, instability, anxiety, lack of self-control and lack of self-sufficiency", and by "care-freeness, shirking responsibility, lack of definite interests, freedom from worry and from self-consciousness". The similarity between these results, obtained from normal students, and our own is so striking that they constitute a powerful argument in favour of Jung's position.

Further evidence comes from a multitude of other studies involving ratings and tests, such as those of Burt (1937), Cattell (1933), Studman (1935), Garnett (1918), who used Webb's data, Oates (1929), Howie (1945), McCloy (1936), Line (1935), Flanagan (1935), and Kelley (1935). These studies all agree in finding a bipolar factor variously called "surgency-desurgency", "aggressive-inhibitive", "c", "cautious-reckless", or whatever term appeared appropriate; in spite of variations in nomenclature, these factors closely resemble each other as well as our own "hysteria-dysthymia" factor.[1]

---

[1] Pride of place in this connection might go to Burt's pioneer investigation into "emotionality" (1915), were it not for certain difficulties of interpretation. If we regard the introvert as the emotional, "deep-narrow" person, and the extravert as the unemotional, "broad-shallow" person, then Burt's general factor of emotionality might be identified with the extravert-introvert dichotomy. However, this interpretation is not the only possible one of Burt's original data, and it is by no means clear that Burt himself would agree with this identification. His further argument that "neuroticism" may be regarded as a result of too much endowment with the "e" factor in the absence of sufficient endowment with the "g" factor, i.e. as a ratio of "emotionality" and "intelligence", makes it unlikely that his scheme and the one proposed here could be directly identified.

Also based on experimental work is a similar dichotomy first put forward by Pavlov, who finds that "with the collision of . . . excitatory and . . . inhibitory processes, there appears either a predominance of the stimulating process, disturbing the inhibition . . . or in other cases a predominance of the inhibitory process . . . disturbing the excitatory process" (1941). Altogether, then, the recognition of some essential bipolarity such as was posited by Jung appears to have found much support from experimental sources.

The question remains, however, whether the general quality of introversion leads to anxiety-depressive states under stress, while the general quality of extraversion leads to hysterical states. Some evidence on this point is available in the work of Slater (1944), who correlated personality traits with corresponding syndrome. Such correlations as he reports in regard to hysteria and anxiety are rather low, viz. in the neighbourhood of ·4; however, in view of the known inaccuracies of routine diagnoses and assessments such as he relied upon we can say little about the unattenuated size of these correlations, or upon the question of how far they might have been influenced by "halo" effects. In any case, no direct evidence is available regarding pre-neurotic personality and neurotic illness; consequently, this part of the Jungian theory cannot be regarded as established.

## 5. THEORIES OF INTROVERSION-EXTRAVERSION

A brief review of some descriptions of extraverts and introverts respectively may be useful in deciding whether these terms can justifiably be applied to our bipolar factor. Jung himself says: "When orientation to the object and the objective facts is so predominant that the most frequent and essential decisions and actions are determined, not by subjective values, but by objective relations, one speaks of an extraverted attitude. When this becomes habitual, one speaks of the extraverted type. Unlike the extraverted type, the introverted type is prevailingly orientated by subjective factors. Introverted consciousness doubtless views the external conditions, but it selects the subjective determinants as the decisive ones."

Similarly, Conklin (1922) defines extraversion "as a more or less prolonged condition in which attention is controlled by the objective conditions of attention more than by the subjective, and in which the content of the subjective conditions is most closely related to the objective". Introversion is defined as "the reverse of the above".

Freyd (1924), whose definition has already been mentioned, thinks of the introvert as "an individual in whom exists an exaggeration of the thought processes in relation to directly observable social behaviour, with an accompanying tendency to withdraw from social contacts". *Per contra*, the extravert is "an individual in whom exists a diminution of the thought processes in relation to directly observable social behaviour with an accompanying tendency to make social contacts".

This view was put into physiological terms by McDougall (1926), who maintained that "the essential mark of the extreme introvert is the tendency to internal activity of the brain, especially to an excess of those activities of the highest level in which self-conscious reflection and control of lower level processes bulk so largely. The essential mark of the extravert is the ready passing over of the effective urge into action and expression, without the modification and control of it by cerebral processes of the highest level."

White (1926) considers introversion a return to a less clearly defined individuality, and a return to a phylogenetically older and more diffuse form of contact with reality, while Tansley (1925), taking the opposite view, calls extraversion a primitive biological function of the mind. Bingham (1925) takes refuge in a behaviouristic definition, maintaining that "(in) introversion (we) stress the exaggerated tendencies to delay response, to inhibit overt emotional expression, and to withdraw from social contacts".

These representative definitions [1] reveal marked differences

---

[1] A full discussion of different definitions is given by Guilford and Braly (1930). Among other writers whose views may be of interest, the following may be quoted: Kempf (1921) believes that the introvert has a more highly developed and more dominant central nervous system, and hence is more subject to inhibitions and delayed responses of a directly adaptative nature. Marston (1925) believes that extraversion can be identified with a tendency towards skeletal expression of emotion, while introversion is identified with the dissipation of emotionally aroused energy within the organism rather than with the adequate discharge of this energy through skeletal channels upon the environment. Hunt (1929) introduces the concepts of "erethitic" and "kolytic" types, which he identifies with inhibition (introversion) and excitation (extraversion) respectively. Washburn (1929) obtained negative results in giving tests of reaction time, cube fluctuation and mirror drawing to "introverts" and "extraverts", while Furukawa (1927) claimed to have distinguished "active" (extraverted) from "passive" (introverted) subjects on the basis of their blood group. These definitions and findings add little to the points made in the text; they are merely included for the sake of completeness.

in outlook, and are all characterized by lack of operational connotation. There seems to be some agreement on these points: (a) the introvert has a more subjective, the extravert a more objective outlook; (b) the introvert shows a higher degree of cerebral activity, the extravert a higher degree of behavioural activity; (c) the introvert shows a tendency to self-control (inhibition), the extravert a tendency to lack of such control. In our experimental work the dysthymic group was found to exhibit the introverted traits, as enumerated above, while the hysterical group was found to exhibit the extraverted traits, and accordingly there need be little hesitation in using the terms Extraversion and Introversion in referring to our two groups.

One difficulty arises, however, in using these terms in relation to our neurotic population. When we contrast the behaviour of a group of dysthymics with the behaviour of a group of hysterics, it must be clear that we are dealing with the contrast between *neurotic* extraverts and *neurotic* introverts; our results cannot immediately be generalized to cover the behaviour of non-neurotic extraverts and introverts. If this qualification is borne in mind, there is perhaps little harm in identifying our two neurotic groups with "extraverts" and "introverts".

The distribution of this bipolar temperament factor for our experimental population may be of interest. No large-scale investigation of such "type" distributions involving ratings would appear to have been carried out with the exception of Burt's important study (1940); he found no evidence of any bimodality in his sample. In the present study, 1,000 male and 1,000 female neurotic patients (unselected) were given a score on the basis of the sixteen items most highly correlated with the bipolar factor, each item being weighted in accordance with the Cowdry-Kelley formula (Guilford, 1936). (Eight of these items were taken from the hysteric end of the distribution, the other eight from the dysthymic end.) Arbitrarily, the dysthymic end of the distribution was regarded as the negative pole, the hysteric end as the positive pole. The mean for the male neurotics was precisely zero, that of the female neurotics was −·04. As the two distributions were not significantly different, they were thrown together and are shown in Figure 5. The combined distribution has a mean of −·02, and a Standard Deviation of 2·36.

The distribution shows no evidence of bimodality; it closely resembles a normal distribution. Consequently, we shall arbitrarily define a person as belonging to the hysteric type if his score on the items chosen to identify this type is more than 1 S.D. below the mean; similarly, a person shall be arbitrarily defined as belonging to the dysthymic type if his score on the items chosen to identify this type is more than 1 S.D. above the mean. In our experimental attempts to study the two types, described in detail in the following chapters, selection was made on the basis of special clinical diagnosis, not on the basis of the item-sheet, which became available only after the patient had left the hospital. However, when the item-sheet analysis was compared with the original clinical classification it was found that in 68% of 150 cases the persons chosen to exemplify each type by the psychiatrist fell into the area of the distribution curve chosen to specify that type on the basis of the item sheet. Only 5% of the cases fell into the wrong half of the curve.

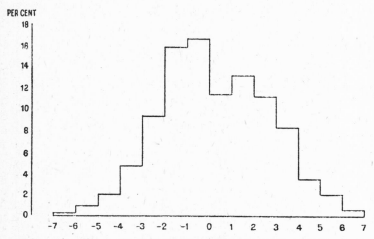

FIG. 5. DISTRIBUTION OF "INTROVERSION-EXTRAVERSION" FOR 1,000 MALE AND 1,000 FEMALE NEUROTICS.

These figures indicate comparatively good agreement between the senior psychiatrists who selected the patients for our experimental groups, and the psychiatrist in charge of the patient, who filled in the item sheet. It is also obvious that the agreement is far from complete, as might indeed have been expected on the basis of such knowledge of the relative unreliability of ratings as psychologists have amassed in the past (Vernon, 1938). We may conclude that such differences as are shown on experimental tests between groups of dysthymic and hysteric patients selected in the manner described will be considerably attenuated because of the relative unreliability of the selection; however, any *marked* differences between the types ought to become obvious in spite of this unreliability.   Thus, positive conclusions would in all probability have been even more significant than they appear in our calculations, if we had to deal with perfectly chosen groups; accordingly, in finding significant differences we are on relatively safe ground, and may justifiably conclude that such differences as are found may be used to define the two types operationally. Failure to find a difference, however, may be due to one of two factors: (1) absence of any such difference, and (2) attenuation of a small difference actually present by unreliability of selection. Consequently, interpretation of negative results must always be more hazardous than interpretation of positive results, and several repetitions of the experiment, with different methods of selection, seem advisable.   This is the course followed with our experiments on suggestibility and colour/form reactions, for instance.

The evidential value of psychiatrists' ratings, of course, is strictly limited.   It might be argued quite justifiably that both our factors delineate syndromes which exist in the minds of the psychiatrists concerned, not in the behaviour of the patients. Webb's "w" factor has often been said to be nothing but a "halo" effect, produced by the general liking or disliking of the ratee by the rater; similarly, our "P" factor is susceptible to this criticism.   Again, in the literature "hysterics" and "dysthymics" are often said to possess certain traits; may it not be that the psychiatrist, having arrived at a diagnosis, simply tends to attribute these various traits to the person so diagnosed?   In fact, our ratings are subject to all the objections and difficulties set forth by the more critical writers on the subject (Symonds, 1931; Vernon, 1938; Greene, 1941).   While we have made efforts to overcome the more obvious snags and pitfalls, there seemed to be no possibility of overcoming the essential subjectivity of ratings, even when made by experienced psychiatrists.

However, it is possible to validate the two factors experimentally by showing that "P +" patients differ from "P—" patients significantly with respect to an operationally definable variable, or that dysthymics differ from hysterics in a similar manner. The rest of this book is devoted to a discussion of experiments in which "P +" patients and "P—" patients, or dysthymics and hysterics, were submitted to a variety of psychological tests chosen because on *a priori* grounds it seemed likely that these tests would discriminate between these groups. Again, a negative result would not have proved in any way that our two factors did not represent real and suitable principles of classification; such a result might have been due to an unsuitable selection of tests. In actual fact, the results obtained were positive in almost every instance, thus showing that the psychiatrists' ratings were not in the main based on subjective opinions lacking objective reference, but did in part correspond to real principles of division in the human material with which they were dealing.

## 6. QUESTIONNAIRE STUDY OF NEUROTICISM

One possible method of obtaining objective evidence with respect to the two factors isolated lies in the use of questionnaires. The word "objective" may be criticized in this connection, because questionnaires are often held to be one of the prime examples of extreme subjectivity. It would appear that one's view of the subjectivity or objectivity of a questionnaire depends entirely on the evidential value one ascribes to the resulting scores. If we argue that because person A answers "Yes" to the question: "Are you easily fatigued?", while person B answers "No", therefore A is more easily fatigued than B, we obviously leave ourselves open to all the criticisms which have rightly been raised against the use of questionnaires. If, however, we look at the behavioural act of underlining "Yes" rather than "No", without necessarily drawing any conclusions as to the motives or underlying reasons which may have prompted this reaction, then we are dealing with a purely objective type of response which may or may not be of importance in the study of personality. To put this argument in another way, the response of the subject to the questionnaire is a purely objective one; the interpretation of the response is usually quite subjective, but may by the adduction of suitable evidence acquire a certain amount of objectivity.

The objection is sure to be made that unless we take interpretation into account, the objective scores are meaningless, and that consequently the argument presented may have logical consistency, but little psychological interest. The value of this objection depends on the use which is to be made of the results of one's experiment. If our aim is the characterization of groups of persons already known to differ with regard to certain personality traits, then we must acknowledge the force of the objection. But if we are dealing with two groups the differences between which are not established in any objective fashion, then the fact that these groups can be shown to differ significantly on a questionnaire in itself establishes the fact that the two groups are different; the original subjective principle of differentiation is therefore strengthened. If in addition we can interpret the observed results on the questionnaire, so much the better; such interpretation, however, is by no means necessary in order to establish the systematic value of the questionnaire study.

The questionnaire used in our work was developed by means of preliminary experimentation; some of these experiments themselves may be of interest. In the main, they consisted in item analyses performed on various existing types of questionnaire, and attempts to validate such results as might be found against objective criteria.

The first questionnaire to be subjected to such analysis was a 46-item Medical Questionnaire, which has been used extensively in this country and abroad. It consists of questions dealing largely with physical complaints, such as are frequently made by neurotic subjects; a few psychological questions are also included. The reason for putting the questionnaire in this form lay in the fact that while most people are suspicious of questions probing into their mental difficulties and symptoms, they are far more likely to be forthcoming when questioned along the more "orthodox" lines dealing with bodily health. The score on this questionnaire consists simply in the number of symptoms shown.

Results were available for 1,500 normal male soldiers;[1]

[1] Here and throughout the book, "normal" does not imply complete absence of neurotic symptoms from all members of a group so designated; an average "normal" group is quite likely to contain a number of potential or actual neurotics.

also tested were 300 male neurotic patients at this hospital. The average score of the normal soldiers on the questionnaire was 5; for the neurotics it was 19. This large difference might be thought to be due to the fact that the normal soldiers would be anxious to hide any defects from the examiner, while the neurotics might be only too keen to bring their complaints to the forefront. Consequently, the neurotic scores were analysed in two groups: 150 neurotics who were boarded out of the army subsequently, and 150 neurotics who were sent back to their units.

These two groups showed significant differences from each other; the "P +" group had an average score of 17, the "P–" group had an average score of 21. The difference between these two scores is significant at the ·01 level of probability. A similar validation method had been used for the normal soldiers. Of those scoring under 10 points, 10% had been given a psychiatric interview; of those scoring 10 points or more, over 80% had been given such an interview.[1] Of those interviewed, 8% with a score of under 10 were found to suffer from an incapacitating neurosis; for those scoring between 10 and 15 and interviewed, the percentage suffering from an incapacitating neurosis was 12, while for those with a score above 15 and interviewed it was over 30.

An item analysis had been carried out on the responses of the normal soldiers, showing which questions showed highest correlation with total score. An item analysis was also carried out on the neurotic subjects, determining which items differentiated best between the "P +" and the "P–" group. The results of these analyses agree extremely well; the tetrachoric correlation between them being $r_t = + 0.66$. Thus we may conclude that this questionnaire (a) distinguishes neurotic soldiers from normal soldiers, (b) distinguishes the more neurotic from the less neurotic in the normal group, (c) distinguishes the more neurotic from the less neurotic in the neurotic group, (d) achieves this result by means of questions covering the same areas of personality in the two groups.

These results are of interest because they show that our "P +" and "P–" groups are not merely artificial creations due to "halo" effects on the part of the psychiatrist, but that these two groups are also differentiated objectively by means of their

[1] The decision to send the candidate to a psychiatrist for an interview was taken on grounds independent of the questionnaire results.

scores on the questionnaire. The other results given above suggest that this quality we have provisionally designated "P" is not confined to the hospital population, but extends to the outside world; the clearest proof for this contention lies in the surprisingly high agreement between the item analyses performed on the normal and the neurotic populations respectively.

Experiments similar to the one described were carried out on questionnaires of the more usual variety, using questions having a psychological rather than a medical import. The numbers of patients involved were always rather small, and little purpose would be served in recounting these preliminary studies. In the end, a questionnaire was drawn up which included the most diagnostic questions from both the psychological and the medical spheres; this questionnaire is reproduced in Table 2. The number of "Yes" answers underlined constitutes the score of the patient.

Mean score of 547 neurotic men on this questionnaire was 19·51 ± 8·66; of 264 neurotic women, it was 16·82 ± 8·54. The difference between the means is significant, the C.R. being 4. This sex difference is in the expected direction; as we have shown in the discussion of the item sheet, the women tend to show a less serious picture of neuroticism than do the men.

As our main interest in the questionnaire lay in its use inside the hospital, i.e. in sorting out the more seriously ill from the less seriously ill, only a small number of normal subjects was tested.[1] The average score of 300 non-neurotic men was 2·81 ± 2·60. While this score is significantly different from the neurotic scores quoted above, little interest attaches to such a ponderous demonstration of the simple fact that neurotics complain about more neurotic symptoms than do normals.

The distributions of scores for the neurotic men and women are curiously platykurtic, and rather skewed in the case of the men. Similarly, the distribution of scores for the normals is rather skewed. However, on the whole the distributions are not too markedly divergent from the general shape of the normal distribution.

[1] In giving the questionnaire to normal subjects, the items were reworded so as to refer to present symptoms and feelings, rather than to symptoms and feelings *prior to admission to hospital*, as in the case of the neurotics. Thus the first item would read: Do you have dizzy turns? not: Did you have dizzy turns? Similarly, the last sentence of the instructions was omitted in the case of the normal subjects.

*Medical Questionnaire*

Name (Block letters and in full): .........................................

Date ..............................

Read through these questions and underline the correct answer, either "Yes" or "No". Do not omit any item. The questions refer to your state of health before your present illness developed and caused you to come into hospital.

| | | | $r_tM$: | $r_tF$: |
|---|---|---|---|---|
| 1. Did you have dizzy turns? | Yes | No | ·71 | ·72 |
| 2. Did you get palpitations or thumping in your heart? | Yes | No | ·76 | ·57 |
| 3. Did you ever have a nervous breakdown? | Yes | No | ·35 | ·51 |
| 4. Have you ever been off work through sickness a good deal? | Yes | No | ·53 | ·65 |
| 5. Did you often use to get "stage fright" in your life? | Yes | No | ·84 | ·22 |
| 6. Did you find it difficult to get into conversation with strangers? | Yes | No | ·80 | ·64 |
| 7. Have you ever been troubled by a stammer or a stutter? | Yes | No | ·55 | ·64 |
| 8. Have you ever been made unconscious for two hours or more by an accident or blow? | Yes | No | ·47 | ·35 |
| 9. Did you worry too long over humilating experiences? | Yes | No | ·80 | ·52 |
| 10. Did you consider yourself rather a nervous person? | Yes | No | ·83 | ·72 |
| 11. Were your feelings easily hurt? | Yes | No | ·87 | ·54 |
| 12. Did you usually keep in the background on social occasions? | Yes | No | ·44 | ·69 |
| 13. Were you subject to attacks of shaking or trembling? | Yes | No | ·79 | ·78 |
| 14. Were you an irritable person? | Yes | No | ·84 | ·85 |
| 15. Did ideas run through your head so that you could not sleep? | Yes | No | ·83 | ·75 |
| 16. Did you use to worry over possible misfortunes? | Yes | No | ·83 | ·66 |
| 17. Were you rather shy? | Yes | No | ·71 | ·84 |
| 18. Did you sometimes feel happy, sometimes depressed without any apparent reason? | Yes | No | ·79 | ·74 |
| 19. Did you daydream a lot? | Yes | No | ·72 | ·53 |
| 20. Didn't you use to have as much life about you as others? | Yes | No | ·61 | ·82 |
| 21. Did you sometimes get a pain over your heart? | Yes | No | ·55 | ·36 |
| 22. Did you have nightmares? | Yes | No | ·69 | ·48 |
| 23. Did you worry about your health? | Yes | No | ·68 | ·78 |
| 24. Have you sometimes walked in your sleep? | Yes | No | ·36 | ·24 |
| 25. Did you sweat a great deal without exercise? | Yes | No | ·58 | ·68 |
| 26. Did you find it difficult to make friends? | Yes | No | ·76 | ·52 |
| 27. Did your mind often wander badly, so that you lost trace of what you were doing? | Yes | No | ·87 | ·75 |
| 28. Did you use to be touchy on various subjects? | Yes | No | ·87 | ·71 |
| 29. Did you often feel disgruntled? | Yes | No | ·82 | ·76 |
| 30. Did you often feel just miserable? | Yes | No | ·80 | ·90 |
| 31. Did you often feel self-conscious in the presence of superiors? | Yes | No | ·79 | ·77 |
| 32. Did you suffer from sleeplessness? | Yes | No | ·83 | ·72 |
| 33. Did you ever get short of breath without having done heavy work? | Yes | No | ·71 | ·81 |
| 34. Did you suffer from severe headaches? | Yes | No | ·81 | ·68 |
| 35. Did you suffer from "nerves"? | Yes | No | ·85 | ·81 |
| 36. Were you troubled by aches and pains? | Yes | No | ·73 | ·79 |
| 37. Did you get nervous in places such as lifts, trains, or tunnels? | Yes | No | ·86 | ·68 |
| 38. Did you suffer from attacks of diarrhoea? | Yes | No | ·57 | ·44 |
| 39. Did you lack self-confidence? | Yes | No | ·81 | ·76 |
| 40. Were you troubled with feelings of inferiority? | Yes | No | ·74 | ·69 |

NOTE: $r_tM$ = correlation of each question with total score for men;
$r_tF$ = correlation of each question with total score for women.

The questionnaire has a rather high internal consistency. Tetrachoric correlations were run, for the neurotic men and the neurotic women separately, between each question and the total scores. The results are shown in Table 2. It will be seen that on the average, each question correlates with the total score rather highly both for the men ($\bar{r}_t = + 0\cdot72$) and for the women ($\bar{r}_t = + 0\cdot65$). These relatively high correlations show that a great deal of generality prevails in the test-responses of our subjects. Presumably, this "generality" is a compound of genuine symptomatology, hypochondriasis, and positive attitude towards answering questionnaires of this type.

There are some rather interesting differences between the men and the women with respect to the degree of diagnostic value of each question. Questions 3, 4, 7, 12, 17, 20, 23, 25, 30, and 33 are more diagnostic for the women than for the men; questions 5, 9, 11, 16, 19, 22, 26, 28, and 37 are more diagnostic for the men. The meaningfulness of these differences is difficult to assess, and no general psychological reason suggests itself which might account for them.

While the internal method of validation implied in an item-analysis such as we have performed throws some light on the question of generality or specificity of the questions included, it tells us nothing regarding the external validity of the test. Nor does it tell us much regarding the reliability of the questionnaire. The latter was calculated by means of the split-halves method, corrected by the Spearman-Brown prophecy formula; it is $+ 0\cdot89$ for the men and $+ 0\cdot87$ for the women. The external validity of the questionnaire was established by correlating the scores of the patients with the psychiatrist's rating.

The patients were divided into two groups, according to the rating of the psychiatrist in charge on the item: "Badly organized personality". Tetrachoric correlations were run between score on the questionnaire and the dichotomous division "Badly organized personality"—"Yes" or "No". High score on the questionnaire was correlated with badly organized personality to the extent of $r_t = + 0\cdot48 \pm \cdot05$ for the men, and $r_t = + 0\cdot43 \pm \cdot08$ for the women. Bearing in mind that we are dealing with a group of people rather alike with respect to the "P" factor, as compared with the total population of which they are a selected sample, this correlation is perhaps not unduly low. It should also be borne in mind, however, that the psychiatrist in his assessment would give a certain amount of weight to the patient's own account of his personality and illness, and thus draw on much the same information as is given in the questionnaire. The wording of the questions was such as to ask for personality traits *before* the onset of the illness which brought them into hospital, and it would be tempting to use the correlation found as evidence that those patients who showed evidence in their pre-army and pre-hospital lives of neurotic traits were those who tended to have less well organized personalities than patients whose pre-illness life was relatively free from such traits. It is doubtful, however, whether such an interpretation would be justified; the distinction between behaviour before the onset of the illness, and behaviour after the onset, is rather a fine one, and one which a patient with below average I.Q. is not likely to draw very successfully.

Differences in average scores between the badly organized personality groups and the others are significant. For the men, the respective scores are $24 \pm 10\cdot8$ and $16 \pm 8\cdot7$; for the women they are $20 \pm 9\cdot6$ and $15 \pm 8\cdot5$. Ratings could not be secured for all the men and women who took the test, and the above figures are derived from 420 male and 200 female neurotics. The C.R.s of the difference are 8 for the men and 4 for the women, leaving no doubt at all that the differences are significant.

The question arises whether hysterics and dysthymics show any differences in the questions they answer "Yes" or "No", i.e. whether the total score on the questionnaire, which we have studied so far, is made up of different sub-scores on the various questions for the two diagnostic types. Questionnaires of 100 male hysterics and 100 male dysthymics were selected, and the percentage of "Yes" answers to each particular question ascertained. A number of the differences observed were statistically significant, and are listed below. A similar enquiry was undertaken with respect to the questionnaires of 50 female hysterics and 50 female dysthymics.

Taking the men first, the most obvious difference between hysterics and dysthymics in connection with their questionnaire answers would seem to lie in the fact that on all questions except two (questions 7 and 8) the percentage of dysthymics answering "Yes" is larger than the percentage of hysterics answering

"Yes". On the whole, dysthymics answer "Yes" in 52% of the cases (2,084 answers out of 4,000); hysterics answer "Yes" in 43% of the cases (1,722 answers out of 4,000). This difference is significant beyond any doubt.

Looking at the individual answers, we find that in 16 cases the differences between the two groups are significant, while in 24 cases the differences are below the level required for significance. The questions on which the dysthymics replied with "Yes" significantly more frequently than did the hysterics were as follows:

(2) Gets palpitations—63% vs. 48%. (11) Feelings easily hurt—83% vs. 68%. (12) Keeps in background on social occasions—76% vs. 62%. (13) Attacks of shaking or trembling—64% vs. 43%. (15) Ideas run through head—67% vs. 52%. (18) Sometimes happy, sometimes depressed—76% vs. 58%. (19) Daydreams—56% vs. 32%. (20) Not much life about him—53% vs. 36%. (31) Self-conscious—72% vs. 55%. (32) Sleeplessness—54% vs. 36%. (35) "Nerves"—60% vs. 45%. (37) Nervous in lifts, etc.—48% vs. 28%. (38) Diarrhoea—25% vs. 9%. (39) Lacks self-confidence—57% vs. 38%. (40) Feelings of inferiority—61% vs. 45%.

These results, if we assume for the moment that they are to some extent reliable, give us a picture of the dysthymic, as compared with the hysteric, which is very much in line with the traditional clinical view. He is variable in mood, nervous, withdrawn into himself, easily subject to physical signs of emotional experiences, such as palpitations, shaking, trembling, shortness of breath, and diarrhoea; lacks self-confidence, feels inferior, and daydreams a lot.

Precisely the same general picture is given by the women. In 46% of the cases (920 answers out of 2,000) the dysthymics answer "Yes", while in 43% of the cases (860 answers out of 2,000) the hysterics answer "Yes". This difference is smaller than was the difference between the two types for the men, but it is in the same direction. In view of the smaller number of cases included, only 7 differences in respect of individual questions are significant between the groups; even where the differences are not significant, however, they are in line with those found for the men.

The 6 significant differences in favour of the dysthymics are:

(2) Gets palpitations—68% vs. 50%. (5) Gets "stage fright"—72% vs. 44%. (10) Considers herself a "nervous" person—60% vs. 38%. (15) Ideas run through head—64% vs. 44%. (22) Nightmares—52% vs. 30%. (28) "Touchy" on various subjects—60% vs. 32%.

On only two questions did the male hysterics give more "Yes" answers than the male dysthymics: (7) Troubled by stammer or stutter, and (8) Ever been made unconscious by blow or accident. The women hysterics also were troubled by a stammer or stutter more frequently than were the women dysthymics; this difference is not significant. With regard to question (8), however, there is a significant difference for the women, the hysterics answering "Yes" in 22% of the cases, the dysthymics in only 4%. This finding would seem to support the view that hysterics tend to be more accident-prone than other types of neurotics.

On several further questions the woman hysterics gave more "Yes" answers than did the dysthymics; none of the differences were significant, however. Among these questions were the following: (1) Dizzy turns; (4) Been off work through sickness a good deal; (29) Often feels disgruntled; (34) Suffers from severe headaches; (36) Troubled by aches and pains. While these results fit in with the asocial, hypochondriacal features of hysteria, little importance attaches to them in view of the small number of cases from which the relative frequencies were derived.

The question must now be faced whether the lower scores of the hysterics on the questionnaire are due to their being less neurotic, or whether this result is due rather to other factors. Two such factors suggest themselves. In the first place, the majority of the symptoms listed in the questionnaire are affective symptoms; indeed, it is almost insuperably difficult to design a questionnaire containing many hysterical symptoms. The dysthymic patient is troubled by the consciousness of emotional disturbances; it is easy to list a number of the more common of these disturbances, and a list of this nature is likely to cover most of the symptoms of which the patient complains. The symptomatology of the hysteric, on the other hand, is more protean; it relates to his attitude to society rather than to individual symptoms, and is, therefore, much more difficult to put into the form of simple "Yes—No" questions. Also, the hysteric has little insight into the pathological character of these attitudes, and is, therefore, unlikely to give very meaningful answers to a simple questionnaire. Thus, in the second place, even if a questionnaire could be drawn up containing equal numbers of dysthymic and hysterical questions, the very personality qualities which make the hysteric what he is would effectively prevent him from giving truthful answers.

This fact would seem to lessen considerably the value of questionnaire studies of this kind. They are of interest and importance only in so far as they give us an idea of what the patient thinks of himself; quite clearly the dysthymic patient has a different picture of himself than has the hysteric. How correct this picture may be in each case it is impossible to know without further evidence of a different kind.

### 7. Questionnaire Study of Persistence and Irritability

Two further questionnaires were given to selected groups of patients, and the results illustrate well the difficulties in interpretation which inevitably arise. The two questionnaires used were shortened versions of Wang's "Persistence" (1932) and Cason's "Annoyances" questionnaire (1938); sixteen of the most diagnostic questions were taken from the former, and thirty from the latter. In the "Persistence" questionnaire, the patients had to answer "Yes" or "No" to questions such as: "Do you usually stick to a task until it is completed?" or "In an argument do you find it difficult to give in?". In the "Annoyances" questionnaire he has to put a number signifying (0) not annoying at all, (1) slightly annoying, (2) moderately annoying, or (3) extremely annoying after descriptions of certain kinds of behaviour, or of certain factual occurrences, such as: "A person talking in an unnecessarily loud voice" or "To see unwashed dishes".

These questionnaires were given to 25 male and 25 female hysterics, and to 25 male and 25 female dysthymics.[1] The results of analysing the 3,000 "annoyances" statements by these 100 patients show that for the hysterics, 12% of the answers are made

[1] In this experiment as well as in all later ones of which this may serve as the paradigm, the influence of intelligence was eliminated from the group-comparisons by equating hysterics and dysthymics for intelligence.

up of "o"s, and 45% of "3"s, while for the anxiety states 10% are made up of "o"s, and 49% of "3"s. Altogether, the actual numbers of answers in each category are shown in Table 3.

TABLE THREE

| | Hysterics. | | Dysthymics. |
|---|---|---|---|
| Not annoying at all(o) . . . . . | 182 | . | 157 |
| Slightly annoying (1) . . . . . | 260 | . | 250 |
| Moderately annoying (2) . . . . | 385 | . | 363 |
| Extremely annoying (3) . . . . | 673 | . | 730 |

These figures show a trend in the expected direction, i.e. towards a greater irritability in the dysthymics as compared with the hysterics; however, this tendency is so much attenuated in these questionnaire answers that for practical purposes we can hardly claim that a questionnaire of this kind will be useful in distinguishing the two types.

The replies to the "Persistence" questionnaire (16 items) show no significant differences between the hysterics and the dysthymics, as can be seen from the figures given in Table 4.

TABLE FOUR

| Male hysterics . . . . . | $7.56 \pm 4.08$ |
|---|---|
| Male dysthymics . . . . | $6.08 \pm 3.93$ |
| Female hysterics . . . . | $9.00 \pm 4.24$ |
| Female dysthymics . . . . | $8.90 \pm 3.01$ |

These figures illustrate the difficulties in interpreting questionnaire answers. As will be shown in a later chapter, experimental tests of persistence bring out particularly clearly the differences between these two types; the hysterics show far less persistence than do the dysthymics. Yet in their answers, the hysterics give a picture of rather superior persistence. How can this finding be reconciled with our experimental results?

In the first place, it will be shown in a later chapter that hysterics tend to judge their own past performances in a much better light than do dysthymics; the hysteric overrates, the dysthymic underrates his assets. Consequently, the hysteric is quite likely to give a better picture of his abilities and attitudes than is justified, and the dysthymic is quite likely to give a worse one. Thus an explanation might be sought in the retrospective falsification, in a positive or negative direction, of the patients' behaviour.

A more likely explanation, however, may lie in the fact that although a questionnaire may be labelled "Persistence", it may actually be measuring some entirely different quality. In this particular instance, it seems quite likely that Wang's questionnaire merely measures "P", rather than the quality (persistence) he sets out to measure. This interpretation is borne out by an analysis of the actual questions used by him; it is also borne out by the fact that the women score significantly higher than do the men. We found a similar sex-difference in connection with our own Medical Questionnaire, and consider that such similarity in results argues in favour of identity of function measured.

However, that may be, there can be little doubt that no definite conclusions can be based on questionnaires of this kind. While the actual scores on these tests are objective enough, it is almost impossible to disentangle the varied reasons which may prompt the patients to answer the questions in one way or in another. At best, we may take the results as confirmation of two facts proved independently by other means, viz. that dysthymics tend to be more irritable than hysterics, and that hysterics tend to over-rate their own performances; at worst, we may consider the results to be quite meaningless. Clearly, no scientific picture of any value can be built on such evidence, and we must turn to more objective studies in order to obtain such a picture.

## 8. Summary

A factorial analysis was undertaken on the intercorrelations of 39 trait ratings, carried out by psychiatrists on 700 neurotic patients. Two main factors emerged from this analysis: (1) A general factor of "neuroticism", characterized by such items as badly organized personality, abnormal before present illness, boarded out of the army, abnormality in parents, unsatisfactory home, poor muscular tone, etc., and (2) a bipolar factor opposing the affective or dysthymic group of symptoms (anxiety, depression, obsessional tendencies, apathy, irritability, autonomic dysfunction, etc.), to the hysterical group of symptoms (conversion symptoms, sex anomalies, low intelligence, bad work history, hypochondriasis, etc.). Further factors appeared of little interest. These factors were discussed in detail, and an attempt was made to relate them to previous factorial studies which had been carried out in the main on normal subjects, students, and children. Many such resemblances were found, relating the general factor of "neuroticism" to Webb's "w" factor, Maller's "readiness to forego an immediate gain for the sake of a remote but greater gain", and various others. The dysthymic-hysteric dichotomy was found to be closely related to Jung's introversion-extraversion dichotomy.

Various questionnaire studies were undertaken of different neurotic groups, and reliable differences found with respect to both factors. A "Neuroticism" questionnaire was shown to discriminate both between neurotics and normals, and between the more seriously ill and the less seriously ill neurotics. This questionnaire also distinguished between hysterics and dysthymics. Other questionnaires, dealing with "persistence" and "irritability", added further data on the differentiation of the types discussed, but raised at the same time many difficulties which are inevitable in the use of subjective instruments of measurement, such as questionnaires, and which can only be overcome by means of more objective, experimental tests.

# CHAPTER THREE

# PHYSIQUE AND CONSTITUTION

## 1. BODY TYPE AND BODY SIZE

THE words "constitution" and "physique" have often been used interchangeably in the literature; recently, however, they have acquired connotations which effectively discriminate the one from the other. Thus Pearl (1933) has defined the modern concept of "constitution" as depending on, and being determined by, "the present functional condition (tonus and balance) and state of activity of the endocrine system, the autonomic nervous system, the vascular and vasomotor system, the central nervous system". These in turn he considered to be dependent upon "the physical chemistry of the blood, and the innate degree of perfection (biological worth) of the anatomical structure in general, and of each particular organ, and the age of the individual". Physique or habitus, on the other hand, is "used in the sense of bodily configuration, somatic structure, or somatic organization, and refers to one aspect of an individual's constitution" (Betz, 1942). Thus physique is a subordinate concept, while constitution is the supraordinate.

In this chapter, investigations will be reported dealing (a) with the correlation between physique and various personality traits, and (b) with correlations between measures of certain constitutional aspects and the personality of the subjects. These constitutional aspects are largely restricted to investigations of autonomic activity.

In classifying habitus into different types, medical men, artists, philosophers, psychologists, poets and anthropologists have vied with each other in producing new and complicated terms, usually linked with some untenable hypothesis implying genotypical validity for phenotypical observations. All of these different typologies, however, do seem to recognize two main types: (a) Persons in whom there is a relative preponderance of vertical over horizontal measurements, and (b) persons in whom there is a relative preponderance of horizontal over vertical measurements. Usually, an intermediate type is also recognized, so that we are finally left with three types in all. The various names by which these types were known have been tabulated by Wertheimer and Hesketh (1926), and a table similar in some respects to theirs is included here. It will be seen that fundamentally all later writers have merely rung the changes on Hippocrates' original conception of a *habitus apoplecticus* and a *habitus phthisicus*, each of which was conceived to be specially linked with susceptibility to certain diseases and with certain temperamental peculiarities.

While the main types distinguished by these writers have frequently been diagnosed by somatoscopic inspection, i.e. in a highly subjective manner, more recent writers have suggested a number of indices which are supposed to give a numerical value to types of bodily habitus. These indices, of which over a hundred have been elaborated, are frequently subject to damaging criticism, particularly with respect to the logic of their derivation, and to their statistical make-up.

### TYPES OF PHYSIQUE

| *Author.* | *Leptomorph.* | *Mesomorph.* | *Eurymorph* |
|---|---|---|---|
| Hippocrates | Habit. Phthicus | | Habit. Apoplecticus |
| Rostan (1828) | Respiratory-Cerebral | Muscular | Digestive |
| Carus (1853) | Asthenic | Athletic | Phlegmatic |
| Mills (1917) | Asthenic | Sthenic | Hypersthenic |
| Brugsch (1918) | Narrow-chested | Normal | Wide-chested |
| Bean (1923) | Hyperontomorph | — | Mesontomorph |
| Stockard (1923) | Linear | | Lateral |
| Davenport (1923) | Slender | Medium | Fleshy |
| Aschner (1924) | Slender | Normal | Broad |
| Pende (1924) | Hypovegetative | — | Hypervegetative |
| Bauer (1924) | Asthenic | | Arthritic |
| Kretschmer (1925) | Asthenic | Athletic | Pyknic |
| Huter (1928) | Empfindungstypus | Krafttypus | Ernährungstypus |
| Viola (1933) | Microsplanchnic | Normosplanchnic | Megalosplanchnic |
| Sheldon (1940) | Ectomorph | Mesomorph | Endomorph |

Body-types roughly corresponding to leptomorph, mesomorph, and eurymorph types, as described and named by fifteen authors. Our terms are explained in the text.

The most usual method of deriving indices of body-build has been the following. The author distinguishes two types of body-build, on a purely subjective basis; he then selects certain measurements which seem to discriminate best between extreme instances, and puts these measurements together into some kind of mathematical formula. Now clearly, the superficial objectivity of a formula does not counterbalance the subjectivity of the original selection; the rather naive joy with which some writers find that certain measurements distinguish significantly between groups originally selected on the basis of being differentiated with respect to precisely these measurements indicates that this fundamental subjectivity of the whole procedure has not always been appreciated.

Even when the measurements which are to be combined into an index have been determined, the method of combination often leaves a good deal to be desired. In many cases, there is a curious belief that multiplying either divisor or dividend by a constant changes the relative standing of individuals in some way; the Wertheimer and Hesketh Index is a case in point. More serious is the fact that many writers fail to appreciate that an unconscious process of weighting takes place in their indices through the fact that the Standard Deviations of the various measurements are not equal; an obvious safeguard would be to use Standard Scores instead of absolute scores.

### Table Five

| Investigator. | Factor I. % | Factor II. % | $h^2$. % | n. | N. |
|---|---|---|---|---|---|
| Cohen, 1 | 44 | 24 | 68 | 50 | 14 |
| „ 2 | 46 | 19 | 65 | 64 | 14 |
| „ 3 | 35 | 25 | 60 | 62 | 12 |
| Hammond | 31 | 9 | 40 | 100 | 12 |
| Dearborn and Rothney | 59 | 8 | 67 | 533 | 8 |
| Mullen | 56 | 19 | 75 | 305 | 8 |
| Rees and Eysenck | 34 | 12 | 46 | 200 | 18 |
| Average | 43 | 17 | 60 | 188 | 12 |

In recent years, a more objective method of arriving at bodily "types" than the usual somatoscopic ones has been elaborated. This method, which was first used by Burt (1944) and his students, has in the main corroborated the fundamental dichotomy underlying all the other typologies. Seven studies altogether have been reported in which correlations between a variety of bodily measurements have been subjected to a factorial analysis; they are listed in Table 5.[1] These studies agree in

[1] In this Table, n=number of subjects, N=number of traits, $h^2$=communality.

finding (I) a general factor of body growth or body size, which accounts for some 40% of the variance, and (II) a type factor distinguishing between growth in length and growth in breadth, which accounts for some 20% of the variance. In view of the differences in age, sex, status, mental health, race, and nationality between the populations studied this agreement is impressive and suggests that here indeed we have found some fundamental aspects of human constitution.

Our view that these factorial studies have isolated a genotypical difference, not merely a phenotypical one, is strengthened by a number of direct studies of the relative growth of the horizontal and the vertical components. Hall (1896), in a study of growth in 2,000 school children, found that when the vertical dimension of the body undergoes an acceleration, the horizontal dimension undergoes a retardation in its rate of growth. More recently, Duckworth (1929) quotes the work of Godin, who found that growth in length alternates with growth in breadth. Friend (1935) found in growing schoolboys that the maximum increase in height occurred during spring, while that for weight occurred in autumn. Finally, the postulation of two factors of growth is consistent with the distinction drawn by Huxley (1932) between *isogonic* and *heterogonic* growth in lowlier animals. These researches seem to lend strong support to the results of the statistical analysis.

Illustrative of the factors thus isolated is an investigation carried out by Rees and Eysenck (1944). 200 male army patients were measured with respect to 17 bodily traits and age; these traits were then correlated. Finally, a factor analysis was carried out on the intercorrelations. The actual measurements carried out, their means and S.D.s, and the factor saturations of each measurement for two factors are given in Table 6. A diagrammatic description of the resulting factor pattern is given in Figure 6.

As the saturations of the various measurements with the second factor correspond to correlations of these measurements with that factor, we are now in a position to make up an index of body build which is based not on subjective appraisal, but entirely on objective measurement. The best measure of body type would, of course, be a regression equation containing the various measurements used as terms, and their saturations as weights; such an equation would be rather unwieldy, however,

## TABLE SIX

| | 100 Normal Soldiers. | | 200 Successive Admissions to Neurosis Centre. | | Factor Saturations: | |
|---|---|---|---|---|---|---|
| | Mean. | S.D. | Mean. | S.D. | I. | II. |
| Age | 29·27 | 6·06 | 28·8 | 5·89 | ·02 | -·09 |
| Stature | 171·01 | 5·32 | 170·9 | 6·77 | ·73 | ·57 |
| Suprasternal height | 139·47 | 4·67 | 139·4 | 5·78 | ·82 | ·56 |
| Symphysis height | 86·30 | 4·55 | 86·5 | 4·81 | ·69 | ·47 |
| Trunk length | 53·41 | 2·05 | 52·9 | 2·58 | ·41 | ·15 |
| Breadth of skull | 15·28 | 0·52 | 14·9 | 0·58 | ·31 | -·27 |
| Length of skull | 19·60 | 0·65 | 19·2 | 0·66 | ·25 | ·00 |
| Biacromial diameter | 39·61 | 2·10 | 38·8 | 1·68 | ·71 | -·11 |
| Transverse chest diameter | 28·77 | 2·12 | 27·9 | 1·85 | ·67 | -·54 |
| Sagittal chest diameter | 20·60 | 1·63 | 20·4 | 1·58 | ·65 | -·23 |
| Bicristal diameter | 29·08 | 1·59 | 28·7 | 1·61 | ·77 | -·05 |
| Sternal length | 21·89 | 2·23 | 21·2 | 1·78 | ·41 | ·06 |
| Arm length to radial styloid | 55·77 | 2·35 | 55·7 | 2·78 | ·58 | ·46 |
| Arm length to tip of medius | 76·45 | 3·23 | 75·3 | 3·57 | ·57 | ·39 |
| Chest circumference at inspiration | 95·79 | 4·87 | 92·2 | 3·57 | ·54 | -·35 |
| Chest circumference at expiration | 87·96 | 5·30 | 86·5 | 4·50 | ·54 | -·41 |
| Hip circumference | 79·93 | 6·64 | 80·2 | 5·27 | ·54 | -·33 |
| Weight | 65·00 | 6·88 | 64·6 | 7·22 | ·64 | -·23 |

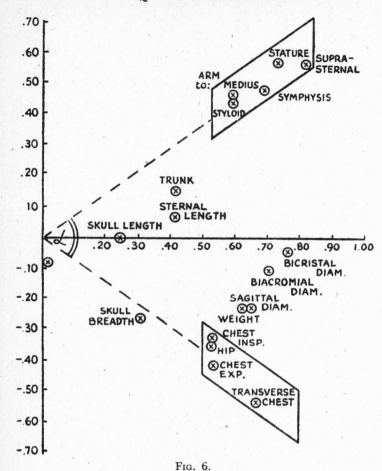

FIG. 6.

and consequently a simpler formula has been derived. Two measurements, viz. Stature and Transverse Chest Diameter, will be seen to have equal saturations with the general factor, as well as saturations of equal size but opposite sign with the 2nd or type factor. The ratio Stature/Transverse Chest will therefore give us an index of body build which is free from the influence of general body size (the general factor), and which indicates clearly the position of the subject with respect to the preponderance of horizontal or vertical measurements. In order to get an index free from decimal points, and with a mean which is easily remembered, it is advisable to multiply the Stature measurement by 100, and the Chest measurement by 6, so that the complete formula for the Index of Body Build (I.B.) reads:

$$\text{I.B.} = \frac{\text{Stature} \times 100}{\text{Transverse Chest Diameter} \times 6}$$

100 normal soldiers, average age 30 ± 6, showed an average I.B. of 100·1 ± 7·6; thus, this index has an average value of 100 and a coefficient of variation of approximately 8. This would seem to show that variations in body form are only ½ as large as

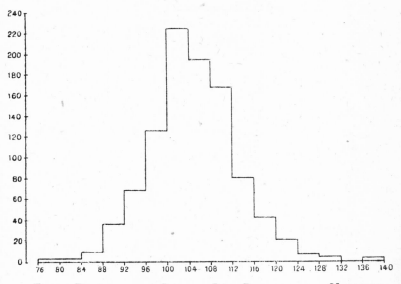

FIG. 7. DISTRIBUTION OF INDEX OF BODY-BUILD FOR 1,000 NEUROTICS.

variations in intelligence, where the Binet test, for instance, gives a mean I.Q. of 100 and a coefficient of variation of approximately 17.[1] Values of the I.B. higher than 100 indicate relative prevalence of vertical measurements, values of the I.B. less than 100 indicate relative prevalence of horizontal measurements.

In Figure 7 is shown the distribution of I.B.s for 1,000 neurotic

[1] This comparison is not strictly accurate, as not all of the conditions required for the use of the C.V. obtain.

men. The average score is 104·4 ± 7·9; this value is considerably above the average Index value of the normal group (C.R. = 5·4), and shows that our neurotics show a preponderance of linear over lateral growth. It will also be seen that the variability of the neurotic group, as shown by the S.D., is slightly higher than that of the normal group.

While the curve of distribution of the I.B. is slightly positively skewed, it approximates the normal curve, and certainly fails to evince any signs of discontinuity. There is, therefore, no evidence for the existence of "types" in the sense of discrete, separate groups of persons showing similarity or identity of body build. However, for the sake of convenience and ease of description, we shall split the continuously graded curve of distribution into three parts, defining three "types" of body build: (1) Those whose I.B. scores are one S.D. or more above the mean (*leptomorphs*); (2) those whose I.B. scores are within one S.D. of the mean (*mesomorphs*); (3) those whose I.B. scores are one S.D. or more below the mean (*eurymorphs*). The terms leptomorph, mesomorph, and eurymorph are purely descriptive, and were chosen because they carry no connotational significance which would imply causation or association with mental or physical disorders. Furthermore, they are purely relative to the population studied; it would be possible to give absolute meaning to these terms only after large-scale testing of normal subjects.

The question of the measurement of the I.B. of women presented certain problems which were dealt with in a special research. Fifteen measurements were taken on 200 female patients, and tetrachoric correlations calculated between the measurements. Two factors were extracted from the resulting table of correlations, accounting for 41% and 16% of the variance respectively. The interpretation of these factors was similar to that of the factors found for the male patients.

The results of this analysis did not lend themselves to the construction of an index of the simple design which characterised the I.B. for males, and it was thought that a regression equation would give a better representation than a simple index. (It has been suggested to us that even in the case of the men a regression equation would be more appropriate than an index. However, the correlation between the I.B. and a regression equation specially constructed was found to be + 0·98 for 400 male patients; this correlation is so high that there seems little gain in employing the more complicated method.)

For the purpose of our equation, four measurements were taken into account: $x_1$ = stature, $x_2$ = symphisis height, $x_3$ = chest circumference, and $x_3$ = hip circumference. If we denote the female Index of Body Build by the letters I.B.$_{(F)}$, then the regression equation runs:

$$\text{I.B.}_{(F)} = \cdot59x_1 + \cdot47x_2 - \cdot31x_3 - \cdot64x_3.$$

While the I.B. enables us to express a subject's body build in terms of the second factor isolated in our analysis, it does not tell us anything with regard to the general factor of body-size. Here also, it would appear possible to carry out measurements, and

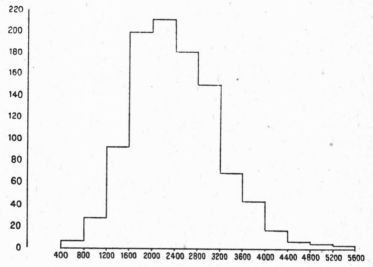

FIG. 8. DISTRIBUTION OF INDEX OF BODY-SIZE FOR 1,000 NEUROTICS.

to study the correlation of this variable with personality traits. In order to measure body size, the same two measurements were used which previously had served to make up the I.B., viz. Stature and Transverse Chest Diameter. The average height of our 1,000 male neurotics was 172·07 ± 6·69 cm., while their average transverse chest measurement was 27·63 ± 1·90 cm. In view of the lack of equality between the S.D.s and the co-efficients of variation of the two measures, direct multiplication was meaningless, and both measures were turned into standard scores, with a mean of 50 and a S.D. of 10. These standard scores were then multiplied, and the product was taken as the best obtainable measure of general body size. The distribution of the results of calculating this product for each of our 1,000 cases is given in Figure 8; the mean is 2397 ± 714. The curve of distribution is relatively normal, but positively skewed.

Although here also there are no disparate "types", we have split the continuous distribution into three parts: (1) those one S.D. or more above the mean (*macrosomatics*); (2) those within ± S.D. of the mean (*mesosomatics*); (3) those one S.D. or more below the mean (*microsomatics*). Again, this division is entirely arbitrary, and relative to the sample studied; no absolute standards are set up, or implied.

## 2. PERSONALITY CORRELATES OF PHYSIQUE

Having thus defined the concepts relating to "body type" operationally, we are in a position to proceed to the next stage of our investigation, and attempt to correlate body type with certain personality traits. The belief that such correlations exist has been held for as long as separate body types have been recognized. Esquirol in 1816 and Morel in 1857 had each pointed out an association between habitus and character of illness in their patients; even earlier, as Ciocco (1936) shows in his excellent review of the historical background of this concept, Hippocrates and his disciples, Aristotle, the Greek Polemonis and the Jewish physician Adamantius (circa 300 A.D.), the philosopher Porta and the Protestant minister Lavater, as well as Gall and Spurzheim and their fellow phrenologists, had postulated a correlation between psyche and soma. Modern work in this field is based on the contributions of Beneke (1878) and Carus (republ. 1925) in Germany, Giovanni, Viola, and Pende in Italy, and Rostan (1828) in France. An excellent review of recent history is given by Schrieder (1937), who gives an extensive bibliography dealing particularly with the French and Italian contributions.

Three main claims appear to have been made regarding the mental correlates of body type. In the first instance, as already adumbrated in Hippocrates' use of the term *habitus phthisicus* and *habitus apoplecticus*, it has been suggested that certain diseases are more liable to attack persons of a certain body type. Cohen (1940) concludes from a review of the literature that there is fairly good evidence indicating that leptomorph individuals are predisposed to tuberculosis, pneumonia, dyspepsia, presbyacusia, hyperthyroidism and brain disorders, while eurymorph individuals are more prone to diabetes, nephritis, apoplexy, dropsy, alimentary disorders, arteriosclerosis, cerebral haemorrhage, cardiac disease, and gall bladder disease. (Indeed, Draper (1928) classifies individuals from the point of view of constitution into "gall bladder" and "ulcer" types!)

While this work is interesting, it is not as relevant to our purpose as are the studies undertaken in order to prove or disprove the second major claim made with respect to psychosomatic correlation. This is that *psychotic mental disorders show clearly marked affinities with certain body types;* in particular, schizophrenic illnesses are correlated with leptomorph body type, and cycloid illnesses with eurymorph body type (Kretschmer, 1926). His work, while in many respects not going beyond a combination of Rostan's and Esquirol's views, has given rise to a large body of research, some of it confirmatory, some of it contradictory. Many of the criticism of Kretschmer's original work have been presented by Burchard (1936), whose own work in part corroborates Kretschmer's views.

Of the many authors whose conclusions favour the Kretschmerian view, perhaps the most convincing are the German writers Sioli and Meyer (1922), Olivier (1922), Jacob and Moser (1922), Michel and Weber (1924), Henckel (1924), Weissenfeld (1925), Rohden (1926) and Wyrsch (1924). Among non-German writers, Shaw (1925), Wertheimer and Hesketh (1926), Matecki and Szpidbaum (1927), Farr (1928), Adler and Mohr (1928), Conolly (1939), Cohen (1940), Betz (1943) and Rees (1943) may be mentioned. Raphael, Ferguson and Searle (1928), Clegg (1935) and Burchard (1936) are more critical, while negative findings are reported by Möllenhoff (1924), Kolle (1925), Gruhle (1926), Garvey (1930), Campbell (1932), Schwerin (1937), Wells (1938) and Farber (1938).

There are several difficulties in the way of accepting these studies as conclusive evidence. In the first place, the cycloid groups are usually considerably older than the schizoid group, thus introducing an obvious error due to the fact that age is often assumed to be positively correlated with eurymorph body build. In the second place, the usual statistical criteria of significance of differences require modification when hundreds of separate measurements are being compared; thus for a level of $P = \cdot 05$, one would expect several differences between two groups to be significant, although the groups were selected entirely at random, if they were compared with respect to a large number of traits. Thirdly, the fact that ratings were often on a somatoscopic basis introduces considerable subjectivity into the work; it can be seen from a table given by Betz (1942) that the percentage of leptomorph individuals in schizophrenic groups may be anywhere from 11 to 64! Fourthly, the possibility cannot be excluded that body build actually played some part in the diagnosis on which the selection of cases originally depended; thus in an institution in which Kretschmer's theories are accepted the diagnosis of schizophrenia might not be entirely uninfluenced by the fact that the patient had a leptomorph habitus.

These considerations introduce serious doubts into an appraisal of much of this work. While investigators very often find significant differences with respect to various measurements on comparing schizophrenic with manic-depressive populations, the alert student will find on looking through many of these reports that differences between various schizophrenic groups are almost equally numerous as differences between schizophrenes and manic depressives. This is shown quite clearly in a table presented by Plattner (1932), in which are summarized various researches. It will be seen that 78 differences are found to be significant between schizophrenic and manic-depressive groups, while 47 differences are significant between one schizophrenic group and another. Manic-depressive groups are not compared with each other.

One possible explanation of the contradictory results reported by different observers may lie in the different symptomatology of leptomorph and eurymorph schizophrenics. From the work of Mauz (1930), Kisselew (1931), Plattner-Heberlein (1932), Vanelli (1932), Langfeldt (1937), and Betz (1942) it would appear that leptomorphs become ill at a relatively early age, show poor rapport, disorientation, shut-in personality, indifference, scattered

G

thinking, mannerisms and habit deterioration, while eurymorphs tend to fall ill rather later, show hallucinations and delusions rather than disorientation and mannerisms, preserve affective relations with the environment better, and deteriorate less frequently. As Vanelli puts it, we find "una notevole preponderanze della brachitipia nelle forme paranoide e parafreniche, mentra trave prevalenza della longitipia negli ebefrenici e nei catatonici".

The third claim often made is that not only psychotics, but also neurotics and normal persons show a certain affinity between temperament and body type. Kretschmer holds, for instance, that his demonstration of schizophrenic-leptomorph and manic-depressive—eurymorph affinity extends also to schizoids and cycloids, i.e. persons showing a tendency towards these two diseases, and to schizothymes and cyclothymes, i.e. persons showing certain quite normal types of temperament resembling in some ways the main features of schizophrenic and manic-depressive illness.

Work on neurotics has been reported by Naccarati (1934), whose investigation contrasted neuroses such as anxiety state and hysteria on the one hand, and neurasthenic neuroses on the other. Lack of definition of his terms makes it impossible to appraise his results, and an absence of statistical analysis of his data leaves the reader doubtful about their significance. It would appear, however, that his neurotic groups showed larger Standard Deviations than did his normal control group, a finding reduplicated in our own work.

Wiersma (1933) collected anatomical, physiological and psychological data on 415 individuals, classifying his subjects into physical types, tempo-types, and autonomic nervous system types. Though his examinations are comprehensive, the statistical treatment of his data is so cursory that no conclusions can be drawn as to the significance of his findings.

Burt's (1937) data, comprising physical measurements and temperamental assessments in school children, show comparatively low correlations between stoutness and cheerful emotions, and thinness and inhibitive and repressive tendencies. In adults he found leptomorph body build to be associated with repressed and introverted temperament, and also with depression. His final conclusion is that measurable correlations between physical and mental characteristics, though frequently positive, are almost always too slight to be trusted for the needs of diagnosis. Greenwood and Smith (1941) report essentially negative conclusions regarding their investigation into the correlation of the Brugsch index with intelligence, occupational efficiency, nervous symptom, and speed and accuracy of movement. Isolated correlations between various mental traits and habitus are almost always insignificant (Paterson, 1930).

More recently than these studies, two reports have appeared of large-scale work carried out in attempts to find relationships between psyche and soma. These reports both come from Harvard, and deal with the work of Sheldon (1940, 1942) and that of Sanford et al. (1943). Sheldon has elaborated two tri-dimensional schemata, dealing respectively with body-build and with temperament; he claims a very close correspondence between these two schemata. He believes that we can distinguish three components[1] in body-build, derived respectively from the endoderm, the mesoderm, and the ectoderm; the relative preponderance of one of these gives rise to endo-, meso-, or ectomorph types. (This scheme owes much to Huter, who put forward a similar theory in 1928.) The three physical components are closely related in Sheldon's view to three mental components, viscerotonia, somatotonia, and cerebrotonia. There is lack of independent verification of the interesting theories put forward, and of the usefulness of the ingenious photographical method of measuring body-build. Only one independent study of Sheldon's claims has come to hand (Fiske, 1944). This is summarized by the author: "The number of significant findings in this study of adolescent boys is not greater than chance expectancy. The use of Sheldon's improved procedure for classifying physique yielded the same paucity of significant relationships to physique that has been found in earlier studies."

The work of Sanford and his colleagues (1943), on the other hand, is of particular interest because it agrees in almost every crucial aspect with the results reached in our own studies. This is of importance because of the great contrast between the conditions under which the two experiments were carried out. Where we dealt with neurotics throughout, they dealt with normals;

[1] This theory of "components" would appear to have originated with Plattner (1938), who describes a "Körperbauspektrum".

where we dealt with adults only, they dealt with children; where we dealt with large numbers of subjects in an inevitably rather superficial manner, they dealt with small numbers of subjects in a very intensive manner; where we used common psychological and psychiatric concepts in ordering our material, they used concepts and terms introduced by H. Murray; where we used factorial methods, they used special methods of their own devising. If, in spite of these differences between our two approaches, similar results emerged, we may justifiably claim that the types delineated in our studies are of general validity, and of fundamental importance in the field of psychological classification.

Sanford and his collaborators give a table of intercorrelations of 18 body measurements which are almost identical with those used by us; from this table they deduce the existence of two contrasted types: tall-narrow and wide-heavy. From the actual figures given by them, it is clear that these types are practically identical with our own leptomorph and eurymorph types.

Measurements of various autonomic reactions (pupillary size dilation, pallor, flushing, sweating, odour, acne, pulse, etc.), disclose the existence of a syndrome of autonomic imbalance, which is positively correlated with tall-narrow body build, and negatively with wide-heavy body build.

Both tall-narrow body build and autonomic imbalance correlate positively with success in various tests of intelligence, and also with school abilities and cultural stimulation in the home. Wide-heavy body build, on the other hand, correlates negatively with intelligence, school abilities, and cultural stimulation.

Lastly, tall-narrow body build and autonomic imbalance correlate positively with personality syndromes characterized by self-sufficiency, guilt-feelings, remorse, and counteractive endocathection; this syndrome is clearly similar to our dysthymic factor. On the other hand, wide-heavy body build and lack of autonomic imbalance correlate positively with good fellowship, social feeling, and lively self-expression. As the authors point out, "it is possible . . . to compose a broader picture of inner life, tallness, thinness, and parasympathetic response, and to contrast this picture with one of social responsiveness, shortness, wideness and absence of parasympathetic activity" (p. 528). The similarity of these findings to our own will become apparent after a discussion of our own results, to which we may now turn.

Our sample of 1,000 unselected neurotics contained 120 eurymorphs, 150 leptomorphs, and 730 mesomorphs. For each of these three groups, the percentage incidence of the various symptoms, diagnoses, traits, etc., in the Item Sheet was established, and significant differences between the eurymorph and the leptomorph groups noted. The results are set out in Table 7.[1] The items are arranged in four groups. In the first group are shown the percentages the various age groups contribute to the

[1] This method of setting out data has been criticized, and requires an explanation. Our data may be used to furnish us with two items of information: In the first place, analysis may be directed towards ascertaining those temperamental qualities, clinical syndromes, etc., which occur with *significantly different frequency* among leptomorphs and eurymorphs; in other words, we may enquire in what ways body type is related to personality. In the second place, analysis may be directed towards ascertaining the *closeness of the association* between body build and the various personality traits sampled; in other words, we may enquire how closely body type is related to personality. The method used by us is capable only of dealing with the first of these points; an analysis by means of tetrachoric correlations would be required before an answer could be given to the second point. It may be asked why such an analysis has not been undertaken.

In answer, we may point to the comparative lack of reliability of the psychiatrists' ratings involved in our calculations. Such lack of reliability will undoubtedly reduce the significance of any correlations which may be found. Now if in spite of the lack of reliability in the original data a significant difference is found, then we may consider that the actual difference is greater than the found difference by an unknown amount; it will certainly not be smaller unless certain prejudices and preconceptions on the part of the psychiatrists could be made responsible for the existence of the difference in the first place. Actually, however, any such preconceptions on the part of the psychiatrists would probably have worked in the opposite direction to that indicated by our results; many Mill Hill psychiatrists held a belief in a close connection or even identity between anxiety states and other "affective disorders", such as manic-depressive insanity. Now in view of the known correlation between manic-depressive insanity and eurymorph body build, the possibility can hardly be ruled out that some psychiatrists might have been influenced in their ratings, diagnoses, etc., by a belief that affective (dysthymic) symptoms would be found in eurymorph patients. In actual fact, as is shown below, our findings indicate rather that dysthymics tend to be of leptomorph body build. We may consequently conclude that while any lack of reliability on the part of the psychiatrist may have attenuated such differences as we found, it could not have created them; consequently, we are on safe ground in incorporating these differences in our book.

The case is quite different, however, as regards the second point, i.e. the question of giving the actual correlations. The only additional information which these correlations could give would be an exact estimate of the closeness of the association found. But from the very unreliable nature of the data, this is precisely what we cannot do; the actual correlations are so heavily attenuated that they are unlikely to bear any close relation to the true values. In other words, we do not consider ourselves justified in printing correlation coefficients whose spurious accuracy might mislead the unwary to infer that we had succeeded in actually measuring the degree of association between personality traits and body build. We merely claim to have shown the existence of such an association; we do not claim to have measured it.

In spite of these objections, the required correlations were in fact calculated, and a general estimate of their size is given on a later page. The interpretation of the figure given there is subject to all the objections mentioned in this footnote; it may, however, serve a salutory purpose in emphasizing the incompleteness of our knowledge, and the impossibility of relying on general trends in assessing the individual case.

eurymorph, leptomorph and mesomorph groups. It will be seen that within the age-range represented by the hospital population there is no consistent trend for body-build to correlate with age.

In the second group are included items which have been found in the factor-analysis to be correlated with the hysterical type. Some of the items in this group were put in although they had not been used in the factor analysis. This was done

### TABLE SEVEN

| Item. | 120 Eury-morphs. | 150 Lepto-morphs. | 730 Meso-morphs. |
|---|---|---|---|
| Age: 16—20 . . . . . . | 1 | 9 | 7 |
| 21—25 . . . . . . | 18 | 25 | 27 |
| 26—30 . . . . . . | 34 | 23 | 28 |
| 31—40 . . . . . . | 42 | 36 | 34 |
| 40+ . . . . . . | 4 | 7 | 4 |
| Hysterical personality . . . . | 30 | 23 | 23 |
| Hysterical attitude . . . . . | 37 | 29 | 32 |
| *Hysterical conversion symptoms . . | 40 | 29 | 33 |
| *Diagnosis: Conversion Hysteria . . | 24 | 11 | 20 |
| Treatment: Hypnosis and/or Barbiturates . | 8 | 3 | 7 |
| *Service occupation unskilled or semiskilled . | 77 | 61 | 73 |
| *Education: Elementary . . . . | 88 | 77 | 84 |
| Delinquent . . . . . . | 6 | 2 | 5 |
| Intelligence average or below . . . | 75 | 66 | 69 |
| Vocabulary above average . . . | 22 | 38 | 28 |
| *Physical disease not trivial . . . | 12 | 3 | 4 |
| *Anxious . . . . . . | 54 | 67 | 60 |
| *Obsessional . . . . . . | 15 | 35 | 23 |
| *Depressed . . . . . . | 56 | 73 | 65 |
| Diagnosis: Severe acute or chronic anxiety | 43 | 47 | 42 |
| Reactive depression . . . . | 13 | 20 | 18 |
| *Treatment: Insulin . . . . | 2 | 14 | 6 |
| N.C.O. . . . . . . | 17 | 23 | 19 |
| Headaches . . . . . . | 56 | 65 | 60 |
| *Dyspepsia . . . . . . | 12 | 21 | 15 |
| Tremor . . . . . . | 25 | 31 | 26 |
| *Irritability . . . . . | 32 | 43 | 30 |
| Apathy . . . . . | 18 | 25 | 21 |
| Boarded out . . . . . . | 58 | 50 | 52 |
| Endogenous depression . . . . | 4 | 1 | 2 |
| *Loss of weight more than ½ stone . . | 4 | 20 | 12 |
| *Muscular tone good . . . . | 40 | 20 | 30 |
| *Single . . . . . . | 23 | 37 | 27 |
| *Teetotal . . . . . . | 39 | 50 | 52 |
| Schizoid, seclusive . . . . . | 31 | 39 | 32 |

Percentage of eurymorphs, leptomorphs and mesomorphs showing various symptoms, traits, etc. For full definition of items see Chapter One.

either (1) because later investigations showed them to be correlated with the hysterical personality; so it will be shown later that the vocabulary of the hysteric is significantly worse, on the average, than that of the dysthymic of similar intelligence, or (2) because it was well known that an item was associated with hysteria; so treatment by hypnosis and/or barbiturates is known to be more usually given to hysterics, while treatment by insulin is more frequently given to dysthymics.

In the third group are shown items associated with the dysthymic type. Selection of items here was carried out on a basis similar to that used for the hysterics. In the fourth group are shown various items of interest which did not seem to fit into any of the previous categories. Not all the items in the table distinguish significantly between eurymorphs and leptomorphs; some are included because they are suggestive, and round off the general picture. Significant differences are marked with an asterisk.

Close study of the table reveals quite clearly two main features. In the first instance, we note a close relation between eurymorph body build and hysterical personality, attitude, symptomatology and intelligence level. In the second instance, we note a similar relation between leptomorph body build and dysthymic personality, attitude, symptomatology and intelligence level. In other words, the typology worked out on the mental and temperamental level is reduplicated on the physical level with surprising accuracy. *Hysterics are distinguished from dysthymics not only on the intellectual and temperamental level, but also with respect to body build.* This would appear to be the main conclusion to be derived from Table 7.

Certain other points from the table may be noted in passing. Thus we see that while the reactive depressions show a tendency towards leptomorphy, the endogenous depressions show a tendency towards eurymorphy; in each case, the incidence of the illness in the mesomorph group is intermediate between incidence in the two extreme groups. This finding is of obvious interest in relation to the discussion in an earlier chapter regarding the question of the unitary nature of affective disturbances; so far as the present result can be regarded as bearing on this problem, it would appear to support those who believe that the endogenous depressions are qualitatively different from the reactive depressions.

It will also be noted that leptomorphs tend to be single, to be teetotal, and to be schizoid and seclusive more frequently than the eurymorphs. These findings might be taken as affording some support for Kretschmer's theories, particularly when taken in conjunction with the results of our comparison of eurymorph and leptomorph endogenous depression cases.[1]

The question thus arises as to the relation of our I.B. to the schizophrenic and manic-depressive disease groups. A small experiment was carried out on 49 schizophrenics and 42 manic-depressives, carefully selected on psychiatric grounds by Dr. Rees (1943). Eighteen different body-measurements were taken, and the I.B. was calculated for all patients. No significant difference was found between the groups, the schizophrenes being slightly more *eurymorph* than the manic-depressives.

It was also found, however, that great differences existed between the two groups with respect to the sagittal chest measurement. The means for schizophrenics and manic-depressives respectively were $19 \cdot 9 \pm 1 \cdot 7$ and $21 \cdot 8 \pm 1 \cdot 8$; the C.R. is $6 \cdot 2$. Thus, there can be no doubt that the two samples measured differed considerably with respect to this particular chest measurement, uncorrected for height or any other variable. (Several corrections were in fact tried out, but did not increase the differentiating value of the simple sagittal measurement.)

These findings suggest that possibly differences in body build in psychotics are significant along a different dimension than are differences in body build in neurotics (and normals). In particular, they suggest that the main difference between schizophrenics and manic-depressives lies in the "thin chest" of the schizophrenic, i.e. in the "third dimension" of body build, while the main difference between introvert and extravert lies in the first and second dimensions, i.e. in the flat, as it were.

This view is obviously no more than a tentative hypothesis, in view of the small number of cases involved. It should be noted, however, that it agrees well with the known affinity between schizophrenia and tuberculosis, and that it finds some additional support in the suggestive discovery by Burt (1944) of a third factor in his studies which he identifies with growth

---

[1] It is interesting to note that leptomorphs tend to be more intelligent than eurymorphs, have a better education, and a better vocabulary. Our conclusions on these points agree perfectly with those of Pillsbury (1936).

in the third dimension. Consideration of previous work by other investigators suggests that most of the differences found between schizophrenics and manic-depressives fit in well with the hypothesis outlined above. Further work is in progress to test the tenability of this view.

As regards the comparison between microsomatics and macrosomatics, certain results are set out in Table 8 with respect to 156 microsomatics, 156 macrosomatics, and 688 mesosomatics. There appears little correlation of this factor with age, except that for the 16–20 age group the big body of the macrosomatic

TABLE EIGHT

| Item. | 156 Microsomatics. | 156 Macrosomatics. | 688 Mesosomatics. |
|---|---|---|---|
| Age: 16—20 | 8 | 3 | 7 |
| 21—25 | 26 | 27 | 25 |
| 26—30 | 25 | 30 | 28 |
| 31—40 | 37 | 37 | 35 |
| 41+ | 4 | 3 | 4 |
| *Modal civilian occupation: unskilled | 51 | 39 | 36 |
| *Education secondary, central, or higher | 15 | 24 | 15 |
| *Sexual activity inhibited | 17 | 9 | 11 |
| *Broad hobbies | 23 | 35 | 25 |
| *Teetotal | 54 | 37 | 52 |
| *Past physical health good | 44 | 68 | 52 |
| *Weak and dependent | 58 | 38 | 50 |
| *Inert | 26 | 18 | 27 |
| *Rebellious, aggressive | 13 | 30 | 17 |
| *Anxious | 61 | 51 | 63 |
| *Hypochondriacal | 27 | 17 | 32 |
| *Slight or no exposure to enemy attack | 61 | 51 | 55 |
| *Depressed | 72 | 58 | 65 |
| Irritability | 30 | 38 | 32 |
| *Muscular tone good | 19 | 49 | 28 |
| *Loss of weight more than ½ stone | 19 | 9 | 13 |
| *Boarded out | 60 | 46 | 51 |
| *Intelligence average or above | 63 | 74 | 70 |
| *Vocabulary average or above | 68 | 89 | 69 |

Percentage of microsomatics, macrosomatics and mesosomatics showing various symptoms, traits, etc. For full definition of items, see Chapter One.

is under-represented. All the differences between microsomatics and macrosomatics reported in the table are significant, with the exception of the item "Irritability".

The picture of the microsomatic person which emerges from

the Table is perhaps not so very different from what one might have expected on general grounds. He is unskilled, of poor education, dull, has a poor vocabulary; his hobbies are narrow, his sexual activity is inhibited, and his physical health bad. His muscular tone is bad, he does not drink much, and has broken down although not so often exposed to enemy attack. He has lost weight, and is likely to be boarded out of the army. Temperamentally, he is weak and dependent, inert, hypochondriacal, anxious and depressed. Altogether, both mentally and physically he is what is popularly called "a poor specimen". The macrosomatic type is the opposite on all the points mentioned, while the mesosomatic type usually comes somewhere in between the extremes. It may, perhaps, be said that these results have value only in so far as they reinforce everyday observation, and disprove Adler's well-known contention of a "masculine protest" compensating for some constitutional "organ inferiority". He cites many examples of microsomatics developing aggressive and rebellious personalities as an overcompensation for their smallness; our figures suggest that such an outcome is the exception rather than the rule in neurotics.

We may close this section with an attempt to evaluate the results reported. We believe that from a theoretical point of view the correlation of the hysteric-dysthymic continuum with the eurymorph-leptomorph continuum is of considerable interest; we also believe, in view of the agreement of our results with those reported by Burt, and by Sanford and his associates, that this relation is not restricted to neurotics, but constitutes a much more general and widespread phenomenon. From the practical point of view, however, we do not believe that these findings are of great importance; correlations between personality traits and body type are not very large, being mostly in the neighbourhood of + 0·30, and are thus quite unsuited to serve the demands of diagnosis or selection. Here also, therefore, our conclusions agree with those of Burt, who dismisses indices of body type as diagnostic criteria. If we wish to obtain information regarding a person's temperament, we must apply direct tests of the particular trait in which we are interested; there are no short-cut methods through body measurement or other similar procedures.

### 3. AUTONOMIC ACTIVITY: SALIVARY SECRETION

The general field of constitution is far too vast to make it possible for us to attempt even a superficial summary of the work done, or to contribute to any great extent to this highly technical sphere bristling with difficulties. In only a few respects have we attempted to trespass on to this ground traditionally reserved to physiologists. In our work on body type we found some slight evidence of correlation of autonomic lability with leptomorph body type and anxiety symptoms (Rees and Eysenck, 1945); consequently it was thought that a direct investigation of the autonomic reactivity of neurotic and psychotic patients might throw some light on this relation.

The view that the autonomic nervous system is causally related to personality type is often identified with the theories of Eppinger and Hess (1917). They conceived of a sort of continuum of individual differences in the method of functioning of this system, varying from one extreme at which the thoraco-lumbar branch was predominant (sympathicotonics), to the other, at which the cranio-sacral branch was predominant (vagotonics). The psychological traits associated with vagotonia are listed by Guillaume (1928) as follows: depression, hesitation, anxiety, apathy, melancholia, liability to phobias. Sympathicotonics on the other hand are impulsive, active, busy, dominating, and liable to lose control over themselves. A good review of pharmaco-dynamic, physiological, clinical and other tests of this supposed general trait is given by Sachs (1936), who also marshals the evidence regarding the nature of this trait, and its significance.

Recently, Darling (1940) and Wenger (1941, 1942) have submitted this dichotomy to a factorial study. Correlating various tests of autonomic functioning, they find that most of these tests are relatively unreliable on retesting, and that correlations between them are rather low; however, Wenger concludes that on the whole the results "offer substantiation for the hypothesis of Eppinger and Hess and the means of measuring the individual differences in autonomic function which they postulated". Most diagnostic of this autonomic factor he finds salivary output, which correlates with long dermographic persistence and short dermographic latency, with slow heart rate and much sinus arrhythmia, with low electric skin-conductance and slow respiration rate, as well as with low systolic blood pressure.

Salivary output, as measured by means of the Lashley disc, was shown by Strongin and Hinsie (1938, 1939) to be considerably lower in manic-depressive subjects than in normal controls, and it appeared possible that similar differences might become apparent in our neurotic population. The test used was similar to that described by Lashley (1914, 1916), while our measuring device was modified from Richter and Wada's description (1924). In this arrangement, a disc is held over the opening of Stenson's duct by suction, and the saliva issuing from the parotid gland drained off through a rubber tube to a measuring device, thus enabling the experimenter to measure secretion per unit of time in cubic centimetres (Eysenck and Yap, 1944).

The population tested consisted of 12 male and 12 female neurotic controls (nearly all hysterics), 26 male and 26 female anxiety and depression cases (dysthymics), and 24 psychotic subjects, 13 of whom were schizophrenic, while the remaining 11 were suffering from affective disorders. The psychotic patients were almost twice as old as the neurotics.

Salivation was measured under various conditions, such as reading, rest, mental work, food imagery, and whilst doing a test involving hand-eye co-ordination (the Triple Tester[1]). The results of these tests are quite definite; in each of the eleven experimental periods the dysthymic group shows less salivation than the hysteric group. The ratio, hysteric-secretion/dysthymic-secretion is 1·41, showing that the H-group secreted almost 50% more saliva than did the D-group. A similar result was found for the psychotics, where the ratio schizophrenics/affectives was 1·36.

The possible explanations of these findings are discussed at length in our original article (Eysenck and Yap, 1944). It would seem reasonable to assume that dysthymics would show more emotional reactions than hysterics to the unpleasant and rather frightening situation of having a foreign body put in their mouths, and having to keep it there for nearly an hour.

Such an emotional experience tends to have an inhibiting effect on salivary secretion, as Wittkower and Pilz (1932) have shown, and consequently the comparative lack of salivary flow in the dysthymics would seem to find an obvious explanation.

[1] This test is described in a later chapter.

An interesting finding of this research is that mental effort has a marked inhibiting effect on salivary secretion; in this respect our results support the work of Brunacci and de Sanctis (1914) and Winsor (1931), as against the view of Lashley (1914, 1916). It may prove possible to invert this relationship, and make the inhibition a measure of effort expended; that such a suggestion is not entirely fanciful may be seen from the interesting and important work of Lehman and Wirth on mental energy, as reviewed for instance by Spearman (1938).

## 4. DARK VISION

One aspect of constitution which might reasonably be expected to show differences between neurotic and non-neurotic patients is sensory functioning. In a well-controlled study, Slater (1944) showed that with respect to both auditory and visual acuity neurotics are inferior to normal controls of similar age, intelligence, and status. In our own work, we have been particularly interested in night visual capacity, as psychological factors enter more markedly into this sensory function than into many others (Rees, 1945).

The ability to see in diminished illumination shows considerable individual variations, and minor degrees of night blindness are common. Maitra and Harris (1937) found that of 200 poor class children, 20–30% were slightly below normal, and a similar number definitely subnormal in dark adaptation. Bishop Harman (1941) found that 14–28% of the normal population see poorly at night, while Rycroft (1942) reported 7–14% of his military subjects as night vision defective. Lister and Bishop (1943) found that 3·9% of 10,333 first-class soldiers had poor scotopic vision.

Deficient dark-adaptation may be due to pathological eye changes, congenital and hereditary causes, vitamin A deficiency, pathological changes in the liver, or over-exposure to light (Duke Elder, 1938). In a number of cases, however, no apparent pathological or nutritional causes are present, and various writers have delimited a hysterical or neurotic type of night-blindness (Smith, 1921; Derby, 1921; Elder, 1938; Livingston and Bolton, 1943; Wittkower et al., 1941).

96 neurotic male patients were tested by means of the

Livingston Rotating Hexagon. This apparatus was designed for testing night visual capacity (Livingstone, 1942). It consists of a hexagonal structure which can be rotated so as to present different panels to the subject tested; there are altogether 96 letters and objects on its six sides. The letters are placed in various positions, and the objects are outlines of aircraft, ships, parallel lines, etc. Preparation for the test includes 30 minutes dark adaptation, with dark goggles, admitting only 3% light, followed by ten minutes in the dark room during which the details of the test are carefully explained. The subject is able to record his interpretation of the objects and letters in the dark by means of special Braille cards.

Four routine tests are given at various levels of illumination, each dealing with 6 letters and 2 objects. In each test one minute is allowed for recording the answers, with a warning after 45 seconds. A fifth test may be given to "detect possible malingerers, or persons with hysterical amblyopia". Three large capital letters are exposed against a background sufficiently illuminated to make certain that they could be easily read except by patients suffering from advanced pathological conditions (Livingstone and Bolton, 1943).

The Hexagon test examines a mixture of photopic and scotopic vision (Lythgoe, 1940), illumination during the test ranging from 0·00015 eq. foot candles to 0·0012 eq. foot candles. The adaptation period is sufficient for the purpose of the test, as shown by Yudkin (1943) who found that there was no improvement in dark adaptation after thirty-five minutes.

Of the neurotic patients examined, 36 were suffering from anxiety state, 33 from depression, and 27 were hysterics. All were on full hospital diet, and none suffered from any marked visual defects. During the explanation of the test the patients were encouraged to do as well as possible and to compete with each other; it was pointed out to them that the result of the test was in no way relevant to their treatment or disposal.

The results obtained from this group of neurotic patients were compared with results obtained from 6,062 R.A.F. personnel with the same apparatus, and under identical conditions. Figure 9 clearly shows the results of the comparison. The average score of the neurotic group, on a scale ranging from 0 to 32, is 7·1; the average score of the normal group is 19·3. The average of the neurotic group is more than three standard deviations lower than the mean of the normal group.

The three neurotic groups are themselves differentiated with respect to test scores. The anxiety states have a mean score of 4·8, the depressives of 7·9, and the hysterics of 8·7. Grading the scores of these three groups according to Steadman's list (1942), we find that 81% of the anxiety states are below average, while only 67% of the depressed and 63% of the hysterics are below average. For the total neurotic group, 72% are below

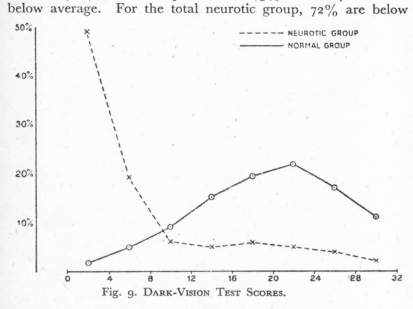

Fig. 9. DARK-VISION TEST SCORES.

average. It would seem, accordingly, that anxious patients are particularly handicapped in tests of night-visual capacity.

Age is a possible factor in these results, as Ferree (1935, 1938), Bishop Harman (1941), Rycroft (1942), and Lister (1943) have shown that night vision becomes worse with increasing age. The correlation between score and age in the test used was −0·394 ± ·086 for the total neurotic group, showing that the older patients have poorer night vision on the average. The only difference in age between the three neurotic groups which is significant is that between the depressives and the hysterics; the depressives are rather older than the hysterics. Intelligence, contrary to the contention of Rycroft (1942) shows little correlation with performance; when night visual capacity was correlated with Matrices score, r was found to be −0·107 ± 0·103. This correlation is not significant.

Scores on this test distinguish significantly not only between neurotics and normals, they also distinguish between the more seriously ill and the less seriously ill within the hospital. 50 men who had poor scores (4 or under) were compared with 13 men with high scores (19 or over) with respect to a variety of items, and the following significant differences were found:

TABLE NINE

| Item Investigated. | Percentage Good Group. | Percentage Bad Group. | C.R. |
|---|---|---|---|
| Considerable unemployment | 0·0 | 28·0 | 4·41 |
| Poor work history | 0·0 | 10·0 | 2·38 |
| Discharged from the army | 15·4 | 46·0 | 2·44 |
| Poor education | 7·7 | 30·0 | 2·29 |
| Good mental health before illness | 61·5 | 16·0 | 3·04 |
| Previous mental illness | 0·0 | 16·0 | 3·08 |
| Well organized personality | 76·9 | 30·0 | 3·40 |
| Very anxious and highly strung | 0·0 | 22·0 | 3·76 |
| Obsessional traits | 0·0 | 14·0 | 2·85 |
| Cyclothymic personality | 7·7 | 52.0 | 3·67 |

These findings show conclusively that the group with poor night vision was inferior with respect to general neurotic tendency to the group with good night vision; they also show that this inferiority was particularly marked with the dysthymic type of personality. No significant differences were observed with respect to the various hysterical traits, nor did schizoid or hypochondriacal traits show any marked differences.

The interpretation of these findings is by no means easy. Kekcheyev (1943) has pointed out that sensitivity of night vision is one of the most fluctuating functions of the human organism, and that such factors as fatigue, distension of visceral organs, and strong stimulation of other sense organs may diminish night vision. These effects he maintains are produced through the sympathetic part of the autonomic system. It seems possible, then, that in this study also we find evidence of the greater lability of autonomic reactivity in patients of the dysthymic type; while such an interpretation would be much in line with our previous discussion more direct evidence on this point would seem desirable before this explanation can be accepted.

One item of information may be thought to lend support to

this argument. Kekcheyev (1943) suggested that poor night vision might be the result of fears associated with darkness. We found that 60% of the men with poor night vision had marked fears of the dark, either in childhood or in adult life, while only 27·3% of the men with good night vision had such fears. This difference (t = 2·3) is of great interest in view of the known close relation between autonomic activity and fear (Cannon, 1929), and would seem to support the explanation put forward above.

## 5. CHOLINE ESTERASE SECRETION

Of great interest in this connection is also the work of Richter and his associates at this hospital, carried out on clinical material selected according to principles similar to those which guided our choice. The most significant of these studies deal with the relation between the serum choline esterase activity and neurotic syndrome; they link up with a number of studies which have been made of the choline esterase activity of the serum in various physiological and pathological conditions, following the work of Dale (1934) and Loewi (1935) on the relationship of choline esterase to the transmission of nervous impulses. There are great inter-personal variations in the activity of the serum esterase, but it generally remains very constant for any one individual, being relatively little affected by changes in diet, exercise, or fatigue. Tod and Jones (1937) and Jones and Stadie (1939) found a high esterase activity in anxiety states, and lowered activity in catatonic stupor, epilepsy, and schizophrenia.

In a preliminary experiment, Richter and Lee (1942) used the method described by Jones and Tod (1935) to estimate the serum choline esterase of 12 normal adults, 12 patients with anxiety symptoms, and 12 non-neurotic patients (mainly surgical cases). The mean esterase activity of the normal group was 74 ± 22, that of the non-neurotic patients, 75 ± 20; this difference is, of course, not significant. The patients suffering from anxiety states showed a mean activity of 104 ± 24; this is markedly different from the two normal groups, and the difference shows a satisfactory degree of significance, as tested by Student's t-test. Subsidiary experiments showed that the high esterase activity in anxiety states was not due to the removal of an inhibitor, but to the increased outpouring of the enzyme from the tissues. No such increase was shown by the serum amylase, serum albumin, serum globulin, or total serum proteins.

In a second experiment, Richter and Lee (1942) used the results of the 24 non-neurotic subjects from their first experiment to compare them with estimates of the serum choline esterase activity of 23 hysterics, 53 anxiety states, 27 depressives, 11 anxiety-depressive states, and certain other groups of no immediate interest to our purpose. Compared with the control group's mean esterase activity of $75 \pm 21$, they found that the hysterics had a score of $86 \pm 17$, the anxiety states of $95 \pm 20$, the depressives of $96 \pm 23$, and the anxiety-depressive states of $103 \pm 19$. As judged by the $t$-test, the hysterics did not differ significantly from the normals; all the other groups did differ from the normal group at the $P = \cdot 01$ level.

Of particular interest in connection with these results is the fact that the (largely reactive) depressive patients show results essentially identical with those given by the anxiety states, while the hysterics do not appear to be significantly differentiated from the normal control group. Superficially, the fact that the depressives were so differentiated appears to contradict the results reported by Tod and Jones (1937) who found normal choline esterase activity in depressive states; however, it should be remembered that their work was carried out on psychotic patients (manic-depressives and involutional melancholias). Two possibilities are suggested by Richter and Lee to account for the difference between these findings on neurotic and psychotic patients respectively: (1) different emotional condition in the two states, and (2) reversion of serum esterase activity to normal in depressive states of long standing.

In summing up their results, the authors suggest a link between their investigations and the theory of autonomic lability in the affective states which has governed our own approach. "It has frequently been pointed out (Whitehorn, 1938) that the main physiological concomitants of emotion are closely similar in anxiety, depression, anger and fear; these physiological reactions depend for the most part on the visceral and circulatory changes due to the increased activity of the autonomic system, particularly in the sympathetic division, and the finding of an increased serum esterase activity in anxiety and depression agrees with many other observations as to the similarity of the physiological changes in these emotions." One possible way in which esterase activity might be linked with autonomic activity has been suggested by Tod and Jones (1937); they believe that the serum choline esterase serves the purpose of destroying any acetyl choline that may escape into the blood from the tissues (Stedman and Russell, 1937), and that thus the raised serum esterase activity in anxiety might act as a physiological mechanism to combat the increased output of acetyl-choline due to increased autonomic activity.

Whatever the ultimate explanation of the differences in serum choline esterase activity between hysterics on the one hand, and dysthymics on the other, the fact that such differences were observed appears to strengthen considerably the arguments in favour of the existence of some such type-differences as are implied in the Hysteric-Dysthymic factor.

## 6. Exercise Response

Another interesting field where conspicuous constitutional differences between dysthymics, hysterics, and normal controls can be observed is that of *exercise response*. One group of dysthymics, the so-called "effort syndrome" group, has often been singled out as showing poor exercise response, but it is doubtful if this group is significantly distinguished from other types of dysthymics in this respect. The question of exercise response in relation to anxiety, hysteria, effort syndrome, and normal personality was studied by Jones and Melhuish (1945).[1]

[1] A summary of previous work along these lines is given by McFarland and Huddleson (1936). The studies of these investigators themselves are of great interest, as they report results almost exactly identical with those found in this hospital. Using the Schneider index, they found the following values for samples of anxiety states (dysthymics), conversion hysterics, various other neurotic states, and controls:

Dysthymics:    M = 7·6 ± 3·4 (N = 73)
               F = 6·7 ± 3·8 (N = 75)
Hysterics:     M = 10·0 ± 3·8 (N = 58)
               F = 10·2 ± 2·9 (N = 45)
Neurotics,     M = 8·6 ± 3·6 (N = 261)
All kinds:     F = 7·2 ± 3·9 (N = 242)
Controls:  M + F = 12·6 ± 2·7 (N = 191)

The investigators conclude: "Whatever its etiological mechanism, a considerable physiologic imbalance seems to be exhibited by the cardiovascular system during the earlier stages of psychoneurotic . . . illness, especially when anxiety is marked." As will be seen below, these words might equally well have been used to sum up our own results.

Twenty normal controls were used, as well as ten anxiety states with no complaint of poor exercise response, ten effort syndrome cases, and ten hysterics. All the patients were free from demonstrable organic disease and had no history of serious respiratory or circulatory illness at any time in their lives. Controls and patients were equated with respect to weight and age. The controls were leading relatively sedentary lives (they were craftsmen from a near-by barracks), and did less physical training, marching, etc., than did the patients.

The task chosen was pedalling on a bicycle ergometer at 42 revolutions per minute, the friction of the brake band being equivalent to a weight of 9 lbs. The subject thus did 6,750 foot pounds of work per minute for five minutes. Three main methods of determining exercise response were used: Oxygen uptake, pulse rise, and lactate rise.

Oxygen uptake was measured in cubic centimetres per minute after standard work by means of a Douglas bag; pulse rise by calculating an index in which the pulse figure for the first four minutes after cessation of the exercise, and the mean of the 8th, 9th, and 10th minutes are added, and five times the resting pulse subtracted from the resulting figure; lactate rise by comparing lactate content of a sample of venous blood removed before and another removed 10 minutes after standard exercise.

These three indices of exercise response correlate together; for the total group of fifty subjects tested the correlations are oxygen consumption and pulse rise = + 0·63 ± ·09; oxygen consumption and lactate rise = + 0·49 ± ·11; pulse rise and lactate rise = + 0·56 ± ·10. The average of these correlations is + 0·56; in other words, the three tests tend to measure the same function, and in combination would correlate with this function to the extent of + 0·80 approximately.

Certain features (which are worth noting) appear in the results of the three tests: (1) The anxiety states with and without effort syndrome show reactions which are not significantly different; (2) The anxiety states with and without effort syndrome show significantly worse exercise response than do the normal subjects; (3) The hysterics are intermediate between the normal subjects and the two groups of anxiety states with respect to their exercise response, the tendency being for them to be differentiated significantly from the anxiety states, but not from the normals.

These tendencies become even clearer when we compare the combined total scores on the three tests. (Before combining the scores, they were turned into standard scores in order to avoid differential weighting because of S.D. differences.) The results are set out in graphical form in Figure 10. The mean scores for the groups are as follows:

TABLE TEN

|  | | | Mean. | | S.D. |
|---|---|---|---|---|---|
| Anxiety states | . | . . | 7·787 | . | 2·542 |
| Hysterics | . | . | 5·858 | . | .1·177 |
| Normal controls | . | . | 4·328 | . | 1·437 |

The three means are significantly different, Student's *t* being 5·2 for the anxiety states and the controls, 3·4 for the hysterics

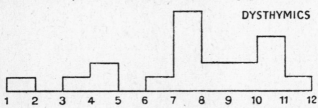

DYSTHYMICS

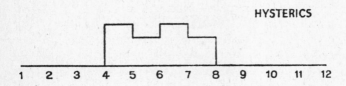

HYSTERICS

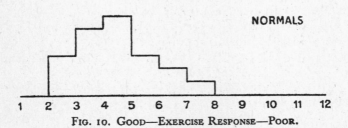

NORMALS

FIG. 10. GOOD—EXERCISE RESPONSE—POOR.

and the controls, and 2·7 for the anxiety states and the hysterics. The S.D. of the anxiety states is significantly larger than that of either of the other groups, $t$ being 2·4 (controls) and 2·9 (hysterics). The hysterics do not differ from the normals in this respect; $t = 0·1$ only.

These results show that the neurotics tested gave significantly worse exercise response than did the normal controls; that anxiety states did even worse than hysterics; and that the anxiety group showed greater inter-personal variability. Admittedly these conclusions are based on very small numbers of patients, but the significance of the findings was established by means of formulae specially devised for small samples. Repetition and verification of these findings would be of great interest.

### 7. Oscillation (Reversal of Perspective)

Among the writers who believe that Introversion has a basis in the physical constitution, McDougall holds a prominent place. In his view, the introverted or extraverted attitude of a person depends on the speed with which nervous impulses travel in the C.N.S., and especially in the higher centres. In the extravert, this rate is slow, and his nervous excitation finds ready expression in overt channels (1926, 1933). McDougall believed that the rate of reversal of perspective of an ambiguous figure (cube, windmill, face-vase, etc.), showed clearly this "speed of nervous action", and adduced a certain amount of experimental evidence to show that high speed of nervous action (rapid rate of reversal) was characteristic of introverts (identified by him with schizophrenes), while a low rate of reversal was characteristic of extraverts (identified by him with manic-depressives).

Hunt and Guilford (1931) tested 25 college students for rate of reversal with the Wheatstone Cube. They found the phenomenon of "rate of reversal" relatively constant from one testing to another, but failed to find any definite correlations of the test with three personality inventories. In view of the many criticisms made of self-rating questionnaires of the kind used by them, this result can hardly be considered fatal to McDougall's theory.

In another study, Guilford and Braly (1931) tested 19 manic-depressive and 26 dementia praecox patients with the reversal of perspective test. The test was given in two forms, with the subject adopting (a) a passive and (b) an inhibitive attitude towards the reversal. A comparison of the results of the normal, the manic-depressive and the dementia praecox groups shows that with the passive attitude normals and dementia praecox patients give 18 and 17 reversals per minute respectively, while manic depressive patients give only 4 reversals. With the inhibitive attitude, normals give 9 reversals, dementia praecox cases 13, and manic depressives 2. Paranoid forms of dementia praecox showed rates intermediate between the other dementia praecox cases and the manic depressives (12 and 5 reversals respectively for passive and inhibitive attitudes). These results show that the differences in reversal rate between manic-depressives and schizophrenes predicted by McDougall actually do manifest themselves, thus giving a certain amount of support to his theory.

Cameron (1936) reports results which tend in the same direction. He used the staircase pattern, and showed that the fluctuation rate of depressive patients increases (i.e. approaches the normal), as patients get better; he also found that the results of the test became more regular. If these results were to be confirmed, they would appear to be of outstanding importance.

A study of a normal group is reported by Denton (1943). Using 5 different tests (cube, duck-rabbit, stairs, pyramid, and vase-face), she tested 41 students on two occasions, giving the five tests twice at each sitting. She reports reliability coefficients between the two sittings of ·86, ·73, ·94, ·76, and ·93 for the five tests; these results are similar to those obtained by Hunt and Guilford (1931). She also correlated the five tests, obtaining an average intercorrelation of ·53 for the first sitting, and an average intercorrelation of ·68 for the second sitting. A factor analysis of the two tables of correlations indicated the presence of one strong, general factor, with saturations varying from ·94 and ·92 (first and second sitting respectively) for the Cube test, to ·66 and ·69 for the Pyramid. This general factor of "oscillation" showed no significant correlation with intelligence, academic attainment, or perseveration; it did show a correlation of + 0·40 with writing speed.

As rate of reversal (oscillation) would, therefore, appear to be a test of considerable reliability, capable of discriminating between schizophrenes and manic-depressives, an effort was made to study its power of discrimination with regard to our hysteric-dysthymic dichotomy. Two tests (face-vase and Maltese cross) were given by A. Petrie to 21 male and 13 female hysterics, as well as to 23 male and 15 female dysthymics. Each test was given twice; once with instructions to be passive, the other time with instructions to attempt to get as many reversals as possible. Correlations between passive and active state were + 0·77 for the Face-Vase test, and + 0·87 for the Maltese Cross test. Correlations between the two tests were + 0·89 for the passive state and + 0·83 for the active state.

The minute reversal rate of these four groups was as follows: Male hysterics, 7·7 and 8·1, female hysterics, 9·6 and 14·1; male dysthymics, 8·4 and 9·6; female dysthymics, 10·6 and 12·3. These results show no significant or suggestive difference between the hysterics and the anxiety states; it is interesting to note, however, that the reversal rate is rather lower for neurotics than for normals.[1] In the absence of a normal control group, this suggestive finding could not be followed up. It would not be at all surprising in terms of McDougall's theory if neurotics were found to have a lower rate of oscillation than normals; McDougall holds that cerebral activity inhibits the activity of the lower centres, and that this cerebral activity, through rate of nervous transmission, is linked causally with rapid rate of reversal. However, this finding requires confirmation in a properly controlled experiment before any attempt at explanation becomes necessary.

It will be seen that in all our tests the female groups show higher rates of reversal than do the males; these differences are statistically significant. There are two possible ways of interpreting these differences. It may be that we are here dealing with a genuine sex difference; or it may be that the women tested were less severely neurotic than the men tested, thus showing reversal rates nearer the normal. From the literature it would not appear likely that any sex differences are shown on this test, so that the second explanation offered above appears more likely to be able to account for the phenomenon. When it is

[1] As found in the literature.

realized that in the questionnaire test already discussed, and in the suggestibility test to be discussed later, female groups of patients showed responses closer to the normal than did male groups, our suggestion may be regarded as not altogether devoid of support.

One further finding may be of interest, viz. the fact that the female patients had more control over their rate of reversal, as shown by the fact that when asked to give as high a rate of reversal as they could, the female patients increased their rate by 3·1 reversals, while the males increased their rate by only ·8 reversals. Again, it would appear that the capacity to change the rate of reversal is weaker in neurotics than normals, and a similar explanation to that given above for sex differences in actual rate of reversal would appear to apply to the present phenomenon also.

In this connection, the results of certain preliminary studies by R. Gordon may be of interest. She found that when normal and neurotic subjects are asked to modify or change their images, some persons show great fluidity, while other have great difficulty in doing so (rigidity). This fluidity-rigidity factor has been studied by her in connection with the formation of conceptual stereotypes, and also in connection with perceptual rigidity. In the experiments dealing with the latter problem, she had the subject record his rate of reversal (a) in the normal state, (b) under instruction to get as many reversals as possible, and (c) under instruction to get as few reversals as possible. Under those conditions, it appeared that the person with fluid imagery succeeded in varying the rate of reversal to a greater extent than did the person with rigid imagery. These findings are of particular interest as suggesting the dependence of imagery on constitutional factors, at least in part, and also because they link the work on reversal of perspective with the extensive work on imagery in relation to typology which has been carried out in Germany (Jaensch, 1930). These studies are not sufficiently advanced to be included here in detail; they are mentioned mainly to show the interrelation of the various "levels" of the personality at which we have attempted to sink our exploratory shafts.

## 8. SUMMARY

In this chapter are reviewed a number of studies carried out on the physique and constitution of neurotic and normal subjects. An objective index of body build was derived on the basis of a factorial analysis, which isolated the main dimensions of body configuration or physique. This index showed hysterics to have a higher preponderance of lateral growth, as compared with the dysthymics, who had a higher preponderance of linear growth. Neurotics as a whole were found to be pronouncedly leptomorph as compared with normals. Certain personality differences were also found with respect to body size.

Autonomic activity was investigated by a study of parotid gland activity, and differences found between hysterics and dysthymics. A dark vision test also showed differences between the two types, but was particularly successful in differentiating between neurotics and normals.

Further significant differences between hysterics and dysthymics, and between neurotics and non-neurotics, were found by the investigation of choline esterase secretion and exercise response.

No difference between hysterics and dysthymics was found on a test of oscillation (reversal of perspective), which had been shown by other investigators to discriminate between schizophrenes and manic-depressive patients. This result argues against an identification of the two dimensions of temperament involved.

# CHAPTER FOUR

# ABILITY AND EFFICIENCY

## 1. INTELLIGENCE AND NEUROSIS

IT HAS been pointed out that "some loss of efficiency is one of the commonest manifestations of disorder in the human being" (Hunt and Cofer, 1944). This loss is recognized in clinical terms such as *dementia, deterioration,* and *regression*; in recent psychological writing the more neutral term *psychological deficit* has come into use for characterizing such loss of efficiency. This psychological deficit may be studied from two points of view. We may look at it from the point of view of deterioration or lack of general, innate, all-round ability, or we may look at it from the point of view of the use which the individual makes of his ability. Thus we may study a group of neurotics by comparing their absolute ability, as shown by the results of intelligence tests, with a group of normals; theoretically this would enable us to study differences in innate, all-round ability.   Alternatively, we may study the persistence, the personal tempo, or the level of aspiration of neurotics; in this way we would be able to throw some light on the more complex question of precisely how the neurotic uses such ability as he has. These two points of view, while they may be distinguished on the theoretical level, are at times difficult to disentangle in practice. The present chapter begins with a consideration of results which are relevant mainly to the question of the actual ability of neurotics; in the later sections, experiments are reported dealing largely with the way this ability is used.

With regard to the *ability* of neurotics, it has often been suggested that it is below the average of non-neurotic subjects.[1]

[1] The first empirical study in this field appears to have been a research by Adrian and Yealland (1917), who showed that the majority of 250 army hysterics scored below average on the Binet test.

Thus Hollingworth (1920, 1931), who applied mental tests to several hundred neurotic soldiers, found that "except for the psychasthenic group, all the classifications of 'psychoneurosis' fall definitely below the mental level of the average recruit". Similar results were obtained by Tendler (1923), who, however, found hysterics superior to other neurotic groups. More recent work, such as the investigations of Michaels and Schilling (1936), Jastak (1937), Kendig and Richmond (1940), Roe and Shakow (1942), Eysenck (1943), Malamud and Gottlieb (1944) and Halstead (1944), leave a confused impression. Most of the average I.Q.s reported would appear to be above the average, thus contradicting the conclusion that psychoneuroses develop mainly in persons of subnormal intelligence.

Some of the contradictions which are apparent in the results quoted may be due to differences in the selection of neurotics. It would appear that neurotic service cases tend to score rather below average, while civilian neurotics tend to score slightly above average. This tendency is explicable on the grounds that army training imposes a considerable stress on the dull person, who may find difficulties in understanding and following instructions; this strain may lead to break-down in persons constitutionally disposed towards neuroticism. On the other hand, the selection of civilian cases often shows an opposite bias; the intelligent person is often subjected to a greater strain in our civilization than is the dullard, and consequently may show neurotic symptoms more readily. He may also be more ready to seek treatment. This argument is purely hypothetical, of course, in view of the lack of precise information regarding the actual stress experienced by different groups in civilian life and in the army; it is put forward mainly to illustrate the dangers of generalizing from insufficient data. Our own results are derived exclusively from service patients, and any interpretation of the results must be made subject to the qualification that the conclusions may not be applicable to civilian neurotics.

The test primarily used in our work has been the Progressive Matrices test, devised by Raven (1941). This test provides a non-verbal series of 60 individual problems, and was constructed in accordance with the theoretical analysis of intelligence given by Spearman (1927). Each problem consists of a design or "matrix" from which part has been removed. The subject is required to examine the matrix and decide which of several pieces given below is the correct one to complete the design. In terms of Spearman's noegenetic laws, the testee must first of all educe the relations obtaining between the different parts of the design, and then educe a correlate, using the incomplete design as a fundament, together with the educed relation, in order to find the piece which will best serve to complete the design. Four different problems, of varying degrees of difficulty, are given in Figure 11 to illustrate the mechanism of this test. Usually the test is given as a group test, but it may also be used individually, and for very young children and for senile dementia patients a special board form has been prepared in which the pieces can actually be fitted into the design (Raven, 1940; Eysenck, 1945).

The sixty problems in this test are divided into 5 sets, A, B, C, D, and E, of 12 problems each. The problems in each set become progressively more difficult, and each succeeding set is more difficult than the previous one. The principle on which the problems are based differs from set to set; thus in one set the principle may be an additive one, in another set it may be subtractive. The test as a whole has been widely used in the army, where over a million men and women have been tested, and where the results have been used for selection and classification purposes. The test has been found to be an almost pure measure of "g", showing hardly any saturation with such group factors as are known to enter into many other intelligence tests. Its reliability lies in the neighbourhood of ·85.

There are two standard methods of administering the Matrix test. It may be given either as a timed test, in which case the subjects are given 20 minutes to do as many problems as they can, or it may be given as an untimed test, in which case the subjects have as much time as they want to finish the problems. Separate norms are available for these two forms of the test. These norms divide the population into five "Selection Grades", for administrative convenience. On the untimed version, Grade I embraces the best 5%, Grade II the next-best 20%, Grade III the middle 50%, Grade IV the next 20%, and Grade V the lowest 5%. On the timed version, the percentages in the five grades are 10, 20, 40, 20, 10.

The untimed version was given to 5,000 male neurotic service

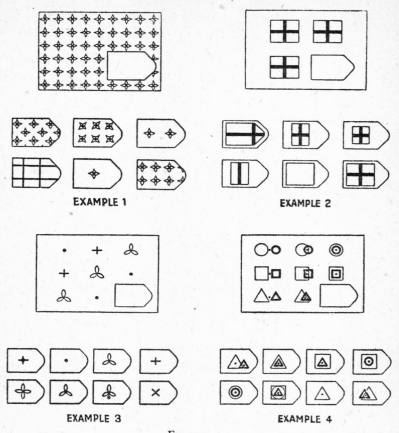

FIG. 11.

patients the day after they arrived at the hospital. As a control
group, the scores of 3,665 men between the ages of 20 and 30
years who had been tested before they began their military
training were kindly put at our disposal by Mr. J. C. Raven.
Also tested were 1,000 female neurotic army patients, under
similar conditions to the males.

The results of comparing the male neurotic and male control
groups show a decided superiority for the normals. The average
scores are 42·24 ± 9·77 for the normals, and 39·36 ± 9·90 for the
neurotics; this difference has a Critical Ratio of 14, and is thus
significant beyond any possible doubt. The percentage distribu-

tions of the two groups are given in Figure 12; it will be seen that up to a score of 40, the percentage of normals is lower than the percentage of neurotics, while above that score, the percentage of neurotics is lower than the percentage of normals. The coefficient of variation is larger for the neurotics than for the normals: 25, as compared with 23. This would seem to indicate that the neurotic group includes a slightly higher percentage of extremes (persons with high or low intelligence) than does the normal group. This is understandable enough in view of the fact that extremely bright or extremely dull persons are more likely to experience difficulties in coping with army routine than are persons of average mentality.

As will be shown later, in a comparison of speeded and un-speeded tests, the average score of our male neurotic group corresponds to an I.Q. of 93. However, this average score is not entirely due to any intellectual inferiority of the neurotic; certain selection factors must be taken into account. Our neurotic group does not contain any officers, while the control group, who had been tested before they began their military career, almost certainly contained a number of men who later rose to officer rank. Thus for a fair comparison it would be necessary to know the number of men from the ranks who become officers, and their average score on the matrix; it would also be necessary to know the average score on the matrix of neurotic officers. In the absence of such information, we cannot correct the I.Q. value obtained for absence of officers; we can only point out that the value obtained is too low by an unknown amount.

A second point to consider is connected with the question of reliability. We have shown that the retest reliability of neurotic groups is lower than the retest reliability of normal groups (Eysenck, 1944); clearly lack of reliability must lower the average score of a group as compared with the average score of another group showing higher retest reliabilities. This is obvious when we consider that chance factors are much more likely to lower than to raise a subject's score on an intelligence test, as compared with its true value. Consequently, we must conclude that part of the difference between neurotics and normals is due to lack of reliability in testing the neurotics, although, again, it is impossible to assign any definite value to the contribution of this factor.

When these two factors are taken into account, it appears

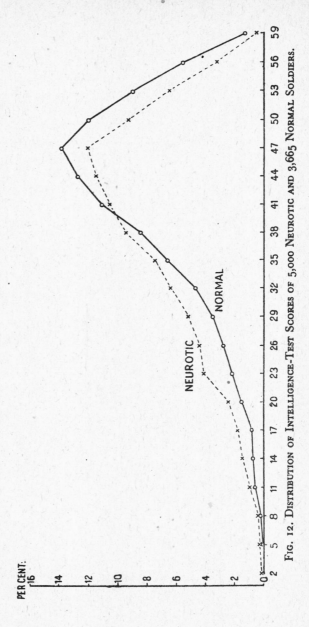

FIG. 12. DISTRIBUTION OF INTELLIGENCE-TEST SCORES OF 5,000 NEUROTIC AND 3,665 NORMAL SOLDIERS.

likely that comparatively little remains of the original difference of three points between the two groups. While it is doubtful if selection and unreliability of neurotic test scores between them can account for all the difference observed, we must conclude that such differences as can be found in the intelligence of neurotics and normals on the untimed Matrix test are small, and no great importance can be attributed to them. This is well in line with the results of the intra-hospital study reported in the second chapter, where low intelligence was shown to be correlated with "P–", but only to a slight degree. "P+" and "g+" appear to be correlated to some extent, but this correlation is rather lower than one would have thought likely in view of some of the early work of Hollingworth, Tendler, and Rivers.

Our results, then are in perfect agreement with the conclusion reached by Vernon in his study of the intelligence of neurotic children; he found "the clinic group as a whole somewhat below the norms on almost all tests of ability", and concluded that "this confirms the existence of a moderate correlation between intelligence and emotional stability" (Vernon, 1937).[1]

The average score of the female neurotics tested was 41·84 ± 9·86, which corresponds to an I.Q. of 97. The women are thus definitely more intelligent on the average than are the men; the Critical Ratio of the difference being 8. This superiority of the women over the men has been commented on in our introductory chapter, where it was pointed out that it represents the result of a more careful selection procedure. It may be noted that the women also showed themselves superior to the men on the speeded (20-minute version) of the Matrix test; in a comparison of 1,691 men and 809 women, the Critical Ratio was found to be 10.

So far, we have treated the neurotic group as a unit, comparing it with outside groups. But as we saw in the factorial study reported in Chapter Two, there are considerable differences between different neurotic groups, viz. the hysterics and the

[1] It had been planned originally to include a study of the memory function at this point, in which neurotics and normals would be compared with respect to their scores on some of the traditional tests of memory. A preliminary study of these tests, however, disclosed that they failed to define any kind of "memory" factor, and that intelligence could account for all the correlations observed (Eysenck & Halstead, 1945). The implications of our conclusion that the usual clinical tests of "memory" measure only "intelligence" and nothing else are perhaps obvious enough to need no discussion. An attempted explanation of our findings is included in our article.

dysthymics, and it becomes important to investigate these differences with respect to intellectual ability. Reports in the literature give conflicting results. Hollingworth (1920, 1931) found psychasthenics more intelligent than hysterics; Tendler (1923) found the opposite. Roe and Shakow (1942) and Malamud and Gottlieb (1944) found no great differences, while Eysenck (1944) reported higher scores for anxiety states than for hysterics. [1] Figure 13 shows the result of testing 904 dysthymics and 474 conversion hysterics. It will be seen that below a score of 25, there are almost twice as many hysterics as anxiety states, while above a score of 50 there are about twice as many anxiety states as hysterics. This is brought out in the respective mean scores, $40 \cdot 12 \pm 10 \cdot 10$ S.D. for the anxiety states, and $37 \cdot 12 \pm 12 \cdot 08$ for the hysterics. This difference is statistically very significant, the Critical Ratio being $4 \cdot 6$. We may conclude that hysterics are more frequently found among the 10% of the population showing the lowest intelligence, while anxiety states (dysthymics) are more frequently found among the 10% of the population showing the highest intelligence. This conclusion is in accordance with clinical experience. The difference, although significant, is not very large; it merely indicates a trend.

## 2. "SCATTER" AS A PERSONALITY VARIABLE

Having thus dealt with the absolute scores of neurotic and normal, hysterical and anxious groups, we may inquire if these groups are distinguished in other ways; for instance, whether the scatter of scores is greater for neurotics than for normals, or for hysterics than for anxiety cases. Wallin (1917), Mateer (1924), Wells (1927), Dearborn (1927), Harris and Shakow (1937), Rabin (1941, 1942), Reichard and Schofer (1943), Gilliland, Wittman and Goldman (1943), and Schafer and Rapaport (1944), have dealt with the problem of scatter in neurotics and psychotics, and the conclusion seems to be that while scatter is larger in psychotics than in normals, neurotics do not differ significantly from normals.

In the Matrix test, scatter is measured in the following way.

[1] More recently still, Slater (1945) reports that obsessional patients significantly surpassed hysterics and other patients on an intelligence test.

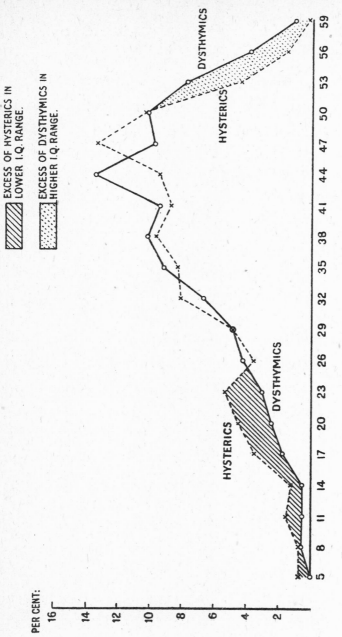

FIG. 13. DISTRIBUTION OF INTELLIGENCE-TEST SCORES OF 904 DYSTHYMICS AND 474 HYSTERICS

Any given total score is made up of the scores in the five sub-tests; these scores should bear a certain relation to each other. Thus for a total score of 45, the subject ought to score 12 points in set A, 10 points in set B, 9 points in sets C and D, and 5 points in set E. This is the scatter of marks on the subtests as determined from several thousand normal scores. Any deviation from this pattern is scored as an irregularity; the sum of such irregularities makes up the subject's "scatter" score. Thus someone scoring 45 points on the total test, made up of sub-scores 10, 10, 10, 8, 7, would have a total scatter-score of 6.

These scatter-scores are useful because they predict with fair accuracy the reliability of a test. A testee having a high scatter-score is likely to show low retest-reliability, while a testee with a low scatter-score is likely to show high retest-reliability. For a group of three hundred subjects, it was found on retesting that those who in the original test had a scatter score of 7 or more showed a change in intelligence score of 6·1 points; those with a scatter-score of between 3 and 6 showed a change in intelligence score of 2·4 points; those with a scatter-score of between 0 and 2 showed a change in intelligence score of only 0·6 points (Eysenck, 1944). Thus it is possible to pick out those subjects most likely to give a widely different score on retesting by a simple considera- tion of their original scores.

This scatter-score does not distinguish between normals and neurotics, nor between hysterics and dysthymics. 100 normal subjects had an average scatter-score of 4·2, as compared with 3·7 for 200 nuerotics. 474 hysterics had an average scatter-score of 3·81, as compared with 904 dysthymics with an average scatter-score of 3·72. Neither of these differences is significant. We must conclude that while the scatter-score is useful in picking out those whose test-scores cannot be relied on, it does not help us in discriminating between neurotics and normals, or between different neurotic syndromes.

This conclusion is contrary to the work of some investigators, and may require amplification. The concept of "scatter" funda- mentally applies to the variability of a person's scores on the sub-tests of a well-standardized intelligence test; this variability may be measured in terms of age-levels over which he scores successes and failures, as in the Binet test, or it may be in terms of variability of the sub-tests about the mean for the whole test.

Now clearly, the meaning and the usefulness of scatter-scores will depend on the character of these sub-tests. When the sub-tests are all very similar in nature, the scatter-score may be regarded simply as a measure of reliability for the whole test; this is the position with respect to the Matrix, for instance. This use of the scatter-score follows directly from a statistical consideration of the Kuder-Richardson method of determining the reliability of a test (1937). The fact that we found neurotics to show less test-retest reliability than normals, while normals showed much the same scatter-score as neurotics, is probably due to the time-intervals involved. The scatter-score gives a minute-to-minute reliability, as it were; the test-retest reliability gives us an idea of the changes which have taken place over a period of four weeks.[1] These two reliabilities are not identical; it is well known that retest reliabilities are usually lower than corrected split-halves reliabilities, for instance. The fact that we found it possible to predict retest-reliability from a knowledge of a person's scatter-score shows that the two kinds of reliability are closely correlated; but this correlation is by no means perfect. The proper conclusion to be drawn, we believe, is that the variability of neurotics with respect to their performance on an intelligence test is greater when moderately lengthy periods are involved; it is not greater when only very short periods are involved.

[1] Ferguson in his discussion of reliability (1941) writes: "Much of the confusion that exists in the literature on test reliability arises from failure to observe the distinction between the reliability of tests and the reliability of persons. . . . The term 'reliability of tests' may be defined as the accuracy (not constancy) with which a test measures the abilities which it measures at the time when it measures them. The 'reliability of persons' may be described as the accuracy with which a person's ability at any point in time approximates to his 'true ability'. On the assumption that errors due to the unreliability of tests are uncorrelated with errors due to the unreliability of persons we may write

$$\sigma_e{}^2 \sigma_t{}^2 + \sigma_p{}^2$$

where $\sigma_e{}^2$ = total error variance,

$\sigma_t{}^2$ = error variance of the test,

$\sigma_e{}^2$ = error variance of the persons."

We would contend that "reliability of tests" cannot experimentally be differentiated from "reliability of persons"; even when, as suggested by Ferguson, we estimate the "reliability of tests" by correlating two parallel forms of a test given on the same day, the "reliability of persons" inevitably enters into the picture, because variations in ability, etc., may take place over a few minutes, as much as over a number of days. Consequently, we cannot grant Ferguson's assumption that "errors due to the unreliability of tests are uncorrelated with errors due to the unreliability of persons"; the experimental data here reported show clearly that a fairly high correlation obtains between the two types of error. Nevertheless, we would agree that "short-term reliability" is differentiated from "long-term reliability", and that although the two are correlated, the correlation is far from perfect.

When the sub-tests which are being studied become relatively unlike, the character of the scatter-score changes. It now becomes less of an index of reliability (although it must always to some extent retain that function), and it becomes more of an index of *differential ability*. To take an extreme case, if we give our subjects a test made up of three sub-tests, constructed to be relatively pure measures of the three group-factors of verbal, mechanical and visuo-spatial ability, a scatter-score will tell us that some people show wide divergencies in their possession of these relatively distinct abilities, while other people tend to have them all in about equal degree. *To the extent to which these three group-factors correlate together and define a general factor, to that extent is the scatter-score a measure of reliability; to the extent that these three group-factors are unrelated, to that extent does the scatter-score define the relatively superior development of one or the other of these abilities.*

We believe that any type of scatter-score can be analysed into these two constituent parts, whose relative importance varies according to the constitution of the whole test. If the sub-tests are relatively homogeneous, then the main use of the scatter-score is clearly in determining its reliability; if the sub-tests are relatively heterogeneous, then the main use of the scatter-score is probably rather in the direction of vocational guidance, industrial selection, and perhaps also of temperamental analysis. A test such as the Wechsler (1941), which is made up of 10 rather divergent sub-tests, clearly falls in the second class; a test such as the Matrix, which is made up of five almost identical sub-tests, clearly falls in the first class. Most other tests fall somewhere in between these comparatively clear instances.

Analysis of scatter-scores should be much more extensive than is usual. To be really complete, such an analysis should embrace the correlations of the various tests, and also a factor-analysis; only when that is done can we know the relative contribution of general factor and group-factors, and therefore the relative importance of scatter-scores for the prediction of reliability or for temperamental and diagnostic analysis.

This rather theoretical discussion of the meaning of scatter-scores may explain why we found no relation between neuroticism or syndrome on the one hand, and scatter-score on the Matrix test on the other; it also suggests that an investigation of rather more heterogeneous tests might prove more interesting. Accordingly, an enquiry was carried out into the verbal ability of neurotics as compared with their ability to use abstract thought.

The verbal test used was the Mill Hill Vocabulary Test (Raven, 1944). This test consists of a series of 44 words graded in difficulty, underneath each of which are printed six alternative choices. One of these six alternatives means much the same as the stimulus word, and has to be underlined. The number of words correctly underlined is the score of the subject. A sample of items from the test is given in Table 11. (In the form of the test given at the hospital, the easiest 10 items were omitted, so that only 34 responses were asked for. Consequently the scores given on the following pages should have 10 added to them in order to make them comparable with scores derived from the full version of the test.)

### TABLE ELEVEN

*Mill Hill Vocabulary Test—Sample of Items from Synonym Selection Part.*

In each group of six words below, underline the word which means the same as the word in heavy type above the group, as it has been done in the first example:

| CONTINUE | | SENSUAL | |
|---|---|---|---|
| clash | clutter | controversial | carnal |
| tilt | keep on | necessary | crucial |
| read | bewail | rational | careful |

| SHRIVEL | | CRITERION | |
|---|---|---|---|
| linger | heed | superior | critic |
| volunteer | haunt | certitude | standard |
| wither | shiver | clarion | crisis |

| PROSPER | | OBDURATE | |
|---|---|---|---|
| imagine | propose | formidable | permanent |
| trespass | beseech | hesitant | obsolete |
| succeed | punish | exorbitant | stubborn |

| FORMIDABLE | | MANUMIT | |
|---|---|---|---|
| tremendous | unexpired | manufacture | liberate |
| feasible | orderly | enumerate | emanate |
| ravishing | remembrance | accomplish | permit |

3,591 male and 1,725 female patients were tested with this test. The mean score for the men was $15\cdot90 \pm 6\cdot15$, that for the women was $16\cdot23 \pm 5\cdot75$. The difference between the means is statistically significant, but is rather smaller than the difference in intelligence between the two groups, as tested by the Matrix test, would have led one to expect.

In order to compare the Intelligence/Vocabulary ratio of various groups, the following method was adopted. 987 female patients and 1,821 male patients were selected who had done both the Vocabulary test and the Untimed Matrix test. For each group, the mean and the standard deviation of the distribution of scores were calculated, and the scores turned into standard scores.[1] The difference in standard scores was then calculated for each person between his or her vocabulary and matrix tests, and the distribution of these differences plotted. The standard deviations of the distributions of difference scores for the men and for the women were calculated (S.D. = 10·00 for the men and 9·77 for the women.) Two groups of men and two groups of women were then selected, viz. those whose difference-scores were more than one S.D. above the mean, and those whose difference-scores were more than one S.D. below the mean. Thus we were left with four groups altogether: 250 men whose intelligence was considerably superior to their vocabulary, 290 men whose intelligence was considerably inferior to their vocabulary, 200 women whose intelligence was considerably superior to their vocabulary, and 140 women whose intelligence was considerably inferior to their vocabulary.

Having established these four groups, the item sheets of the persons falling into them were consulted to establish the percentage of persons in each group showing certain traits, symptoms, etc. The results of this comparison, for men and women separately, are given in Table 12, together with an estimate of the significance of the differences. A more detailed table is given by Himmelweit (1945).

It will be seen from the table that there are certain important differences between the two main neurotic groups distinguished in this research. The patients with hysterical conversion symptoms, with hysterical attitudes to their symptoms, and those with unskilled civilian background show a high intelligence-vocabulary ratio; in other words, the extraverts are found to have

[1] Various methods were tried to offset the effect of the skewed distribution of matrix scores on the selection (cf. Tippet, 1941, for an account of the methods used), but as these methods did not to any appreciable extent change the identity of the persons included as representative of the extremes they were discarded, and the direct method preferred.

a bad vocabulary relative to their intelligence. On the other hand, the anxious, depressive, obsessional, irritable patients, i.e. the dysthymic group, show a low intelligence/vocabulary ratio; in other words, the introverts are found to have a good vocabulary relative to their intelligence.

Certain other items should also be noted. Thus the table shows that those relatively young, badly educated, and in the low income groups have high intelligence/vocabulary ratios, while those whose illness has lasted more than 1 year, and those who

TABLE TWELVE

| Item. | Men. 250 Int. Voc. | Men. 290 Voc. Int. | t. | Women. 200 Int. Voc. | Women. 140 Voc. Int. | t. |
|---|---|---|---|---|---|---|
| (A) Temperamental Traits | | | | | | |
| Hysterical attitude | 38 | 26 | 2·9 | 41 | 34 | 1·3 |
| Hysterical conversion | 44 | 27 | 4·0 | 33 | 28 | 1·0 |
| Depression | 54 | 75 | 5·1 | 73 | 82 | 2·2 |
| Suicidal | 6 | 12 | 2·5 | 8 | 19 | 2·9 |
| Anxiety | 78 | 80 | ·6 | 75 | 78 | ·6 |
| Obsessional | 22 | 25 | ·8 | 27 | 39 | 2·3 |
| Effort intolerance | 39 | 47 | 1·9 | 61 | 70 | 1·7 |
| Irritable | 23 | 45 | 5·5 | 37 | 46 | 1·7 |
| Unstable | 58 | 53 | 1·2 | 55 | 39 | 3·0 |
| Retarded | 23 | 45 | 5·5 | 28 | 26 | ·4 |
| (B) Other Findings | | | | | | |
| Age 21—30 | 57 | 32 | 6.4 | 66 | 59 | 1·3 |
| Unskilled | 44 | 26 | 6·7 | 52 | 38 | 2·6 |
| Illness lasting more than one year | 66 | 72 | 1·5 | 21 | 42 | 4·1 |
| Earnings less than £3 | 38 | 22 | 4·1 | 84 | 74 | 2·2 |
| Education: | | | | | | |
| Poor elementary | 19 | 12 | 2·2 | 7 | 13 | 1·8 |
| Good elementary | 70 | 65 | 1·2 | 68 | 46 | 4·2 |
| Central, secondary | 10 | 20 | 3·3 | 24 | 38 | 2·9 |
| Higher | 1 | 3 | 1·7 | 2 | 3 | ·6 |

Comparison of Percentage Incidence of Various Items in Groups Showing High and Low Intelligence/Vocabulary Ratios.

are retarded, tend towards a low intelligence/vocabulary ratio. These relations are perhaps not unexpected: it is known that vocabulary continues to grow beyond the age of 30, thus putting the 20–30 age group at a disadvantage; similarly, retardation would be expected to affect the intelligence test scores rather than the vocabulary scores. When these differences are adjusted, the two clinical groups still show the differences described above, although in an attenuated form (Himmelweit, 1945).

### 3. Speeded vs. Unspeeded Tests

The data so far considered already throw some light on what Babcock calls the "efficiency" phase of mental organization. In her view (Babcock, 1930, 1941, 1944) unspeeded tests give us a measure of a person's underlying *ability*, while speeded tests give us a measure of his *efficiency*, i.e. of his capacity for using his ability. It is her belief that neurotics are deficient, not in their underlying ability, but in the efficiency with which they make use of such ability as they possess. Our own use of the term efficiency is much wider than Babcock's, covering the whole attitude of a person towards the test, his personal tempo, his perseverative tendencies—in short, all the temperamental aspects of mental functioning. However, as Babcock's view of a correlation between the ability/efficiency ratio and a person's neurotic tendencies appeared to offer a possible explanation of such divergent results in the realm of intelligence testing of neurotic subjects as are reported by Hollingworth (1931) and Michaels and Schilling (1936), a special experiment was carried out in order to test the applicability of her concept to our patients.

The test consisted in comparing the reactions of 500 neurotic subjects (300 men and 200 women) on tests of *ability* and of *efficiency*. Our test of ability was the untimed version of the Matrix test; our test of efficiency was the N.I.I.P. Group Test 33. This test is a verbal intelligence test which has been used extensively in this country. It was drawn up for the Institute of Industrial Psychology by Professor Burt, and is suitable for testing adult subjects. The test consists of five parts, each timed separately. Part I (3 minutes) consists of an Opposites test; part II (3 minutes) of an Analogies test; part III (3 minutes) of a Mixed Sentences test; part IV (10 minutes) of a Completing Sentences test; and part V (10 minutes) of a Reasoning test. The correlation between these two tests is $r = +0.66 \pm 0.02$ for our group.

It is possible to convert scores on the Group Test 33 into I.Q.s, by using conversion formulae prepared by Smith (1940).[1] Although it is difficult to know just how accurate such a conversion may be, the scores of our male and female groups were transformed into I.Q.s, using his formula. On the average, the men showed an I.Q. of 92, the women one of 97. Thus on

[1] The S.D. of the I.Q. in this conversion is assumed to be 15.

his test we observe precisely the same effects as we did previously on the Matrix test: neurotic men show slightly less intellectual ability then normal men, and neurotic women are superior to neurotic men, because of higher requirements in the selection process. The inferiority of neurotic men is not conspicuously more marked on this test of efficiency than it was on the test of ability; the scores of neurotics on both tests are $\frac{1}{3}$ to $\frac{1}{2}$ of a Standard Deviation below the mean.

We can make this comparison rather more precise by transforming the neurotics' scores on the Matrix test into I.Q. equivalents. This was done by calculating for each sex the percentage of normal subjects scoring as low or lower than the average neurotic, transforming this percentage into a sigma score, and this score again into an I.Q., assuming the S.D. of the I.Q. to be 15.[1]

Calculated in this fashion, the average I.Q. for the neurotic men on the Matrix (untimed) is 93, while for the women it is 97. These values are almost identical with those given by the Group Test 33, showing that the neurotic group is equally inferior to the normal group on these two tests.

These experiments, however they may be evaluated, do not support the Babcock hypothesis that *efficiency*, as measured by time-limited tests, is lowered in neurotics as compared with their *ability*, as measured by some test not involving time-limits. It is possible that the neurotics tested were less seriously ill than those on whose responses Babcock based her view; indeed, our results are not offered as disproof of her general theory. This theory of *intrapsychic deviation*—which would seem to constitute a special case of the general theory of scatter discussed previously—will require much concentrated work before its scientific value can be properly appraised. Certain data pertinent to this discussion, derived from an experimental investigation of mental organization in senile patients, are given elsewhere

---

[1] It is quite justifiable to make this assumption, as we are concerned with a comparison between these tests; obviously, such a comparison has no value unless the distributions are equated for S.D. In any case, the concept of the I.Q. is quite artificial so far as adults are concerned; it inevitably loses its basis of ratio or quotient and becomes the equivalent of a S.D. score. We have carried out this transformation merely because (1) the concept of the I.Q. is so well-known that results stated in terms of it may appear more meaningful than results stated in terms of the actual distribution, and (2) because the distribution of scores on the Matrix test is very skew, thus making direct comparison of distribution scores difficult.

(Eysenck, 1945); the conclusion to be derived from those data, and the results presented in this chapter, would appear to be that while Babcock's methods may possess considerable usefulness in the field of the major personality disorders, they are not likely to help very much in the analysis and diagnosis of the minor disorders.

## 4. LEVEL OF ASPIRATION

Two people may possess the same absolute amount of ability in a certain sphere, yet one may set his standards very high, while the other may be content to aim at nothing higher than a maintenance of the *status quo ante*. Again, in evaluating their performances two people may differ radically; one may tend to under-rate his own achievements, while the other may over-rate his performance. These methods of integrating ability and achievement with the rest of the personality are of the greatest interest to the psychologist, and there would appear to be little doubt that studies of this kind have done much to make us understand the dynamics of goal-setting behaviour.

Although in a competitive society like ours goal-directed behaviour and the factors entering into the setting up of goals are clearly of great importance, measurement of these aspects of test-situation behaviour was begun only comparatively recently (Hoppe, 1930; Dembo, 1931). Frank (1941), Rotter (1942), and Lewin (1944) have given exhaustive discussions and bibliographies of the considerable amount of experimental work which has since been carried out.

Understanding of these studies, and of the terms used in describing the results, may be furthered by a brief description of a typical experiment involving "level of aspiration". A task is chosen which has the following characteristics: (1) It gives a wide range of scores; (2) It allows ample practice effects to appear; (3) It shows moderately high correlations between successive trials, so that anticipation of future scores is possible within a certain range of scores; (4) Success as shown in scores cannot be evaluated accurately by the subject himself, but only by the experimenter; (5) It possesses a certain intrinsic interest-value, so that no outside motivation is necessary, although the latter may be supplied for experimental purposes. Not all the tasks used in work on level of aspiration fulfil these conditions, but we have found that if any of these conditions are neglected, experimental difficulties arise.

Two different tasks were finally selected by us for experimentation, after nearly a dozen other tasks had been discarded. These were (1) the Triple Tester, and (2) the Punch test. The Triple Tester is an adaptation of the pursuit-meter, constructed by the late Dr. Craik of Cambridge University. The apparatus consists of a brass drum carrying an Ivorine cover, rotating towards the subject. This Ivorine cover is marked out as a helical "road" with holes punched in it. A "vehicle" in the form of a bronze ball moved sideways on a rack is steered along this road by a steering wheel. The purpose is to keep the ball on the line of holes; each "hit" is scored on an electric counter. The steering wheel operates the rack through an integrating gear instead of directly. Instantaneous deflection of the vehicle from its path is impossible with this method of transmission, and the subject is forced to anticipate the necessary moves. The more he anticipates, the smoother will be the path which he describes, whereas rapid movements made at the last moment will result in violent oscillation or wobbling of the vehicle which requires correction and leads to still worse scores. The test resembles in some ways penny-in-the-slot machines seen at fun-fairs, and has a certain fascination for most subjects which often makes them loath to abandon the machine after the testing session is over.

The Punch test is an adaptation of the Hollerith Punch, which is used for punching holes in cards, for future sorting by Hollerith machines. Ten punch keys make it possible to punch holes on a card in ten different places; each punch pushes the card along a certain distance, exposing a new part which may be punched. This machine was transformed into a code-substitution test by (1) putting before the subject a chart giving equivalent letters for the numbers appearing on the keys of the punch, and (2) exposing automatically a certain letter whenever the punch is depressed. Thus the subject would look at the letter exposed, read off the corresponding number from the card, depress the key bearing the correct number, thus exposing the next letter. This test was timed to continue for 1 minute; after this time, the subject was stopped, the punched card extracted from the machine, and the position of the holes compared with a key.

The number of correctly-punched holes constituted the score of the subject on this test. (In the Triple Tester test, the test came to an end automatically when the whole "road" had been traversed; this took exactly two minutes.)

The actual test-conditions were identical for the two tests. The subject was shown the apparatus, had the method of working it explained to him till he thoroughly understood it, and was given a few short trials to make sure of his comprehension. Then he was told of the highest possible score on the test, and asked what score he thought he would get. His answer was noted, he was made to do the test, and asked what he thought his score actually had been. His score, and his estimate of his score, were both noted, and then he was told what his score had actually been. Again, he was asked to say what he thought he would get next time, and the whole circle of estimate, performance, judgment of past performance gone through. Altogether, each task was performed ten times, and the resulting aspiration scores, performance scores, and judgment scores noted each time. Little interest attaches to the first aspiration score, as this was given in ignorance of the possible performance on the test, and consequently this score was not used in calculations.

The scores made on this test can best be shown in the form of a graph, and further kinds of scores, derived from those already described, can be explained most easily in connection with a concrete example. Consequently, in Figure 14, are presented the score-patterns of two patients. One of these patients was a severe case of conversion hysteria, the other a severe case of anxiety neurosis; the score-patterns shown are representative, as we shall see later, of those characterizing these two types of neurotics. They were selected to bring out as clearly as possible the differences found in a more attenuated form in groups of hysterics and dysthymics tested on our two tests.

The two main differences between the two records, D and H, spring to the eye without any statistical calculation. In record D, the aspiration score is considerably above the performance score, and remains quite rigidly at one value. The judgment score is considerably below the performance score, and is only slightly modified by the success or failure of the subject, as indicated by his performance score. In record H, the aspiration score is very slightly, if at all, above the performance score,

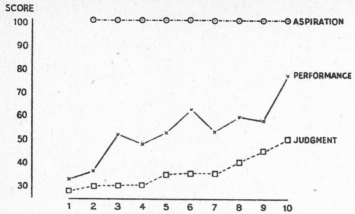

FIG. 14A. ASPIRATION, PERFORMANCE AND JUDGMENT OF DYSTHYMIC PATIENT

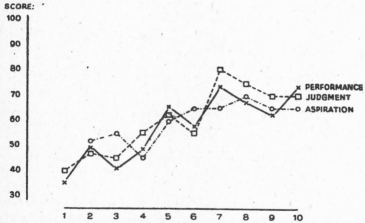

FIG. 14B. ASPIRATION, PERFORMANCE AND JUDGMENT OF HYSTERIC PATIENT.

and the judgment score is very slightly, if at all, below the performance score. Both aspiration and judgment score follow the performance score in a rather regular manner.

While in individual records such facts as these are immediately apparent, examination of groups of scores requires more quantitative variables. Consequently, a number of concepts will next be defined which are intended to relate aspiration and judgment to performance, thus giving a more adequate picture of the subject's achievement than do his performance, aspiration and judgmen scores in isolation.

We may relate, for instance, a person's performance to his aspiration as expressed by him after learning what his performance has been. Thus in record H, the patient scored 49 points on his second trial, and his aspiration score for the next trial was 55. The difference between these two values is called the "goal discrepancy score" (Lewin, 1944); it is positive when the aspiration is above the performance score, and negative when it is below. Thus in our case, the goal discrepancy score would be +6.

Related to the above concept is the "attainment discrepancy". H, having aspired to a score of 55 on his third trial, achieves only 41; the difference between these two scores is his attainment discrepancy. This score is positive if performance is higher than aspiration, negative when aspiration is higher than performance. In our example, it would be −14. Attainment discrepancy is so highly correlated with goal discrepancy (correlations of −0·95 and higher have been reported, cf. Eysenck and Himmelweit, 1945) that in our work we have retained only the concept of goal discrepancy.

The difference between performance and judgment we have called "judgment discrepancy"; it is said to be positive when judgment is higher than performance, and negative when performance is higher than judgment. Thus the judgment discrepancies for D would be consistently negative, as he consistently under-rates his real performance; for H, the discrepancy scores would be partly negative, partly positive, as he both over-rates and under-rates his own performance.

As will be shown later, we found that goal discrepancies and judgment discrepancies correlated fairly highly, correlations of between ·6 and ·7 being observed (Eysenck and Himmelweit, 1945). These correlations were negative, showing that a person who sets himself a very high goal tends to under-rate his own performance, while a person who pitches his aspirations low tends to over-rate his own performance. A combined score, called "Affective Discrepancy", was therefore derived by subtracting the judgment discrepancy from the goal discrepancy; this score may be considered roughly as an index of subjectivity, because in it the difference between aspiration and performance is added to the difference between performance and judgment. Thus a person having a high affective discrepancy score is a person who is unable to keep aspiration and judgment in touch with reality, as represented by the performance; he aims too high and he misjudges his own success. On the assumption that such departure from objective reality is in all likelihood due to affective factors, this discrepancy score was named "affective" discrepancy.

Two further measures were used, viz. an Index of Flexibility and an Index of Responsiveness. Flexibility was defined as a tendency to shift the level of aspiration, and the *Index of Flexibility* is the simple sum of all shifts in the level of aspiration during the test. This index does not take into account the direction of the changes which occur in aspiration scores, nor does it differentiate between changes of level of aspiration which occur after success, and those which occur after failure. The *Index of Responsiveness* makes use of the fact that most people tend to raise the level of aspiration after success, and to lower it after failure. These typical reactions are opposed to certain atypical reactions, in which the goal may be lowered after success, raised after failure, or kept constant after success or failure. The percentage of "typical" reactions constitutes the index of responsiveness. Failure of *typical reactions* to appear shows a certain *rigidity* in the reactions of the subject.

These various concepts are of value only if they have some kind of general validity, i.e. if they are to a certain extent independent of the actual test employed, and of the abilities measured by the test. Studies with normal subjects had shown that correlations between the discrepancy scores of subjects on different tests tended to correlate together; correlations varying between + 0·29 (Gould, 1939) and + 0·65 (Frank, 1935) have been reported. The actual size of the correlation would appear to depend on three points:

(1) The similarity of the two tests, as regards the ability measured.

(2) Similarity of the scale on which goodness of performance is measured.

(3) Similarity of the experimental situation, i.e. whether the two tests are given in the same experimental session or not.

Forty neurotic subjects, all of them male, were given both the Triple Tester and the Punch test. These tests involve quite different abilities, as shown by the fact that performance on the

K

two tests correlates only + 0·12 ± ·16. The index of improvement[1] showed a correlation of + 0·29 ± ·15. Other correlations were: Affective discrepancy = + 0·40 ± ·14, Index of Responsiveness = + 0·45 ± ·13, Goal discrepancy = + 0·25 ± ·16, and Judgment discrepancy = + 0·13 ± ·16.

When we consider that in terms of the conditions which influence the correlation of two tests, as enumerated above, the Triple Tester and the Punch test are as unlike as possible, both with respect to the abilities involved, and the scale on which goodness of performance is measured, and that the tests were carried out on different days, these correlations are seen not to be below correlations as found for normal subjects, and to prove that the measures employed have at least a certain degree of generality.

We are now in a position to summarize the results of our first experiment (Eysenck and Himmelweit, 1945). In this experiment, fifty hysterics and fifty dysthymics, all male service patients, were tested on the Triple Tester as described above. These two groups were equated for age, intelligence, and ability in the test, as shown by their actual performance scores. They were also found to be equal with respect to practice efforts; these were calculated by dividing the average scores of the 8th, 9th and 10th trials by the average scores of the 2nd, 3rd and 4th trials for each person. This "index of improvement" was 1·30 ± ·32 for the D group, and 1·29 ± ·24 for the H group. It is interesting to note that the difference between the S.D.s of the two groups is significant (C.R. = 2·00); in other words, there is considerably greater interpersonal variability in the dysthymic group.

On the other hand, intrapersonal variability is greater in the hysterical group. This can be shown by calculating the average intercorrelations between successive "discrepancy" scores for the 50 patients in each group; the values show that successive scores show less variability for the D group than for the H group.

Inspection of the average aspiration, performance and judgment scores of hysterics and dysthymics shows that (1) the aspiration scores of the D group are higher, compared to performance, than are the aspiration scores of the H group, and (2) the judgment scores of the D group are lower, compared to performance, than are the judgment scores of the H group. These facts ar

[1] Defined below.

brought out more clearly in Figure 15, where the average goal, judgment, and affective discrepancies are plotted. It will be seen that the affective discrepancy scores of the D group are nearly twice as large as the scores of the H group. These differences are statistically significant.

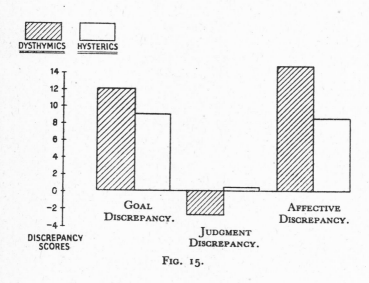

FIG. 15.

Significantly larger S.D.s were found in the D group, as compared with the H group, in each of the discrepancy scores except the judgment discrepancy; these results show a greater interpersonal variability in the dysthymic group. The reason for this greater variability seems to lie in the distribution of the scores: while the majority of dysthymics have high positive goal discrepancies, a small number have negative goal discrepancy scores; the hysterics, on the other hand, tend to have low positive goal discrepancies. Thus the curve of distribution of the dysthymics shows a slight bimodality. This effect may be explicable in terms of Maslow and Mittelman's statement that "anxiety attack is always a person's reaction to a situation which he evaluates in terms of his image of himself (self-esteem) and of other individuals (security feeling)" (1941). High positive discrepancy scores may be interpreted as attempts to bolster up self-esteem, negative discrepancy scores as attempts to maintain security feeling.

Apart from showing greater *subjectivity*, as evidenced by their higher affective discrepancy scores, the dysthymics showed greater *rigidity*, as evidenced by their refusal to modify their aspiration in accordance with their performance (Index of Responsiveness). After failure to reach their aspiration, the hysterics lowered their level of aspiration 56% of the times, while dysthymics did so only 47% of the times. Similarly, the hysterics raised their aspiration level after success in 81% of the cases, while the dysthymics did so in only 72% of the cases. These differences are statistically significant, and indicate that hysterics are less rigid, more modifiable through experience, than are dysthymics. Similarly, the dysthymics showed a lower level of flexibility than the hysterics, the respective average Indices being 4·6 and 5·3 (C.R. = 2·02).

Correlations of the various scores used in this study with intelligence are low throughout. Performance is slightly correlated with intelligence ($r = + 0·38$), while affective discrepancy just fails to correlate significantly ($r = + 0·18$). The judgment discrepancy score, which depends rather more on intellectual factors than do the other discrepancy scores, correlates fairly highly with intelligence ($r = -0·57$). There is also a significant but low correlation between intelligence and the Index of Responsiveness ($r = + 0·21$).

High affective discrepancies were found to correlate with several selected items from the Item Sheet, such as failure to secure promotion to N.C.O. status ($r_t = + 0·58$), unsatisfactory home conditions ($r_t = + 0·40$), aggressiveness ($r_t = + 0·38$), abnormality in parents or siblings ($r_t = + 0·24$). On the whole these correlations suggest that high affective discrepancy scores are symptomatic of "P–" personalities, while low affective discrepancy scores are symptomatic of "P+" personalities. This conclusion would fit in well with results found in working with normal subjects (Jucknat, 1937; Sears, 1940), and convict. (Rotter, quoted Lewin, 1944).

It appeared possible that the results reported so far might have been linked with the use of the particular measuring device used, i.e. the Triple Tester, and might fail to reappear when some other test was used; or again, it might be thought that results which hold for men might not hold for women. Consequently, 34 male and 35 female dysthymic patients, and 29 male and 29 female hysterical patients were tested in a similar manner with the Punch test described above (Himmelweit, 1945).

For both men and women, the dysthymics were found on this test to have a higher goal discrepancy; thus results on this test bear out the findings on the Triple Tester. The affective discrepancy was again found to be higher for the dysthymics than for the hysterics. And lastly, the dysthymic groups were more *rigid* than the hysterics in their attitudes towards success and failure. No significant difference was observed, however, with regard to the judgment discrepancy.

High affective discrepancy scores were again found to correlate with various personality traits. For the men, tetrachoric correlations were found with abnormality in parents and siblings ($r_t = \cdot31$), unstable personality ($r_t = \cdot53$), touchy and suspicious ($r_t = \cdot61$), obsessional features ($r_t = \cdot58$), and discharged from the army ($r_t = \cdot38$). For the women, tetrachoric correlations were found with rebellious and aggressive ($r_t = \cdot45$), obsessional features ($r_t = \cdot42$), headaches ($r_t = \cdot44$), suicidal thoughts ($r_t = \cdot46$), and discharged from the army ($r_t = \cdot42$). These results agree with those reported for the first experiment in emphasizing that subjects with high affective discrepancy scores show a distinctive tendency towards a "P—" personality.

TABLE THIRTEEN

| Correlations Between Discrepancy Scores. | Punch Test (127 Neurotics). | Triple Tester. (100 Neurotics) |
|---|---|---|
| Goal vs. Attainment . . . . | $-\cdot96$ | $-\cdot95$ |
| Goal vs. Judgment . . . . | $-\cdot29$ | $-\cdot68$ |
| Goal vs. Affective . . . . | $+\cdot62$ | $+\cdot83$ |
| Goal vs. Index of Responsiveness . | $-\cdot44$ | $-\cdot59$ |
| Judgment vs. Affective . . . | $-\cdot64$ | $-\cdot78$ |
| Judgment vs. Index of Responsiveness . | $+\cdot28$ | $+\cdot35$ |
| Affective vs. Index of Responsiveness . | $-\cdot32$ | $-\cdot42$ |

The correlations between various discrepancy scores are of interest, and are given in Table 13, both for the Triple Tester (n = 100) and for the Punch (n = 127). It will be seen that in the great majority of cases, correlations are similar for the two tests; they are slightly higher in almost every instance for the Triple Tester.

If the theory on which the concept of affective discrepancy is based is correct, we should expect that such differences as are found between hysterics and affectives would become accentuated under conditions which stimulate and increase the affective relation of the patient to the task. An attempt to find out whether this prediction would be borne out was made by offering the patients incentives if they succeeded in beating their scores, as made at a previous testing, by a certain number of points. The incentive offered was sufficient to arouse definite interest; it amounted to about half a week's hospital pay (Himmelweit, 1945).

The set-up of the experiment was as follows. In the first place, twenty-two male dysthymics and twenty male hysterics were tested on the Triple Tester in the manner described. A week later, they were retested in the same manner, but before the test began they were offered 50 cigarettes, or 5 shilling in money, if they succeeded in beating their previous best score by thirty points. The assumption was made that the incentive thus provided would secure greater ego-involvement of the patients in the task.

The following results were obtained. The average scores on the actual test rose very significantly from first to second testing for the dysthymics, but failed to show a significant rise for the hysterics. The affective discrepancy was larger on the second testing for the dysthymics, smaller for the hysterics. Lastly, the judgment discrepancy on the second testing was considerably lower for the dysthymics, and considerably higher for the hysterics. In other words, the dysthymics under conditions of special motivation tended to under-rate their performance even more than usual, while under these conditions the hysterics over-rated their performance even more.

Further confirmation for our theory is given by the correlation between goal discrepancy and judgment discrepancy, i.e. the two scores which together make up the affective discrepancy. While on the occasion of the first testing this correlation was $-0.46 \pm .12$, it rose to $-0.63 \pm .09$ on the second testing. This rise in the correlation suggests that the factors which are responsible for the existence of the correlation in the first place become stronger when greater ego-involvement is secured through the provision of incentives.

A last finding which supports our theory is that while the rigidity of the hysterics did not change to any extent from first to second testing, the dysthymics became considerably more rigid. Thus on the whole, the dysthymies tended to change their reactions to the test in the direction of emphasising more strongly the tendencies previously manifested, while the hysterics either did not change at all, or changed in a direction opposite to that taken by the dysthymics.

In addition to the neurotic groups mentioned, two small groups of normal subjects were tested. One of these groups consisted of 20 male soldiers, the other of 33 female nurses. The number of subjects is so small that no great reliance can be placed on the results; yet certain marked and very significant differences were observed between the normal and the neurotic groups (Himmelweit, 1945).

TABLE FOURTEEN

| Discrepancy Scores. | 100 Male Neurotics. | 32 Female Neurotics. | 20 Male Normals. | 33 Female Normals. |
|---|---|---|---|---|
| Goal vs. Judgment | −·68 | −·39 | +·59 | +·39 |
| Goal vs. Index of Responsiveness | −·59 | −·27 | −·25 | +·13 |
| Judgement vs. Index of Responsiveness | +·35 | +·36 | −·53 | −·22 |

In the first place, the normal men showed a much higher performance than did the neurotic men, and the normal women than the neurotic women. Secondly, the neurotic groups showed far greater interpersonal variability on all scores than the normal groups. Thirdly, both male and female neurotics showed a significantly smaller negative Judgment discrepancy score than the normal men and women. Fourthly, the variability of the neurotics on all the discrepancy measures was significantly larger. Fifthly, as can be seen from Table 14, while the correlation between goal and judgment discrepancy is negative for the neurotic groups, it is positive for the normal groups. Sixthly, the correlation between Judgment discrepancy and Index of Responsiveness, which is positive for the neurotics, is negative for the normals (cf. Table 14).

Certain interesting sex differences were also found both in the normal and in the neurotic groups. In particular, men tended to have higher Goal discrepancies than the women, and to under-estimate their past performance less. The question remains whether the nature of the task may have conditioned these differences, or whether regardless of the nature of the task similar differences may be customary in our culture pattern.

These experiments, it may perhaps be claimed, throw a certain amount of light on the dynamics of goal-setting, and of the reaction to success and failure, of our neurotic and normal subjects. We find that (a) normals are clearly distinguished from neurotics, (b) the hysterics are clearly distinguished from dysthymics, and (c) that men are clearly distinguished from women in their behaviour on these tests. These differences are very profound, extending not only to score-patterns, but also to the actual mental organization of our subjects. This is brought out by the fact that while for both male and female neurotics the correlation between goal discrepancy and judgment dis-crepancy is *negative*, implying that a person with a high level of aspiration tends to evince a tendency to under-rate his own performance, this correlation is *positive* in the case of the normal men and women tested, implying a contrary tendency. We consider evidence of this kind, showing differences in the *interaction* of the various dynamic factors which go towards the formulation of goals and judgments, as even more important than evidence regarding simple score-differences. While these differences in organization present great difficulties in inter-pretation, their existence would appear to be an undoubted fact.

One criticism is frequently made of experiments of this kind, and as this criticism applies with equal strength to many later experiments recorded on these pages, a few words may be said here in defence. The critic may point out that while our conclus-ions are perhaps justified regarding the extremely artificial task set up in the laboratory, they can hardly be of any great im-portance, seeing that most tasks which the individual encounters in his life-history are of quite a different kind, and are of much greater importance to him. Consequently, his reaction to the laboratory experiment can hardly throw any light on his reaction to entirely different conditions encountered outside the laboratory.

Several answers may be made. In the first instance, similar criticisms have often been made of intelligence tests, where the artificial and "trivial" nature of the test-items has been contrasted with the kind of problem set to the individual by his environment. Yet the trivial and artificial intelligence test has been shown to predict with a certain amount of accuracy the success of the individual in dealing with his environment, be it in school and college, or in the army, in business, or in industry. A sharp distinction must be made between the *nature of the task*, which may be trivial and artificial, or important and real, and the *mental mechanism* which is being studied. If we are studying the ability of a person to act intelligently, the mechanics involved seem to be identical regardless of the material with which the individual is furnished, and on which he uses his intelligence. A similar argument may be put forward with respect to Level of Aspiration experiments, and many other temperament tests in use nowadays.

Fortunately, we do not have to rely on merely theoretical arguments with regard to this point. There is ample evidence to show that the reactions of individuals on the Level of Aspiration test are closely related to the dynamics of their everyday behaviour. Gould (1941) showed that goal discrepancies are related to socio-economic background. Jucknat (1937) showed the effect of habitual success or failure in school on Level of Aspiration, and so did Sears (1940). In a clinical study of a number of children, Sears (1941) found a relationship between Level of Aspiration scores and general self-confidence. Rotter (1945) divided prison inmates into three groups: (a) a "normal" group, in which goals had in actual behaviour been held fairly close to the experiences of achievement, (b) a "defeated" group, whose behaviour was characterised by lack of self-confidence, strong fear of failure, and protection against failure by setting very low explicit goals in actual behaviour, and (c) a "conflict-tension" group, characterised by inability to reach a decision in problem situations. These three groups were clearly distinguished by their Level of Aspiration score-patterns. The same writer showed that college cripples showed different reactions from normal college students, and that hospital employees also differed from the students. Lastly, our own demonstration that certain reliable differences exist in response to this test between neurotics and

normals, hysterics and dysthymics, men and women, shows that
*a priori* objections to the "artificial" nature of the test fail to take
into account the dynamics of the total situation. The very
tendency of the subject to accept or reject the task as a "trial of
strength" is of fundamental importance, and his whole behaviour
in dealing with the total situation makes it possible to gain
important insight into habitual methods and modes of reacting.

Flugel (1945), in a very suggestive discussion of the origin and
functions of the ego-ideal, relates Level of Aspiration experiments
to Freudian theory. He points out that in the realm of ideals,
"much depends on what might be termed the distance between the
real self and the ego-ideal. If there is an immense gulf between
the ideal and reality, we shall inevitably feel dissatisfied, guilty,
and inferior. . . . Here we see a vindication of Adler's contention
as to the widespread desire for superiority, and at the same time
a justification of Freud's theory of 'secondary narcissism', attaching not to the real self but to the ideal one. . . . There is little
doubt that a vast amount of psychogenic misery is caused by this
setting of too high a standard for one's own self." Flugel goes on
to insist on the dangers inherent in the attitude of those who
pitch their ideals too low, and proceeds to support his theoretical
position by reference to Brahmachari's experimental studies into
"Moral Attitudes in Relation to Upbringing, Personal Adjustment, and Social Opinion" (1937).

This interpretation of unduly high level of aspiration as
caused by the hyperdevelopment of the super-ego, and of unduly
low level of aspiration as caused by the hyperdevelopment of the
id in relation to the super-ego, may be regarded as one possible
explanation of our differential findings with respect to hysterics
and dysthymics. If this argument could be worded in such a
way as to avoid the personification of mental mechanism inevitable in Freudian terminology, it might offer a satisfactory
beginning of a theory to account for our findings. This point will
be taken up again in the last chapter.

One further result proved of suggestive value in connection
with the scores obtained from the performances of the various
groups studied in our Level of Aspiration experiments. In
comparing the shape of the curve of performance of neurotics
with that of normals, it appeared that the curve of performance
of the normals was much smoother and more regular than that

oj the neurotics. A special experiment was performed by A. Petrie to validate this finding. Using as a test the well-known mirror-drawing test, she had her subjects trace a star six times, keeping account of the time taken, number of mistakes, etc. The groups consisted of male and female patients selected as being either relatively non-neurotic, or as being particularly neurotic. Thirty-one patients belonged to the former group, thirty-six to the latter, the sexes being approximately equally represented.

Evenness of improvement was scored in terms of "relapses". A "relapse" was defined as any trial which took longer than a previous trial. The amount of the "relapse" was the difference in time between two such adjacent trials. For both males and females, the amount of "relapse" was almost exactly twice as large for the more neurotic group than for the less neurotic group; the means being $8\cdot6 \pm 15\cdot3$ for the less neurotic and $15\cdot3 \pm 30\cdot5$ for the more neurotic group. $52\%$ of the less neurotic subjects had no relapses, while only $36\%$ of the more neurotic subjects had no relapses.

Also tested in this manner were two further groups of patients. 21 patients showed a history of neurotic symptoms, but an absence of any pronounced symptoms at the time of testing, while 33 patients showed serious neurotic symptoms at the time of testing, but a history which gave no indication of neurotic personality. These groups were tested because it was thought that some evidence might thus be obtained on the question, seldom explicitly formulated in psychological inquiries, of whether the performance of a neurotic on a test is conditioned more by his underlying personality structure, or rather by the presence of symptoms at the time of testing.

The results in this case are quite clear-cut. The "symptom" group was seen to score even worse, in terms of "relapse" than the more neurotic group, while the "history" group scored almost exactly the same as the less neurotic group. Scores were $30\cdot8 \pm 45\cdot2$ and $8\cdot7 \pm 17\cdot9$, respectively; percentages without relapse were 43 and 52. Thus it is seen that in the case of this particular test the work curve of neurotics is less even than that of less neurotic patients, and that this unevenness is related more closely to the presence of symptoms than to the underlying personality structure. How far this finding can be generalized to the other tests used in our studies cannot be decided on the basis of our information; other experiments summarized by Petrie (1946) suggest that such a generalization would be decidedly premature.

Thus in an experiment carried out on the same four groups of patients, Petrie used the body sway test of suggestibility and found that while the test differentiated significantly between the more and the less neurotic groups, the "history" group showed greater suggestibility than did the "symptom" group. It would appear, therefore, that in this test the underlying personality of the subject exerts more influence on the result than does his momentary symptomatology. A variety of other tests used by her showed intermediate results. In view of the paucity of the data at hand, we can arrive at no definite conclusion; it may be suggested, however, that a large-scale investigation along these lines might be of great interest and importance in helping us decide on the degree to which a given test reveals the underlying personality of the patient.

## 5. PERSONAL TEMPO

The concept of "personal tempo" as a temperament-variable is relatively old, but in spite of the hundred or so experiments which have been carried out in this field since Wissler's (1901) original paper, many of the problems connected with it have remained unsettled. In particular, the battle between the "specific" school, which believes that mental acts are specific, and uncorrelated, and the "general" school, which believes that mental acts are interrelated, and define higher-order concepts, has not yet been decided with any degree of finality.

Wissler (1901) had shown that speed of reaction in several "perceptive and associative processes" was relatively specific to each process, and that the tests showed little correlation. This conclusion was supported a year later by Aiken, Thorndike, and Hubbel (1902); as Lanier (1934) points out, this was the first expression of Thorndike's theory of "specificity of mental functions". Krüger and Spearman (1914) investigated the relation between speed and intelligence, and concluded, as did Bernstein (1924) somewhat later, that there was no "speed" factor independent of intelligence.

Since then, a number of writers have come to the conclusion that there is a general "speed" factor which characterizes human beings, and which is of importance in the determination of their temperamental characteristics; prominent among these workers are Braun (1927), Frischeisen-Köhler (1933), Meumann (1913), Reymert (1923), Wu (1937), and Slater (1938). The experimental results which have been reported in this connection are divergent, and leave rather a confusing picture. Some workers report high correlations among measurements of speed in different processes, and between speed in simple motor reaction (or even reflexes) and intelligence test scores (McFarland, 1930; Kennedy, 1930; Peak and Boring, 1926; Rounds, 1928; Travis and Hunter, 1928); others entirely fail to find any relationship between speed of reaction and intelligence, and also between different measures of speed itself (Farnsworth, 1927; Seashore, 1930; Sisk, 1926; Travis and Young, 1930; Whitehorn, 1930). Among the reasons for these differences may be the following: too few subjects, insufficient number of measurements, different processes studied, experimental errors, and differences in the homogeneity of subjects.

Certain facts, however, do seem to have been established in this field. Thus different types of reaction times yield high correlations (Lanier, 1934), even when measurements are taken from different parts of the individual. Simple and discriminate reaction times correlate together moderately highly (Lemmon, 1927; Perrin, 1921; Kennedy, 1930; Lanier, 1934), but are not closely related with serial reaction time (Beck, 1932; Farnsworth, 1927; Hansen, 1922; Lanier, 1934). Tapping shows little relation with reaction times (Perrin, 1921; Ream, 1922; Reymert, 1923; Seashore, 1930). Serial motor responses show low positive correlations, and are only slightly related to rate of tapping.

Different types of discriminative reaction are closely related (Lanier, 1934), even when various distractions and complications are involved (Farmer, 1926). Word association times are correlated (Lanier, 1934), but are independent of reaction time or rate of discriminative response (Lanier, 1934; Kennedy, 1930; Wissler, 1901; cf. however Hüberl, 1930). Intercorrelations between motor functions depend to some extent on whether they are executed by members at the same end of the body (Campbell, 1934; Gates, 1931; Lewitan, 1927).

Speeds of higher-order mental functions have been reported to show low correlations (Gates, 1921; Jones, 1917; Sutherland, 1934); they have also been reported to show high correlations (Clark, 1924; Courthial, 1932; Garrison, 1929; Hunsicker, 1925; Longstaff, 1928; McFarland, 1930). Speed of decision tasks show low but positive correlations (Filter, 1921; Trow, 1925; Uhrbrock, 1928).

Mental fluency (the "f" factor of the London school) seems to be defined by tests giving substantial correlations (Studman, 1935; Cattell, 1933; Notcutt, 1943); it is also correlated with speed of association. Cattell (1940) and Frischeisen-Köhler (1933) suggest a heritable basis for this trait.

These many findings cannot at present be explained in terms of a single concept or theory. Efforts have been made to account for them by reference to the "similarity of function" hypothesis, i.e. to the view that the more similar two mental processes are, the more closely will they be related. This theory, which corresponds to the theory of "identical elements" in the field of learning and transfer of training, is subject to the same criticisms as the latter theory. If similarity is defined in terms of what might be called "naive" similarity, i.e. in terms of obvious resemblances such as movement of a limb, or association to various stimuli, the theory is obviously false (Harrison, 1941). If similarity is defined in more dynamic terms, then the correlations between the activities considered become themselves part of the evidence regarding "similarity" or "identity", and thus we begin to reason in a circle. These objections render untenable the efforts of Carothers (1922), Dowd (1926), Farnsworth (1927), Gates (1931), Lewitan (1927), Line (1932) and others to resolve the difficulty.

A further difficulty is introduced through the fact that many of the experimenters have dealt with maximum rather than with voluntary speed. Of those who worked with voluntary speed tests, Baxter (1927), Braun (1927), Harrison (1938, 1941), Allport and Vernon (1933), Lauer (1933) and Wu (1934), some reached results favouring specificity, other results favouring generality.

The most extensive study in this connection is probably that of Harrison (1941), and his results may be taken as a fair indication of the kind of results to be found in this field. Using 50 students, he gave them 12 tasks to do at their preferred (voluntary) speed, and another set of 12 partly identical tasks to do at maximal speed. The average intercorrelations of the voluntary speed tests was + 0·20, of the maximum speed tests + 0·15. The 6 tasks included in both series correlated on the average + 0·37. Between personal tempo as measured by the whole battery, and the subject's self-estimate of his own personal tempo, a correlation of + 0·51 was found.

These results are interpreted by the author as favouring the specificity theory, but they would seem rather to provide a certain support for the view that a general speed factor of a motor type does exist. This limited factor should be differentiated sharply from other "personal tempos" with which it has frequently been confused. Thus it does not appear to be related to (1) reaction times, to (2) fluency, or to (3) intelligence; nor can the possibility be ruled out that a proper factorial study would succeed in breaking this factor up into yet smaller group factors.

*Speed* of performance is often contrasted with *accuracy*; in popular belief, at least, the quick worker is the inaccurate worker, and "slow but sure" remains a recommendation in favour of the slow but painstaking craftsman.[1] Hartmann (1928) did not find any evidence that "accuracy" any more than "speed" constituted a functional unit of behaviour; he concluded his examination of eleven tests of "accuracy" by saying that "in general the results indicate that there is no ground for the belief that an individual's accuracy of performance in a certain group of tasks enables us to predict his accuracy in other fields of work".

This conclusion, of course, is qualified by the selection of tests used by Hartmann, and by his choice of subjects. Thorndike's results (1915) on comparing speed and accuracy of work in 671 students are even more damaging to the belief that the quick worker is frequently inaccurate; he found that the faster students tended to be more accurate than the slower ones. This result is presumably due to the fact that brighter students tend to be more accurate and quicker than dull ones (Mudge, 1921).

Longstaff and Porter (1928) found very little correlation between speed and accuracy ($\bar{r}$ = + 0·07). Sturt (1921) on the

---

[1] A detailed study of motor adaptation and accuracy is given by McNeill (1934); his volume deals with the psychological factors underlying the elimination of errors.

other hand concluded that speed and accuracy were inter-dependent. Similarly, Burtt and Fry (1934) concluded from an experimental study of a small group of subjects that "reckless-ness" constitutes a unitary personality trait; this concept of "recklessness" appears to be nothing else but a preference for speed over accuracy. Lastly, Tiffin (1943) showed that in tin plate inspection there is a highly significant correlation between accuracy and speed of −0·49.[1]

In considering the relation between speed and accuracy, we again find the same bewildering multiplicity of contradictory findings as we did previously in considering "personal tempo". However, these contradictions themselves may give us important clues to the relation between these two factors. Roughly speaking, it appears that in tasks depending largely on intelligence, speed is related directly to accuracy (Thorndike, 1915), while in tasks depending very little on intelligence, i.e. tasks of a manual or discriminatory nature, speed is related inversely to accuracy (Tiffin, 1943; Burtt and Fry, 1934). Tasks involving medium amounts of intelligence show small positive or small negative correlations, depending on the exact amount of intelligence involved (Longstaff and Porter, 1928). It may be presumed, although there is no direct proof of this contention, that if in-telligence were to be partialled out of the correlations involving the more intellectual tasks, the positive correlation between speed and accuracy would disappear.

Two separate investigations were carried out in an attempt to study the differential personal tempo of hysterics and dysthymics. The assumption which underlay our work was that hysterics would prove to be quick but inaccurate in their work, while dysthymics would be rather slower, but more accurate. The experimental work, while in general supporting these contentions, also imposed certain qualifications which will be considered presently.

In a preliminary investigation, Eysenck (1943) failed to find any differences in the number of letters written, or figures drawn, in unit time by hysterics and dysthymics; he also found a correlation of + 0·60 between the two tasks, showing that a person who is quick in one task tends to be quick in the other also.

---

[1] The early work of Brown (1924) and Manson (1925) on "Impulsiveness" should also be mentioned here, as well as Snow's studies on "caution" (1926).

The number of subjects in this study was only 60. A rather more complete study was undertaken by A. Petrie (1945), who tested a total of 75 male and female hysterics and dysthymics with 8 tests of Fluency. In each test, the subject was asked to give as many responses as possible in the time at his disposal (usually 1 minute), the number of responses constituting his score.

The tests used were: (1) Number of round things S could think of. (2) Number of birds S could think of. (3) Number of things which might reasonably be on a certain spot in a picture (Cattell, 1938; Tree picture); (4) Number of responses to a coloured Rorschach ink blot. (5) Number of things which might reasonably be on a certain spot in a picture (Street Corner). (6) Number of things to eat which S could think of. (7) Number of responses to black-and-white Rorschach ink blot. (8) Number of flowers S could think of.

That these tests define a general factor of "Fluency" can be seen from the intercorrelations between them, which are given in Table 15. Also given there are the first factor saturations for each test, showing how highly each test correlates with the general factor, this factor accounts for 43% of the variance.[1]

TABLE FIFTEEN

| | | | | | | | | Factor-Saturation. | Correlation with Intelligence. |
|---|---|---|---|---|---|---|---|---|---|
| 1. Flowers | ·41 | ·13 | ·55 | ·33 | ·51 | ·62 | ·49 | ·69 | ·03 |
| 2. Rorschach col. | | ·20 | ·33 | ·47 | ·39 | ·33 | ·69 | ·63 | ·25 |
| 3. Round things | | | ·22 | ·23 | ·21 | ·11 | ·27 | ·28 | −·02 |
| 4. Birds | | | | ·44 | ·39 | ·43 | ·45 | ·63 | ·07 |
| 5. Tree | | | | | ·48 | ·47 | ·47 | ·65 | ·11 |
| 6. Street corner | | | | | | ·58 | ·60 | ·72 | ·36 |
| 7. Things to eat | | | | | | | ·52 | ·69 | −·03 |
| 8. Rorschach uncol. | | | | | | | — | ·81 | ·04 |
| | | | | | | | | ·43 | |

Intercorrelations of eight fluency tests, and factor saturations.

This factor does not differentiate at all between hysterics and dysthymics, as can be seen from the results given in Table 16. On none of the tests are the differences even suggestive, and we can only conclude that fluency of associative processes does not play any part in the trait-constellation which distinguishes between our two temperamental groups.

A study of personal tempo along rather different lines was

[1] Intelligence was not found to be highly correlated with this type of test in our group, and cannot account for the correlations in Table 15. It is interesting to note that in her investigation of Senile Dementia patients, Eysenck (1945) found fluency tests highly correlated with various other tests of mental ability.

carried out by H. Himmelweit (1945). She used five different tests on 25 male and 25 female hysterics, and on 25 male and 25 female dysthymics. These tests were designed in such a way that they could be done with special attention to speed, or with special attention to accuracy. Each test was done twice: once, with instruction to work as quickly and as accurately as possible on a task of predetermined length (choice test), the second time, with instruction to work as quickly as possible for a predetermined length of time (speed test). In the first case, scoring was (1) with

TABLE SIXTEEN

|  | Male Hysterics. | Female Hysterics. | Male Dysthymics. | Female Dysthymics |
|---|---|---|---|---|
| Round things . | $9\cdot7 \pm 4\cdot4$ | $8\cdot6 \pm 3\cdot4$ | $9\cdot2 \pm 4\cdot8$ | $8\cdot8 \pm 3\cdot8$ |
| Birds . | $14\cdot5 \pm 6\cdot4$ | $14\cdot8 \pm 4\cdot5$ | $17\cdot8 \pm 5\cdot6$ | $15\cdot3 \pm 4\cdot5$ |
| Tree . | $10\cdot5 \pm 6\cdot1$ | $12\cdot2 \pm 5\cdot0$ | $10\cdot2 \pm 5\cdot1$ | $11\cdot7 \pm 4\cdot5$ |
| Rorschach . | $4\cdot7 \pm 2\cdot9$ | $6\cdot2 \pm 3\cdot8$ | $4\cdot7 \pm 3\cdot5$ | $6\cdot6 \pm 3\cdot2$ |
| Street corner . | $9\cdot6 \pm 6\cdot2$ | $10\cdot8 \pm 7\cdot3$ | $9\cdot3 \pm 3\cdot7$ | $11\cdot8 \pm 5\cdot5$ |
| Things to eat . | $18\cdot0 \pm 6\cdot5$ | $18\cdot7 \pm 7\cdot4$ | $18\cdot7 \pm 5\cdot8$ | $22\cdot7 \pm 9\cdot7$ |
| Rorschach . | $4\cdot5 \pm 4\cdot2$ | $4\cdot7 \pm 2\cdot3$ | $4\cdot6 \pm 3\cdot3$ | $5\cdot4 \pm 2\cdot3$ |
| Flowers . | $12\cdot6 \pm 4\cdot0$ | $16\cdot8 \pm 5\cdot1$ | $12\cdot9 \pm 3\cdot9$ | $18\cdot0 \pm 5\cdot0$ |

respect to time taken on the task, and (2) with respect to number of mistakes; in the second case, scoring was (1) with respect to amount of work accomplished, and (2) with respect to number of mistakes. The following five tests were used:

*Word test* (*W*). The subject is presented with a list of 3-letter words, some of which are nonsense words, while others are actually existing English words. The sense words are to be underlined.

*Cancellation test* (*C*). On a sheet full of isolated letters, A and B are to be crossed out alternately.

*Addition test* (*A*). The subject is presented with a series of two-digit numbers; he has to add 7 to each.

*Track-tracer* (*T*). On an ivorine sheet a path is marked out between rows of holes. This path is to be traced with a metal stylus. Each time the stylus touches a hole, a connection is made through a metal plate underneath the ivorine cover, a buzzer sounds, and an electric counter is activated.

*Measurement test* (*M*). With a pair of dividers set at a certain angle, the subject has to measure off equal divisions on a sheet of paper. This test is given only under the second condition set down above, viz. with instructions to work as quickly as possible for a predetermined length of time (speed test).

The correlations between these tests, separately for Speed and for Mistakes, may be of interest. They are given in Table 17 for condition I (Choice) and in Table 18 for condition II (Speed). Also given in these tables are the correlations of the various tests with intelligence ("g"); only the .Word and the Addition tests correlate at all highly with intelligence. Intelligence was partialled out from the intercorrelations between the tests, and the partial correlations are given in the lower half of each table, the raw correlations being in the upper half in each case.

## TABLE SEVENTEEN

| Time: | | W. | C. | A. | T. | Correlation with "g". | First Factor Saturation. |
|---|---|---|---|---|---|---|---|
| W | . . | — | ·64 | ·43 | ·54 | −·51 | ·84 |
| C | . . | ·67 | — | ·23 | ·15 | ·19 | ·63 |
| A | . . | ·23 | ·28 | — | ·30 | −·32 | ·41 |
| T | . . | ·47 | ·16 | ·28 | — | −·03 | ·48 |
| | | | | | | | ·38 |
| Mistakes: | | | | | | | |
| W | . . | — | ·22 | ·46 | ·15 | −·32 | ·34 |
| C | . . | ·14 | — | ·50 | ·32 | −·21 | ·48 |
| A | .. . | ·36 | ·43 | — | ·64 | −·23 | ·90 |
| T | . . | ·20 | ·36 | ·68 | — | ·19 | ·70 |
| | | | | | | | ·41 |

## TABLE EIGHTEEN

| Scores: | W. | C. | A. | T. | M. | Correlation with "g". | First Factor Saturation. |
|---|---|---|---|---|---|---|---|
| W | . — | ·29 | ·41 | ·59 | ·62 | ·61 | ·65 |
| C | . ·31 | — | ·35 | ·31 | ·33 | −·03 | ·53 |
| A | . ·08 | ·37 | — | ·34 | ·35 | ·59 | ·42 |
| T | . ·54 | ·31 | ·29 | — | ·42 | ·08 | ·65 |
| M | . ·62 | ·33 | ·35 | ·42 | — | ·00 | ·74 |
| | | | | | | | ·37 |
| Mistakes: | | | | | | | |
| W | . — | ·27 | ·32 | ·41 | ·25 | −·13 | ·81 |
| C | . ·26 | — | ·16 | ·23 | ·21 | −·09 | ·49 |
| A | . ·29 | ·14 | — | ·19 | −·18 | −·22 | ·22 |
| T. | . ·39 | ·22 | ·16 | — | ·05 | −·12 | ·48 |
| M | . ·25 | ·21 | −·17 | ·05 | — | ·03 | ·17 |
| | | | | | | | ·24 |

A factorial analysis was carried out on the partial correlations, and the results are given in Tables 17 and 18. It will be seen that both under condition I and under condition II a general speed and a general accuracy factor is found, accounting for 38% and 37% of the variance in the case of the speed factor, and 41% and 24% of the variance in the case of the accuracy factor. In the tests studied, therefore, we find that an individual who is a quick worker in one also tends to be a quick worker in the other tests, and the individual who tends to be an accurate worker in one also tends to be an accurate worker in the other tests.

The question arises next as to the relation between the two factors. In Table 19 are given the correlations between Time and Mistakes for the tests under condition I (Choice), and the correlations between Scores and Mistakes under condition II (Speed). As these correlations are affected to some extent by the intelligence factor, intelligence was partialled out, and the partial correlations are given in brackets after the raw correlations. It will be seen that only in the case of the Track Tracer is there a significant correlation between Speed and Accuracy; in this test the quick person tends also to be inaccurate. On the other tests, there are only slight and non-significant correlations.

TABLE NINETEEN

| | | | Choice. | | Speed. |
|---|---|---|---|---|---|
| W | . | . | −·04 ( −·24) | . | ·04 (·15) |
| C | . | . | ·11 ( ·16) | . | ·05 (·05) |
| A | . | . | ·13 ( ·07) | . | ·14 (·34) |
| T | . | . | −·38 ( −·37) | . | ·56 (·57) |
| M | . | . | — — | . | ·10 (·10) |

These results seem to clarify the position. We find that on the tests used, there is a general tendency to work quickly or slowly; there is also a general tendency to work accurately or inaccurately. These two tendencies are only slightly correlated with intelligence, and in all but one test are relatively independent of each other. We may now turn to the question of whether hysterics are differentiated from dysthymics with respect to either the speed or the accuracy factor.

The detailed results are given by Himmelweit (1945). We find that on the whole the dysthymics are somewhat slower than the hysterics, both when the tests are given in the "Choice" and in the "Speed" form; this difference, however, is only suggestive, and does not reach the required limit of significance. We also find that the dysthymics are more accurate than the hysterics, and this result is definitely significant, both for the "Choice" and the "Speed" forms of the tests used. In every test the hysterics made a greater number of mistakes. The Critical Ratios found are given in Table 20. The scores in all the tests were turned into standard scores and summed, and the Critical Ratios of the resulting distributions compared; they also are given in Table 20.

TABLE TWENTY

| Test. | Critical Ratios, Accuracy Scores, "Choice" Form. | | "Speed" Form. |
|---|---|---|---|
| Word Test . . . . | 1·42 | . | 2·26 |
| Cancellation Test . . . | ·14 | . | 1·51 |
| Addition Test . . . | 1·81 | . | 1·85 |
| Track Tracer . . . | 1·76 | . | 1·87 |
| Measurement Test . . . | — | . | 1·21 |
| | | | |
| Combined Tests . . . | 2·08 | . | 2·53 |

The results reported so far suggested that significant differences might become apparent between our two diagnostic groups on a test in which mistakes were automatically penalized. The test chosen to verify this deduction was the O'Connor Tweezers Test. The subject sits in front of a metal plate with a large number of small holes in it, and is required to pick up one small metal pin at a time with a pair of tweezers and put it in a hole in the plate. Any mistake is penalized in the sense that the subject has to repeat the whole process if he drops the pin, fails to pick it up properly, etc., thus losing part of the time he is given. This test is given as a speed test, and the score is the number of pins correctly placed in unit time.

This test was given to 25 male and 25 female hysterics, and 25 male and 25 female dysthymics (Petrie, 1945). The results bore out the hypothesis which caused us to select this test; the average number of pins correctly placed by the hysterics was 10·2 ± 3·2, while the dysthymics placed 12·6 ± 3·8 pins. The C.R. is 3·00, showing that this difference is beyond the chance level.

We may, perhaps, summarize our findings in the light of the

literature. The general concept "personal tempo" would appear to cover several different spheres which are relatively independent. The speed with which a person reacts to a signal (reaction time experiments) defines one form of personal tempo; a quite unrelated form of personal tempo would appear to be the rate of associative production of the subject (fluency experiments). A third type of personal tempo is defined by tasks which can be done by the subject at different rates, his relative quickness or slowness being independent apparently of his reaction time or his fluency. Correlated with quick reaction times, high fluency, and quick performance is intelligence, which requires to be partialled out before any fruitful comparison between different tests becomes possible.

In addition to personal tempo of the third type, we have another temperamental factor, that of "accuracy". On most tasks, accuracy is independent of personal tempo (quickness), but on tasks of a manipulative nature (track-tracer, tweezers test, tin-plate inspection, etc.), a negative correlation appears to exist between quickness and accuracy. Again, the factor of intelligence has to be eliminated before the relations obtaining between the other factors can be viewed without distortion. When this is done, we find that quickness and accuracy are related to the temperamental peculiarities of our main neurotic types.

## 6. Perseveration

The history of the concept of "perseveration" is rather a chequered one. As Foster (1914) points out, the term originated with the psychiatrist Neisser in 1894, who used it to describe the clinical symptoms of "abnormally persistent repetition or continuation of an activity after the activity had been once begun or recently completed". Later, Müller and Pilzecker (1900) added the process of "interference" to Neisser's two processes of "continuation" and "repetition". Spearman attempted to subsume all these processes under his concept of "mental inertia"; where intelligence or "g" is the total mental energy available to a person, perseveration or "p" is the inertia of that energy. "p" was conceived as varying independently of "g", and as lying at the basis of an individual's temperament

Tests of this alleged mental function have been very numerous, and may be divided into five main groups, although no claim is made that these groups are in any sense absolute and non-overlapping.

(1) *Sensory perseveration.* Tests falling into this group are based on the various theories of "secondary function" (Groos, 1902; Wiersma, 1906) discussed in the first chapter. According to these writers, individuals differ with respect to the length of the after-effects of sensory stimulation, and these individual differences are closely related to the individual's temperament. The rate at which a colour-wheel bearing black and white stripes has to be rotated in order to make the "flicker" sensation disappear is one of the most frequently used measures of this function.

(2) *Associative perseveration.* This type of perseveration test is characterized by the tendency for ideas to occur involuntarily to the mind once they have been aroused; Stroop's (1935) colour naming test may be cited as an example. In this test the names of four colours are printed on cards in a colour other than the one named; subjects are required to name the colour of the ink in which the word is printed.

(3) *Creative effort perseveration (motor).* Tests falling in this group attempt to measure the ease with which the subject can break up an established habit; the mirror-drawing test may be quoted as an example. Here the subject has to trace a star without looking at the paper directly; he follows the movements of his hand in the mirror. The speed with which he succeeds in adapting to the reversal of direction caused by viewing his actions in the mirror constitutes his score.

(4) *Alternation perseveration (motor).* This kind of test measures the ease with which the subject is able to do two opposite tasks independently, and in alternation. Thus the subject may be given the task of writing sssss for 30 seconds, writing zzzzz for 30 seconds, and then of writing szszszsz for 60 seconds. Comparison of the last score with the sum of the two previous ones indicates perseveration.

(5) *"Umstellbarkeit" type of perseveration.* In tests of this kind, the ability of a person to switch without effort from one activity to another is measured, and a score for his "Umstellbarkeit" derived (Zillig, 1925; Kügelgen, 1932).

Early workers of the London school reported that tests of these various types of perseveration, and more particularly of the two "motor" types, correlated together and defined a factor other than "g". On this body of work by Lankes (1915), Jones (1915), Pinard (1932), Cattell (1933), Clarke (1934), Howard (1930), Bernstein (1924), Rangachar (1932) and others, Spearman based his "law of inertia" (1927).[1] More recent work, however, has been rather critical of these claims. Kelley (1928) has criticised the early researches on the grounds that the correlations were not large enough to give unequivocal results; Burri (1935) has argued that certain inconsistencies are implied in the statistical treatment; and Walker et al. (1943) have pointed out that there are certain weaknesses in interpretation which seriously lessen the evidential value of the work.

More damaging than these criticisms are the experimental results of Jasper (1931), Hargreaves (1927), Hamilton (1940), Walker et al. (1943), and Notcutt (1943), all of whom failed to find any evidence for the existence of a general factor of perseveration in their well-controlled studies. Shevach (1937) in his research found that "perseveration manifests functional unity amongst some people; amongst others, its functional unity is either very weak or non-existent".

Taking the evidence as a whole, there seems little doubt that these is no general perseverative tendency covering all the fields subsumed by Spearman's law. There is a certain amount of evidence that tests of the "motor alternation" type define a group factor; however, correlations between different tests of this function are disappointingly low, and the reliability of there tests is not very high. It is also possible that the "creative effort" type of motor perseveration defines a second group factor; the evidence on this point is not conclusive.

No survey of perseveration tests, however brief, would be complete without a mention of certain concepts which are not usually thought of in connection with perseveration, but which clearly are related to it. One of these concepts, that of conditioning, has been advanced by Walker et al. in part-explanation of some of the phenomena of perseveration; he makes much play with the derived concept of disposition-rigidity. Another field of psychology closely related to perseveration is the study of retro-

[1] Yule's (1935) works with twins even suggests a hereditary basis of perseveration.

active inhibition (Britt, 1935), where indeed interference can be seen in its clearest form.

In our own work, preliminary experiments on 15 male and 15 female hysterics, and 15 male and 15 female dysthymics, showed no differences of any kind on the "SZ" test described above, or on the similar "Triangle-Triangle reversed" test. Another attempt to show differences in "perseveration" between our two syndrome-groups was undertaken by A. Petrie. Using groups of 25 male and 25 female hysterics, and 25 male and 25 female dysthymics, she gave altogether four tests of perseveration:

(1) The SZSZSZ test;

(2) The 234 test, in which these numbers have to be written in the ordinary way, and then in reverse (i.e. by reversing the direction of each stroke).

(3) The AaBbCc test, in which capitals alternate with small letters.

(4) The Colour Reversal test, in which the subject points to coloured circles on a board, and has to say the name of the colour complementary to that to which he is pointing.

The perseveration score on each of these tests was determined by dividing the sum of the scores achieved when doing the customary, straightforward activity by the sum of the scores for the unusual, inverted activity. This method of scoring has been justly criticised by Darroch (1938), and Walker et al. (1945), but has been retained here because this is the method which had been used by the original investigators whose results suggested to us the possibility that perseveration might differentiate between hysterics and dysthymics.

The intercorrelations between the four tests are given in Table 21; as the subjects taking part in the experiment varied slightly from test to test, the number on which the correlations are based is only 74. It will be seen, however, that only one correlation is significantly positive, viz. that between the SZSZSZ test and the 234 test; the others are very small or even negative.

TABLE TWENTY-ONE

| | 234. | AaBbCc. | Colour Reversal. |
|---|---|---|---|
| SZSZSZ . . | ·62 | ·11 | −·01 |
| 234 . . | | ·01 | ·21 |
| AaBbCc . . | | | −·33 |

Thus our results lend further support to those who argue against the existence of a general factor of perseveration.

The detailed results of the four tests for our four groups of subjects are given in Table 22. It will be seen that in none of the tests do even suggestive differences appear; we may conclude that as regards whatever abilities or temperamental characteristics may be measured by these tests, hysterics and dysthymics react in precisely the same fashion.

### TABLE TWENTY-TWO

| | Male Hysterics. | Female Hysterics. | Male Dysthymics. | Female Dysthymics. |
|---|---|---|---|---|
| SZSZSZ | $1\cdot3 \pm \cdot5$ | $1\cdot2 \pm \cdot3$ | $1\cdot3 \pm \cdot4$ | $1\cdot2 \pm \cdot4$ |
| 234 . . | $1\cdot1 \pm \cdot3$ | $1\cdot2 \pm \cdot3$ | $1\cdot2 \pm \cdot3$ | $1\cdot1 \pm \cdot3$ |
| AaBbCc . . | $1\cdot3 \pm \cdot3$ | $1\cdot3 \pm \cdot3$ | $1\cdot3 \pm \cdot4$ | $1\cdot4 \pm \cdot4$ |
| Colour Reversal . | $1\cdot3 \pm \cdot3$ | $1\cdot4 \pm \cdot3$ | $1\cdot4 \pm \cdot3$ | $1\cdot4 \pm \cdot3$ |

## 7. PERSISTENCE

Among the qualities which make for the efficient use of a person's ability is his *persistence*; "the success or failure of individuals depends largely on the ability to endure and to continue to strive for the sake of achievement, in spite of fatigue and discouragement" (Fernald, 1912). Much effort has been devoted by psychologists to the delineation and measurement of this trait.

The original work of Fernald (1912) and Bronner (1914) was directed towards showing that normal and delinquent groups differed with respect to their persistence, as measured by the subject's continuance of a painful, tiresome task in spite of the fact that he was free to discontinue that task. The tasks chosen were mainly of a fatiguing nature, such as standing on tiptoe, or holding out one's arm as long as possible. The large differences in group-average found between normals and delinquents are explicable on other grounds, of course, than those of the greater "persistence" of normals, but the methods of measurement introduced by these workers have led to many interesting developments.

Many writers have devised different types of tests, and applied these to widely different populations. Among the more important contributors, Burtt (1923), Chapman (1924), Hartshorne, May and Maller (1930), Cushing (1929), Nelson (1931), Howells (1933), Porter (1933), Crutcher (1934), and Clark (1935) are, perhaps, the best known. Apart from using the measures of persistence on the physical level (standing on tiptoe, etc.), they have introduced measures of persistence on the ideational level (continuance of reading in spite of the fact that letters are run together, etc.), and in other spheres, and have shown that persistence is to a large extent independent of intelligence.

Other writers have used factorial methods in an attempt to answer the question of the unitary nature of the trait under consideration. Ryans (1939) reports studies suggesting the existence of one general factor of "persistence", while Thornton and Guilford (1938) report results favouring a multiple-factor theory. Rethlingshafer (1942) also reports the existence of several factors, such as "the habit of finishing whatever is started", endurance, etc. These differences in interpretation are presumably due largely to the fact that some of the writers mentioned used some form of rotation in their analyses, while others did not; ultimately we may hope to reach agreement between these different schools along the lines indicated in the first chapter of this book.

However the evidence regarding the existence of a general factor covering the whole field of persistence may be evaluated, there is little doubt that various tests involving the continuance of a bodily posture in spite of fatigue and pain induced by that posture correlate together, and define a group-factor which can be measured with relative ease. It is with regard to this factor that our work has been carried out.

The test used was an extremely simple one, requiring the subject to sit on a chair, and to hold one of his legs over another chair, keeping the heel of his shoe about an inch from the seat of the second chair. He was asked to hold his leg up as long as he could, and the time till his shoe touched the seat of the chair was taken in seconds.

This test was given by A. Petrie to 25 male and 25 female hysterics, and to 25 male and 25 female dysthymics. The results in seconds were as follows. The two hysteric groups gave average scores of $14 \cdot 1 \pm 9 \cdot 6$ and $13 \cdot 9 \pm 9 \cdot 2$ secs., while the two dysthymic groups gave scores of $29 \cdot 1 \pm 20 \cdot 8$ and $32 \cdot 5 \pm 25 \cdot 9$ secs. respectively. Altogether the hysterics persevered for $14 \cdot 0 \pm 9 \cdot 4$ secs., while the dysthymics persevered over twice as long, viz. 30·8 ± 25·9 secs. This difference is well beyond the P = ·01 level of significance, and shows that as measured by this test, the hysterics are considerably less persistent than are the dysthymics. This conclusion agrees well with clinical impression. Kraepelin (1899) pointed out that hysterics usually attack a new task with great energy, but tire very soon, show no tendency to perserve, regard everything as a game, without seriousness or persistence. Many other psychiatrists could be quoted to the same effect.

## 8. SUMMARY

In this chapter, comparisons have been presented between neurotics and non-neurotics, and between hysterics and dysthymics, of the ability and the efficiency of these various groups. We found that on the whole the neurotics tended to be slightly below average in intelligence, both when speeded and when non-speeded tests were used. Hysterics were found to be inferior to dysthymics with respect to intelligence, and an even more marked inferiority became apparent when the two groups were compared with respect to their vocabulary. No differences were found in the scatter of scores between any of the groups studied.

Level of aspiration was found to be considerably higher for dysthymics than for hysterics, and dysthymics were also found to under-rate their own performances, while hysterics tended if anything to over-rate their performances. Dysthymics showed greater rigidity in their reactions. Normal groups showed interesting differences from the neurotic groups tested particularly with respect to the *organization* of the mental processes involved. Incentives were found to bring out the general tendencies discovered even more clearly.

Personal tempo was shown to have relatively little relation to the hysteric-dysthymic dichotomy, although it was found to define a general factor. It was discovered, however, that a general factor of *accuracy* exists in relative independence of the *tempo* factor, and that dysthymics were differentiated significantly from hysterics by the greater accuracy of their work.

No differences were discovered in various tests of perseveration, but with respect to persistence dysthymics were shown to be superior to hysterics.

# CHAPTER FIVE

# SUGGESTIBILITY AND HYPNOSIS

## 1. PROBLEMS IN THE STUDY OF SUGGESTIBILITY

NONE of the personality traits which we have studied so far has been linked so closely in the past with both the "neuroticism" factor and with the extravert-introvert dichotomy as has suggestibility. So interwoven are the concepts of "hysteria" and "suggestibility" in the history of psychiatry that some writers have even gone so far as to regard them as inseparable or identical. Over three hundred years ago Weyer pointed out that those who "possess a temperament or a complection which makes them easily obey a persuasion succumb most frequently to the prevailing mental diseases" (quoted by Zilboorg, 1941), and the view that suggestibility is correlated with neuroticism is still widespread.

The view that suggestibility and hysteria are connected in some specially close way has been set forth most persuasively by Janet, whose writings on this subject have had a profound influence on psychiatry. He maintained that "suggestion is a precise and relatively rare phenomenon; it presents itself experimentally or accidentally only with hystericals, and, inversely, all hystericals, when we study them from this standpoint, present this same phenomenon in a higher or lower degree. . . . The most important mental stigma of hysteria is *suggestibility*" (Janet, 1907). This view was espoused and developed by Babinski, who believed that hysteria consists in manifestations which are brought into existence by the influence of suggestion, and that the essential feature of the hysterical personality is abnormal suggestibility (Babinski and Froment, 1918).

The adherents of the Nancy school, while maintaining that all men are suggestible under favourable conditions, and that suggestibility by and in itself is not a morbid condition, nevertheless agreed with the Salpetrière school in believing that in hysterical patients an increased and exaggerated state of suggestibility can usually be found (Bernheim, 1887).

While this view of a very special relationship between hysteria and suggestibility originated in France, and was most widely popular in that country, its influence has been universal. Thus McDougall (1911) points out that "a high degree of 'Suggestibility' is a leading feature of hysteria"; Jacoby (1912) speaks of "the special relationship between suggestion and hysteria", quoting Morton Prince in support; Rosanoff (1920) quotes Babinski with approval, as does Noyes (1939). Shaffer (1936), speaking of the personality of hysterics, asserts that they tend to be more suggestible; Morgan (1936) lists suggestibility among the most characteristic features of hysteria; Hirschlaff (1919), Tuckey (1921), Satow (1923), Fisher (1937), Ewen (1934), Cameron (1929), and many others could be quoted in support, while Bleuler (1924) points out that hysterical suggestibility may often be negative.

This general theory has recently been extended along Freudian lines by Rosenzweig, in the form of a "triadic hypothesis" (1942). He argues that "in the long history of hysteria this illness has been almost invariably associated with hypnosis. Moreover, in Freudian psychoanalysis hysteria has from the first been linked with repression. There was thus an obviously implied association between repression as a mechanism of defense and hypnotizability as a personality trait." Formally stated, the triadic hypothesis runs: "Hypnotizability as a personality trait is to be found in positive association with repression as a preferred mechanism of defense and with impunitiveness as a characteristic type of immediate reaction to frustration." As a corollary to this hypothesis, non-hypnotizability would be associated with such other defense mechanisms as displacement and projection, and with other types of reaction to frustration, viz. intropunitiveness and extrapunitiveness. (It should be added that Rosenzweig regards hypnotizability and suggestibility as concepts referring to similar if not identical underlying traits, and he has attempted to verify his hypothesis by using both hypnosis and suggestibility tests.)

Attempts to verify the view that hysteria and suggestibility are closely related have usually taken the form of comparing groups of students, whose scores on some of the common introversion-extraversion tests were known, with respect to suggestibility as measured by the body-sway type of test, which will be described in detail below. Results are conflicting; thus White (1930) found a high correlation of + 0·70 between extraversion and suggestibility; Davis and Husband (1931) found low negative correlations in two groups, while Barry, MacKinnon, and Murray (1931) found no significant correlation of any kind. These contradictions are not surprising in view of the fact that only very small numbers of subjects were used in these investigations, and that questionnaires of the kind employed are not very reliable research instruments.

Rosenzweig and Sarason (1942) report results from three rather small student groups, two of which were studied by means of suggestibility tests, while one was investigated with regard to hypnotizability. These groups were also tested with a test of "tendency to repression", which consisted essentially of a number of tests on half of which the subject was praised for his performance, while on the other half he was given the impression that he had failed. "Tendency to repression" was inferred from the fact that tests on which the subject failed tended to be remembered less well than tests on which he succeeded; the ratio of the two was used as in index of "repression". Significant positive correlations were found between suggestibility and "repression", and the writers consider that these results support their hypothesis.[1]

Apart from this rather indirect proof, there appears to be no experimental evidence on the view that hysteria is related to suggestibility. A certain amount of evidence is available, however, on the question of the relation of neuroticism to suggestibility; unfortunately, most of the studies to be reviewed under this heading also used questionnaires in order to estimate the personality trait whose correlation with suggestibility is under investigation. Davis and Husband (1931), who applied Thurstone's personality schedule, found that their 55 subjects showed a correlation between hypnotic susceptibility and the

[1] This hypothesis, which links "repression" with "hysteria", is discussed below in some detail.

presence of neurotic symptoms of only + 0·04. Messer, Hinckley, and Mosier (1938), working with 129 college students, found that "not only is suggestibility not correlated with total score on the neurotic inventory type of test, but that it exhibits no correlation with any of the several traits known to be measured by such tests." Baumgartner (1931), who had 56 pupil-nurses rated on various temperamental traits, concluded from a comparison of these ratings with scores on the body-sway test of suggestibility that "suggestibility, instead of being an undesirable trait is in reality a desirable one with some indication of being a component of several eminently desirable traits".

Rather more satisfactory than these studies, in the sense that neither questionnaire responses nor ratings by unskilled raters formed the validating criterion, are two experiments by Bartlett (1936a, 1936b) who compared neurotics and normals with respect to their body-sway suggestibility. In the first of these studies, she compared the scores of 21 neurotics and 26 normals and concluded that "psychoneurotic subjects are no more suggestible than are normal individuals". The conclusion of her second study, in which she compared 16 neurotics and 20 normals, was that "it would appear that there is little relation between suggestibility and neurotic tendency". While these two studies are more satisfactory technically than those reviewed above, the number of subjects is too small to justify so far-reaching a conclusion. We are left, then, with no very clear picture of the personality correlates of suggestibility.

Nor is the position much better with regard to the question of the relative generality or specificity of suggestibility. In speaking about "suggestibility" we imply the existence of some unitary trait which is displayed in all the various tests of this trait which have been devised and described by psychologists; yet the evidence on this point is of very doubtful value.

Aveling and Hargreaves, in discussing their experimental findings, "consider that . . . the most probable explanation of (the) results is . . . the existence of a general factor of suggestibility, combined with group factors common to two or more tests" (1921, p. 73). Similarly, Otis believes in the existence of a general trait of "ability to resist suggestion", a belief also based on experimental evidence (1923).

Brown (1916), on the other hand, found little evidence of such generality in his pioneer studies, and Estabrooks (1929) also had to report that the majority of correlations found by him were around zero. Allport (1937) believes that suggestibility is a trait which may characterize a few people consistently, but that it is not otherwise a "unitary" trait, while Britt (1941) also is sceptical with regard to the existence of a general trait of this nature.

Many investigators believe in the existence of different types of suggestibility, and various schemes of such typological division have been worked out by Prideaux (1919) and later writers. Thus Hull (1933) distinguishes prestige and non-prestige suggestion, identifying the first-named with that found in his body-sway test, and the latter with the Binet Progressive Weights and Progressive Lines tests. Murphy et al. (1937) discuss three common psychological principles underlying many "suggestion" tests, and Bird (1941) speaks of direct and indirect suggestibility.

## 2. TYPES OF SUGGESTIBILITY

Our own researches have led us to the view that there is no general trait of suggestibility, but that there are at least two, and probably three, main factors involved in the tests commonly used to measure suggestibility. These factors mark out three different kinds of "suggestibility", which may best be presented by describing some of the tests used in defining them. In so doing, we are presenting merely a conceptual scheme to accommodate our data; the evidence on which this scheme rests will be presented later.

The first type of suggestibility to be discussed has been called "Primary Suggestibility" (Eysenck, 1943), and is of the ideo-motor kind. The main feature in the tests which go to define this trait is the execution of a motor movement by the subject consequent upon the repeated suggestion by the experimenter that such a movement will take place, without conscious participation in the movement on the subject's part. Several of the procedures adopted by Mesmer, Puységur, Faria, Braid, Liébeault and other early hypnotists come close to being regarded as "tests" of this type of suggestibility, but the first to produce a simple, objective measure of suggestibility was Chevreul (1854), with his *Pendule Explorateur.*

M

The basic idea of this test is this: The subject holds in his hand a thread, from which hangs a small weight; he attempts to hold this weight dead over the centre of a line drawn on the table in front of him, while the experimenter tells him repeatedly that he will not be able to hold the weight still, but that it will start swinging along the line on the table. The amount of swing imparted to the weight along this line during the experiment constitutes the score of the subject. The test is effective with nearly 100% of young children, and with a surprisingly large number of adults. Under the name of "Chevreul's Pendulum" it has been used frequently in experimental studies.

Another well-known test is the so-called Body-Sway test, introduced by Hull (1933). The subject is told to stand quite still and relaxed, with his eyes closed, while the experimenter says to him: "You are falling forward, you are falling all the time, you are falling forward, you are falling forward now, you are falling. . . ." The amount of sway consequent upon this suggestion is measured, and constitutes the suggestibility score of the subject.

In the Press-Release test (Eysenck and Furneaux, 1945), the subject lies on a couch, and holds on to a rubber bulb. He is told to close his eyes, and to keep on holding the bulb just as he is holding it now; then the experimenter repeats several times a suggestion to the effect that the subject is squeezing the bulb. The amount of pressure applied is measured, and constitutes the score of the subject. In the second part of this test, the subject is asked to squeeze the bulb as tightly as he can, and the suggestion is given that he cannot hold it any longer, that he is relaxing and getting tired. Decrease in pressure exerted constitutes the score on this part of the test.

The same principle as is embodied in these tests can be found in various others, such as the Arm Levitation test, in which the arm is held out sideways and the suggestion is made that it is getting heavier, and becomes too heavy to hold it up, or that is getting lighter, and is moving upwards. In fact, almost any movement which can be carried out voluntarily can be made into a test of primary suggestibility, as long as a method can be found for measuring the extent of the movement.

The second type of suggestibility to be discussed has been called "Secondary Suggestibility" (Eysenck, 1943), and is of the "indirection" kind. The main feature in the tests which go to define this trait is the experience on the part of the subject of a sensation or perception consequent upon the direct or implied suggestion by the experimenter that such an experience will take place, in the absence of any objective basis for the sensation or perception. In other words, the experimenter uses indirection (i.e. deceit or trickery, as the dictionary defines the term) in order to give the subject an impression which the latter then claims as his own (Young, 1931).

Perhaps the best known tests of secondary suggestibility are Binet's Progressive Lines and Progressive Weights tests (Binet, 1900). The basic idea in these tests is that a subject is asked to discriminate between successive weights or lines, reporting whether they are heavier or longer than previous weights or lines. Usually about 15 stimuli are given in such an order that the first five stimuli all vary in the same direction (getting heavier, or getting longer), thus setting up a set or expectation that the following ten lines, which are objectively equal, will go on varying in the same direction as the first five. The number of objectively equal weights or lines which are called heavier or longer, or some function of that number, constitutes the score of the subject.

Many other writers have used similar tests in other sense modalities. A test may be made of olfactory suggestibility by asking the subject to give the name of an odour the moment he recognizes it, then bringing a bottle filled with some odoriferous substance near him. This is repeated three times, using a different odour each time; then bottles containing plain water are substituted, and the number of positive responses to these nonodoriferous substances constitute the subject's score. Visual stimuli, such as very light tints, may be employed instead of the odours, using plain white sheets as the "catch" tests. Auditory stimuli also may be used, the test stimuli being made up of very soft sounds, the "catch" periods containing no sound at all.

Slightly different from the above sensory tests are tests involving memory or imagination. The subject may be shown a picture; then asked to answer various questions regarding what he has seen. Several suggestive questions are slipped in among perfectly straight-forward ones; thus the question may be: "What colour was the cat in the window?" when there was no cat in the picture at all. The number of suggestions of this kind which are accepted by the subject constitutes his score. This type of picture test is described extensively by Whipple (1921). In the ink blot test, which uses imagination rather than memory for its field, the subject is shown an ink-blot and is told that people often see objects in these blots, such as bats, butterflies, etc. He is told two objects which people often see in the ink blot he is being shown, and asked if he can see them. Then he is told three further objects which are as unlike anything in the ink blot as possible, but which are presented to him as quite usual responses, and he is asked whether he can see these things in the blot. The number of unusual responses seen constitutes his score on the test.

The last type of suggestibility which we are going to distinguish is of the prestige kind. The main feature in the tests which go to define this trait is the change of attitude on the part of the subject on being told of the different attitude of someone whose opinion for him has prestige value. Thus, for instance, a group of college students may be given a questionnaire requiring them to express their opinions on a variety of issues; after a few days, they may be asked to fill in the same questionnaire again, but this time they may be provided with a set of answers said to be the average response of the whole group, or the considered judgment of a group of businessmen, politicians, educators or film stars. The degree to which their second set of answers deviates from their previous answers, and approximates to the "prestige" group is an index of their suggestibility.

Much work has been done along these lines by Sorokin and Boldyreff (1932), Arnett et al. (1931), Bowden (1934), Kulp (1934), Moore (1921), Barry (1930), Marple (1933), Wheeler and Jordan (1929), and Ferguson (1944). The last-named has presented some evidence to show that there is a certain amount of functional unity in this trait of prestige suggestibility. While primary and secondary suggestibility have been shown to be quite uncorrelated and independent (Eysenck, 1943; Eysenck and Furneaux, 1945), the "prestige" kind of suggestibility has not yet been shown to be independent of the other two types of suggestibility, and its independent position must, therefore, remain doubtful; however, it is probable that when this question is tackled experimentally prestige suggestibility will show little connection with primary suggestibility. It is more difficult to be certain that is does not correlate with secondary suggestibility.

The evidence on the independence of primary and secondary suggestibility mentioned above rests on two correlational studies involving altogether 14 different tests of suggestibility. In the first of these, 60 patients at the Hospital, 30 male and 30 female, were given the Body Sway test, the Chevreul Pendulum test, an Arm Levitation Up and an Arm Levitation Down test, and the Progressive Lines and Progressive Weights tests, both in the impersonal form as described above, and also with a special system of scoring so as to measure the influence of personal prestige (Eysenck, 1943).

The average intercorrelation of tests of primary suggestibility was + 0·27; the average intercorrelation of tests of secondary suggestibility was + 0·29. The intercorrelations between tests of primary and secondary suggestibility averaged —·04. These results show clearly that the two types of suggestibility are essentially different in nature, and constitute separate traits. This impression was confirmed by a factor-analysis of the intercorrelations.

This preliminary study possessed certain obvious weaknesses, which made it desirable to repeat it with various modifications. The number of different tests of suggestibility was too small to give any definitive results; the tests of secondary suggestibility were too similar to make this concept very meaningful; no effort was made to include hypnosis among the variables, in spite of the acknowledged close relation between hypnosis and suggestibility. An attempt to remedy these faults was therefore made in another experiment along similar lines (Eysenck and Furneaux, 1945).

In this experiment, twelve tests of primary and secondary suggestibility were used. The tests of primary suggestibility included the Body Sway test, the Press and the Release tests, the Chevreul Pendulum, a Hypnotic and a Post-hypnotic test; the tests of secondary suggestibility included a Picture Report test, the Ink Blot and the Odour Suggestion tests, the Progressive Weights test, both in its personal and its impersonal form. Also used was the Heat Illusion test, whose position with respect to primary or secondary suggestibility was doubtful. This test, which had been used previously in a variety of different forms by Seashore (1895), Small (1896), Guidi (1908), Scott

(1910), and Chojecki (1911), was given as follows. The subject is asked to hold on to a metal handle which is slowly heated by an electric current passing through a resistance box; he is asked to report when he begins to feel the heat. By turning the indicator on the resistance box, the current is increased till the subject feels the heat; the indicator is then turned back to zero, and the procedure repeated. Finally, the experimenter switches the current off by means of a secret switch, and again invites the subject to report when he begins to feel the heat. The number of times the subject reports a feeling of heat when objectively no heat is present constitutes his score.

60 male neurotic subjects were tested altogether; their I.Q.s were between 90 and 110. The scoring of the hypnotic and the post-hypnotic tests was done on a point-scale; 21 suggestions were made to the subjects; a complete acceptance of the suggestion was counted 2, a half-hearted acceptance of the suggestion was counted 1, and a refusal to carry out the suggestion was counted 0. Weights were attached to the items roughly in accordance with the "difficulty" of the item, so that spontaneous amnesia at the conclusion of the experiment is weighted four times as heavily in making up the total score of the subject as the fact that he is incapable of raising his arm. The post-hypnotic items were scored similarly. The subjects were kept in ignorance of the fact that they were being hypnotized, but were told they were going to learn how to relax. (The actual suggestions made are given in our paper.)

Tetrachoric correlations were run between these twelve tests. The six tests of primary suggestibility intercorrelated to the extent of + 0·50 on the average. The Heat Illusion test did not correlate with any of the tests of primary suggestibility except hypnosis; consequently it was, with some misgivings, put with the tests of secondary suggestibility. These intercorrelated to the extent of + 0·15; the two groups of tests did not show any correlation on the average ($\bar{r}_{I, II}$ = + 0·02). Factorial analyses were carried out for the two sets of six tests independently. The Body Sway test was found to correlate with primary suggestibility + 0·92, while hypnosis correlated with primary suggestibility + 0·89. The Ink Blot and the Odour suggestion tests correlated with secondary suggestibility to the extent of + 0·71 and + 0·62 respectively. The primary suggestibility factor accounted for 55% of the variance, the secondary suggestibility factor for 20% of the variance (Eysenck and Furneaux, 1945). In other words, primary suggestibility showed considerably greater functional unity than did secondary suggestibility, and can, therefore, lay claim to be regarded as a unitary factor; the claims of secondary suggestibility to the status of a unitary trait are more doubtful.

One difficulty clearly arises from these results. Provisionally, the Heat Illusion test had been assigned to the tests defining secondary suggestibility, as it failed to correlate with primary suggestibility tests such as the Body Sway test (r = −0·07). Yet the Heat Illusion test correlated with Hypnosis to the extent of + 0·51, while body sway correlated with hypnosis to the extent of + 0·71; the multiple correlation between these two tests and hypnosis being + 0·96. The possibility that the Heat Illusion test had been assigned to the wrong battery could not be neglected; neither could the possibility that the correlation between heat illusion and hypnosis was spurious, arising from the small number of subjects tested.

Accordingly, another sample of 50 male patients was tested; the tests used being the Heat Illusion, the Body Sway, the Ink Blot, the Odour, and the Hypnosis tests (Furneaux, 1945). Again, the Heat Illusion test correlated significantly with Hypnosis (r = + 0·69); equally, the Body Sway test correlated significantly with Hypnosis (r = + 0·64). A combination of the two sets of results seemed likely to give more exact data than either set alone, so tetrachoric correlations were calculated for 100 male patients on these five tests. The results are given in Table 23.

TABLE TWENTY-THREE

|  |  |  |  | Body Sway. | Heat Ill. | Odour. | Ink Blot. |
|---|---|---|---|---|---|---|---|
| Hypnosis | . | . | . | ·73 | ·59 | ·08 | −·22 |
| Body Sway | . | . | . |  | ·04 | −·24 | −·28 |
| Heat Illusion | . | . | . |  |  | −·24 | ·03 |
| Odour | . | . | . |  |  |  | ·29 |

(Significant correlations in italics.)

The multiple correlation between body sway/heat illusion and hypnosis is + 0·92. Again, the Heat Illusion test fails to correlate to any extent with the Body Sway test, but this time it shows even less inclination to correlate with the tests of secondary suggestibility. We must, therefore, leave open the question of its attribution, maintaining only that it correlates beyond any doubt with "hypnotizability".

The degree of predictability of this quality of "hypnotizability" would appear to be rather high; yet caution must be observed in interpreting multiple correlation coefficients. The difficulty arises in applying a very delicate statistical technique which is easily and markedly disturbed by chance errors in the original correlational data. Small differences in the original correlations may give rise to great differences in the final multiple correlation. Also, a multiple r tends to exaggerate the amount of relation found. The optimum weights attached to each component of the battery of tests are those found to be best in the particular small group of subjects studied; in another group other weights might be found to give better predictions.

It might be regarded almost as axiomatic that no multiple r should be greater than the reliability of the test predicted. The reliability of the hypnotic scale used, when given to the same subjects by two hypnotists, working independently, is $+ 0.85 \pm .08$ (n = 15). This value is satisfactorily high, as a reliability score, but it is below the multiple r predictive of hypnosis. Taking these considerations into account, we may perhaps say that the predictive accuracy of the two tests under examination is not very much different from the reliability of the hypnotic scale, and that, therefore, these two tests between them appear to account for most of the factors making for "hypnotizability".

The actual effects of such prediction may be illustrated by reference to the hypnotizability of two groups of subjects. 19 non-suggestible subjects were selected from among the 100 patients who had been subjected to the Hypnosis test, as well as 22 suggestible subjects. A subject was classed as non-suggestible if he gave a negative reaction to the heat illusion, and swayed only 2 inches or less on the Body Sway test. A subject was classed as suggestible if he responded positively to the Heat Illusion test, and fell outright on the Body Sway test. The scores on the hypnosis-scale of these two groups of patients are illustrated in Figure 16. None of the suggestible subjects had a hypnosis score of less than 20; only one of the non-suggestible subjects had a hypnosis score of more than 20. The average score of the suggestible subjects was 42; that of the non-suggestible subjects, 6. Thus between the most and the least suggestible 20% of our subjects, as determined by the Body Sway and the Heat Illusion tests, there is only a 2% overlap on the Hypnosis test.

No evidence is yet available to enable us to explain the fact that the Body Sway test and the Heat Illusion test do not correlate together, but yet increase each other's predictive value to almost double the original amount. A possible approach to this difficult question may lie in a consideration of the nature of the two tests. The Body Sway test measures the motor effect of a suggestion; the Heat Illusion measures the sensory effect of a suggestion. Both these effects form part of the hypnotic scale; possibly the hypnotic score is a combination of two relatively separable part-scores—a motor and a sensory part. It should be easy to test this hypothesis; however, further consideration of this point would clearly be a digression from our main argument.

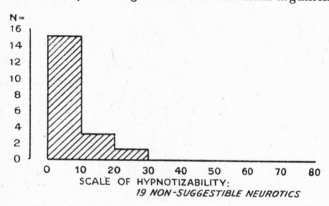

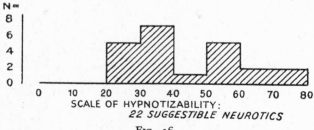

Fig. 16.

Having established the relative independence of primary and secondary suggestibility, we may revert to our main problem and ask which of these two kinds of suggestibility is invoked by psychiatrists when they maintain that hysteria and suggestibility, or suggestibility and neuroticism, show a particularly close relation. According to Janet (1924), "suggestion is a particular reaction to certain perceptions; this reaction consists in the more or less complete activation of the tendency that has been evoked, without this activation being completed by collaboration with the whole personality". This definition would seem to cover primary suggestibility, but it does not seem particularly appropriate with respect to secondary suggestibility.

Again, there can be no doubt from Janet's own writings, and from the views advanced by his associates and successors, that he considered hypnotic suggestibility the prototype of suggestibility in general. Consequently we do not believe that we should do violence to the theory we are testing if we used a test of primary suggestibility in our investigation. Hypnotizability itself would no doubt be the most satisfactory test to use, but as that would be impracticable we selected the test most highly correlated with primary suggestibility, viz. the Body Sway test.

## 3. The Nature of Primary Suggestibility

Before we are ready to use this test in investigating the various theories regarding the relation between suggestibility and personality, however, it is important to investigate certain features of the test itself. We must know its retest reliability, the distribution of scores, the correlation with intelligence, the existence or not of sex-differences, the best methods of standardising its application, and various other facts regarding the mechanics of the test, as it were, before using it as an instrument. A variety of experiments were performed in an attempt to obtain data on these various points, and these will be examined briefly.

There can be no doubt that the retest reliability of the test is very high indeed for the subjects on whom we have tried it out. For 60 neurotic service patients who were given the test in the form "You are falling forward", and immediately afterwards in the form "You are falling backward", the correlation between the two forms was + 0·91. For 60 non-service patients who were given the test under two conditions, standing on the ground and standing on a low stool, the correlation was + 0·89. These retests were carried out immediately following the original test.) The passage of time tends to lower retest reliability to some extent. 30 neurotic men and 30 neurotic women were tested and retested immediately afterwards; the retest reliability of the whole group was + 0·93. 40 men and 40 women were tested and retested the following day; the retest reliability of the whole group was + 0·91. 30 men and 30 women were tested and retested after four weeks. The retest reliability of the whole group was + 0·84. In the first-mentioned experiment, the suggestion was given by the experimenter in person; in the other experiments, it was given by means of a gramophone record. The upshot of these experiments seems to be that the test is highly reliable, both as given personally and as given by means of a gramophone record.

The question of the distribution of a trait in the population, and the problem of estimating this distribution from a knowledge of the distribution of scores on a supposed test of that trait, has already been touched upon in the introductory chapter. It arises with particular insistence in relation to suggestibility, because it has been found quite generally that tests of primary suggestibility, and the Body Sway test in particular, tend to give U-shaped curves of distribution, thus lending support to the old and discredited "type" view which would divide people up into two groups, the suggestible and the non-suggestible. Experimental evidence and statistical examination are necessary before we can adhere to such a view.

In Figure 17, C, is shown the distribution of scores on the Body Sway test of 150 neurotic men and 150 neurotic women. It will be seen that the curve is of the U-shaped kind, 29% swaying less than two inches, and 24% falling outright. None of the intermediate groups contains more than 12% of the cases.

It is possible to account for this fact in two ways. We may assume that the underlying trait which is measured by the Body Sway test is really distributed in the population in the fashion illustrated, showing about a third of the population as non-suggestible and another third as very suggestible. Alternatively, we may assume that the actual form of distribution found is

merely an experimental and statistical artefact, of no ultima
significance. One way in which a U-shaped curve of distributic
might have arisen from a normal curve of distribution of tl
underlying trait is illustrated in Figure 17, A and B.

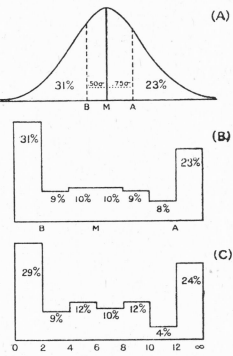

FIG. 17. (A) NORMAL CURVE OF DISTRIBUTION FOR SUGGESTIBILITY:
THRESHOLD AT B, CEILING AT A. (B) U-SHAPED CURVE OF DISTRIBUTION
DERIVED FROM (A). (C) EXPERIMENTALLY FOUND CURVE OF DISTRIBUTION
FOR 300 NEUROTICS; SWAY IN INCHES.

Let us assume that primary suggestibility is distributed i
the population in the form of a normal curve, as in Figure 17, *
Let us also assume that the test used has a threshold and *
ceiling, i.e. that the test is sensitive only over part of the tot*
range, being unable to discriminate between persons showin*
less of the trait which is being measured than a person at th*
31st percentile, or more of the trait than the person at the 77t*
percentile. In other words, the test lumps together all tho*

whose scores are more than ·50 S.D. below the mean, and all those whose scores are more than ·75 S.D. above the mean. On this assumption, the observed distribution of scores on the test would be as in Figure 17, B; it will be clear from casual inspection that this form of distribution is very nearly identical with that actually found in our experiment (Figure 17, C).

So far we have shown only that a distribution such as that actually found is not incompatible with a normal distribution of the underlying trait; it remains to be shown that this theory is in accordance with the facts, and more likely to be true than the "type" theory of distribution. The decision between the two theories hinges on the relative homogeneity of the two extreme groups, i.e. the "suggestibles" and the "non-suggestibles". According to the "type" theory, these two groups are homogeneous with regard to the trait which is being investigated, members of either group showing a certain identical amount of the trait, i.e. either very little or very much. According to the view advocated here, the members of these two groups are heterogeneous with regard to the trait under investigation, appearing homogeneous only because of the high threshold and the low ceiling of the test. Therefore, we can decide between the theories by investigating the relative homogeneity of the two extreme groups.

This was done by means of the following experiment. 70 male and female patients altogether were given the Body Sway test (gramophone record) for 30 seconds, and their sway noted; they were then given the same test for 2½ minutes, and again their sway was noted. From test I to test II the average amount of sway increased from 4 to 5 inches; 35 of the patients swayed over an inch more the second time, while only 1 swayed less the second time. 20 patients fell outright during the 30 second run, while an additional 6 fell when the run was extended to 2½ minutes. 39 men swayed less than 2 inches during the short run; only 15 swayed less than 2 inches during the long run. (These differences are not due to practice effects; a repetition on 100 patients of the Body Sway test in its full (2½ minute) version did not show any greater sway the second time as compared with the first.)

These results show clearly that neither the suggestible nor the non-suggestible group is in the least homogeneous; by simply

increasing the time of the test some patients who in the short te
seemed to belong to the non-suggestible group were shown t
be moderately suggestible, while other patients who had n
in the short version belonged to the very suggestible group wer
shown to belong to it when the time of the test was extended
Thus both the suggestible and the non-suggestible groups ar
heterogeneous in their make-up, and we may regard the "type
theory as disproved.

Another method of proof may be used to show a simila
result. If the U-shaped distribution found in tests of primar
suggestibility is due to the fact that these tests have a threshol
and a ceiling which restrict the discriminative ability of the tes
then combining the scores of several different tests, whose thresh
olds and ceilings may be presumed to lie at different level
should result in a curve of distribution approaching the norma
When such a combination of scores, weighted by the respectiv
saturation of the tests combined with the factor of primar
suggestibility, was carried out, the resulting curve of distributio
was found to have lost its U-shaped appearance, and to b
unimodal (Eysenck and Furneaux, 1945). This method of proc
thus supports the conclusion derived from the other experimen
and we may conclude that the U-shaped form of distributio
often found with tests of primary suggestibility is an experiment
artefact, and that the true distribution is probably of a unimoda
form.

The question of the correlation of primary suggestibilit
with intelligence is a vexed one. Hull (1933) presents a tabl
setting out the results of eight investigations into this question
in which altogether 296 subjects were used; none of the resultin
correlations between intelligence and suggestibility are negative
and he concludes that "this array of positive values should g
far to dissipate the somewhat vague but widespread belie
that for a person to be susceptible to hypnosis is an indicatio
of feeble intelligence". In some preliminary work carried ou
at this hospital, the correlation between intelligence and suggesti
bility was found to be curvilinear rather than linear, patient
of average intelligence being more suggestible than the dull o
the bright (Eysenck, 1943, 1944).

Although the significance of the divergence of these dat
from linearity was established by reference to Blakeman's test

this test has been criticized by Fisher (1932), and it appeared essential to amass further data before deciding finally on the linearity or non-linearity of the correlation.    Scores on the suggestibility test and on the Matrix test of intelligence are now available for 865 male and 324 female neurotic army patients, and the distribution of scores argues definitely against curvilinearity.    Consequently, tetrachoric correlations were run for the males and the females separately, and the correlation between intelligence and suggestibility was found to be $-0.15 \pm .04$ for the men, and $+ 0.04 \pm .07$ for the women.    These correlations are significantly different, the Critical Ratio being 2·4. Taking men and women together, the tetrachoric correlation between intelligence and suggestibility is $-0.10 \pm .04$.

These results do not leave any clear-cut impression, except that the relation between intelligence and suggestibility is negligible.    As far as they go, they seem to indicate that duller subjects are very slightly more likely to be suggestible than very bright ones; but even this tendency cannot be regarded as established because in the case of the women this generalization does not hold true.    In view of the fact that previous workers have tended to find very low positive correlations between the two variables, our own discovery of a very low, if significant negative correlation on the rather atypical population of an Army hospital cannot be taken as final.[1]    We have no suggestion to offer concerning the observed sex-difference in correlation; although significant it is too small to be of any practical importance.

The data just quoted may account for the fact that in our preliminary work a curvilinear correlation was suspected between the variables; in these studies, correlations were run on populations containing equal numbers of men and women; the low suggestibility of Grade I males and of Grade V females might

[1] One obvious method of proving or disproving this point is the examination of the suggestibility of mental defectives; if there is even a slight tendency for suggestibility to increase as intelligence decreases, a group of subjects with I.Q.'s. between 50 and 70 should differ significantly from a group of normal intelligence.    The experiment was performed by M. Brady, who tested 106 male and 94 female M.D.'s. within the stated range of intelligence.    She also tested 100 male and 100 female epileptics, mainly of subnormal intelligence.    Her results showed that epileptics did not differ significantly from M.D.'s., both groups being less suggestible than a normal control group, and very significantly less suggestible than a neurotic control group. Women epileptics and M.D.'s. were found to be less suggestible than men.    These results would seem to disprove the existence of any negative correlation between intelligence and primary suggestibility.

produce apparent curvilinearity, which disappears on separating the sexes.

The question of sex-differences thus raised must, of course, be answered also with respect to the actual suggestibility scores of the two sexes. Hull (1933) reviews a number of studies and comes to the conclusion that "women and girls upon the whole are truly but very slightly more suggestible than are men and boys under the experimental conditions usually employed". In our own work on neurotic patients it became clear very soon that the men were more suggestible than the women; this impression became strengthened in the course of time till now the data admit of no doubt whatever. Counting as "suggestible" those who sway two inches or more, we found that of 1,000 male neurotics 76% were suggestible, while of 400 female neurotics only 52% were suggestible. The Critical Ratio of the difference is 8, leaving no doubt that the phenomenon observed is a real one for this population.

It would not be admissible, however, to deduce from these values that women are less suggestible than men. When the test was given to 60 male and 60 female non-neurotic subjects, 20% of the females and 18% of the males were suggestible by the criterion employed above; in other words, no significant difference was observed between the two sexes when non-neurotic subjects were tested. It seems likely, therefore, that an explanation for the observed differences in the neurotic groups must be sought for in the differential method of selection of male and female neurotics sent to this hospital. An attempt at such an explanation will be made later in this chapter.

A discussion of sex differences with respect to suggestibility inevitably raises the question of the influence of the experimenter. It has often been maintained that the fact that the experimenter is usually a man may account for the frequent finding of greater female suggestibility; this view is somewhat related to the Freudian theory which links suggestibility and hypnosis with sexual factors. Again, much is made by writers such as McDougall (1926) of the "prestige" of the experimenter, and the success or failure of the suggestion is thought to be due to the presence or absence of "prestige" in the eyes of the subject. Thus, clearly it is important to investigate this question, and to decide to what extent prestige may be said to play a part, to what extent the sex of the experimenter influences the results of the test, and whether any completely objective technique can be designed which will standardize many of the otherwise uncontrolled forces which may play on the mind of the subject. Our observations on these points are rather unsystematic, and were collected in the course of researches having other ends in view; they are given here merely for the sake of the light they throw on the problem of objectifying the test, and may serve to stress the necessity of investigating the problem by means of experiments specifically designed for the purpose.

Of 900 male patients tested by means of the record (male voice), 16% ± 1·2% fell outright, while of 100 male patients tested by a male experimenter in person, and of 60 male patients tested by a female experimenter in person, 40% ± 3·9% fell outright. This difference is highly significant, the C.R. being 6. It would appear, accordingly, that personal administration of the test is more effective than the playing of a record.

That this is not universally so was shown in another experiment, however, in which 30 men and 30 women were tested by another male experimenter, 30 men and 30 women by a female experimenter, and 100 men and 100 women by means of the record (Eysenck, 1943). For the men, the record was found to be more effective than either experimenter; for the women, it was found to be slightly less effective. The male experimenter was more effective than the female for both male and female patients. Thus, clearly the personality of the experimenter has something to do with the outcome of the test; personal administration may be more effective, less effective, or equally effective as compared with administration of the test by record, depending on the personality of the experimenter. His or her sex seems to have little to do with the final result.

In view of these results, it was decided to employ a record rather than using a more personal method of administration. This standardization of procedure eliminated many possible subjective influences of mood, preconceived ideas, and so forth, and made it possible to have the experimental results checked by other workers. This latter point is important; it is possible to obtain the record we used, thus reduplicating the essentials of the experimental situation.

To make such repetition and confirmation possible, a detailed and complete description is given below of the test as it has

N

been used in our investigations. The patient is brought into the room and told that he is to be given a short test. He is told to stand quite still, with his eyes closed, his feet together, and his arms hanging loosely by his side. While he is standing thus, a thread is attached to his collar by means of a pin. This thread runs back to the wall, over a hook fixed to the wall at a height of exactly 5 feet, and after running over another hook fixed one foot higher and two inches to the side of the first, supports a pointer which runs on a scale marked in half-inches which is fixed to the wall. Any forward movement of the patient is shown by a corresponding upward move of the pointer on the scale; any backward movement of the patient is shown by a downward movement of the pointer. The extent of the movement can be read off the scale in inches.

A slight inaccuracy is introduced in this method of recording because a difference in height of the person whose body sway is being measured changes the exact equivalence of sway and pointer movement. This inaccuracy can be allowed for by a simple mathematical formula, or it can be eliminated by fixing the thread at uniform height in every case. As this inaccuracy is trifling in comparison with the wide individual differences observed, and as the method of grading (to the nearest half-inch) is rather rough, no correction has been made in our data.

When the thread is fastened in position, the patient's body sway is observed for 30 seconds, and his maximum sway forward and backward noted. If an individual sways 1 inch forward and $\frac{1}{2}$ inch backward during this time, his total non-suggestion body sway is $1\frac{1}{2}$ inches.

When this 30-second period is over, the subject is told that a record is now going to be played to him. "I want you to listen carefully to what the record says, while you go on just standing there, quite still and relaxed, with your eyes closed. Listen carefully, and just keep on standing as you are standing now. I am putting the record on now."

The record is an ordinary, commercially produced gramophone record, made by, and obtainable from, the Star Sound Recording Studios, Cavendish Square, London. The text was spoken by the writer, and runs as follows: "Now just keep standing there, please, quite still and relaxed, with your eyes closed, and think of nothing in particular. Just keep standing quite still and relaxed, and listen to *me*. Now I want you to imagine that you are falling forward, you *are* falling, falling forward, falling forward all the time. Falling, falling forward, you are falling forward now. You are falling, falling forward, falling forward all the time. . . ." These suggestion are repeated for a total of $2\frac{1}{2}$ minutes, and are then slowly faded out.

The body sway of the patient in response to the record is observed, and his maximum sway from the original position, either in the forward or in the backward direction, is recorded. If a patient sways 5 inches forward and 2 inches back, then his score would be + 5; if he swayed 1 inch forward and 2 inches back, his score would be −2. Scores were recorded to the nearest half inch. A complete fall, when the patient either had to put a foot forward to catch himself, or when he had to be caught by the experimenter, was arbitrarily counted as + 12 when forward or as −12 when backward. [1]

After the test is over, the patient is told to open his eyes, the pin is removed, and he is interrogated on various points connected with his subjective experiences. He is asked whether he felt affected by the record, i.e. whether he felt any tendency to fall forward; whether he tried to resist this tendency; whether he thought he had actually swayed more than in the non-suggestion stage; and quite generally what he had thought about the test, and what he had felt like during it. While these introspections do not have any high objective value, they are important and interesting because (1) they reveal how the subject interpreted the instructions, and whether he failed to understand that he was supposed to try to resist the suggestion; (2) they throw some light on his attitude to the test, and on his own evaluation of the result; (3) they help us in evolving hypotheses regarding the dynamic interplay of opposed tendencies at work in the mind of the patient subjected to this rather traumatic experience. These introspections are entered on the score-card of the patient, together with his suggestion- and his non-suggestion body sway, his intelligence rating, and a summary of observations of his behaviour while the test was in progress, dealing with such matters as sweating, clenching of fists, shaking of head, trembling, grimacing, laughing, fainting, tics, and so forth.

[1] Different methods of scoring this test are discussed in Appendix B, where a justification is given for the method adopted here.

## 4. Personality Correlates of Primary Suggestibility

The test in this standardized form was given to 900 male and 330 female neurotic service patients, as well as to 60 male and 60 female non-neurotic service personnel. An analysis of the results derived from the scores of these 1,450 subjects constitutes the bulk of our evidence regarding the personality correlates of suggestibility.

In Figure 18 are given histograms showing the distribution of scores for male neurotics, female neurotics, and normals separately. Suggestibility scores are given along the base-

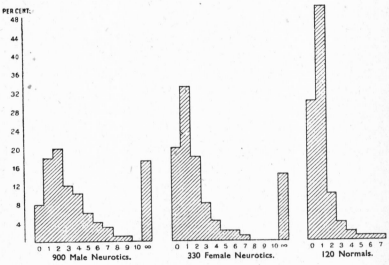

FIG. 18. DISTRIBUTION OF SUGGESTIBILITY IN THREE GROUPS.

line; these scores refer to amount of sway regardless of direction, i.e. both a sway of + 5 inches and a sway of —5 inches would be entered as 5 inches. The reason for thus neglecting to different-iate between positive and negative suggestibility will become clear later on; an analysis of negative as opposed to positive suggestibility will be given below.

As was shown in Chapter 2, it is possible to grade the patients with respect to the general trait of "neuroticism". The neurotics were divided into six groups according to the amount of "neuroticism" shown; Group I was made up of the least neurotic patients, Group VI of the most neurotic patients, the intermediate Groups showing intermediate degrees of neuroticism. A seventh group, presumably less neurotic even than Group I, was made up of the "normal" service personnel. Average amount of suggesti-

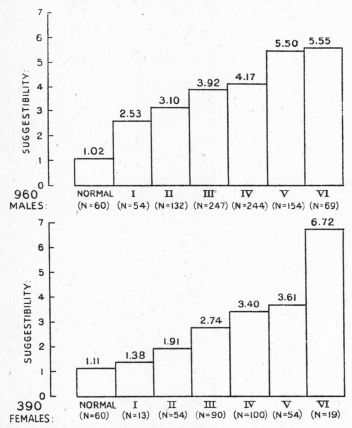

Fig. 19. Average Suggestibility of Normals and Neurotics, Showing Increase in Suggestibility Correlated with Increase in "Neuroticism".

bility (sway in inches) of these seven groups is shown in Figure 19, separately for men and women.

It will be seen that as we proceed from the normals through the slightly and moderately neurotic to the most severely ill patients, suggestibility goes up fairly evenly from 1·02 inches to 5·55 inches for the men, and from 1·11 inches to 6·72 inches for the women. There is not one single reversal in this steady progression, but it should be noted that some of the averages given are not based on sufficient numbers of patients to be considered very reliable; e.g. two averages are based on less than fifty cases. Average sway of the neurotic men is 4·18 inches, as compared with 1·02 inches of the normal men; total average sway of the neurotic women is 3·13, as compared with 1·11 inches of the normal women.

A more detailed analysis of the findings is given in Table 24.

TABLE TWENTY-FOUR

| Items. | Males. | | | | | Females. | | | | |
|---|---|---|---|---|---|---|---|---|---|---|
| | 1 | 2 | 3 | 4 | 5 | 1 | 2 | 3 | 4 | 5 |
| 1. Affected by record | 97 | 86 | 64 | 34 | 45 | 93 | 74 | 46 | 21 | 27 |
| 2. Age below 30 | 62 | 56 | 56 | 52 | 58 | 91 | 85 | 91 | 81 | 88 |
| 3. Service more than 1 year | 92 | 91 | 90 | 91 | 91 | 76 | 48 | 63 | 73 | 65 |
| 4. Rank: N.C.O. | 14 | 19 | 16 | 11 | 18 | 12 | 11 | 13 | 21 | 19 |
| 5. Discharged from army | 65 | 54 | 46 | 33 | 45 | 69 | 63 | 44 | 49 | 35 |
| 6. Skilled civilian occupation | 61 | 66 | 59 | 62 | 61 | 44 | 56 | 56 | 48 | 42 |
| 7. Has been unemployed | 39 | 41 | 30 | 34 | 28 | 42 | 55 | 41 | 35 | 46 |
| 8. Bad work history | 7 | 6 | 7 | 8 | 5 | 13 | 4 | 8 | 4 | 4 |
| 9. Abnormality in family | 66 | 67 | 55 | 55 | 50 | 69 | 63 | 58 | 49 | 50 |
| 10. Unsatisfactory home | 40 | 32 | 28 | 20 | 26 | 24 | 37 | 33 | 24 | 23 |
| 11. Education—elementary or higher | 71 | 77 | 82 | 78 | 81 | 93 | 78 | 96 | 92 | 92 |
| 12. Narrow hobbies | 78 | 77 | 72 | 68 | 69 | 67 | 75 | 56 | 54 | 62 |
| 13. Drinks (alcohol) | 55 | 54 | 51 | 51 | 54 | 20 | 18 | 17 | 29 | 19 |
| 14. Past physical health good | 54 | 57 | 57 | 57 | 68 | 64 | 51 | 60 | 73 | 46 |
| 15. Abnormal before present illness | 78 | 72 | 60 | 66 | 57 | 87 | 70 | 74 | 53 | 85 |
| 16. Badly organised personality | 62 | 46 | 49 | 53 | 44 | 62 | 63 | 62 | 49 | 73 |
| 17. Weak: dependent | 64 | 58 | 59 | 50 | 51 | 69 | 56 | 60 | 47 | 69 |
| 18. Little energy | 28 | 22 | 25 | 24 | 24 | 18 | 37 | 25 | 14 | 31 |
| 19. Rebellious, aggressive | 25 | 15 | 15 | 26 | 15 | 18 | 7 | 22 | 16 | 23 |
| 20. Touchy, suspicious | 36 | 27 | 28 | 27 | 21 | 33 | 19 | 28 | 27 | 38 |
| 21. Seclusive, schizoid | 43 | 43 | 48 | 39 | 34 | 29 | 38 | 30 | 27 | 35 |
| 22. Hysterical personality | 29 | 30 | 22 | 28 | 28 | 40 | 51 | 35 | 31 | 35 |
| 23. Anxious, highly strung | 70 | 68 | 61 | 55 | 57 | 78 | 59 | 65 | 56 | 88 |
| 24. Hypochondriacal | 34 | 30 | 28 | 30 | 28 | 33 | 22 | 22 | 20 | 27 |
| 25. Obsessional, meticulous | 26 | 25 | 26 | 27 | 18 | 36 | 26 | 30 | 27 | 27 |
| 26. Autonomic imbalance | 48 | 51 | 46 | 45 | 44 | 36 | 26 | 25 | 19 | 38 |
| 27. Headaches | 57 | 68 | 59 | 55 | 54 | 62 | 51 | 55 | 52 | 47 |
| 28. Effort intolerance | 56 | 57 | 48 | 50 | 42 | 71 | 44 | 47 | 46 | 38 |
| 29. Dyspepsia, vomiting | 20 | 21 | 13 | 14 | 14 | 20 | 4 | 11 | 9 | 0 |
| 30. Fainting, fits | 14 | 16 | 15 | 12 | 17 | 16 | 15 | 14 | 14 | 12 |
| 31. Tremor | 34 | 30 | 25 | 20 | 18 | 36 | 15 | 14 | 15 | 8 |
| 32. Sexual anomalies | 17 | 14 | 16 | 15 | 13 | 11 | 4 | 4 | 5 | 15 |
| 33. Anxiety | 45 | 43 | 36 | 26 | 44 | 58 | 38 | 48 | 33 | 50 |
| 34. Depression | 24 | 28 | 25 | 18 | 29 | 27 | 33 | 29 | 24 | 38 |
| 35. Irritability | 45 | 34 | 33 | 36 | 44 | 31 | 18 | 28 | 25 | 38 |
| 36. Apathy, retardation | 20 | 22 | 22 | 20 | 17 | 29 | 22 | 22 | 20 | 23 |
| 37. Hysterical attitude to symptoms | 40 | 40 | 33 | 35 | 51 | 44 | 56 | 47 | 39 | 42 |
| 38. Hysterical conversion symptoms | 30 | 35 | 30 | 28 | 33 | 38 | 48 | 33 | 39 | 31 |
| 39. Good muscular tone | 91 | 93 | 91 | 91 | 86 | 91 | 74 | 91 | 95 | 81 |
| 40. Hypnosis or narcosis | 4 | 7 | 7 | 2 | 9 | 7 | 0 | 3 | 7 | 0 |
| Number of subjects | 169 | 191 | 239 | 214 | 87 | 46 | 22 | 74 | 159 | 29 |

The subjects were divided into five groups, according to the amount of suggestion body sway they showed in response to the test: Group I swayed more than 8 inches, or fell outright;

Group II swayed 3½ inches or more; Group III swayed 1½ inches or more; Group IV swayed 1 inch or less forward, or ½ inch or less backward; Group V swayed more than ½ inch backward. Information was also available with regard to 40 items concerning the patient's family history, symptomatology, adjustment to work and army life, age, marital status, disposal, physical health, and various personality traits. The percentage was calculated of patients in the five groups showing the various traits listed, and these percentages are given in Table 24, separately for men and women. It will be seen, for instance, that of the male patients who were very suggestible (Group I) 65% were discharged from the army, while of those who were non-suggestible (Group IV) only 33% were discharged from the army (see item 5). Similarly, of the female patients in Group I, 87% had been abnormal before the present illness, while of those in Group IV, only 53% had been abnormal (item 15).

It will be noted that for the majority of neurotic symptoms the percentages are highest in the extremely suggestible group, slightly less in the very suggestible group, less still in the suggestible group, least in the non-suggestible group, and rising again in the negatively suggestible group. In other words, negative suggestibility shows the same correlation with these various items as does positive suggestibility, and we may, therefore, justifiably calculate our index of suggestibility without taking into account the direction of body sway.

Some of the conclusions which can be derived from this table may be briefly indicated. The age factor appears to be relatively unimportant; on the whole, the young are slightly more suggestible than the over-thirties. This is in good accord with the usual findings that after the age of eight or so there is a marked decline in suggestibility as age increases; our data seem to show that this decline is continued even after adolescence is passed. Tetrachoric correlations between age and suggestibility are $-\cdot12$ for the men and $-\cdot29$ for the women.

Length of service is clearly not correlated with suggestibility. This point is important because McDougall has maintained that suggestibility is increased considerably in the soldier because of his acquired habit of obedience; our data do not bear this theory out at all.

The fact that the percentage of those who feel affected by

the record is larger among the suggestible than among the non-suggestible is hardly surprising; even so, 1 in 3 of the non-suggestible admits that he was affected. Rather more surprising is the fact that good muscular tone appears quite unrelated to suggestibility; past physical health also does not seem to have any influence on a person's suggestibility.

We may now turn to a comparison between the hysterics and the dysthymics, in an attempt to secure evidence regarding Janet's and Babinski's theory of the close connection between suggestibility and hysteria. The evidence is fairly clear. Tetrachoric correlations between hysterical personality and suggestibility are ·14 for the men and ·19 for the women; correlations between anxious personality and suggestibility are ·28 for men and ·46 for women. Similarly, correlations between anxiety as a symptom and suggestibility are ·26 for men and ·33 for women, while for conversion hysteria the correlations are ·12 for men and −·08 for women. Thus both for hysterical personality and for conversion hysteria as a diagnosis correlations with suggestibility are smaller than for anxious personality and for anxiety as a diagnosis. These figures give no support to Janet's view.

The greater suggestibility of the dysthymics as compared with the hysterics is apparent also in those items which in the factor analysis presented in Chapter II were found to be most significant of the hysteric and the dysthymic groups. Thus the items concerned with bad work history, hypochondriasis, abnormal sex activities, lack of energy, and narrow interests show less correlation with suggestibility than do items concerned with somatic anxiety, tremor, effort intolerance, irritability, depression, and dyspepsia. The data even suggest that hysterics may show a greater tendency than dysthymics to be negatively suggestible, while dysthymics tend to be more positively suggestible; this would be well in line with Bleuler's (1924) dictum that the suggestibility of hysterics often tends to act in the negative direction.

Using the point-scale described in Chapter II, 229 comparatively pure cases of dysthymia and 166 cases of relatively pure hysteria were singled out from among the male patients, as well as 80 dysthymics and 65 hysterics from among the females. The average suggestibility score of the male dysthymics was

4·66, that of the male hysterics 3·93. Among the females, the dysthymics score 3·61 on the average, the hysterics 3·09. In view of the abnormal distribution of suggestibility scores, the usual tests of significance of differences between means are not admissible, and an analysis by means of Chi Square methods is presented in Table 25.

In this Table are given the numbers of dysthymics and hysterics respectively who fall into the five groups (extremely suggestible, very suggestible, suggestible, non-suggestible, and negatively suggestible) defined above. The results show that the differences between dysthymics and hysterics could have arisen by chance, although for both men and women the difference lies in the same direction.

TABLE TWENTY-FIVE

|  | 1. | 2. | 3. | 4. | 5. | Total. |
|---|---|---|---|---|---|---|
| Dysthymics, male | 54 | 4 | 56 | 58 | 20 | 229 |
| Hysterics, male | 26 | 39 | 44 | 39 | 18 | 166 |
| Dysthymics, female | 16 | 4 | 21 | 33 | 6 | 80 |
| Hysterics, female | 9 | 7 | 12 | 33 | 4 | 65 |

Chi square, males: 4·888.
Chi square, females: 0·402.
Number of degrees of freedom: 4.

The only one of the groups which appears to show a definite difference between dysthymics and hysterics is the first group, giving the number of extremely suggestible patients. Taking men and women together, we find that 22% of the dysthymics and only 15% of the hysterics belong to this group; this difference is significant (C.R. = 2·12). However, as this comparison is selected from five possible comparisons, we can only conclude that although the data suggest strongly that dysthymics are more suggestible than hysterics, they do not prove it. They do appear to disprove the view, however, that hysterics are more suggestible than dysthymics.

So far, then, our data seem to lead to two conclusions: (1) Suggestibility is closely related to neuroticism, and (2) Suggestibility is not related more closely to hysteria than it is to other neurotic disorders. While we believe that the experimental design of our investigation is of such a kind as to establish the truth of our first conclusion, there are two possible argument which may be advanced against our second conclusion.

In the first place, it may justly be objected that hysteric are said to be particularly suggestible only to *personal suggestions* and that the impersonal kind of suggestion issuing from a record does not give the hypothesis a fair trial. This objection is al the more weighty as our demonstration that the effect of the record was no less marked than the effect of personal suggestion was not sufficiently rigorous to be convincing. It is quite possible that had the experiment been carried out by the experimenter in person, differences in the expected direction would have been observed.

In the second place, it might be argued that the selection of hysterics and non-hysterics on the simple basis of taking the routine diagnosis of a psychiatrist who did not have very much time to give to each patient, even when widened so as to include certain other personality ratings, is unlikely to be highly reliable. Lack of reliability in the choice of the two diagnostic groups would lead to an attenuation of such differences as might exist, and might turn a significant difference into a non-significant difference (but would be unlikely to reverse the difference).

## 5. HYSTERIA AND SUGGESTIBILITY

Two special experiments were performed in which the design was of such a kind as to obviate these two objections. 15 male and 15 female hysterics were selected very carefully by the most experienced and senior psychiatrists at the hospital; in each case definite conversion symptoms were present, and the patient was considered to have an hysterical personality. Similarly, 15 male and 15 female neurotics were selected by the same psychiatrists on the understanding that they should choose patients who showed no hysterical symptoms and who did not have "hysterical personality". All the case-notes were read carefully by the writer, and the crucial cases, i.e. non-suggestible hysterics and highly suggestible non-hysterics were seen by the Clinical Director who in each case confirmed the original diagnosis.

These 60 patients were given 8 suggestibility tests, 4 tests of primary and four tests of secondary suggestibility, by the experimenter in person. In none of the tests were any significant differences observed, and the conclusion was drawn that hysterics are no more suggestible than non-hysterics (Eysenck, 1943).

In the other experiment, an attempt was made to provide some evidence with respect to the "triadic hypothesis" of Rosenzweig mentioned earlier in the chapter. 21 male and 13 female hysterics, and 23 male and 15 female dysthymics were selected as the most typical 10% of these two classes of patients in the hospital by the Superintendent, his deputy, or the Clinical Director. These patients were given individually a battery of 19 short tests in the morning, followed by the Body Sway test, administered in person by the experimenter (Mrs. A. Petrie). On 9 of the tests, the patients were told they had done very well; on the other 10 tests, they were made aware of the experimenter's displeasure at how badly they had done. After the Body Sway test, they were asked to make a list of all the tests they had done that morning.

Similarly, each patient was tested in the afternoon with 19 short tests, on 9 of which he was told he had done well, and on 10 of which he was told he had done badly. Again the Body Sway test was given, and again he was asked to make a list of the tests he had done. Finally, after a week each patient was asked to make a list of all the tests he had been asked to do on the two previous occasions, and when he had recalled as many tests as he could he was given a test of recognition, consisting of a list of all the tests used.

A more detailed description of the various short tests used, and of the results reached, is given elsewhere (Petrie, 1945). We may note, however, the main outcome of the experiment. In the first instance, it is important to establish the reliability of the "repression" test; clearly, unless this test has a reasonable reliability, not much attention need be paid to the correlations it may show with other variables. We have correlated three versions of the test: (1) The test given in the morning, (2) the test given in the afternoon, and (3) the delayed memory test. In each case, the score consisted in the number of "discouraged" tests remembered minus the number of "encouraged" tests remembered. The three correlations are all positive, but

extremely small; they average + 0·14.[1] None of them is statistically significant.  We may doubt, therefore, if "tendency to
repression", as measured by the Rosenzweig type of test, represents a real unitary personality trait.  In this connection, attention
may also be drawn to the theoretical criticisms advanced by
Rappaport (1942) of the possibility of testing Freudian concepts
by means of tests of this type; he concludes that these tests have
little relevance to Freudian theories.  With this position we are
in full agreement.

In view of the unreliability of the test, it can hardly be
expected that "repression" scores would differentiate between
hysterics and dysthymics, and indeed the scores of the two
groups are almost identical when the scores for the three tests
are summed (1·22 and 1·24 respectively for the hysterics and the
dysthymics).  Neither were the two groups of patients differentiated with respect to their suggestibility; the respective scores
being 7·0 ins. for the hysterics and 7·4 ins. for the dysthymics.
Thus the hysterics are slightly less suggestible on this test than
are the dysthymics; the difference is, of course, well below the
level of significance.

The correlations between repression scores and suggestibility
are in the direction which accords with Rosenzweig's theory;
for a combination of the morning and afternoon tests, the correlation with suggestibility is $r_t = -0.12 \pm .18$, and for the delayed
memory test, $r_t = -0.32 \pm .16$.  The latter correlation is
significant statistically, the former is not.  Correction for attenuation raises the "delayed memory" vs. suggestibility correlation
to + 0·64.

These results would seem to lead us to the following conclusions.  There are theoretical objections to the use of tests
of the kind employed as "repression" tests.  Even if this objection
is waived, the tests show comparatively little reliability.  In
addition, they fail to discriminate hysterics from dysthymics

---

[1] It is possible that the smallness of these correlations is due to the intervention o
a time-interval in the case of the delayed memory; thus if we consider that repressio
may be a cumulative, time-conditioned process the two immediate memory tests may
be too close to the semi-traumatic experience temporally for repression to get to
work; in the case of delayed memory, we would then expect repression to show more
obvious effects.  It should be noted that the delayed memory score correlates more
highly with other scores (suggestibility, etc.), than do the immediate memory scores
and also that the split-half reliability of the delayed memory test, though still unsatisfactory, is +0·33 (corrected).

'hus the part of the "triadic hypothesis" which links "repression-
bility" to hysteria receives no support from our data.

It is possible, however, to rephrase that theory so as to account
or the facts. If we use "neuroticism" as the link between
uggestibility and "repressionability", then our results become
erfectly intelligible; the neurotic person is suggestible, and
also likely to react with repression to a situation threatening
is security. In support of this view we may quote the fact that
vhen our subjects were devided into a "repressed" and an
unrepressed" group, the incidence of neurotic symptoms and
ther indicators of a "P—" personality was significantly higher
n the "repressed" group. Indeed, a perusal of Freud's classi-
icatory system makes it appear quite possible that he would
ave called the majority of our neurotics "hysterics", dividing
hem into "conversion hysterics" and "anxiety hysterics". It is
iseless to speculate on this point, but if the possibility be granted,
hen there are no points at issue between Rosenzweig's results
nd our own. Beyond that we cannot go at the moment; clearly
urther research is urgently needed to corroborate the views put
orward.

## 6. Ideo-Motor Action

We are now in a position to attempt a theoretical account
of our findings which will give them a much-needed coherence.
The main concept on which we shall rely is one which has in
one form or another played a very important part indeed in the
history of psychology, although it did not receive the name by
which it is known nowadays until comparatively recently, when
Carpenter (1852) coined the word "ideo-motor action". In one
of its earliest versions, the ideo-motor theory of action may be
said to have been formulated by Isaac, the abbot of Stella, who
lived in the 12th century and defined imagination as "intelligence
clothed in sensation" (Zilboorg, 1941). A modern behaviorist
would have little fault to find with that definition!

The further history of the concept, well reviewed and
documented can be found in Klinckowstroem's book (1913),
and more specifically in Tischner's paper (1929). Throughout,
ideo-motor action was linked with various kinds of magic, with
water-divining, thought-reading, and similar parapsychological

phenomena. Many writers, such as Kirscher (1678), Lebrun (1693), Zeidler (1700) and others stress the influence of the imagination of the holder on the movement of the divining rod but do not relinquish entirely the belief that God or the Devil may play some part in the action.

The first to give an adequate version of this theory, according to Tischner, was an anonymous author writing in 1807, who discussed the force of imagination by describing a variety of experiments, and dilated upon "die Macht ihres inneren Schauens und Bildens auf den Körper und seine Bewegungen". At this time, early versions of the Chevreul pendulum began to attract attention, and a variety of experiments were performed (Gilbert, 1808) which attracted the attention of such men as Chevreul, Ampère, Braid, Faraday, and others. G. C. Beireiss, an eccentric genius, is reported to have known and used the principle of ideo-motor action in a variety of experiments and demonstrations, designed mostly to impress and awe his visitors (Sybel, 1811).

W. B. Carpenter (1852) named this type of movement in a lecture "On the influence of suggestion in modifying and directing muscular movement independently of volition", and both name and explanation were taken over by most of the psychologists of his day; James's advocacy established it as "orthodox" (1890). Thorndike's presidential address to the American Psychological Association in 1913 was devoted largely to a criticism of the principle, and marked the beginning of an era in which more stress was to be put on the "motor" than on the "ideo-" side of the phenomenon.

This period is marked by the extremism and the exaggerations of orthodox behaviorism, which reduced thought to "incipient motor movement of the speech organs", and refused to allow such concepts as "imagination", "ideas", or "consciousness" (Watson, 1924). Experimental attempts to verify these theories were not as numerous as one might have expected from a school which was based so firmly on observation and experiment, and such attempts as were made were largely unsuccessful. A full review of these earlier studies is given by Thorson (1925), and reasons for their failure are advanced by Max (1934).

More recent studies have reopened the field of ideo-motor interaction, particularly with respect to thought and muscular tension (Stauffacher, 1937; McTeer, 1933; Clites, 1935, 1936;

Stroud, 1931; Ghiselli, 1936; Reed, 1931; Bills, 1937; Cason, 1938; Zartman, 1934; Block, 1936; Freeman, 1931, 1933; Max, 1935; Reiter, 1933; Kanner, 1930; Allers, 1926). Using more up-to-date methods, such as measurements of action-currents in the muscle, these workers have gone a long way towards re-establishing the ideo-motor theory in its previous commanding position.

Of particular importance in this connection has been the work of Jacobson (1927, 1929, 1932). He found that "contraction of specific muscles is not only concomitant with the occurrence of certain mental activities, but is essential to their occurrence, since imagination of a particular act failed to occur if the muscles involved in it were completely relaxed".

He also found that when arm-movements were magnified 80-fold and photographed, imaged arm-movements were always accompanied by actual movements of between ·07 and ·32 mm. in extent. He observed during his studies of action currents that "large deflections . . . following the signal to imagine are markedly increased in all cases, having a value from 340 to 530 per cent. of that during complete relaxation. No increase occurs in the control tests". "Microvoltage during recollection is about equal to that during . . . various acts of imagination." Concerning thought, he found that "the series of vibrations during the mental activity occur in patterns evidently corresponding with those present during actual speech."

These studies leave little doubt that the thought or image of a movement is closely related to the muscles which carry out that movement; in other words, the idea of a movement is frequently, if not always, followed or accompanied by an incipient movement employing the same muscle-groups as are involved in the imagined movement. By thus postulating a close connection, we do not imply identity; it is not suggested that the thought and the movement are actually one and the same thing.

In a test such as the Body Sway test, it is easy to show that the active factor which causes the movement is the image of that movement in the patient's mind. Berreman and Hilgard (1936) tested 30 students under the following three conditions: (a) Personal heterosuggestion, (b) Verbal autosuggestion, and (c) Subvocal autosuggestion. The differences in amount of sway caused by these three different methods were too small to be significant, and the correlations between the three methods averaged over + 0·7. Similarly, in our own work we had 60 patients tested once by personal heterosuggestion, and twice by simply asking them to imagine to themselves that they were falling forward (Eysenck and Furneaux, 1945). The intercorrelations between the three tests averaged over + 0·9, and no significant differences were observed in the total amount of body sway.

We believe, then, that the effective part of a suggestibility experiment such as the Body Sway test consists in implanting the idea or the image of the desired movement in the mind of the subject; this can be done by means of repeated heterosuggestion, by means of autosuggestion, vocal or subvocal, by means of asking the subject to imagine the movement, by means of getting the subject to witness the movement being carried out by somebody else (Hull, 1933), or by means of getting him to listen to two people discussing the movement (Eysenck, 1944). The method used appears unimportant; what matters is that the idea or the image should be firmly implanted in the subject's mind.

We submit, then, that experimental evidence is overwhelmingly in support of the contention that an idea, or image, of a movement tends to produce the precise movement imagined, or a modified form of it. The strength of this tendency varies from person to person; in some persons, it is very strong, producing easily-observed movements, in other persons, it is very weak, making it necessary to employ refined physical and electrical methods in order to detect the movements. This trait of possessing a strong or weak ideo-motor tendency we shall call a person's "aptitude" in the remainder of this chapter; this trait will be contrasted with "attitude", which also plays an important part in our theory of suggestibility.

When a person is put in a situation which calls forth his ideo-motor aptitude, e.g. when he is given the Body Sway test, his response will be determined not merely by his aptitude, but also by his attitude. Although he may feel a distinct tendency to fall forward in response to the suggestion; although, in other words, his aptitude for ideo-motor action is brought into action, he may be able to check this tendency by an effort of will. Thus a person's aptitude may be veiled by a negative or hostile attitude, and the end-result of the test may be identical for a person of high aptitude, but negative attitude, and for a person with low aptitude, but positive attitude. The result of a test of primary suggestibility is thus determined by two factors, aptitude and attitude.

While aptitude is a comparatively simple, straightforward concept, attitude is a very complex concept indeed. It embraces not only the desire of the subject to resist or not to resist the suggestion, but also his power to do so. Again, it is possible that the subject may consciously desire to resist, but unconsciously wish to comply. Thus a variety of complications arise which make the detailed analysis of test-results difficult. In order to simplify matters as far as possible, the instructions to our patients emphasize that they are expected to keep standing; i.e. an attempt is made to force them into a negative attitude towards the test. They regard the test as a direct conflict of wills between themselves and the experimenter, and try as hard as they can to avoid any sway. This desire to resist the suggestion is obvious both from their introspections (we found that only those who did not sway at all said they had not tried to resist; in terms of our theory, aptitude was absent, and consequently attitude did not matter to the outcome of the experiment) and also from their actual behaviour: very many subjects clenched their fists, shook their heads, clenched their teeth, or audibly said, "No, no!" to the suggestion.

Consequently, we may regard our tests as giving us information on the ability of the subjects to overcome ideo-motor tendencies aroused by the experimenter in varying strength; this ability is closely akin to what in popular parlance might be called "will-power" or "strength of character". Unfortunately, our test does not enable us to measure this ability directly, but only in the form of a ratio of which the subject's aptitude is the divisor. We must ask ourselves, therefore, whether the high correlation between suggestibility and neuroticism is due to the fact that neurotics may have greater ideo-motor ability, or whether they are inferior to normals rather with regard to their ability to counteract voluntarily the ideo-motor tendencies aroused no more strongly in them than in non-neurotics. In other words, do neurotics differ from normals with respect to aptitude, to attitude, or to both combined?

This question cannot be answered at present. Those who believe with Salter (1944) that hypnosis and suggestibility are simply phenomena due to conditioning would presumably hold the first-mentioned view, arguing that the neurotic is more easily conditioned to react to inappropriate stimuli. The view that neurosis and conditioning are causally related concepts was

o

adumbrated in Watson's paper on the conditioning and de-conditioning of a phobia, and finds some support in recent work on "experimental neuroses" (Masserman, 1943). Certainly the conditioning experiments of Hudgins (1933) on the pupillary reflex, and of Menzies (1941) on vasomotor responses bear a resemblance to hypnotic experiments which presumably is due to a similarity of underlying factors.

A priori arguments of this kind, however, can have little force, particularly in view of the demonstration by Berreman and Hilgard (1936) that there is no correlation between body-sway suggestibility and amplitude or frequency of conditioned eyelid-response in 19 students studied by them. This experiment is not conclusive, however, because of the small number of persons involved, and because of the homogeneity of the population tested. Further work is needed in this connection, and no assessment can be given at present of the differences in "aptitude" between neurotics and normals.

The view that suggestibility is due rather to defective voluntary control than to strong ideo-motor tendencies is perhaps more in line with orthodox psychological teaching. The theories of McDougall and Freud agree in regarding the "will" as the outcome of the integration of early instinctual tendencies, organized into hierarchical structure through the influence of the environment; neurosis, in these terms, is then considered as a regression towards a less integrated state. It follows quite naturally from a view such as this that neurosis should be accompanied by a weakening of "will-power", and consequently by greater suggestibility. Again, experimental support is lacking, and it is impossible at the present moment to come to a decision on the merits of this theory.[1]

[1] One further item of evidence which might be used to indicate that it is with respect to *attitude*, not *aptitude*, that neurotics differ from normal subjects, comes from the generally accepted belief that neurotics cannot be hypnotized more easily than normal subjects. While in our suggestibility tests we attempt to make the subject oppose the suggestion with the full strength of his will, thus measuring the effectiveness of his will-power, the typical procedure in hypnosis emphasizes co-operation with the experimenter, and a positive attitude. In hypnosis, therefore, we have a situation where aptitude alone is being measured, attitude (except in a few recalcitrant cases) being positive. If we can accept the common belief that under these conditions there are no differences in hypnotizability between neurotics and normal subjects, it would follow that as regards aptitude there was little difference between the two groups. The whole question, of course, deserves a more experimental treatment than it has received so far, and raises the whole question of the nature of hypnosis (Eysenck, 1941). There should be no difficulty in designing a crucial experiment along the lines indicated to validate or invalidate our theory.

## 7. NARCOSIS AND SUGGESTIBILITY

An attempt was made to adduce experimental evidence on this point by a study of the effects of certain drugs (sodium amytal injection; nitrous oxide inhalation) on suggestibility (Eysenck and Rees, 1945). These drugs are known to diminish conscious control, while there is no reason to suppose that they act on the underlying neural structures mediating ideo-motor tendencies; consequently the suggestibility scores of patients tested before and after administration of the drug should throw some light on the part played by conscious control in these tests.[1]

Groups of patients were selected according to their body-sway scores; those swaying less than 2 inches were called "non-suggestible", those swaying more than 3 inches were called "suggestible". The test used for the experiment proper was the "Press" test described earlier on in this chapter; it will be remembered that in this test the subject is asked to hold on to a rubber-bulb, while a record suggests to him that he is squeezing the bulb, the actual pressure on the bulb being recorded on a kymograph. This test was used because it can be administered while the patient is lying on a bed; both sodium amytal and nitrous oxide have such pronounced effects on patients that it would be impossible to subject them to a test requiring them to stand up for any length of time.

10 suggestible patients and 10 non-suggestible patients were given the press test, first in the normal state, then a few minutes later in the narcotic state, having been given an intravenous injection of sodium amytal till they could no longer count backwards without making gross mistakes. The results of the experiment are quite clear-cut. None of the non-suggestible patients became suggestible under the drug; the records do not show a single case of pressure in either the normal or the drugged state. On the other hand, all the suggestible patients became more suggestible; tracings of their actual kymograph records are given in our paper. In the narcotic state pressure is exerted earlier, more strongly, and for a longer period, than in the normal state. The probability of such a clear differentiation between suggestible and non-suggestible patients with regard to the effects of the drug being due to chance is less than 1 in a million.

[1] Earlier works on this point is discussed critically in our paper.

In a control experiment, 10 suggestible patients were first tested in the normal state, then had an intravenous injection with saline solution, and were retested to discover the suggestive effect of the injection by itself. 2 out of the 10 showed an increase in suggestibility; consequently we may deduce that the suggestive effect of the procedure employed (intravenous injection) has a certain effect by itself in raising the suggestibility scores of the patients, but that this effect is not sufficient to explain fully the effects of the administration of sodium amytal.

Similar results were obtained when 10 suggestible and 10 non-suggestible patients were given nitrous oxide to breathe until they could no longer hold the mask up by themselves. The non-suggestible patients did not increase their suggestibility scores in a single case; 9 out of the 10 suggestible patients did increase their suggestibility scores. The results for the suggestible patients clearly confirm our previous results and show that *decrease in conscious control is followed in suggestible subjects by an increase in suggestibility*.

These experiments thus indicate that attitude plays an important part in the reaction of the patient to the total test situation, and strongly support our analysis of primary suggestibility into aptitude and attitude. The non-suggestible patient may be conceived of as lacking in aptitude; removal of conscious control by means of the narcotic does not affect their response at all, because there is no aptitude on which the suggestion could play. For the suggestible patients, however, who have a measure of aptitude, removal of conscious control gives this aptitude freer play, and thus creates the condition necessary for heightened degrees of suggestibility.

It is along these lines that we would look for an explanation of the phenomena, and while there can be little doubt that our general theory of suggestibility will require many modification before it can be accepted as an all-embracing account of the facts we believe that such modifications are unlikely to alter the theory in any fundamental respect.

## 8. SUMMARY

In this chapter an attempt has been made to distinguish various types of suggestibility, to establish the relation between suggestibility and hypnosis, to discover personality correlates of suggestibility (particularly by investigating its relation to hysteria and neuroticism), and to elaborate a theory of suggestibility.

In two factorial studies of altogether 16 different tests of suggestibility, it was shown that these tests define two entirely different and separate types of suggestibility: (1) Primary suggestibility, characterized by dependence on ideo-motor action, and (2) Secondary suggestibility, characterized by dependence on indirection. Primary suggestibility was shown to be closely related to hypnosis; secondary suggestibility showed no such relation.

In a variety of studies, it was shown that contrary to common psychiatric assumptions hysterics were not more suggestible than other types of neurotics; indeed, it appeared that dysthymics were slightly more suggestible on the average than were hysterics. Suggestibility was found to be strongly correlated with neuroticism; both when comparing neurotics with normals, and when comparing the more seriously ill with the less seriously ill it was found that degree of neuroticism was reflected in the suggestibility test scores.

On the basis of these and other results a theory of suggestibility was put forward which emphasized the two functions of *aptitude* and *attitude*. Conceiving of ideo-motor action as an aptitude present in varying degree in different people, we considered this aptitude to lie at the basis of all manifestations of primary suggestibility, including hypnosis. Attitude was conceived of as a controlling mechanism which inhibited the ideo-motor activity, except in cases where this inhibiting mechanism was too weak to control the activity (e.g. in neurotics).

An attempt was made to provide evidence for this theory by studying the behaviour of neurotics on a suggestibility test before and after the injection or inhalation of a narcotic (sodium amytal or nitrous oxide). This experiment showed that, as was predicted on the basis of the theory, suggestible patients became more suggestible under the narcotic, while non-suggestible patients remained unaffected.

# CHAPTER SIX

## APPRECIATION AND EXPRESSION

1. Temperament and "Weltanschauung"   2. Appreciation: General Theory
3. Conformity: The Ranking Rorschach Test
4. Types of Aesthetic Appreciation
5. Coloui/Form Attitudes   6. Sense of Humour
7. Expression Tests: Mosaic Construction and Graphology   8. Summary

### 1. Temperament and "Weltanschauung"

It has often been maintained by the more philosophically inclined psychologists, such as Mueller-Freienfels (1919), Adickes (1907), James (1910), Jung (1923) and others, that a person's whole Weltanschauung, his approach to scientific, aesthetic, political and moral problems, is determined by his temperament. In particular, it is often maintained that the "tender-minded" introvert will tend towards an idealistic philosophy, while the "tough-minded" extravert will tend rather towards materialism. Some would go even further than this and correlate Weltanschauung with body-build (Kretschmer, 1926); in an interesting study Boldrini and Mengarelli claimed that of one thousand university professors the asthenics tended to have "abstract thought", while the pyknics tended to have "concrete thought" (1933).

That the problem is not quite so straightforward as this is indicated by a study of the philosophical attitudes and the temperamental traits of 107 philosophers (Eysenck and Gilmour, 1944). These philosophers filled in a questionnaire listing nine questions regarding causality, the independent existence of universals, the teleological view of the universe, absolute values, the semantic view of philosophy, and *a priori* knowledge; the answers to these questions were intercorrelated, and the resulting matrix factor-analysed. The first factor extracted from the matrix accounted for 51% of the variance, and was clearly an idealism-materialism factor; the second factor, accounting for only 13% of the variance, opposed *monism* and *dualism*.

When the questions were weighted according to their saturation with the idealism-materialism factor, and weighted scores
given to the participants, it was found that 48 qualified as
materialists, and 47 as idealists, the remaining 12 subjects being
classed as "undecided". All the 107 philosophers had been given
a temperamental questionnaire, made up from the most diagnostic
items of Guilford's "Personality Factors" (1936, 1939, 1939),
purporting to measure introversion, social shyness, overt
emotionality, nervousness, general drive, and depression. When
the idealists and the materialists were compared with respect to
these various items, no significant differences were found on any
of these characteristics; such small differences as did exist were
found to contradict rather than to support the hypothesis that
introverts tend towards an idealistic philosophy.

While these results may be of interest as indicating that the
question of the relation of *Weltanschauung* to temperament is
rather more complicated than was at first thought, they are of ·
little help in the study of temperamental peculiarities in the
ordinary population whose interest in, and knowledge of,
philosophical subtleties is minimal. Of more relevance perhaps
would be a demonstration that some of the recently demonstrated
general social attitudes (Eysenck, 1944) showed some affinity to
temperamental traits; unfortunately, this aspect has not been
studied sufficiently to make a lengthy discussion fruitful.

In a field related to that of social attitudes, however, namely
in the measurement of human aversions and satisfactions, recent
work has shown certain interesting correlations with temperament
(Eysenck, 1943). In the type of research referred to, the subject
is required to rank a number of items in order of "pleasantness";
i.e. he has to indicate which item he would like most to have
happen, which second-most, and so on down to the item he
would like least. He may have to choose, for instance between
items such as having his work praised and acknowledged, being
allowed to read all the books banned for indecency, having
complete security in his job, living in perpetual sunshine, believing in a life after death, and so on. Alternately, he may be
required to say which of several displeasing items he would
like most to avoid, the choice being between such occurrences as
having his intelligence reduced below average, becoming incapable of taking part in athletic pastimes, giving up social affairs

involving more than four people, becoming totally bald, or blind,
or living quite alone in a friendless city.

Results of the study, when compared with the scores on a
questionnaire, showed that while introverts would particularly
like to own every book they cared for, extraverts would like to
read books banned for indecency. Introverts would hate
particularly to live with uncongenial people, get a job which
involved making speeches, or work under someone who criticized
them constantly; extraverts would dislike particularly to become
bald and to have their teeth extracted.

These results may be of interest in suggesting a novel method
of attacking the thorny problem of how to make people give an
accurate picture of themselves in a questionnaire; an indirect
method such as asking them to rank the satisfactions they would
derive from a variety of situations and contingencies, or to rank
their aversions to certain courses of action, would seem more
likely to receive a truthful answer than a more direct approach.
Thus to ask a number of subjects whether they were particularly
keen on indecent books would put them on their guard, and the
results would be doubtful in their validity; by putting this item
in with some twenty others, and asking for a relative value-
judgment, less hostility and suspicion is aroused, and the results
are more likely to be trustworthy. As a proof of this latter contention, we would like to draw attention to the experimental support
in a later section of the contention that extraverts are more
overtly interested in sexual matters than are introverts.

Although this approach may thus be useful in developing the
questionnaire into a weapon less obvious than a bludgeon, many
of the defects of the questionnaire remain, and more strictly
experimental results are preferable. Such results are most easily
obtained, perhaps, when using tests involving the perceptual
and ideational spheres, and consequently the material in this
chapter will come in the main from these spheres. In particular,
it is proposed to study the aesthetic reactions of our subjects,
using that word in its widest sense, and including both aesthetic
appreciation and aesthetic production (expression) under this
concept. As mentioned at the beginning of this chapter, it has
often been maintained that personality and art-production and
appreciation are closely related; it is the burden of this section
to determine on a very low level of complexity whether it may

be possible to find any evidence for this contention. The results are of interest, partly because to the best of our knowledge this is the first time that a determined attempt has been made to adduce experimental proof with regard to the general problem, but mainly because our work has been done both on neurotic and on normal subjects, and thus the results may throw some light on the question of whether our results are valid only for the limited population with which we have been dealing in the main, or whether they have a wider significance.

Such rather subjective evaluations of the field as have been made suggest that artistic style and aesthetic appreciation are both linked with temperamental factors, in addition to such cultural and social factors as are universally recognized. Worringer's distinction between *abstraction* and *empathy* (1906, 1912), has been taken up by Jung and related to the Introversion-Extraversion dichotomy; Read has also shown that it fits in well with Jaensch's work on eidetic imagery (1943). Quite generally, Jaensch (1926) has more and more based his types on perceptual reactivity, thus relating them very closely to appreciation (Eysenck, 1942). Löwenfeld's "visual" and "haptic" types (1939) must also be mentioned in this connection; although his work deals largely with the artistic productions of blind or weak-sighted children, it is generalized to cover those with normal sight as well.

Joan Evans (1939) has attempted to relate artistic productivity and appreciation to Jung's typology in detail, as has Read (1943). In so doing, the last-named draws on the work of Riegl (1893, 1927), who distinguishes geometric and naturalistic types of art, Wölfflin's (1915) well-known "contrasts", Dvorak's (1918) distinction between idealism and naturalism, and Verworn's (1914) and Kühn's (1923) studies of primitive art, resulting in distinctions between ideoplastic and physioplastic, or imaginative and sensorial types.

Read also draws on the well-known work of Bullough (1906, 1921), Meyers and Valentine (1914), and Downey (1923), identifying Bullough's perceptive types with Jung's four basic psychic functions. Apparently, he would also extend this identification to Binet's (1903) perceptive types, which were later investigated by Muller (1912).

Along rather different lines lies the work of Spearman (1931), which is based on his Noegenetic laws. But again, the analysis is purely *a priori*, and lacks any experimental verification. In Spearman's case, this is probably inevitable as he is concerned with proving that artistic phenomena are capable of being subsumed under the more general concepts he has advanced elsewhere; consequently, a deductive rather than an inductive procedure appears indicated. No similar reason can be given for the subjective and non-experimental nature of the work of the other writers quoted, i.e. Jung, Evans, and Read; they attempt to establish a correlation between temperament and artistic activity by means of argument by analogy. While highly suggestive, their contributions cannot be regarded as convincing.

Almost the only writer to eschew theoretical argument, and to substitute experimental fact for reasoning by analogy, has been Burt (1939); his contribution will be discussed in connection with our own studies. Much work has also been done with psychotic patients, but although most of this is of a semi-experimental kind, it has little relevance to our subject. Good summaries are available in the monographs by Hrdlicka (1899), Fursac (1905), Prinzhorn (1923) and Anastasi and Foley (1940, 1941).

## 2. APPRECIATION: GENERAL THEORY

The principles on which our experiments are based are derived from an objective examination of the various factors which determine aesthetic appreciation (Eysenck, 1942). The typical experiment from which this analysis derives is the following: A number of objects having aesthetic value (paintings, photographs, statues, vases, book-bindings, flowers, odours, polygonal figures) are presented to the subject; he is told to rank them in order of *personal liking*, independently of what he conceives to be their *conventional value*. (Care is taken to ensure that he should be ignorant of this conventional value in any case.) He may be asked to repeat his ranking after a certain amount of time has elapsed. His ranking is then compared with rankings of others obtained under similar conditions, and the results are analysed by means of various statistical techniques.

When observers of different ages, different degrees of aesthetic sophistication, different sex, different race and nationality are asked to rank in order of liking objects having aesthetic value, the most striking fact is that there is a good deal of agreement between their rankings. The existence of such agreement has often been denied, both on *a priori* and on experimental grounds; yet recent evidence leaves little room for doubt on this point.

The development of the argument is, perhaps, clearest with respect to simple colour preference. Cohn (1894) in his pioneer work denied the existence of any general order of preference for colours; he found that for equally saturated colours preference depends exclusively upon individual taste. Dorcus (1926) agreed with this statement, saying that "we must be rather skeptical as to whether there is such a thing as colour preference". Von Allesch (1924), whose work has been accepted as the standard text in this field (Chandler, 1935), maintains that in view of the chaotic diversity of preference among colours, it is impossible to arrive at any objective and generally valid order. Others, however, such as Walton (1933), St. George (1938), and Garth (1922) maintain the opposite point of view.

In a critical and experimental study, Eysenck (1941) showed that colour preference rankings tended to correlate together positively; he also found that Allesch's conclusion was not justified by his own data, as a statistical analysis of the rankings given by his subjects showed them to correlate to the extent of + 0·26. Going through the whole literature on colour preference judgments, he showed that for the six main colours which had been used by most investigators the rankings of 12,175 white subjects correlated with the rankings of 8,885 coloured subjects to the extent of + 0·96. Similarly, rankings by 7,378 men and 6,247 women correlated to the extent of + 0·95. Thus there appeared no racial or sexual differences of any importance in the ranking of these colours.

These figures indicate not only that there exists what has been called a "general factor of aesthetic appreciation", but they also indicate that this factor is likely to have a biological foundation. It has often been suggested that colour preferences are conditioned entirely by associations and personal experience; such factors are obviously important in individual cases, and must not be neglected. But it is difficult to see how individual or specific factors of this kind could result in almost identical orders of preference for white and coloured subjects, having widely different backgrounds, associations, and experiences with these colours. It is difficult to avoid the conclusion that some fundamental biological factor is at work here, connected in some way with the functioning of the central nervous system.

Such a conclusion seems even more inevitable when we examine the data regarding preference judgments of odours (Beebe-Center, 1933; Stephenson, 1936; Eysenck, 1944). Here, agreement is even closer, and few would doubt the existence of some physiological mechanism relatively independent of environment. Again, however, we do not deny that environment does, in fact, exert a certain amount of influence; we are concerned merely to point out that this influence would appear to be exerted on the basis of an inherited predisposition.

When we begin to deal with more complex stimuli than simple colours or odours, the assumption of such a neural origin for preference judgments becomes more speculative. It remains possible, however, to study the bases of judgment from which the rankings are derived, and even to construct an objective formula which can be used to predict the reactions of subjects to any given stimulus. Work along this line was begun originally by Birkhoff (1932), whose "Aesthetic Measure" has aroused much interest in the analysis of the formal properties of works of art. However, as Beebe-Center (1937), Davis (1936), Harsh (1939), Brighouse (1939), Wilson (1939) and others have shown, Birkhoff's *a priori* formulae do not correlate well with actual preference judgments. Eysenck (1941) attempted to base an aesthetic formula on regression equations derived from the correlations of various objective properties of the polygonal figures used in his research with actual preference judgments; he was able to account for almost all the non-chance variance by means of this formula. This study, as well as another, on the predictability of the pleasantness of colour-combinations from a knowledge of the pleasantness of single colours (Eysenck, 1941), shows that although more complex stimuli may involve environmental influences more than do simple stimuli, yet aesthetic ratings still remain subject to scientific and objective analysis.

While the work quoted hitherto has been concerned largely with the properties of the stimuli, results of another study (Eysenck, 1940) leave little doubt that this method of approach is also of interest in the study of individual differences, because it was possible to show that once an average order of preference is established for various series of aesthetic stimuli, then a person whose rankings agree with the average in one of these series tends to give rankings in the other series which agree with the average to the same extent. To phrase it in another way, if we regard agreement with the average ranking as a "high" score, then there is a tendency for a subject who scores highly on one test also to score highly on all the other tests. This factor is not dependent to more than a small extent on intelligence, but seems to constitute a more or less separate group-factor of "aesthetic appreciation" within the cognitive sphere. In another paper, it has been shown that this factor has properties which link it closely with the concept of the "good gestalt", and that there is a certain amount of evidence to show that its existence may possibly be due to certain neural laws connected with the postulate of "isomorphism" (Eysenck, 1942).

While this general factor seems to be of interest to the aesthetician, in one aspect, certainly, it should prove of importance to the psychologist interested in individual differences. As Peters (1942) writes in his review of these studies, "regardless of what the ultimate explanation of (this) factor may be, it certainly evidences the generality of a trait of conformity". Leaving aside, then, the question of the interpretation of our general factor in terms of aesthetics, we may use the techniques and the materials of these researches in investigating this general trait of "conformity".

In doing so, we are much helped by a property of our data which links them closely to a much better explored and understood field of research, viz. that of perceptual discrimination. In an investigation into the discrimination of subliminal weight-differences, Gordon (1924) had her subjects rank a number of weights in order of heaviness; this involved much "guessing", as the differences in weight were subliminal. She found that while the correlation of one subject's ranking with the true ranking (as obtained by actually weighing the weights) was comparatively low, the correlation increased when the average of 5 subjects' rankings was taken. Further increases were obtained as the number of subjects whose rankings were averaged was increased, till finally the average ranking of all her 200 subjects correlated perfectly with the true ranking.

In an experiment performed to investigate whether a similar relation obtains in the field of aesthetic judgment, Eysenck (1939) had 900 non-neurotic judges rank 12 uncoloured pictures in order of preference.  Using 700 rankings, averaged, to serve as the criterion or "true" ranking, correlations were calculated between the criterion and single rankings, grouped rankings of 5, 10, 20, 50 and 200 subjects.  The results show that exactly the same effect is observable in this study as in Gordon's, namely an increase in the validity of judgments as the number of judges increases.

The fact that the validity of judgments is thus a function of the number of judges suggests the possibility of expressing this function it mathematical terms.  Let us call the correlation of the average order of n judges with the true order $r_{\bar{k}g}$; let $\bar{r}_{kk'}$ be the average intercorrelation of the n rankings.  Then

$$r_{\bar{k}g} = \sqrt{\frac{n\,\bar{r}_{kk'}}{1 + (n-1)\,\bar{r}_{kk'}}}$$

This formula is only an approximation formula (Eysenck, 1941), but the amount of inaccuracy it introduces is very small indeed.  The only difficulty which it gives rise to lies in the fact that the correlation of the average order with the true order presupposes the *existence* of a "true order", and while in the case of the weight-experiment the existence of such an order is apparent, it may be doubted whether aestheticians would be ready to grant that the average judgment of a large unselected group can serve as the criterion for a "true order".  It seems to us that the aesthetician is unduly skeptical of the aesthetic abilities of the man in the street; thus Bulley (1933), Dewar (1938) and Semeonoff (1940) have shown that laymen and even young children tend to agree on the average with experts.

However, if we are content to regard our general factor as one of "conformity" only, leaving aside for the moment the question of its aesthetic significance, the criterion proposed will probably be more acceptable, and we shall be able to use the formula given above, and the fundamental law which it expresses, to aid us in our further analysis.

So far, we have concentrated on the general factor; there

are, however, other factors in aesthetic judgments which are of equal importance for our work. We can eliminate the general factor, either experimentally or statistically, and when that is done there emerges a very strong bipolar group or type factor (Eysenck, 1941). This type factor has been found in the study of paintings, photographs, poetry (Eysenck, 1940), odours (Eysenck, 1944), statues and various other stimuli, and seems to show a considerable amount of functional unity. Suggestive evidence for its existence has also come from Dewar (1938) and Williams et al. (1938), and Stephenson (1935, 1936), whose results failed, however, to reach statistical significance (Eysenck, 1939).

The nature of this factor is difficult to indicate in the absence of the actual stimuli which define its two poles. On the one hand, we have a type of person who shows preferences for the simple, highly unified, vividly coloured, modern type of picture; the poem with the obvious rhyming scheme and the definite, unvarying, simple rhythm; the polygon with simple, straightforward outline; the strong, obvious odour. On the other hand, we have the type of person who prefers the complex, less "poster-colour", more diversified picture, the more complex polygon; the poem with a less obvious rhythm and a more variable and loose rhyming scheme; the more subtle odour. Investigation by means of questionnaires shows that there is a marked tendency for the extravert to prefer the simple, vivid, strong type of art, while the introvert prefers rather the complex, refined, subtle type of art (Eysenck, 1942). Burt (1939) had previously reported similar correlations.

General and group factor together account for only part of the variance—usually less than a third. Specific factors, i.e. factors peculiar to the individual, make up approximately one half of the variance, while error factors, i.e. factors which change from day to day, account for the remaining sixth. While these non-communal factors are of great interest in the study of aesthetic preferences, they are probably of less importance in the analysis of temperamental "types", and we may leave them aside without doing more than acknowledge their existence.

It may now be asked how the communal factors—i.e. general and type factors—can help us in our study of the neurotic. The answer is that the use which can be made of these two factors

is closely associated with their actual constitution.  Regarding the
general factor as one of "conformity", it seems possible that lack
of such conformity might be related closely to neuroticism.  The
Kent-Rosanoff test (1910), in which the unusualness of the
word-reaction to a stimulus word is scored as a neurotic response,
shows that this hypothesis is not without support.  The "lack of
social adjustment" which is usually quoted as the distinguishing
mark of the neurotic ought to become apparent in any test in
which scores are determined by "conformity" with the social
environment.

In the case of the group or type factor, the connection with
our studies of temperament is even easier to establish.  We have
evidence that this type factor is correlated with introversion-
extraversion in normal subjects; this fact makes it reasonable
to assume that in our neurotic population also certain differences
will become apparent between different syndromes.

In a preliminary study, an effort was made to prove the
theory underlying our use of the "lack of conformity" score
as an index of neuroticism (Eysenck, 1942).  In this study, the
subjects were required to rank certain words in order of preference; conspicuous deviations from the average order were
analysed in order to find the motivation behind the unusual
rankings.  In many cases, it was possible to show that such
abnormal rankings are as diagnostic of some kind of "complex"
as are the usual "complex" signs in the Jung word-reaction test,
and that the "complex" is closely related to the word thus dis-
placed.  This conclusion was confirmed by Anthony (1943) in a
study of school children.


### 3.  Conformity:  The Ranking Rorschach Test

The principle that "lack of conformity" may be correlated
with neuroticism was made use of principally in an effort to
make the Rorschach test into an objective, reliable and valid
test of temperament.  As is well known, this test in its usual
form consists of a set of ten ink-blots; these are presented to
the subject one by one, and he is required to tell the examiner
what they remind him of, or what they look like to him.  These
reactions are then analyzed by the Rorschach expert, and it is

claimed that this analysis reveals something of the total personality of the subject. The extreme subjectivity of the procedure, far from arousing misgivings, is actually claimed as an advantage of this test (Rorschach, 1942).

Opinion regarding the value of the Rorschach test in its orthodox form is sharply divided. To many Rorschach experts, this test seems to fulfil in the realm of psychology the functions which in physics fall to the cyclotrone, the Wilson cloud chamber, the thermionic valve, and the spectroscope all in one; in other words, the test is used for a great variety of disparate measurements which make it seem likely that if any of the fields is accurately covered by the test, none of the others can very well be so covered. To many more cautious psychologists, the test appears as one whose reliability is known to be low, whose validity has never been established with regard to most of the claims made in its favour, and whose subjective nature does not attract the scientific worker.

Efforts have been made to remedy these faults, and to convert the test into one which can be scored objectively, and which can be given to groups of people at a time. Outstanding in this field has been the work of Harrower-Erickson (1945), who devised a test based on the Rorschach cards which may be said to overcome many of the difficulties of the original test. In brief, her procedure is to present the subjects with a slide of each of the Rorschach cards, and to get them to pick out a response which to them appears most definitely suggested by the ink-blot as seen on the screen. Half of the possible responses, which are printed on a sheet the subjects have in front of them, are typically neurotic responses, the other half are typically normal responses. The total number of neurotic responses chosen constitutes the subject's neuroticism score, ranging from 0 (for the most normal) to 10 (for the most neurotic); a score of 4 is considered as the critical score, above which the subject is considered in need of a psychiatric check-up.

In spite of its many good features, such as its objectivity, and its attempt to measure one trait at a time, this test has been reported on adversely by workers who have been using it for the purpose of screening (Jensen and Rotter (1945), Wittson et al. (1944); they maintain that it does not segregate the neurotic from the non-neurotic group with sufficient accuracy. This

P

fault seems to be due in large measure to two facts: (1) The test as presented by Harrower-Erickson is not reliable enough to be acceptable; its split-half reliability, corrected by the Spearman-Brown prophecy formula, was found by us to be only $+ 0\cdot64$ (n $= 300$). A reliability as low as this would require a very high selection-ratio[1] before the test could be considered adequate for selection purposes. In military work, and in civilian work also, such selection ratios are seldom found, and consequently a way must be sought to improve the reliability of the test. (2) The set of items from which the subject is required to choose could probably be improved by active experimentation.

It appeared to us that these faults could be remedied by applying the theory and the statistical techniques of our "conformity" studies to the problem. Ultimately, what causes a response to be labelled "neurotic" and another to be labelled "normal" is precisely this quality of "conforming". That this line of reasoning is justified can be shown by the fact that with the above-mentioned methods we were able to raise the reliability of the test from $0\cdot64$ to $0\cdot84$.

In the new form which we gave to the test, it becomes a simple *ranking* test. The subject is shown a slide of one of the Rorschach cards; he is also furnished with a list of nine possible answers which might be suggested by the ink-blot. He is required to write a 1 after the response which seems to him most like the ink-blot, a 2 after the response which seems to him second-most like the ink-blot, and so on down to 9 after the response which seems to him to be least like the ink-blot. The same procedure is repeated, with different sets of responses, for the other nine ink-blots. The actual responses used we took from Harrower-Erickson's list; they are given overleaf. There are four neurotic and five normal responses to choose from.

The scoring of the test is very simple. If the theory on which the test is based is sound, then the completely normal person would rank the four neurotic responses 6th, 7th, 8th, and 9th; the completely neurotic person would rank them 1st, 2nd, 3rd, and 4th. The summed ranks of the four neurotic answers for each of the ten cards is the person's score. In the above example, the completely normal person would have a score of 9 + 8 + 7 +

---

[1] For a discussion of the Selection Ratio as a measure of the effectiveness of selection, see Taylor and Russell (1939) and Tiffin (1943).

6 = 30, while the completely neurotic person would have a score of $1 + 2 + 3 + 4 = 10$. On the total ten cards, the normal person would then have a score of 30 times $10 = 300$, and the neurotic person would have a score of 100; all possible scores lie between those limits.

Does any real meaning attach to these scores? In particular, does the person who has a high score on one card tend to have a high score on the other cards also? This question can be answered by correlating the ten scores obtained for each subject, and factor analyzing the resulting table. This was done for 300 neurotic subjects. All the correlations were positive, giving rise to a general factor which accounted for 34% of the variance. No significant residual correlations were left after removal of this general factor.

These results prove that the test is measuring something very definite, which we may call "lack of conformity" until we know more about it, and that it measures this something with considerable reliability—the split-half reliability, corrected by the Spearman-Brown formula, is $+ 0.84$. They also show that the different cards do not measure this lack of conformity with equal success; card seven is superior to cards one or two, for instance, as evidenced by the respective factor saturations of these cards. The scores contributed by the ten cards separately were weighted by their factor-saturations, using the formula

$$W = \frac{r_{ug}}{1 - r_{ug}^2},$$

in which W stands for the weight, and $r_{ug}$ for the factor saturation of card u. When this was done, the reliability of the test went up to $+ 0.87$; this increase is not sufficient in practical work to compensate for the additional labour expended in calculating the scores.

While we thus have here an instrument of considerable reliability and objectivity, it must be asked whether the results given by this test are valid in terms of personality structure. Correlation with the Progressive Matrices test of intelligence is very low ($r = + 0.08$); correlation with the Vocabulary test is slightly higher ($r = + 0.27$) but still insufficient to account for the variance of the test. It appears likely, therefore, that "lack of conformity" may in some measure be related to temperamental or characteriological features of the personality.

## RANKING RORSCHACH TEST

Name .....................................    Date ................. Sex ..............
                                      I.Q. .................. Voc. .............

### CARD ONE

An army or navy emblem      .   ( )
*Mud and dirt             ( )
A bat                .   .   ( )
Two people           .   ( )
A pelvis            .   .   ( )
*An X-ray picture      .   .   ( )
Pinchers of a crab   .   .   ( )
*A dirty mess         .   .   ( )
*Part of my body    .   .   ( )

### CARD TWO

*An insect somebody stepped on   .   ( )
Two Scottie dogs   .   .   .   ( )
Little faces on the sides .   ( )
*A blood-stained spinal column   ( )
A white top        .   .   .   ( )
*A bursting bomb  .   .   .   ( )
Two elephants     .   .   ( )
Two clowns   .   .   .   .   ( )
*Black and red    .   .   .   ( )

### CARD THREE

Two birds   .   .   .   ( )
*Meat in a butcher's shop  .   .   ( )
Two men     .   .   .   ( )
*Part of my body  .   .   ( )
*Red and black   .   .   .   ( )
A coloured butterfly  .   ( )
*Spots of blood or paint .   .   ( )
Monkeys hanging by their tails  ( )
A red bow-tie   .   .   ( )

### CARD FOUR

Head of an animal  .   .   ( )
*Lungs and chest   .   .   .   ( )
*A nasty mess   .   .   .   ( )
A pair of boots   .   .   ( )
*Black smoke and dirt  .   .   ( )
A man in a fur coat  .   .   ( )
An animal skin   .   .   ( )
A big gorilla   .   .   .   ( )
*An X-ray picture  .   .   ( )

### CARD FIVE

An alligator's head.  .   .   ( )
*A smashed body  .   .   .   ( )
A fan dancer.   .   .   ( )
*An X-ray picture  .   .   ( )
Legs   .   .   .   .   ( )
A bat or butterfly  .   .   ( )
*Lungs and chest   .   .   ( )
*Black clouds   .   .   ( )
A pair of pliers  .   .   ( )

### CARD SIX

Two kings' heads with crowns   ...   ( )
*An X-ray picture  .   .   ( )
*Sex organs   .   .   .   ( )
Pagan idol on a pole  .   ( )
A fur rug   .   .   .   ( )
*Mud and water   .   .   ( )
A polished post   .   .   ( )
A turtle   .   .   .   ( )
*A gray smudge  .   .   ( )

### CARD SEVEN

*Smoke or clouds  .   .   ( )
Two women talking  .   .   ( )
Part of my body   .   .   ( )
*Animals or animal heads  .   ( )
A map   .   .   .   ( )
*Dirty ice and snow  .   .   ( )
Lambs' tails or feathers  .   ( )
*An X-ray picture  .   .   ( )
Bookends   .   .   .   ( )

### CARD EIGHT

Flower or leaves   .   .   ( )
*An X-ray picture  .   .   ( )
*Pink, blue, and orange  .   .   ( )
A horseshoe crab  .   .   ( )
A coloured coat of arms  .   ( )
*Fire and ice, life and death  .   ( )
Two animals.   .   .   ( )
Blue flags   .   .   .   ( )
*Parts of my body  .   .   ( )

### CARD NINE

*Red, green, and orange  .   ( )
Sea horses, or lobsters  .   ( )
Flowers or underwater vegetation   .   ( )
*Parts of my body  .   ( )
*Smoke, flames, or an explosion  .   ( )
Deer or horns of a deer  .   ( )
Two people—witches or Santa Clauses ( )
*Clouds with blood  .   .   ( )
A candle   .   .   .   ( )

### CARD TEN

Two people   .   .   .   ( )
*Spilt paint   .   .   .   ( )
A Chinese print   .   .   ( )
*An X-ray picture  .   .   ( )
*Red, blue and green  .   ( )
Spiders, caterpillars, crabs and insects ( )
*Parts of my inside  .   .   ( )
A coloured chart or map  .   ( )
A flower garden or gay tropical fish  .   ( )

---

**(The items are taken by permission from Harrower-Erickson and Steiner (1945). "Neurotic" items are marked with an asterisk.)**

We took the 50 patients who had obtained the highest (most normal) scores, and compared them with the 50 patients who had obtained the lowest (most neurotic) scores. The results of this comparison are given in Table 26; it will be seen that in almost all the neurotic traits the low scoring group shows twice as high a percentage as the high scoring group. This result is highly significant statistically, and shows that the test can successfully distinguish within a hospital population between the more severely neurotic and the less severely ill.

A comparison between hospitalized neurotics and a normal, non-hospitalized group, also gives support to our view that "lack of conformity" as measured by this test is an index of neuroticism. In Figure 20 are given two histograms showing the distribution of scores for 300 neurotics and for 150 normals, both groups containing male and females in the proportion of 2 to 1.

TABLE TWENTY-SIX

| Item. | "Good" Ranking Rorschach Group. | | "Bad" Ranking Rorschach Group. |
|---|---|---|---|
| N. C. O. status . . . . | 34% | . | 18% |
| Abnormality in parents, etc. . . | 20% | | 44% |
| Abnormal sex activity . . . | 16% | | 32% |
| Unstable . . . . . | 30% | | 46% |
| Weak, dependent . . . . | 30% | | 58% |
| Aggressive . . . . . | 12% | | 24% |
| Anxious . . . . . | 26% | . | 54% |
| Conversion hysteria . . . | 12% | | 56% |

The mean score of the neurotic group is 205 $\pm$ 26, while that of the normal group is 231 $\pm$ 26. The C.R. is 3·2, and we may conclude that the difference is significant beyond any reasonable doubt. It will be noted that 12% of the neurotics have scores lower than even the lowest normal score, and that 18% of the normals have scores higher than even the highest neurotic score. There is a good deal of overlap between the two distributions, and while we may conclude that the test does significantly discriminate between the two groups, clearly it is in need of improvement. Such improvement must lie in the selection of better choice-answers; comparing the rankings of normals and neurotics for each card, we can select those answers which show the greatest difference in rank-order, and reject those

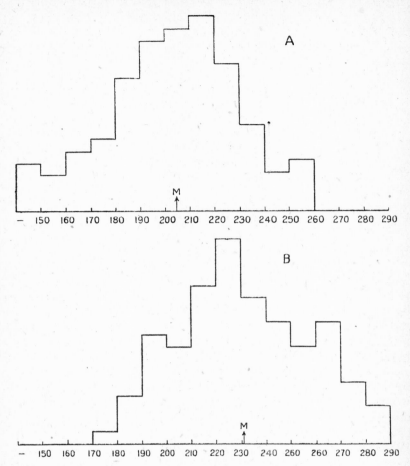

FIG. 20. SCORES ON "RANKING RORSCHACH" TEST OF NEUROTICS (A)
AND NORMALS (B).

which fail to show such differences. In due course, the selectivity
of the test may be greatly improved by such methods; even in its
present form, however, the test may be of some value.[1]

---

[1] At an A.T.S. reallocation centre, 50 girls of doubtful "general adjustment"
were compared with 50 girls of excellent "general adjustment". The scores on the
ranking Rorschach of the two groups were $217 \pm 21$ and $233 \pm 23$, with a C.R. of
3.56. These figures are typical of results obtained with various samples of service
personnel.

## 4. TYPES OF AESTHETIC APPRECIATION

Having thus shown that the general factor of "conformity" in perceptual-aesthetic tests is related to neuroticism, we may turn to the bipolar or type factor described briefly earlier in this chapter and attempt to confirm the finding on normal subjects that the extraversion-introversion dichotomy is related to the type of aesthetic appreciation. The test used has been described in detail elsewhere (Eysenck, 1941); it consists of 16 pairs of coloured landscape paintings, each pair depicting roughly the same kind of subject—a windmill, say, or a waterfall. The two pictures making up each pair differ profoundly in execution; one is painted in the colourful, simple, modern manner, the other in the more detailed, less colourful, older manner. Representative of the modern type of painter in our test are van Gogh, Gauguin, Cezanne, Vlaminck, Corinth, and Derain; of the older type, Hobbema, Constable, Wilson, Corot, Boudin, and Crawford. The score on the test is simply the number of modern pictures preferred to the older; the highest score possible is thus 16, the lowest is 0. The pictures are all post-card reproductions, and are pasted on to pieces of cardboard in pairs; in 8 cases the modern picture is on top, in 8 cases it is at the bottom. Simple preference judgments are asked for.

In a test so obviously influenced to a considerable extent by environmental influences, we did not dare hope that the results would be very definite; at best we expected a slight tendency one way or the other. 25 male and 25 female hysterics were given this test, and also 25 male and 25 female dysthymics. We thus have 400 judgments in each of the four groups; 1,600 judgments in all. Of these, 367 (23%) were in favour of the modern kind of picture; the men showed a greater preference for modern pictures than did the women, the respective figures being 236 (30%) and 131 (16%). Hysteric males preferred the modern pictures as compared with dysthymic males (130 or 32% as compared with 106 or 26%); similarly, hysteric females preferred the modern pictures as compared with dysthymic females (77 or 19% as compared with 54 or 14%). Altogether, the hysterics preferred 207 modern pictures, the dysthymics 160 (26% and 20% respectively). While these differences are not very large they are congruent and in the expected direction; they are also

quite definitely statistically significant.    We may conclude,
therefore, that in respect to this test, hysterics behave in a similar
manner to normal extraverts, and dysthymics in a similar manner
to normal introverts.

## 5. Colour Form Attitudes

One possible explanation of the preference of hysterics for
the modern pictures might be that these pictures usually contain
much brighter colours; in other words, the hypothesis might be
entertained that hysterics are more sensitive to colour, dysthymics
to form.    Lindberg has shown that among manic-depressive
patients the colour-attitude is more prevalent than among
schizophrenes (1938).

Interest in colour-reactions and form-reactions may be said
to have begun with the work of Kuhlman (1904) and Külpe
(1904), who came to the conclusion that there are *Formbeachter*,
*Farbbeachter*, and intermediate types.    Much work has since
been done along these lines, both on animals (Engel, 1935;
Revesz, 1926) and on children (Katz, 1913; Descoeudres, 1914;
Kuenberg, 1920; Volkelt, 1925; Segers, 1926; Tobie, 1926;
Eljasch, 1928; Hazlitt, 1930; Engel, 1935); the results seem to
indicate a decrease in colour-reaction with increase in age.

More interesting than these experiments are a series of
studies in which an effort has been made to link up the colour
reaction with temperament.    Scholl (1927) has attempted to
connect colour reaction with Kretschmer's typology; he has
been followed by Dambach (1929), Lutz (1929), Ritter (1930),
Popinga (1931), Oeser (1932), Kibler (1925), Enke (1928),
Braat (1936), Schmidt (1936), Lüth (1936), and Lindberg
(1938).    In general, these studies leave the reader with the
impression that schizoid personalities are more frequently
characterized by non-colour attitude, while cycloids are more
frequently characterized by colour attitude; a correlation seems
also to have been established between asthenic body-build and
non-colour attitude, and between pyknic body-build and colour
attitude (Lindberg, 1938).

In our work, three different tests of colour-attitude were
used; two of these, the "Similarities" test and the" Ranking"
test were specially devised for the purpose, while the third, the

"Ring" test, was taken from Lindberg's study. These tests share the characteristic feature that the subject is presented with a choice between different alternatives, a choice which is governed by his colour or non-colour attitude; in all other ways they are as different as possible.

The "Similarities" test consists of four pieces of cardboard each of which contains eight coloured shapes arranged in a circle. The first of these cards is used merely to demonstrate to the subject the method of the experiment; the other three cards, A, B, and C, constitute the test proper. On each of these three cards, there are three figures which are identical with regard to colour, but different with regard to shape, and three figures which are identical or similar with regard to shape, but different with regard to colour. In the card used to demonstrate the method of the experiment, there are three figures which are identical with regard to both colour and shape, and in showing the card to the subject, the experimenter is careful to lay stress only on the similarity between the three figures, without mentioning either form or colour. Having thus demonstrated to the subject that on each card to be presented to him he will find three figures which are similar, the experimenter presents one by one the three test cards and records the subject's decision. In the great majority of cases we found that the subject judges similarity either by colour or by form, without even realizing that another possibility exists.

The three cards which constitute the test differ from one another in their choice of colours and in their choice of figures which are similar or identical. In card A, the colour identical to three figures is a strong black which stands out with great insistence from the background, while the three forms are not identical but only similar, all three being triangles of one kind or another. In card C, the three forms which are similar are in fact identical, all three being squares, and the colour which is identical for three of the figures is a rather pale, unsaturated blue. In card B, the stress is laid no more strongly on colour than on form; it is intermediate in this respect between A and C.

In the "Ranking" test, the subject is asked to rank in order of preference 10 polygons (black outline on white background), and 10 colours (coloured paper pasted on pieces of cardboard without a margin). Having obtained these rankings, the experimenter selects from a prepared set 10 polygons cut out in coloured paper, pasted onto white cardboard, in such a way that the best-liked polygon appears in the least-liked colour, the second polygon in the least-liked but one colour, and so on. The subject is then required to rank these coloured polygons, and his final ranking is correlated with his ranking of the uncoloured polygons. If this correlation is positive, it indicates that in his final ranking, form was more important than colour; if it is negative, it indicates that colour was more influential than form. The size of the correlation indicates the strength of the influence exerted by either colour or form.

The "Ring" test was given in exactly the manner described by Lindberg (1938). It consists of a coloured plate, divided into two parts. Both parts contain two figures, a circle with an arrow and a square with a smaller square inside it. The upper figures are blue, the lower figures are red. There are many differences between the upper and the lower figures, such as the direction of the arrow, the background, the position of circle and square, and so on. The subject is simply asked to tell the examiner in what way the upper and the lower figures differ. If the subject mentions the colour difference as either his first or his second response, he is rated as having positive colour attitude; if the colour difference is mentioned later, or not at all, he is rated as having negative colour attitude.

Each of these three tests was carried out on 25 male and 25 female hysterics, and on 25 male and 25 female dysthymics. The subjects used in these three studies overlapped partially; altogether about 200 neurotic subjects were tested. Tetrachoric correlations were obtained between the three tests on 53 patients who had done all three tests; these averaage only ·24, thus indicating that the three tests measure relatively specific attitudes, while not excluding the possibility of a general factor of "colour attitude". A more extensive study of the intercorrelation of a variety of "colour attitude tests" would appear desirable in order to decide this question; our data are not extensive enough to be more than suggestive.[1]

In spite of the relatively low intercorrelations between the three tests, the results are in very close agreement. In the

[1] Huang (1945) reports moderately high correlations between different tests; however, these are too similar in design to settle the question.

"Similarities" test, everyone who gives a colour response on any
of the three cards is scored as having a "Colour attitude". When
his is done, we find that the male hysterics give 5 colour responses,
he female hysterics 4 colour responses, while the male dysthymics
give 6 and the female dysthymics 3 colour responses. Dysthymics
thus give 9 colour responses, and hysterics the same number;
here is no evidence here of any difference between the two groups.
There appears a slight male superiority in colour responses, the
figures being for male and female, respectively, 11 and 7; this
difference is not significant statistically.

As regards the "Ranking" test, we find an average correlation
with form in the male hysteric group of −0·26, and in the female
hysteric group of + 0·17; for the male dysthymics the correlation
is + 0·11, and for the female dysthymics it is + 0·14. These
correlations suggest a conclusion identical with that set out above;
here are no consistent differences between the hysterics and the
dysthymics, but the males are slightly more colour-reactive than
are the females. Again, this difference is far from significant.

As regards the "Ring" test, the male hysterics show 9 colour
reactors, the female hysterics 10; the male dysthymics have 11
colour reactors, the female dysthymics 8. Both hysterics and
dysthymics thus contain 38% of colour reactors; there is no
evidence here of any difference between the two groups. Again,
the males are slightly more colour-reactive; 20 of the men and
18 of the women belong to this category. This difference is, of
course, not significant. In view of the congruent results obtained
from these three experiments, we may conclude that hysterics
are not markedly different from dysthymics with respect to their
colour attitude, but that possibly men tend to be more colour-
reactive than women.

Certain comparison figures are available for the "Ring" test
from Lindberg's researches in which the same test was used
(1938). It will be remembered that in our work altogether 38%
of 100 neurotics were colour-reactive on this test; this is considerably above Lindberg's norm for normal adults. He finds 26%
of normal males, and 16% of normal females to be colour-
reactive (n = 218); on the average, 22% of his normals were
colour reactive. This figure is significantly lower than our own,
and suggests that *neurotics tend to be more colour-reactive than normals.*
This conclusion would fit in well with Rorschach's view of

"colour-shock" (1942). However, in view of the differen
nationality of the comparison groups, and possible differences in
social status and intelligence this finding cannot be regarded a
more than suggestive; a separate research would be needed in
order to establish it. It is interesting to note, however, that in
Lindberg's work he found 62 schizophrenic patients to contain
29% of colour reactors, i.e. a larger percentage than his norma
control group, and that he found the percentage of colour
reactors among the school children he tested to decrease with
advancing age, from 74% among the 7-year olds, through 66%
(8 years), 53% (9 years), 50% (10 years), 45% (11 years) down
to 36% for the 12-, 13-, and 14-year olds. It will also have been
noticed that he also found men more colour-reactive than women
the Critical Ratio being 1·8 for his figures.

One interesting question raised by the results of our work
relates to the well-known Freudian concept of *regression*. If
it be true that neurosis and psychosis constitute some form of
libidinal regression, one would expect this regression to show
itself experimentally in a variety of temperamental tests where the
age factor is important. Thus, for instance, Hull (1933) has
shown that during childhood primary suggestibility decreases
with increasing age, and our own figures have shown that this
trend continues even in adolescence and early adulthood. Now
libidinal regression to an infantile level, if it were a relatively
generalized phenomenon, would be expected to produce increased suggestibility as a concomitant; this, of course, is precisely
what we do find. Similarly, if colour-reactivity is found to decrease
with increasing age, then we would expect the neurotic who has
regressed to an earlier level, to show greater colour-reactivity
as compared with normal adults of equal age. Again, this is
what we actually find. Here, then, we may have an important
experimental method which may enable us to investigate this
highly speculative realm of Freudian psychopathology.[1]

At present, of course, this cannot be more than a suggestion;
there is as yet no proof that we are not dealing with an unsound
analogy which may be disproved by further research. If our
suggestion could be placed on a firmer footing, it should be
possible to develop a series of tests to measure "depth of regres-

[1] A discussion of the different meanings attaching to the term "regression" is
given by Hollingworth (1931).

ion", and to subject to objective study Freud's views regarding "depth of regression" as determining the type of mental disease.

## 6. SENSE OF HUMOUR

So far we have been dealing with tests of appreciation which are perceptual in the main. However, similar methods to those discussed may also be used in other spheres. Sense of humour for instance, is a personality trait which it should be possible to investigate in this manner, and indeed some very suggestive results have been obtained, both for normal and for neurotic subjects.

It is generally agreed, among psychologists as well as among laymen, that "sense of humour" is an important and valuable personality trait. It has been equated with "insight" (Allport, 1938), and it has been made into a fundamental philosophical "Lebensgefühl" (Hoffding, 1918); it has been ascribed to various nations (Egner, 1932) and races (Kadner, 1939) in varying proportions, usually determined by the nationality or race of the writer; it has been used as an aid in classifying and diagnosing mental illness (Coriat, 1939; Elste, 1940; Haggard, 1942; Mayer-Gross, 1921; Rebatel, 1908; Senise, 1941); it has been correlated with personality and temperament (Gregg, 1929; Kambouro-poulou, 1926, 1930; Landis, 1933; Omwake, 1937), as well as with scholastic aptitude, emotional maturity, height, and weight (Stump, 1939). Yet in spite of these manifold uses of the term, scientific measurement of the trait, and its theoretical analysis, have lagged seriously behind.

Before we can attempt to measure a trait of this kind, we must have at least some idea of precisely what it is we are attempting to measure. As regards "sense of humour", there are quite clearly at least two factors involved: appreciation and production. We say a person has a good sense of humour because he laughs in the right places (i.e. when we laugh); this meaning would be covered by the term "appreciation". We also say a person has a good sense of humour because he makes others laugh; this meaning of the term would involve "production". In our work we have restricted ourselves to appreciation; attempts have been made to study production too by having subjects supply captions to cartoons, or endings to unfinished jokes, but this aspect of our work has not yielded definite enough results to warrant inclusion here. Of great importance in this field of production of humorous material has been the work of Claparède (1934) and Harrower (1932). Even when we restrict ourselves to appreciation, we find little guidance from the professed experts in the field. Philosophers and psychologists who have worked out theories of humour do not show much agreement.

When we look more closely at the best-known theories of humour and laughter, however, we do discern three main trends running through them. The three principal theories in this field stress respectively the cognitive, the conative, or the affective aspect of humour and laughter. Most numerous of all are those theories which stress cognitive elements such as incongruity, contrast between ideas, deceived ideational expectation, and the like. The long list of writers who have held such theories contains among others the names of Cicero, Quintilian, Dryden, Locke, Marmontel, Gerard, Campbell, Beattie, Priestley, Kant, Jean Paul (Richter), Hazlitt, Brown, Schopenhauer, Everett, and those who, following Spencer, introduced the added requirement that the incongruity should be descending—Lipps, Sidis, Marshall, and Renouvier and Pratt. Willmann (1940) may be quoted as a modern champion of some form of cognitive theory, and so may Maier (1932).

Almost equally numerous is another group of writers who stress the conative aspect of laughter, relating it to the satisfaction of the desire for superiority, or "self-glory" as Hobbes has it. In this class are, for instance, Plato, Aristotle, Trissino, Hobbes, Hegel, Lamenais, Hunt, Bain, Philbert, Michiels, Carus, and Bergson. Chandler (1902) and Kimmins (1932) have provided a certain amount of experimental proof in favour of this theory, which finds its latest champion in Ludovici (1932). Following Wrench (1908), Ludovici has suggested the term "superior adaptation" as characteristic of all instances of laughter, such laughter in his view being due to the consciousness of superior adaptation on the part of the person laughing.

The affective aspect of laughter and humour is stressed by those who have directed their attention more to its emotional components. This is usually conceived to be pure joy, or else joy in combination with some other emotion, such as fear or anger. Alternatively, a contrast of feeling is posited as being essential to laughter. Joubert, Descartes, Hartley, Laprade, Dumont, Höffding, and McDougall may be mentioned here. Occasionally, writers such as Ribot, Sully, and Santayana have advanced theories which recognize two of the aspects of humour; Freud (1916) may even be said to have recognized all three aspects to some extent. His definition of wit as being due to an economy of expenditure of inhibition stresses the conative aspect, his definition of the comic as being due to an economy of thought stresses the cognitive aspect, and his definition of humour as being due to an economy of feeling stresses the affective aspect. His theory is vitiated, as Eastman (1921) points out, by his uncritical acceptance of the mechanical Spencer-Lipps theory of "economy", which is really foreign to the remainder of his views.

The eclectic theory here advanced may be represented by a triangle, as in Figure 21. Using "joke" as a generic term for all items, occurrences, and ideas which may be called humorous, we see that each joke is determined by all three elements, i.e. the cognitive, the affective, and the conative. In any particular case, the influence of one of these elements may be stronger than that of the others, in which case the position of the "joke" in the triangle would be close to the corner representing the preponderant ingredient. In general, the affective element may be called "humour", the conative "wit", and the cognitive "comic"; while these terms are far from perfect, they do give some indication of which of the three components they are intended to represent. It will be seen that in the triangle, the affective and the conative aspects are closer together than either of them is to the cognitive aspect; the reason for this lies in the fact that the two orectic aspects of the mind appear to interact more definitely and more obviously than either of them does with the cognitive aspect.

An analysis can be undertaken of the elements entering into the cognitive aspect of humour by studying jokes ranked high by a representative sample of subjects, as opposed to jokes ranked low. When this was done (Eysenck, 1942), it was found that on the cognitive side, *laughter results from the sudden, insightful integration of contradictory or incongruous ideas, attitudes, or sentiments which are experienced objectively.* Other things being equal, the funniness

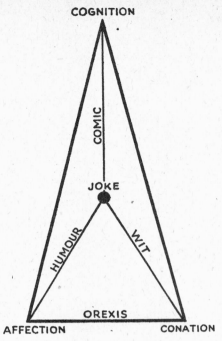

FIG. 21. DIAGRAM REPRESENTING THE STRUCTURE OF THE JOKE, SHOWING
THE THREE-FOLD DETERMINATION OF LAUGHTER BY COGNITIVE, CONATIVE,
AND AFFECTIVE FACTORS.

of a joke is a direct function of the degree of contradiction or incongruity between the main ideas, attitudes, or sentiments contained in it, and the quality of the integration of these elements, as measured by the suddenness of, and the degree of insight resulting from this integration.

Here, then, we would appear to have a trait which should reveal with particular clarity our factor of "conformity", and which should also give rise to interesting and important type differences. Investigations involving altogether 250 humorous items, such as jokes, cartoons, limericks, verses, and so forth, which were ranked by over 100 unselected normal subjects, both male and female, disclosed a surprisingly small amount of agreement on the goodness or otherwise of these items. The average intercorrelations between persons taking part in these investigations ranged from + 0·10 to + 0·15; in other words, there was hardly any agreement at all (Eysenck, 1942, 1943). And even worse, when the scores of 100 persons on five different tests were correlated, these intercorrelations were throughout small and insignificant (Eysenck, 1943). It would appear, therefore, that the standard to which people are expected to conform is so uncertain that conformity ceases to be a useful concept here. Possibly a careful selection of jokes, using particularly good and particularly poor specimens, might give more promising results; further research is clearly needed.

It was found, however, that one characteristic reaction did emerge from all these tests, a reaction which remained relatively constant, and which gave rise to intercorrelations of between + 0·55 and + 0·57 in two separate experiments, involving 3 and 5 tests respectively (Eysenck, 1942, 1943). This reaction was the total amount of "fun" the persons concerned managed to get out of all the material presented. Thus a person who found many limericks funny tended to find many jokes, cartoons, and verses funny; similarly, the person who found few cartoons funny, in general did not enjoy the limericks, the jokes, or the verses either. This affective reaction does seem to constitute a genuine personality trait, and its correlation with other traits should prove of interest.

Thus, while the general factor of "conformity" yielded disappointing results on the whole, the examination of one of the orectic features of the appreciation of humour suggested that more positive results might be forthcoming in that sphere. Accordingly, factorial studies were undertaken in an effort to discover further evidence on this point, particularly with reference to type factors. The main outcome of this work appeared to be a bipolar factor contrasting persons who preferred rather simple, "funny", sex and aggressive jokes with persons who preferred more complex, "clever" jokes not dealing with sexual matters. In other words, one type of person consistently preferred more orectic jokes, another type of person consistently preferred more cognitive types of jokes. When correlations were run between results of an introversion-extraversion questionnaire and these "types", it was found that the extravert tended to prefer the orectic type of humour, while the introvert preferred the cognitive type (Eysenck, 1942). These results are in good agreement with

Q

the finding of Kambouropoulou (1930) that "the more extraverted subjects have a greater proportion of the superiority class among the items they find most amusing. Extraversion and preference for the superiority class of humorous items go together". In her terminology, "superiority" corresponds to our concept of "conative" humour or "wit".

Our conclusions are also in agreement with those of Sears (1934), who analysed jokes into two sets of factors: *schematic* (corresponding to our cognitive) and *thematic* (corresponding to our orectic). Thematic elements "constitute the meaningful human content, or plot, of the joke, and it is this which evokes the asocial or repressed needs: principally Aggression, Superiority, and Sex" (Murray, 1938). Sears selected jokes according to certain themes which released various commonly repressed tendencies: self-enhancement, degradation, sexual and anal. He found liking for jokes of these types highly correlated with repressed aggression, as estimated by members of the clinical staff.

In the study described below, an effort was made to trace connections between the various factors discussed above, and our two main neurotic disease-syndromes. The population tested consisted of 25 male and 25 female hysterics, and of 25 male and 25 female dysthymics. Each one of these 100 subjects was given 60 cartoons, in chance order, and asked to mark each as "very funny" (3 points), "funny" (2 points), "not at all funny" (1 point), or "don't understand" (marked "X" on the answer sheet). These cartoons were selected in the following way: 15 depicted strongly sexual scenes ("S" cartoons), 15 depicted scenes in which an officer or some aspect of the army, navy, or air-force, was made fun of ("A" cartoons), 10 depicted scenes depending for their humour on differences in social class ("C" cartoons), 10 cartoons were of the relatively meaningless kind where the joke consists in introducing an octopus into a bar, for instance ("M" cartoons), and 10 cartoons were picked at random to give an average sort of sample ("R" cartoons).

The results of this study are given in Table 27. It will be seen that for each of the five sub-groups of jokes, the male hysterics score more highly than the male dysthymics, and the female hysterics more highly than the female dysthymics. The average preference score for all 60 cartoons is $1 \cdot 87 \pm \cdot 19$ S.D. for the hysterics, and $1\cdot73 \pm \cdot28$ S.D. for the dysthymics. Both the difference in mean score and the difference in S.D. are significant at the P $= \cdot01$ level; we may, therefore, conclude that hysterics like cartoons such as appear daily in our humorous papers significantly better than do dysthymics, and that, as so often before, here also the hysterics show less interpersonal variation than do dysthymics.

While the hysterics are superior to the dysthymics in their preference scores for each of the five categories, this superiority is most strikingly evident with respect to the 15 "S" cartoons. Here, the difference between the scores of hysterics and dysthymics is over fifteen times as great as in the other categories. This is true for both men and women; consequently, we may conclude that our analysis fully bears out the theory suggested by our previous work, namely that *extraversion (hysteria) correlates with preference for the sexual kind of humour.* The second-strongest difference between hysterics and anxiety states is found with reference to the "A" cartoons, which come nearest as a class to the "superiority" type of humour mentioned by Kambouropoulou (1926, 1930); this fact also is in accordance with our theory.

Sex differences are much less clearly marked than are temperamental differences; on the average, male patients have a score of $1\cdot77$, while female patients have a score of $1\cdot83$. The difference, $\cdot06$, is insignificant, and less than half the difference observed between hysterics and dysthymics, $\cdot14$. It should be noted, however, that while for "A" cartoons, "M" cartoons, "C" cartoons, and "R" cartoons, women have consistently higher scores, both for hysterics and for dysthymics, men show markedly higher preference for "S" cartoons than do women. This finding is intelligible enough in terms of one's every-day experience; while sex-jokes are not entirely the prerogative of men, women do not seem to enjoy them overtly to quite the same extent.

Taking all the groups of patients together, we find that on the average the "A" cartoons are liked best, followed by the "R" cartoons, the "C" cartoons, the "S" cartoons, and last of all the "M" cartoons. The differences between adjacent groups are throughout small and insignificant statistically; differences between the "A" cartoons and the "M" cartoons are significant, however. It would be of great interest to know if this special liking for cartoons dealing with the army would be found in civilians of similar intelligence, background, and age; no data are available, unfortunately, on this point. The theory that here we are dealing with some form of aggressive action camouflaged by the socially accepted form of the joke appears tempting.

TABLE TWENTY-SEVEN

| Joke Category. | Male: H. | Male: D. | Female: H. | Female: D. |
|---|---|---|---|---|
| Random selection. | 1·85 | 1·81 | 1·94 | 1·87 |
| Meaningless jokes | 1·64 | 1·60 | 1·69 | 1·68 |
| Social class | 1·71 | 1·69 | 1·93 | 1·80 |
| Army | 1·88 | 1·78 | 2·06 | 1·97 |
| Sex | 2·05 | 1·58 | 1·82 | 1·51 |
| Average . | 1·85 | 1·69 | 1·90 | 1·76 |

An interesting confirmation of our finding that liking for *cognitive* types of humour goes with an *introverted* temperament, while liking for *oretic* types of humour goes with an *extraverted* temperament, comes from the unpublished work of J. M. Williams on humour in children. [1] She used three different humour tests— pictures, pictures with captions, and verbal jokes—which were based on the contributions of some 300 children who were asked (1) to give an account of their funniest experience, (2) to bring a picture which they thought very funny, and (3) to write out the funniest joke they had heard or read. Each of the three tests as finally used consisted of thirty items which had to be ranked in order of funniness.

A special investigation was then carried out on 12 children (6 boys and 6 girls), whose temperament was investigated intensively by means of teachers' ratings and the Rorschach test. Intelligence tests were also used. In the first instance, the rankings of these children for the items in each of the three tests were intercorrelated, and the tables of correlations factor-analyzed. From each table, two factors were extracted. The first factor was positive throughout in each case, and contributed 16%, 18%, and 36% respectively to the variance. The second factor was bipolar in each case, and contributed 10%, 8% and 5% respectively to the variance.

[1] Williams, J. M. An experimental and theoretical study of humour in children. Thesis, Univ. of London, 1945.

The intercorrelations of the factor saturations for the three tests bring out the same points emphasized in connection with our own experiment. (These correlations were carried out by the writer on data kindly supplied by Mrs. Williams.) The first factor saturations show only insignificant intercorrelations, two of them being actually negative; the average of the three correlations is $-0.21$. Intercorrelations of the second factor saturations, however, reveal a different picture. All three correlations are positive; in order of enumeration, they are $+0.38$, $+0.67$, and $+0.62$. We may, therefore, conclude that in children, as in adults, there is no general factor running through different tests of humour; there is, however, some general principle of choice dividing the subjects into two groups which retain their identity from test to test.

The nature of this general principle was determined by reference to the items most clearly differentiating the two groups of subjects, and by reference to the introspections of the subjects. To quote Mrs. Williams, the one group of children "almost always picked out the joke or picture that, in their view at any rate, showed up the foolishness of other people, and jokes deflating authority were popular with them". "Another characteristic of this group was that they very rarely saw a joke apart from their own lives. It was these children who often twisted the joke to give it a meaning of their own."

The other group of children tended to choose the jokes and pictures showing "humour of incongruity and the fantastic"; in general, these children showed "an approach to humour (which) was generally impersonal", and they also "showed a marked ability to judge the humour situation as a whole". It is clear from the descriptions given by Williams, and by the introspections quoted, that the humour which characterizes her first group of children is of the kind called "orectic" by us, while that which characterizes her second group is of the kind called "cognitive" by us. Williams herself partly recognizes this similarity, but prefers to seek the main distinguishing mark between the two groups in the "personal" attitude of the first group, as contrasted with the "impersonal" attitude of the second.

On the basis of our own work, we would expect Williams' "personal" type to be temperamentally extraverted, and her "impersonal" type to be temperamentally introverted. In actual fact, she does find a close correspondence of temperament and humour type in the predicted direction. To quote again, "there is here a fairly close correspondence between introversion and impersonality in attitude to humour appreciation and between extraversion and the 'personal' attitude to humour".

When it is borne in mind that Williams' study was carried out on subjects differing widely from those used in our own experiments, and that her investigation and our own proceeded along completely independent lines, the close agreement in the conclusions reached makes us hopeful that our results represent, at least, a first approximation to the correct solution of the problem of "sense of humour".

## 7.   EXPRESSION TESTS: MOSAIC CONSTRUCTION AND GRAPHOLOGY

As was pointed out in the section on "Sense of Humour", appreciation, which is essentially passive, finds a counterpart in production or expression, which is creative.  And while our work on "Sense of Humour" has not progressed far enough in the expressive sphere to be strictly quantifiable, tests of production or expression have been published and advertised in such profusion that an experimental examination of some of these, however superficial, is obviously desirable.  In the main, tests of expression are covered by the term "*projection*", the theory being that in these tests, which consist usually of unstructured material of one kind or another, the subject will "project" his own conflicts, difficulties and complexes onto the test material, and that later these conflicts, difficulties and complexes can be diagnosed from his productions.   Typical projection tests are the Rorschach test in its usual form, the Thematic Apperception test, the Mosaic test, any form of Drawing test which aims at temperamental analysis, Composition tests, and so on and so forth.

We prefer to use the term "expression" rather than the term "projection", both because it does not involve a theory tinged with psychoanalytic colour, and because it is more clearly descriptive of the kind of test included.  Thus it is doubtful if tests of expressive movement could properly be called "projective"; they clearly belong in the same class as drawing tests, however, and fall, of course, under the heading "expressive".

"Appreciation" and "expression" are rather closely related, and may blend one into the other; thus the little Chinese boy who chooses from the five systems of calligraphy the one which he prefers (appreciation) will thereafter try to mould his writing according to the precepts of this system (expression) (Chao, 1939). It is for this reason that both types of test are treated in one chapter.

Mostly, tests of expression are analysed by exclusively subjective methods, although attempts have been made to quantify results. Thus in one study of the Thematic Apperception Test, Balken and Mittelmann (1940) found when they had their patients write stories about the various pictures constituting the test that many differences became apparent between the hysterics, anxiety states, and obsessive-compulsives. They took the verb/adjective quotient to indicate dramatic action, and to express libidinal tension and anxiety; they used the fraction: statements· of possibility or probability over statements of impossibility or improbability (pro/con quotient) to indicate smooth narration, expressing superficial emotional equanimity; they considered the certainty/uncertainty quotient to express emotional or defensive positiveness of assertion; finally, they considered the use of qualifications to indicate doubt, hesitation, or self-criticism. Using these measures, which are largely objective, they found the following results for their three groups of patients:

TABLE TWENTY-EIGHT

| | HYSTERICS: (Conversion Hysteria). | DYSTHYMICS: (Anxiety State). | (Obsessive-Compulsive). |
|---|---|---|---|
| Verb/adjective quotient . . | 1·35 | 3·11 | 2·17 |
| Pro/con quotient . . . | 6·7 | 4·1 | 2·4 |
| Certainty/uncertainty quotient . | 3·56 | 1·83 | 0·67 |
| Qualifications . . . | 1·25 | 2·68 | 3·69 |

These results show the anxiety states and the obsessive-compulsive patients on the one hand opposed to the conversion hysterics on the other; thus they lend support to our "type" factor of dysthymia-hysteria. If the interpretation by the authors of the study be admitted, they would suggest that hysterics show less libidinal tension, and a greater superficial emotional equanimity; more positive self-assertion, and less doubt, hesita-

tion, and self-criticism. Whether such psychological interpretations of certain grammatical and semantic usages are
themselves well-founded, itself awaits experimental verification.

In tests of expression, then, we are faced with two problems.
In the first place, we must determine whether the claims of the
expert in the test to diagnose personality traits by means of his
subjective methods are justified, and to what extent they are
justified. In the second place, we must seek for objective criteria
which will correlate significantly with such traits as we may wish
to measure. Both these problems were investigated in relation
to the so-called Mosaic test.

This test, invented by Lowenfeld (no date), consists of a box
of wooden pieces which are standardized so that each of 5 shapes
is available in each of 6 colours. The collection of pieces consists
of 228 pieces altogether; the 5 shapes are as shown in Figure 22.
The 6 colours used are black, white, red, green, blue, and yellow.
In addition to these mosaic blocks, a wooden tray is used which
has a raised edge, and measures 13 inches by $10\frac{1}{2}$ inches.

The subject is seated in front of the tray, which is covered
by a white sheet of paper, and told to make something with the
blocks, which are shown to him in order to make him familiar
with the various shapes and colours. He is told he is quite free to
make anything he likes, to use any colours he likes, and to take
as long over it as he likes.

The finished pattern is either photographed in colour
(Diamond and Schmale, 1944), or more usually simply copied
from the original by the use of coloured pencils. The patterns
can be classified in various ways, such as concrete vs. abstract,
compact vs. scattered, successful vs. unsuccessful, and so forth.
It is claimed that certain relations hold between features of the
completed pattern and the personality of the person constructing
them. Among these claims are the following:

(1) In children and young people, the use of many black
pieces is associated with depression.

(2) Designs edged with projecting red pieces tend to be made
by excitable and impulsive people.

(3) Patterns occurring particularly in children and adults
suffering from emotional disturbances are edge designs, frame
designs, winged designs, arrow designs, and incoherent patterns.

Little has been written about this test, but such reports

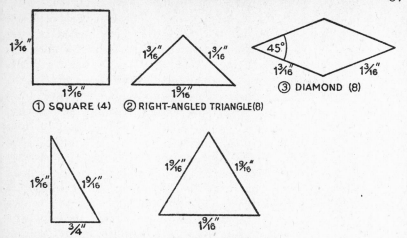

FIG. 22. THE LOWENFELD MOSAIC TEST: FIVE SHAPES USED. EACH SHAPE IS AVAILABLE IN SIX COLOURS: RUBY, EMERALD, SAPPHIRE, TOPAZ, BLACK AND WHITE. THE NUMBER OF PIECES OF EACH OF THE SHAPES AVAILABLE IN THE SIX COLOURS IS GIVEN IN BRACKETS AFTER THE NAME OF THE SHAPE.

as those of Wertham and Golden (1941), Diamond and Schmale (1944), and Kerr (1939) suggest that certain temperamental traits do express themselves in the construction of patterns and the choice of colours. Thus Diamond and Schmale found, for instance, a much greater insistence on colour-balance in the patterns of manic-depressive patients than in those of schizophrenics, and clearly this finding may be linked up with the defective colour appreciation of schizophrenics as demonstrated by Scholl (1927) and Lindberg (1938). Wertham and Golden found that by using 23 criteria of evaluation they were able to determine characteristic patterns for schizophrenics, manic depressives, mental defectives, and for those suffering from organic brain lesions. These criteria are analogous in many ways to Diamond and Schmale's single criterion of "completeness of the Gestalt of the patterns", which links this work with Bender's experiments on visual perception (1938). It would appear from these studies that those conditions in which personality structure is least disordered show the smallest degree of abnormality in the designs.

Two separate studies were carried out in an attempt to

validate this test. In the first, subjective evaluations were made by an expert in the use of this test (Miss Traill), and various matching experiments were undertaken. In the second, comparisons were made between different clinical groups regarding their use of colour, the prevalence of certain types of designs, and so forth. The matching experiments involved (1) matching by Miss Traill of mosaics and personality sketches of patients, written by the psychiatrist; (2) matching by the psychiatrist of personality sketches written by Miss Traill on the basis of the patients' mosaics with his clinical impression of the patient; (3) comparison on questionnaire answers given by the patients regarding themselves, and by Miss Traill from an inspection of the mosaics. The first two of these methods showed results significantly above chance, thus to some extent validating the test against psychiatric opinion; the third method led to negative results (Himmelweit and Eysenck, 1945). The success of the expert in matching was above chance, but not sufficiently so to suggest that this test without much further study could be of psychiatric usefulness.

Regarding the comparison of certain objective features in the patterns for different psychiatric groups, interest centres in the comparison of hysterics and dysthymics. 30 hysterics and 31 dysthymics produced two patterns each; also tested were 39 effort syndrome cases, the great majority of whom were dysthymics also. Altogether, 200 designs were thus available from 100 subjects.

No differences whatever were found in the use of colour; the percentages of the different colours used by the three groups are almost identical. This finding agrees well with our results from appreciation experiments that colour-attitude does not differentiate between hysterics and dysthymics.

Significant differences did appear, however, between the types of patterns produced by the various groups. Thus it was found that 60% of the patterns produced by dysthymics were compact, i.e. were constructed in such a way that all the elements of the design were fitted closely together, leaving no ·spaces between the pieces. 38% of the effort syndrome cases also produced compact designs, but only 27% of the hysterics did so. We may conclude that dysthymics tend to produce compact designs, while hysterics tend to produce scattered and intermediate designs. Another significant difference was found when designs were analysed with respect to concreteness or abstractness. 80% of the hysterics produced abstract designs, while only 63% of the dysthymics and 58% of the effort syndromes did so.

These results probably do not exhaust the number of objectively discoverable differences between dysthymics and hysterics on this test; however, no other differences were found by us in spite of many attempts to do so. To take but one example: The aesthetic quality of the mosaics was examined by six judges, whose rankings correlated to the extent of + 0·45 on the average, thus giving their average ranking a comparatively high validity (the correlation between the average ranking and the "true order" being + 0·91). The ability to create aesthetically beautiful designs was not correlated significantly with intelligence (r = −0·18 ± ·07), and did not differentiate between hysterics and dysthymics.

*Graphology.* A study similar to the one described above was carried out in connection with the analysis of handwriting (Eysenck, 1945; Marum, 1945).

The claims of graphologists that expressive movements as recorded through a person's handwriting can give us information regarding his character and temperament have been so insistent that psychologists have undertaken several experimental studies to investigate these claims. A review of such work as had been done to date was undertaken by Allport and Vernon (1933) in their "Studies in Expressive Movements"; more recent work has been summarized by the writer (Eysenck, 1945). These reviews show two things fairly clearly: whenever attempts are made to correlate specific "signs" in the handwriting and certain temperamental qualities, correlations are usually very low and insignificant. Whenever the graphologist is allowed to use more holistic methods of analysis, although still strictly controlled by the experimental design, then results which are well above chance usually emerge. Unfortunately, many of the more broadly-based experiments have not been sufficiently strictly controlled, and consequently the results have not been accepted universally; indeed the majority of psychologists are still rather hostile to the claims of graphology. This hostility has not been lessened by the exaggerated claims of many graphologists, who have tended to form a circle apart from the main stream of psychology, and who have consequently developed to a high degree the feelings and attitudes so often found in such circles.

In our own experiment, we attempted to fulfil two conditions which are difficult to reconcile. We tried to give the graphologist full scope to employ her art without any external restraints, and we tried to make the conditions of the experiment so stringent that any extra-chance success observed would not be explicable through experimental errors. Where these two claims came into conflict, the former was unhesitatingly sacrificed to the latter.

50 patients at the hospital were made to provide specimens of their handwriting, on uniform paper, and written in ink, by having them copy a personality questionnaire; they were also made to answer this questionnaire, which is given in full elsewhere (Eysenck, 1945). The answers were detached, and the copies of the questionnaire given to the graphologist as samples of the patients' handwriting. Apart from several tasks not relevant to our main point, she was asked (1) to answer the questionnaire for each patient as she thought, from his handwriting, he would have answered it, and (2) to match each patient's handwriting with a personality sketch written by the psychiatrist in charge of him. Thus her view of the patient's personality, entirely derived from his handwriting, was validated against the patient's self-description, and against the psychiatrist's rating.

Both these experiments showed results considerably above chance. By chance, 50% of the questionnaire answers of patient and graphologist should have agreed; in actual fact, 62% $\pm$ 1% agreed. Taking only those judgments on which the graphologist felt particularly sure, the number of agreements rises to 68% $\pm$ 3%. As these percentages are derived from altogether 1,350 comparisons, we feel that considerable confidence can be placed in the accuracy of these results. When it is remembered that the patients' answers to the questions may often have been false to fact, in other words, that the graphologist's opinion was being compared with a validating criterion itself far from perfect, then we must surely conclude that graphology does to some extent at least, succeed in correlating handwriting and personality traits.

The matchings of the handwritings and the psychiatrist's personality sketch were carried out in ten groups of five each.

By chance, one matching out of five ought to have been correct; as a matter of fact, 2·4 matchings were correct on the average. This figure is very significant statistically, and confirms our previous conclusion regarding the value of graphology. As a comparison we may cite the attempts of non-graphologists to match writings and sketches; the average success of twenty such matchings was 0·7, i.e. rather less than chance would allow.

No positive findings resulted from the attempts of the graphologist to judge the patients' intelligence from their handwritings; it was found, however, that those patients whose intelligence she succeeded in judging correctly were also the patients whose temperament she had judged correctly in relation to the questionnaire and the psychiatrists' rating experiment. Consequently, it would appear that some persons' handwritings are more easily interpreted than others'; this is an important point which should be followed up by suitable experiments.

The actual handwriting-symptoms on which the graphologist based her interpretations are discussed at length elsewhere (Marum, 1945), on the basis of a number of selected samples. Here, perhaps, we may give just a summary of the main points.

(1) *Depression:* Falling or fluctuating lines; very heavy or particularly thin, timid and irregular pressure; slanting to the left; small letters; diminished height of capital letters; corrections; slow writing.

(2) *Anxiety:* Narrow distances between words, and between lines; words end abruptly; writing is small and slow; pressure either heavy or irregular; slant and flourishes may be to the left.

(3) *Hysteria:* Irregularity of height, width and slant; fluctuation of lines; indistinct, mixed ligatures. Occasionally, grotesque slant to the left; exaggerated flourishes; heavy pressure; covering strokes; irregular connectedness and lack of proportion in the accentuation of some letters, particularly initials.

Clearly, the fact that the graphologist's judgments ostensibly based on these characteristics were successful above the chance level does not prove by itself that any connection actually exists between the graphological sign and the psychological trait. It was planned to furnish such direct proof by correlational analyses and objective measurement; the tragic death of Dr. Marum in a Flying Bomb incident prevented the completion of this project. Her co-operative and scientific attitude in this field where neither is the rule made her irreplaceable, and we must leave the subject, conscious that the work of relating handwriting to our personality dimensions has not advanced beyond the first preliminary steps.

## 8. Summary

The theory that both in the appreciation of art and in expression through artistic creation certain personality traits are manifested has frequently been put forward, but largely without any experimental backing. Various tests were developed and used in an effort to provide empirical evidence on this point.

Our work was based on an experimental analysis of preference judgments which isolated four groups of factors: (1) A general factor of agreement or conformity, (2) a group factor, opposing preference for certain types of art to preferences for certain other types, (3) factors specific to each subject, and (4) error factors.

On the basis of the "conformity" factor, an objective group version of the Rorschach test, similar to the Harrower-Erickson test, was developed. This test was shown to discriminate well between neurotics and normals, and also between the more seriously ill and the less seriously ill neurotics.

With respect to the group factor, it was found that hysterics tended to prefer paintings different from those preferred by dysthymics; the kind of painting preferred by these two types of neurotics respectively had previously been shown to differentiate between non-neurotic introverts and extraverts.

The colour/form reactivity of neurotics was studied by means of three different tests. No differences were found between hysterics and dysthymics, but as compared with a normal sample the neurotics appeared to be definitely more colour-reactive.

An extension was made of the four-factor theory of aesthetics to sense of humour, and it was shown that hysterics differ from dysthymics on various points. The latter professed to feel less amusement on all kinds of jokes, and this difference in the appreciation of humour was particularly striking with respect to sex jokes. These results also found their counterpart in work with non-neurotic extraverts and introverts.

Two tests of expression were used, the Mosaic test and a Graphology (handwriting) test. On both these tests, reliable differences were observed between contrasted groups of neurotics. Thus, for instance, dysthymics were found to produce "compact" mosaic patterns, while the hysterics tended to produce rather "scattered" designs. These results argued in favour of the general use of "expression" methods, but the accuracy of prediction of these tests, in the present state of development, was not considered sufficient for any practical use to be made of them.

# CHAPTER SEVEN

# SYNTHESIS AND CONCLUSIONS

IN THIS last chapter, an attempt will be made to take stock of the position reached, to relate the dimensions of personality isolated to other "typological" descriptions, and to answer certain criticisms which are likely to be put forward. We will take the opportunity also to give an interpretation of the purely factual results reported so far, and to relate this interpretation to the conceptual framework outlined in the first chapter.

Starting from the position that measurement in the field of personality is impossible until the dimensions along which such measurement can take place are known, a large-scale factorial study was carried out on a variety of personality traits whose presence or absence in 700 male neurotic soldiers was recorded by the psychiatrist in charge of the case. This study resulted in the discovery of two main factors, both of which bore a close relation to similar factors previously discovered in normal subjects by numerous investigators. Subject to various reservations noted at the time, these factors were labelled "neuroticism" and "extraversion-introversion".

Having isolated these factors, which appeared to indicate two dimensions of personality along which measurement might fruitfully be undertaken, an effort was made to discover objective tests which would make possible such measurement, and which would at the same time give empirical support to the essential correctness of the original subjective determination of the factors. In this way it was hoped, (a) that it might be possible to construct a battery of tests for each of the two dimensions isolated, and (b) that the tests useful in measuring neuroticism and introversion would throw some light on the nature of these factors.

A comparatively large number of tests was found to be discriminative in this connection; almost equally important, however, was the fact that certain other tests failed to give such positive results. As will be shown presently, both negative and

244

## TABLE TWENTY-NINE

| | Introversion. | Extraversion. |
|---|---|---|
| Clinical syndrome | Anxiety, depression. Autonomic dysfunction. | Hysterical conversion. |
| Personality traits | Irritability, apathy, obsessional tendencies. | Little energy, narrow interests, hypochondriasis. |
| Self assessments | Feelings easily hurt, keeps in background on social occasions, moody, daydreams, self-conscious, nervous, inferiority feelings. | Accident-prone, troubled by stammer or stutter, off work through illness, disgruntled, aches and pains. |
| Constitution | Physique: Leptomorph. Effort response: poor. (high oxygen uptake (high lactate level (high pulse rate High choline esterase. Salivary secretion inhibited. | Physique: Eurymorph. Effort response: good. low oxygen uptake) low lactate level) low pulse rate) Low choline esterase. Salivary secretion non-inhibited. |
| Intellectual functions | High intelligence. Intell./vocab. ratio low. | Low intelligence. Intell./vocab. ratio high. |
| Persistence | Good. | Bad. |
| Speed/accuracy ratio | Low. | High. |
| Performance on "Tweezers" test | Good. | Bad. |
| Level of aspiration | High. | Low. |
| Past performance | Underrated. | Overrated. |
| Rigidity | High. | Low. |
| Inter-personal variability. | High. | Low. |
| Intra-personal variability. | Low. | High. |
| Aesthetic preferences. | Distinctive. | Distinctive. |
| Mosaic construction. | Compact design. Concrete design. | Scattered design. Abstract design. |
| Sense of humour | Does not appreciate jokes. Dislikes sex jokes particularly. | Does appreciate jokes. Likes sex jokes particularly. |
| Graphology | Special type of handwriting. | Special type of handwriting. |

positive results are useful in suggesting heuristic hypotheses regarding the nature of the factors we are dealing with.

In Tables 29 and 32 are set out, in synoptic form, the main differences which were found between persons at opposite ends of the respective dimensions. These tables will be useful in giving a comprehensive summary of our findings in brief space; there are certain dangers in putting our findings in this form, however, which must be borne in mind. In the first place, the terms used in the table (suggestibility, persistence, intelligence, rigidity) are not used in a popular sense; they are operationally defined, and have reference to exact, quantitative variables.

R

It is only in this precise sense that they ought to be understood; there is no intention to enlarge our findings beyond this limitation. In the second place, our results are restricted to the kind of population with which we have been dealing, that is to say, neurotic service personnel. While we consider it likely that similar differences would be found with other types of population, and while we have throughout the book drawn attention to parallels from experimentation with normal subjects, definite proof that we are justified in extending our results in this way is lacking. In the third place, a table of the kind presented suggests a dichotomous, bimodal differentiation between the extremes; as has been explained at length in the introductory chapter, our own view of the "types" isolated is not founded on any consideration of unimodal or bimodal distribution, but rather on the intercorrelations between different ratings, tests, etc. Consequently, the items in the list should be taken as personality characteristics which show a certain tendency to cohere together; nothing is implied with respect to the actual distribution of the traits measured in the population.

With all these reservations in mind, we offer first of all the synoptic table embodying the data relating to the extravert-introvert dichotomy. An attempt has been made to group the data (Clinical syndrome, self-assessments, constitution, etc.), but this grouping is only a matter of convenience. It will be appreciated that although the statements in the table are categorical, they should be understood as being essentially relative; when we say that "introverts show good persistence", we mean that "introverts are more persistent than extraverts".

Putting the results given in this table into a descriptive paragraph, we find that (neurotic) introverts show a tendency to develop anxiety and depression symptoms, that they are characterized by obsessional tendencies, irritability, apathy, and that they suffer from a lability of the autonomic system. According to their own statement, their feelings are easily hurt, they are self-conscious, nervous, given to feelings of inferiority, moody, day-dream easily, keep in the background on social occasions, and suffer from sleeplessness. In their body-build vertical growth predominates over horizontal growth; their effort response is poor, and their choline esterase activity is high. Salivary secretion is inhibited. Their intelligence is comparatively high, their vocabulary excellent, and they tend to be persistent. They are generally accurate, but slow; they excel at finicking work (Tweezers test). Their level of aspiration is unduly high, but they tend to under-rate their own performance. Withal, they are rather rigid, and show little intrapersonal variability. Their aesthetic preferences are towards the quiet, old-fashioned type of picture. In aesthetic creation, they produce compact designs, often having a concrete subject. They do not appreciate jokes very much, and sex jokes in particular are not much favoured. Their handwriting is distinctive.

In comparison, (neurotic) extraverts show a tendency to develop hysterical conversion symptoms, and a hysterical attitude to their symptoms. Furthermore, they show little energy, narrow interests, have a bad work-history, and are hypochondriacal. According to their own statement, they are troubled by stammer or stutter, are accident prone, frequently off work through illness, disgruntled, and troubled by aches and pains. In their body-build, horizontal growth predominates over vertical growth; their effort response is quite good, and their choline esterase activity low. Salivary secretion is not inhibited. Their intelligence is comparatively low, their vocabulary poor, and they show extreme lack of persistence. They tend to be quick but inaccurate; they are bad at finicking work (Tweezers test). Their level of aspiration is low, but they tend to over-rate their own perform-ance. They are not very rigid, and show great intrapersonal variability. Their aesthetic preferences are towards the colourful, modern type of picture. In aesthetic creation, they produce scattered designs, often having abstract subjects. They appreciate jokes, and are particularly fond of sex jokes. Their handwriting is distinctive.

In contrasting these two descriptions, one is almost inevitably reminded of the Freudian trilogy of id, ego, and super-ego. In the conflict between id and super-ego, it would appear that in the extravert (hysteric) the id had achieved a superior position, while in the introvert (dysthymic) the super-ego had gained the upper hand. While it is quite possible that this comparison is nothing more than a picturesque but inaccurate analogy, it may be worth while to point out briefly on what basis such an analogy could be drawn.

In the first place, the attitude to work is obviously different for these two types. The hysteric has a bad work history, a low level of aspiration, is apt to over-rate his performance, is slapdash (quick but inaccurate), and lacks persistence. The dysthymic has a good work history, a high level of aspiration, is apt to under-rate his performance, is thorough (slow but accurate), and very persistent. Now the qualities which characterize the dysthymic are precisely the "socialized" qualities which one would expect to be favoured by the super-ego, while the qualities which characterize the hysteric are the immediate pleasure-producing qualities which in Freud's teaching are associated with the id.

In the second place, greater structural rigidity is usually associated with super-ego dominance, and such rigidity is found both in the reactions of dysthymics to success and failure experiences, as also in their tendency to produce compact designs in the mosaic test. On the other hand, the hysterics show less rigidity, and favour scattered designs.

In the third place, the attitude of hysterics and dysthymics to sex jokes is highly revealing. In terms of the Freudian theory, the id would be expected to rate this type of humour very high, while the super-ego would be expected to repress rigorously the enjoyment of this type of material.

Whatever may be thought of this interpretation, the inadequacies of which can be obvious to no one more than to the author, it seems fairly clear that the dysthymic represents the more socialized, inhibited type of neurotic, while the hysteric appears as a more asocial, uninhibited type. Beyond this we can hardly go without losing the firm ground from under our feet.

We must now face a question which is of great importance, and which may have troubled the reader already. In Table 1, we have shown that "Introversion" has in the past been identified both with "schizoid" personality and with "psychasthenia"; similarly, "Extraversion" has been identified both with "syntonic" or "cycloid" personality, and with "hysteria". What, then, is the relation of our extravert-introvert dichotomy to the schizoid-cycloid scale?

Jung, who speaks of an essential relation between schizophrenia and psychasthenia, would presumably maintain that both the schemes of classification mentioned stress the same underlying differences. Those who believe in the essential identity of the affective states, both in their "neurotic" and their "psychotic" form, would deny any underlying similarity between the two schemes, and would point out that in the one the affective states are presented as "introverts", while in the other they appear as "extraverts".

Three answers to the general question of the relation between the two schemes of classification appear possible. We may assume identity, we may assume that the schemes refer to quite different and distinct dimensions of personality, or we may assume that we have to do with three main reaction-types, the hysteric, the affective (dysthymic), and the schizoid, only two of which appear in our study because of selection of subjects and tests.

Unfortunately, our experimental data do not allow us to answer the questions raised in any definitive sense. We may, however, quote certain findings in support of the view that identity between the hysteric-dysthymic and the schizoid-cycloid dimensions cannot be assumed. The argument rests on three main points, relating to the colour-form reaction test, the reversal of perspective test, and the investigations of physique.

From a variety of studies already quoted, it appears that cycloid personalities are colour-reactive, while schizoid personalities are form-reactive. This conclusion is well authenticated, and such studies as the mosaic construction test in its application to schizophrene and manic-depressive patients bear it out in the expressive as well as in the appreciative aspect.

On the other hand, three distinct studies with appreciation tests, and one study with the Mosaic expression test, failed entirely to show any differences between hysterics and dysthymics in this field. We may, therefore, state with considerable confidence that with respect to this type of reaction at least, the two dimensions under consideration fail to show any degree of identity.

With regard to the reversal of perspective test, we have found that hysterics and dysthymics are not differentiated by their scores on this test, while similar studies with schizophrenes and manic-depressives have shown that these two types of patients react very differently to the test. This finding would appear to show an important difference between the two dichotomies, and makes it difficult to accept any argument regarding their identity.

Lastly, it is well-known that there is a distinct tendency for schizophrenes to be leptomorph, and for manic-depressives to be eurymorph. In our work, the dysthymics were found to be leptomorph, while the hysterics tended to have eurymorph body-build. This result makes it very difficult to equate the manic-depressive and the dysthymic ends of the two scales, seeing that the body-types of these groups are exactly opposed to each other.

The argument outlined above is not conclusive, but it suggests that there are certain difficulties in maintaining the "identity" view regarding the two schemes of classification. As this view had also been attacked from the psychiatric stand point (Bowlby, 1940), we believe that we are justified in turning our attention to the other two possibilities mentioned above.

The choice between these two alternatives depends, of course, on one's standpoint with respect to the debate on the "qualitative difference" alleged to exist between neurotic and psychotic "affective states", and on the wider question of the differences between psychoses and neuroses generally. Those who believe in the essential dissimilarity between "anxiety states" and "reactive depressions" on the one hand, and "endogenous depressions" and "manic depressive illness" on the other, will find no difficulty in assuming that the schizoid-cycloid dichotomy forms a third dimension of personality, essentially unrelated to the two dimensions discussed in this book.

Those who refuse to acknowledge any such qualitative difference would presumably choose the third alternative, and consider the "schizoid" reaction type as a third, additional corner of a triangle the two other corners of which are marked "hysteric" and "affective". We have already discussed at some length the various possibilities, and the arguments advanced in favour of these various views, and shall not repeat this discussion here.

In the absence of any experimental evidence on the point, we find it impossible to choose between these conflicting views. We should like to point out, however, that an experimental solution to this problem is by no means impossible. If a battery of tests could be found which distinguished reliably between "reactive" and "endogenous" depressions, or between "neurotics" and "psychotics", presumably the difference in opinion could be settled amicably by reference to the kind of distribution of scores on this battery given by an unselected sample of "mentally ill" people.

Similarly, a direct answer to the question of the identity of the schizoid-cycloid and the hysteric-dysthymic dimensions could be obtained by testing representative samples of schizoid and cycloid personalities with the battery of tests used in our work; if the cycloids behaved in a manner similar to the dysthymics, while the schizoids behaved in a manner similar to the hysterics, then clearly the two classifications would seem to stress the same dichotomy. If, however, the tests which are discriminative in one dichotomy failed to be discriminative in the other, in a manner similar to the colour-form test, or the reversal of perspective test, then identity would be definitely disproved. Such developments, however, lie in the future, and we must end our discussion of this important question on a note of uncertainty.

One further point may be relevant here. In our work, we found repeatedly that the dysthymic groups showed higher Standard Deviations than did the hysteric groups. This was as true of the psychological tests, such as the Level of Aspiration tests, as it was of the physiological tests, such as the tests of effort response. Several explanations suggest themselves. In the first place, this obvious lack of homogeneity in the dysthymic group as compared with the hysteric group may be due to difficulties in diagnosis; accurate diagnosis of a conversion hysteria may be simpler than an accurate diagnosis of an anxiety state. In the second place, it is possible that the dysthymic group contains several distinct sub-groups which could be distinguished by further investigation, while the hysteric group does not contain such sub-groups. In the third place, the possibility cannot be ruled out that among the patients genuinely belonging to the dysthymic classification, several endogenous depressions may have been included. If this were so, and if endogenous and reactive depressions could be shown to differ significantly with respect to their reactions to psychological tests of the kind used, then the larger S.D.s of the dysthymics would find an obvious explanation. In the absence of such proof, we cannot answer the question raised, but must leave it to the reader to decide which explanation appears the most reasonable in the circumstances.

We may now turn to the general factor of neuroticism. In the course of the book, a number of tests have been described which showed considerable differences between normal and neurotic groups, and between neurotic groups of different degrees of severity of illness. On four of these tests sufficient data have been accumulated to evaluate their discriminatory usefulness, and to compare their efficiency. The four tests used for this comparison are the suggestibility test, the dark vision test, the ranking (Rorschach) test, and the questionnaire. These tests had all been given to numbers of normal and neurotic subjects, and, therefore, could be compared with one another in terms of their ability to discriminate between these two groups. The hospital groups used in these comparisons were all unselected, and consequently very similar and homogeneous; the normal groups have been characterized in previous chapters, and may be considered as a rather more heterogeneous population, probably slightly above average with respect to intelligence and stability.

Comparison was effected by means of two different formulae. In the first place, an Index of Screening Efficiency (S) was elaborated, on the basis of the coefficient of correlation for point distributions (Eysenck, 1945). While this Index, like every other Index, makes certain assumptions regarding the distribution of the underlying traits which are being measured, and while these assumptions cannot be shown with certainty to apply, we believe that for a comparison such as the present no serious distortion will be introduced by its use. The formula for the Index is as follows:

$$\text{Index of Screening Efficiency (S)} = \frac{a\delta - \beta\gamma}{\sqrt{p_n \, p \, q_n \, q}}$$

in which  $a$ = percentage of neurotics with neurotic scores,
$\beta$ = percentage of normals with neurotic scores,
$\gamma$ = percentage of neurotics with normal scores,
$\delta$ = percentage of normals with normal scores,
$p_n$ = percentage of neurotic scores,
$p$ = percentage of normal scores,
$q_n$ = percentage of neurotics,
$q$ = percentage of normals.

Also used was the so-called Selection Index (D) elaborated by Hunt et al. (1944). The formula for this index is:

$$\text{Selection Index (D)} = \frac{P}{P + P_m + P_f}$$

in which  $P$ = proportion of neurotics with neurotic scores,
$P_m$ = proportion of neurotics with normal scores,
$P_f$ = proportion of normals with neurotic scores.

For the purpose of this Index, the critical level (i.e. the point at which the continuous scoring range is divided into a "neurotic" and a "normal" part), was set at a point where 75% of the neurotic scores fell into the "neurotic" range, and 25% fell into the "normal" range.

The results of the comparison between the four tests is given in Table 30, together with the numbers of subjects on which each Index value is based. It will be seen that both Indices agree on the order of the tests; the most discriminative test is the dark vision test, followed by the suggestibility test. The questionnaire and the ranking (Rorschach) test follow in that order; there is little to choose between them.

### TABLE THIRTY

| Test. | S. | D. | Normal. | Number: Neurotic. | Total. |
|---|---|---|---|---|---|
| Suggestibility | ·40 | ·62 | 120 | 900 | 1,020 |
| Dark vision | ·64 | ·65 | 6,063 | 96 | 6,159 |
| Questionnaire | ·34 | ·50 | 1,500 | 300 | 1,800 |
| Ranking (Rorschach) | ·31 | ·48 | 150 | 300 | 450 |
| Total | | | 7,833 | 1,596 | 9,429 |

These results are confirmed by a similar analysis carried out on our data dealing with the ability of the tests to discriminate between the inmates of the hospital, i.e. between those who were more seriously ill and those who were less seriously ill. The numbers used in this comparison are not sufficiently large to make it desirable to lay too much stress on the agreement, however.

It is more important, perhaps, to emphasize that while each test by itself correlates to some extent with the general factor of neuroticism, a combination of the four tests would without a doubt be a much better measure than any of them would be singly. This is true not only because of the obvious statistical point that four tests are better than one (unless they correlate very highly together), but because the ranking (Rorschach) test appears to be more diagnostic with respect to hysteria than to dysthymia, while the other tests are more diagnostic with respect to dysthymia than to hysteria.

However, these are merely theoretical considerations, and a more direct proof of the discriminatory value of a battery of neuroticism tests would obviously be desirable. Such a direct proof might also help to close a gap in the chain of reasoning which led us to posit the existence of a general factor of neuroticism. We have shown (a) that the factor-analysis of psychiatric ratings gives rise to a general factor of neuroticism, (b) that certain tests, such as the suggestibility test, the Ranking Rorschach test, the Dark Vision test, and the questionnaire correlate significantly with estimates of a kind similar to those used in step (a) above; (c), we have deduced from these facts that these tests, and others like them, would intercorrelate in such a way as to give rise directly, and without the addition of outside, subjective judgments, to a general factor of neuroticism. This conclusion was tested experimentally in a special study carried out by Drs. Himmelweit, Desai, and Petrie at the Southern Hospital in Dartford.[1]

A battery of tests was administered to 198 male army patients at this hospital; 105 patients were returned prisoners of war who had been sent to the special neuropsychiatric section of the hospital for psychotherapeutic treatment, the other 93 were surgical cases without any notation of "neurosis". It was originally thought that the difference in degree of "neuroticism" between these groups would be similar to that between the Mill Hill neurotic groups studied in the main part of the book, and the "normal" army controls. This expectation, however, was not borne out in fact. Psychiatrists with experience of both the Mill Hill and the Dartford type of neurotic were unanimous in their view that the latter were much less seriously ill than the former; similarly, there is little doubt that the group of surgical cases was less "normal" than the non-hospitalized control groups studied previously, in that it contained a number of "compensation neuroses" and other pathological cases. The extent to which the difference in amount of neuroticism between the normal and the neurotic groups was reduced in passing from Mill Hill to Dartford can be seen by comparing the scores of the various groups on such tests as were given in both hospitals; in terms of the S.D. of the normal group as a unit, there is a reduction in difference between the means of the normal and the

[1] We are indebted to the Superintendent of the Southern Hospital for his permission to test the patients there. We are also grateful to Dr. M. Jones, in charge of the Neuropsychiatric section of the hospital, for his co-operation, help, and suggestions. A full account of this experiment is being published.

neurotic groups of approximately 60% on such tests as the questionnaire, the suggestibility test, and the dark vision test. It follows from these considerations that the criterion against which our tests will be evaluated—the difference between the surgical and the neurotic cases—is very far from perfect.

This admittedly imperfect differentiation of our group of 198 subjects into "normals" and "neurotics" will be referred to as "Psychiatric Diagnosis"; it is recognized, of course, that strictly speaking only the neurotic patients had been diagnosed by a psychiatrist, while the surgical cases had not been diagnosed by a psychiatrist. In addition to this Psychiatric Diagnosis, seventeen scores were obtained on objective tests which will be described in brief below.

Several of the tests used have already been described in former chapters, and need only be enumerated here. In this category belong the Body Sway test of suggestibility, the Persistence test (holding up of the leg), the questionnaire, perseveration,[1] fluency, and static ataxia. In addition, slight modifications were made in other tests already described. The Dark Vision test was given, using not the Livingstone Rotating Hexagon, but the U.S. Navy Radium Plaque Adaptometer, kindly loaned by the R.A.F. Physiological Laboratory. A second persistence test was given, using a Mercury column which had to be kept up by the subject's breath. A personal tempo test was given, using as a score the number of triangles drawn by the subject in unit time. A Level of Aspiration test was given, using the O'Connor Tweezers test instead of the Triple Tester or the Punch; goal discrepancy, judgment discrepancy, and rigidity scores were derived from this test. Also used as a score was the "best score" on the test during the ten successive trials. The Track Tracer speed-accuracy test was given, and the following scores used: speed spontaneously adopted, mistake/score ratio, and improvement from first to last trial in number of mistakes. Last, a "breakdown" test was given, in which the Triple Tester was used in a modified form. A variable-speed integrating disc was interpolated between the motor and the drum, and the course which had to be traced was laid out differently, so that the holes had to be avoided instead of aimed at.

---

[1] It should be noted that this test was scored for *extreme* (high or low) response versus average perseveration.

The test was given, first at the normal speed, then at ever-increasing speeds until a speed was reached at which no subject could score better than chance. After this, the speed was brought down to normal again, and the effect of the speeding-up measured by the reduction (if any) in efficiency as compared with the first trial.

The scores on these seventeen tests were intercorrelated with each other, and with the Psychiatric Diagnosis, tetrachoric correlation coefficients being used throughout. The table of intercorrelations between these eighteen variables was factor-analyzed, and two factors extracted. The results of this factor-analysis are shown in Table 31; also given there are the correlations of the seventeen tests with the Psychiatric Diagnosis. (These correlations are given in the column headed: $r_{aN}$, indicating that the values in this column are an estimate of the correlation of each test with neuroticism.)

TABLE THIRTY-ONE

| | | | Factor: | | |
|---|---|---|---|---|---|
| | | | I. | II. | $r_{aN}$ |
| 1. | Psychiatric diagnosis | . . . | ·71 | ·08 | — |
| 2. | Suggestibility | . . . . | ·69 | ·13 | ·51 |
| 3. | Persistence—leg | . . . | ·55 | ·17 | ·46 |
| 4. | Dark vision | . . . . | ·25 | ·28 | ·27 |
| 5. | Persistence—breath | . . . | ·44 | ·22 | ·26 |
| 6. | Questionnaire | . . . | ·29 | ·24 | ·23 |
| 7. | Speed, track tracer | . . . | ·33 | —·10 | ·27 |
| 8. | Personal tempo | . . . . | ·50 | —·34 | ·30 |
| 9. | Perseveration | . . . | ·42 | ·05 | ·21 |
| 10. | Fluency | . . . . | ·40 | —·01 | ·03 |
| 11. | Static ataxia | . . . | ·64 | ·11 | ·54 |
| 12. | Breakdown test | . . . . | ·14 | —·14 | ·24 |
| 13. | Goal discrepancy | . . | ·17 | —·50 | ·06 |
| 14. | Judgment discrepancy | . . | ·23 | —·17 | —·10 |
| 15. | Rigidity | . . . . | ·05 | —·50 | ·05 |
| 16. | Mistake/score ratio | . . | ·40 | ·02 | ·19 |
| 17. | Improvement, track tracer | . . | ·30 | ·52 | ·26 |
| 18. | Best score, tweezers test | . . | ·41 | —·26 | ·57 |
| | Variance | . . . . | ·18 | ·07 | — |

[Factor saturations of eighteen tests for Factors I and II, and correlations of seventeen tests with neuroticism ($r_{aN}$). Only the nature of the test is indicated; the direction of measurement will be obvious on consideration of the discussion of the tests in the relevant chapters. Thus *high* suggestibility correlates positively with neuroticism, as does *low* persistence and *extreme* (either very high or very low) perseveration.]

Looking at the first, general factor which emerges from our analysis, we find that it accounts for 18% of the variance. It is possible to interpret this factor without recourse to subjective evaluations of the kind which have been criticized so strongly in the past. In the first place, we may note that the item "Psychiatric diagnosis-neurotic" has the highest saturation for this factor, followed in order by other tests known to be indicative of neuroticism, such as, for instance, the Body Sway test of suggestibility. In the second place, if the interpretation suggested by these facts is correct, and if we are dealing with a general factor of neuroticism, then we should expect (a) that the factor saturations of the seventeen tests would be proportional to the correlations of these tests with the Psychiatric Diagnosis, and (b) that the latter values would be smaller on the average than the former to an extent determined by the "reliability" of the Psychiatric Diagnosis ($= \cdot71^2 = \cdot50$).

Both these predictions are verified in actual fact. The correlation between columns I and $r_{aN}$ is $+ 0\cdot74$, which indicates a fairly close correspondence between factor saturations and correlations with Psychiatric Diagnosis. The correlations in column J, when averaged by way of the inverse hyperbolic tangent function (z), are larger than the correlations in column $r_{aN}$, averaged in the same manner; when the latter are corrected for attenuation of the criterion, they are almost identical with the former on the average.

These results suggest strongly that here we have a general factor of neuroticism, similar in mode of derivation and general interpretation on the orectic side to the general factor of intelligence on the cognitive side. There is little reason to assume that intelligence has played any prominent part in giving rise to the intercorrelations analysed. While it was impossible to give tests of intelligence to all the subjects tested, it is unlikely that any marked differences existed between the surgical and the neurotic groups with respect to intelligence. Also, tests with high factor saturations for "neuroticism" such as suggestibility, have been shown elsewhere not to correlate with intelligence.

We may now go a step further and ask ourselves just how accurately the tests in this battery enable us to measure neuroticism. For this purpose two groups of five tests each were made up in such a way that the tests in the two groups were matched for the size of their general factor saturation; each test was weighted roughly in accordance with its factor saturation. The two batteries are referred to as $N_1$ and $N_2$, and are given below; the number, in brackets after each test, refers to the weight given that test in the battery. Standardized scores were used in working with these batteries.

| $N_1$: | $N_2$: |
|---|---|
| Suggestibility (3) | Static Ataxia (3) |
| Persistence—Leg (2) | Personal Tempo (2) |
| Best Score (1) | Persistence—Breath (1) |
| Perseveration (1) | Fluency (1) |
| Slow Speed (1) | Mistake/Speed Ratio (1) |

The correlation between these two batteries is $r = + 0.60$; when corrected by means of the Spearman-Brown prophecy formula, this gives us an estimated reliability for the whole battery of 10 tests of $r = + 0.75$. Looked at from a different point of view, we may regard this coefficient as a correlation of the test-battery with an imperfect criterion; we can then estimate what its correlation would be with a perfect criterion. This correlation reaches the comparatively high value of $+ 0.87$;[1] this figure is likely to represent an overestimate of the true value because of the method used in matching the tests in $N_1$ and $N_2$.

We may attempt to estimate the predictive value of our battery in another way. Correlating the total battery of ten tests with Psychiatric Diagnosis, we obtain a coefficient of $+ 0.73$. Distribution of scores of the normal and the neurotic groups on an eight-point scale gives mean scores of the two groups of respectively $5.0 \pm 1.5$ and $3.0 \pm 1.8$, the C.R. being 8. When the distributions are plotted, it can be seen that 75% of all the cases are allocated correctly to their proper half of the scale; this indicates an improvement of 50% over chance, when measured against the imperfect criterion of the Psychiatric Diagnosis. Presumably with a better criterion the correlation would have been higher, and so would the percentage of correct allocations.

Taking the value of $+ 0.73$ as an minimum estimate of the

---

[1] The formula used is $r_{kg} = \sqrt{\bar{r}_{kk'}}$, where $r_{kg}$ is the correlation of test (or battery of tests) k with a true criterion, g, while $\bar{r}_{kk'}$, is the average intercorrelation of a number of tests (or batteries of tests) of the type k. We may regard the reliability of our battery $N_1 + N_2$ ($r = +0.75$) as an estimate of $\bar{r}_{kk'}$, and thus obtain $r_{kg} = \sqrt{.75}$ (approx.). For a discussion of the reasoning behind this formula, c Hartshorne and May (1928), and Eysenck (1939, 1941).

validity coefficient, and the value of $+ 0.87$ as a maximum estimate of the validity coefficient, we may, perhaps, conclude that the actual validity of the battery is likely to lie in the neighbourhood of $+ 0.80$. This value compares favourably with the validity coefficients reported for tests of special ability by industrial psychologists, and suggests that tests of temperament and personality may have reached a stage where they can take their place with the usual tests of cognitive function and special abilities.

It should be noted in this connection that the correlations quoted so far have not been multiple correlations. It is well-known that when multiple correlations are calculated for a battery of tests, and that battery is used with a different group of subjects, a definite shrinkage occurs in the size of the correlations with the criterion. It is for this reason that we used only a rough system of weighting, and used the factor saturations rather than the correlations with the criterion ($r_{aN}$) in order to determine the weights.[1] While the values quoted are presumably still subject to shrinkage, it is unlikely that they would change to any considerable extent. Indeed, it may be predicted that if the tests were to be used for discriminating between a truly "normal" group and a group as seriously neurotic as the Mill Hill groups reported earlier in the book, the correlations found would be larger, rather than smaller, than those reported here.

Before closing our account of this experiment, a few words may be apposite regarding the interpretation of the second, bipolar factor which emerged from our analysis, making a contribution of $7\%$ to the variance. In view of the fact that the tests with the highest factor saturations are Goal Discrepancy and Rigidity, and one score from the Speed/Accuracy test, it seems probable that here we are dealing with the Introvert-Extravert factor which was previously shown to correlate highly with these tests. However, too few saturations are above the chance level to make us feel confident in the interpretation just given, and in the absence of an external criterion we consider it best not to stress this point.

---

[1] Multiple correlations were actually calculated, but are not given in detail for the reason stated. It may be noted that a combination of two tests (Static Ataxia and Best Score) gave a multiple correlation of $+ 0.72$ with Psychiatric Diagnosis, while the best combination of several tests gave correlations in the neighbourhood of $+ 0.80$. Little was added to the multiple correlations by the other tests over and above the contribution of the four tests having the highest correlations with the criterion.

We may now attempt to summarize the knowledge gained in the course of our experiments with respect to the personality of the neurotic. In Table 32 are set out in detail the experimental findings; interpretation of the Table is, of course, subject to the same qualifications as was interpretation of the Table setting out the experimental findings regarding the hysteric and the dysthymic personality. In brief, the neurotic soldier, on the

TABLE THIRTY-TWO

| | |
|---|---|
| *Clinical ratings* . . | Badly organised personality; dependent; abnormal before illness; narrow interests; little energy; dyspepsia; abnormality in parents; poor muscular tone; unsatisfactory home; hypochondriasis; no group membership |
| *Self-assessments* . . | Inferiority feelings; touchy; nervous; autonomic symptoms; disgruntled; accident-prone; effort-intolerant; etc. (Cf. data on Questionnaire.) |
| *Constitution* . . | Physique: Leptomorph. Effort response: Poor. Dark vision: Poor. Static equilibrum: Poor. |
| *Intellectual functions:* . | Low intelligence. Low retest reliability. |
| *Test responses* . . | High suggestibility. Little persistence. Slow personal tempo. Low fluency. Extreme perseveration (high or low). Uneven curve of practice (learning). Little improvement during practice. Abnormal ranking Rorschach responses. High colour/form ratio. Abnormal lack of sociability. Tendency to repression. |

average, is a person defective in mind and body; below average in intelligence, will, emotional control, sensory acuity, and capacity to exert himself. He is suggestible, lacks persistence, is slow in thought and action, unsociable, and tends to repress unpleasant facts. While some of the results suggest that this general picture owes much to hereditary influence, environmental factors are also indicated; in fact, our results are not of a kind to make it possible to disentangle nature and nurture. Both hereditary "liability to succumb to stress" and environmental "amount of stress experienced" would appear necessary to account for the particular aggregation of patients found in a Neurosis Centre.

It is difficult to know to what extent our results throw light on the vexed question of the theory of neurosis. It is possible to point out that our data can be fitted easily into the conceptual schemata elaborated by various authors; we may seek an explanation of our results in Janet's "lack of psychic tension" (*la misère psychologique*), in Luria's "functional barrier", in Freud's concept of failure of the "ego", in Slater's "neurotic constitution", in Pavlov's "weakness of nervous functioning", in Watson's faulty "conditioning", in Adler's "organ inferiority", or in McDougall's "failure to achieve integration through the 'self-regarding sentiment' ". This very multiplicity of explanations suggests (1) that all these authors are concerned, on the descriptive level, with the same fundamental dimension of personality, and (2) that none of our experiments provides data crucial for a choice between the conflicting theories. Beyond that it would not be wise to go.

It may be permissible, however, to indicate that much of the evidence appears to favour a view which would stress an explanation or description of neuroticism in terms of the *conative* component of personality. Thus, suggestibility tests measure the ability of the patient to overcome by an effort of will the tendency to sway; persistence tests similarly measure the strength of his will to overcome fatigue and stress in order to keep on. Many other test findings can be similarly interpreted, although it cannot be said that the total picture does not contain elements of a cognitive and of an affective nature also. This is hardly surprising in view of the artificiality of isolating conation, affection and cognition in theory; in actual fact they must inevitably influence each other closely.

It is possible to show a similar correspondence between the extravert-introvert dichotomy and the *affective* component of personality. To put the heuristic theory proposed here in a form consonant with the scheme drawn up in the first chapter, we would maintain that there is a certain amount of evidence in favour of the view that as "g" or intelligence is a general factor in the cognitive sphere, so "neuroticism" is a general factor in the

s

conative sphere, while "introversion" is a general factor in the affective sphere. These factors are conceived as relatively orthogonal, although a slight obliqueness may have to be admitted in view of our findings, e.g. with respect to the slight correlation between intelligence and neuroticism. Personality is then conceived as the integration and interaction of these three factors within the general frame·work of the person's physical make-up. Little is known about the method of interaction of these variables, and it would appear that much work remains to be done in filling in the details of the general scheme proposed.

It will be clear that the isolation of a number of tests which may be used for measuring introversion and neuroticism is only the first step on a very long road, and that a large number of problems come to mind immediately to none of which can an answer be given. We know next to nothing about the relative contribution of hereditary and environmental factors to the development of a neurotic, or an introverted personality. We know nothing about the relative fixity with which a person is likely to retain his position on the neurotic continuum, or on the introverted continuum. We know little about the predictive value of these tests. What we can say, however, is that once the problems have been made amenable to quantitative treatment by the development of a sufficient number of personality tests, there is no reason why these questions should not find an answer through specially devised experiments. Thus, there seems to be no obstacle in the way of investigating the contribution of hereditary factors to personality traits by a comparison of the sibling-correlations of monozygotic and heterozygotic twins. Similarly, the predictive value of these tests can be tested in the usual way.

In brief, we believe that the researches here summarized have succeeded in isolating two main personality dimensions and in discovering a series of tests which enable us to perform quantitative investigations along these two dimensions. And while the batteries of tests suggested for this purpose are only very provisional, and are capable of much improvement, there can be little doubt that they do measure, in a rough and ready way, two variables which have in the past proved extremely elusive.

# APPENDIX A

## An Experimental Study in the Methodology of Factor Analysis

In the course of the second chapter two assertions were made with respect to the factorizations carried out by the writer of Guilford's and Mosier's tables of correlations between questionnaire items. In the first place, it was shown that the demonstration of these writers that there was no general factor in their tables was contingent on the method of analysis employed; using Burt's Summation Method the writer found a very strongly marked general factor in each of the tables examined, as well as group factors very similar to those isolated by Guilford. In the second place, it was suggested that this general factor could be identified with "neuroticism". The critical reader may wish to be shown the evidence on which this identification is based, and he may also wish to see on which grounds the writer believes that the "general factor solution" is superior to the type of solution preferred by Guilford, Mosier and others who have used rotated factors. Consequently, an experiment will be described in this appendix which was set up with the dual purpose of (a) providing evidence on these points, and of (b) giving an alternative proof of the correlation of suggestibility with neuroticism.

As a first step, the writer consulted his re-factorizations of Guilford's and Mosier's tables, and selected items most highly saturated with the general factor. In view of the overlap which existed between the items in these different tables, duplicate items, and items which were duplicate in sense if not in wording, were rejected; the remaining sixteen items were reworded and constitute the main basis of a personality inventory. (It was necessary to reword many of the items because the original items had been drawn up for use with college students; also, American expressions had to be eliminated.) The sixteen items finally

263

chosen are stated in full in Table 33, together with other items which were added in an attempt to widen the field of investigation, and to study certain personality correlates of suggestibility. The sixteen Guilford-Mosier items can be identified by numbers from Table 34, where a cross has been put against these items in the column headed "G.M."

The total questionnaire was given to 300 subjects altogether. Fifty male and fifty female soldiers and A.T.S. represent the normal, non-neurotic population; one hundred male and one hundred female soldiers and A.T.S. from Mill Hill Emergency Hospital represent the neurotic population. In addition to being given the questionnaire, the neurotic subjects were also given the Body Sway test of suggestibility; on the basis of this test, the male and the female groups were divided into a "suggestible" and a "non-suggestible" group, each consisting of fifty subjects. We are, then, dealing with six groups of fifty persons: normal men, normal women, suggestible neurotic men, suggestible neurotic women, non-suggestible neurotic men, and non-suggestible neurotic women. The normal and the neurotic groups had been equated for intelligence on the basis of the Matrices test.

The per cent. answering "Yes" to each of the 47 questions in the questionnaire are given, for each of the six groups, in Table 34. We are now in a position to analyze these data with a view to obtaining evidence on the points at issue. The argument on which this analysis is based may be put in the following way. If the writer's contention that the sixteen items from Guilford's and Mosier's questionnaires measure a general factor of neuroticism is correct, then *all* these questions ought to show marked differences between the normals and the neurotics in our sample. If the general factor has no real existence, but is a mere statistical artefact; or if the general factor does exist, but does not measure neuroticism, then the questions included should not show a marked difference between neurotics and normals. Thus, for instance, if the general factor were to be identified with "introversion" rather than with "neuroticism", no marked differences should become apparent in view of the fact that the neurotic population was evenly made up of hysterics and dysthymics. On the whole, therefore, the writer believes that the experiment provides a crucial test of the explanatory and predictive value of the two rival hypotheses.

## TABLE THIRTY-THREE

1. Are you more interested in sports than in intellectual things, such as books, politics, theatre, music, etc.? . . . . Yes No

2. Do you have a particular dislike of being "bossed" and ordered around generally? . . . . . . . Yes No

3. Do you usually feel like "kicking up hell" when you don't get a square deal, or when you feel you are being taken advantage of? Yes No

4. Do you like and enjoy having responsibility (as a foreman or N.C.O., for instance)? . . . . . . . Yes No

5. Are you inclined to worry over possible future misfortunes that may happen to you? . . . . . . . . Yes No

6. Do you often act on the impulse of the moment? . . . Yes No

7. Are you inclined to ponder over your past? . . . . Yes No

8. Do you tend to be very conscientious in your work? . . . Yes No

9. Do you enjoy thinking about complex and complicated problems? . Yes No

10. Do you adapt yourself easily to new conditions? . . . Yes No

11. In exciting situations, do you get rattled easily? . . . Yes No

12. Do you often lack self-confidence, and feel inferior? . . . Yes No

13. Do you often feel self-conscious? . . . . . . Yes No

14. Are you easily distracted from your work? . . . . Yes No

15. When you are sitting or lying down, can you relax easily? . . Yes No

16. When something unexpected happens, are you easily startled? . Yes No

17. Do you often sleep badly? . . . . . . . Yes No

18. Are you quick and agile, bodily? . . . . . . Yes No

19. Do you often rush from one activity to another? . . . Yes No

20. When out with your friends, do you usually talk a lot? . . Yes No

21. Do you like meeting new people, and look forward to it? . . Yes No

22. When you and your friends are doing something, do you often take the lead? . . . . . . . . . Yes No

23. Do you have frequent ups and downs in mood? . . . Yes No

TABLE THIRTY-THREE—CONTD.

24. Are your feelings easily hurt? . . . . . . . Yes No

25. Do you express such emotions as delight, sorrow, etc., readily? . Yes No

26. When you are out with friends, do you enter into the fun whole-heartedly? . . . . . . . . . Yes No

27. Would you prefer going through thrilling experiences and adventures yourself to reading about them, or to seeing them at the pictures? . . . . . . . . Yes No

28. Do you worry about your health whenever you feel off-colour? . Yes No

29. Are you easily put off by difficulties? . . . . . Yes No

30. Do you tend to be influenced by other people's opinions? . . Yes No

31. Have you original or unconventional ideas on any subject? . Yes No

32. Do you hold any strong religious views? . . . . . Yes No

33. Has your father been a very steady sort of person? . . . Yes No

34. Has your mother been a very steady sort of person? . . . Yes No

35. Did your parents have any quarrels? . . . . . Yes No

36. Were your relations with your father generally friendly? . . Yes No

37. Were your relations with your mother generally friendly? . . Yes No

38. Were you often nagged when you were a child? . . . . Yes No

39. Which of your parents did you prefer? . . Father Mother Neither[1]

40. Where you brought up rather strictly? . . . . . Yes No

41. Did you resent your parents' punishments? . . . . Yes No

42. Were you a very obedient child? . Very Middling Definitely not[2]

43. In general, did you like your teachers? . . . . . Yes No

44. Were they rather strict? . . . . . . . . Yes No

45. In your civilian work, were your superiors rather "bossy"? . . Yes No

46. In the Army, did you have very strict officers and N.C.O.'s? . Yes No

47. Have you had many "conquests" among the opposite sex? . Yes No

---

[1] Scored as per cent. who prefer mother.

[2] Scored as per cent. who were very obedient.

## TABLE THIRTY-FOUR

| | NORMALS. | | NEUROTICS. | | | | G.M. | Diff. n. | Diff. s. |
| | Men. | Women. | Sug. Men. | Non.-S. Men. | Sug. Women. | Non.-S· Women. | | | |
|---|---|---|---|---|---|---|---|---|---|
| 1. | 36 | 14 | 26 | 36 | 44 | 34 | | — | — |
| 2. | 72 | 84 | 80 | 70 | 62 | 72 | | — | — |
| 3. | 88 | 88 | 76 | 80 | 72 | 82 | | — | — |
| 4. | 96 | 96 | 44 | 48 | 44 | 50 | + | 50 | 5 |
| 5. | 30 | 22 | 78 | 64 | 70 | 54 | + | 40 | 15 |
| 6. | 52 | 68 | 70 | 68 | 70 | 72 | | — | — |
| 7. | 34 | 32 | 78 | 62 | 68 | 72 | +. | 37 | 6 |
| 8. | 88 | 86 | 84 | 94 | 90 | 92 | | — | — |
| 9. | 74 | 72 | 30 | 42 | 40 | 44 | | 34 | 8 |
| 10. | 86 | 96 | 36 | 44 | 64 | 62 | + | 40 | 2 |
| 11. | 6 | 14 | 70 | 56 | 48 | 40 | + | 43 | 11 |
| 12. | 22 | 42 | 82 | 80 | 70 | 64 | + | 44 | 4 |
| 13. | 44 | 52 | 84 | 80 | 84 | 68 | + | 31 | 10 |
| 14. | 10 | 20 | 66 | 42 | 34 | 36 | | 29 | 11 |
| 15. | 92 | 88 | 20 | 36 | 34 | 58 | + | 53 | 20 |
| 16. | 22 | 24 | 88 | 76 | 70 | 60 | | 50 | 11 |
| 17. | 10 | 8 | 80 | 72 | 66 | 52 | + | 59 | 11 |
| 18. | 86 | 80 | 34 | 46 | 66 | 74 | | 28 | 10 |
| 19. | 52 | 76 | 42 | 44 | 58 | 56 | | — | — |
| 20. | 54 | 78 | 32 | 30 | 48 | 54 | | 25 | 2 |
| 21. | 78 | 94 | 24 | 36 | 44 | 48 | + | 48 | 8 |
| 22. | 90 | 88 | 16 | 30 | 42 | 52 | + | 54 | 12 |
| 23. | 40 | 66 | 84 | 86 | 72 | 72 | + | 25 | -1 |
| 24. | 46 | 64 | 88 | 82 | 90 | 84 | + | 31 | 6 |
| 25. | 56 | 68 | 60 | 60 | 68 | 60 | | — | — |
| 26. | 90 | 98 | 42 | 42 | 64 | 82 | + | 36 | 9 |
| 27. | 76 | 88 | 18 | 44 | 56 | 52 | + | 40 | 11 |
| 28. | 30 | 4 | 78 | 60 | 36 | 34 | + | 35 | 10 |
| 29. | 2 | 0 | 66 | 48 | 32 | 18 | | 41 | 16 |
| 30. | 22 | 32 | 48 | 42 | 38 | 30 | | — | — |
| 31. | 62 | 72 | 32 | 38 | 48 | 50 | | 25 | 4 |
| 32. | 24 | 36 | 24 | 30 | 28 | 26 | | — | — |
| 33. | 86 | 86 | 60 | 80 | 82 | 88 | | — | — |
| 34. | 96 | 88 | 92 | 90 | 82 | 86 | | — | — |
| 35. | 12 | 16 | 36 | 24 | 28 | 20 | | — | — |
| 36. | 86 | 90 | 70 | 88 | 80 | 80 | | — | — |
| 37. | 96 | 96 | 86 | 96 | 90 | 82 | | — | — |
| 38. | 8 | 6 | 30 | 32 | 26 | 24 | | 21 | 0 |
| 39. | 42 | 42 | 40 | 42 | 44 | 20 | | — | — |
| 40. | 58 | 46 | 52 | 48 | 56 | 64 | | — | — |
| 41. | 16 | 22 | 36 | 36 | 32 | 44 | | — | — |
| 42. | 12 | 4 | 36 | 30 | 20 | 18 | | — | — |
| 43. | 90 | 92 | 78 | 84 | 86 | 92 | | — | — |
| 44. | 62 | 50 | 60 | 50 | 70 | 62 | | — | — |
| 45. | 14 | 10 | 28 | 14 | 22 | 22 | | — | — |
| 46. | 48 | 34 | 72 | 70 | 54 | 60 | | 23 | 2 |
| 47. | 32 | 56 | 8 | 12 | 46 | 32 | | — | — |

Items marked with a cross in the column headed "G.M." were taken from Guilford or Mosier.

The difference in the percentage of "Yes" answers between the 100 normal and the 200 neurotic subjects is given in Table 34 under the heading: "Diff. n." It will be seen that in every single case the neurotic group gives the neurotic answer with considerably greater frequency than does the normal group; the differences vary from 24 to 59, with a mean of 42. Each one of these differences is fully significant statistically. There can accordingly be no doubt that questionnaire items highly saturated with the general factor discriminate with great efficiency between normal and neurotic subjects. It is difficult to see how this finding can be explained on Guilford's hypothesis of a number of orthogonal personality factors.

It might be argued that Guilford's factors are probably not entirely orthogonal, but oblique, and that consequently from correlations among the first-order factors might arise a second-order factor similar in meaning to our general factor. This view is strengthened by the fact that Guilford himself reports correlations ranging up to + 0·85 between scores on the various factors. Admittedly, these correlations are derived from scorings and do not directly imply similar correlations among the factors themselves; however, it is impossible to obtain correlations of this size without correlations existing between the actual factors. The writer factor-analyzed the table of correlations between the five personality factors given by Guilford, [1] and found a strong general factor responsible for 41% of the variance. The saturations with this factor ranged from ·23 (factor T) to ·69 (factor S) and ·92 (factor D). This analysis strongly supports the view that Guilford's results, however analyzed, give rise to a general factor; in the type of analysis favoured by the writer, this general factor emerges as the first factor, while in Guilford's type of analysis it only emerges after all the other factors have been extracted. In either case, however, we are left with (a) a general factor, and (b) a number of group factors, identical from one analysis to the other. This identity of results, even though reached by divergent paths, is highly satisfactory in that it shows that different methods of factorial analysis are far from being in any way incompatible, but on the contrary are likely to give essentially identical results. If in spite of this identity we may express a preference for one method over the other, it must be

[1] In his "Manual of Directions and Norms" to *An Inventory of Factors STDCR*.

on the grounds that the so-called general factor method gives us an item of information not so easily obtained from the Thurstone-Guilford type of analysis, viz. the actual general-factor saturations of the individual items used in the questionnaire.

Having thus attempted to justify our use of the general-factor method, and our interpretation of the emerging factor as one of "neuroticism", we may turn to the further analysis of our data. Apart from the sixteen items taken from the Guilford-Mosier scales, there were another nine items in our questionnaire which showed differences between the normal and the neurotic subjects in excess of 20 points. The actual differences are given in Table 34, in the column "Diff. n." We have then altogether 25 items which distinguish significantly between the normals and the neurotics; these 25 items will be denoted "neuroticism items" in the rest of the appendix.

These neuroticism items have been used in the following alternative proof of the correlation between neuroticism and suggestibility. In the first place, differences on these 25 items were calculated between suggestible neurotics on the one hand, and non-suggestible neurotics on the other; these differences are given in Table 34, under the heading "Diff. s." Now if the neuroticism items give us a reliable and valid measure of degree of neuroticism, and if suggestibility is correlated with neuroticism, then clearly the differences between the suggestible and the non-suggestible neurotics should be in the same direction as the differences between the normals and the neurotics. To take one instance: 90% of the normals report that they can relax easily, while only 37% of the neurotics report that they can relax easily. If our theory is correct, we should expect that the non-suggestible neurotics report a greater ability to relax than do the suggestible neurotics. In actual fact, the figures show that 36% of the non-suggestible men relax easily, as compared with 20% of the suggestible men; similarly, 58% of the non-suggestible women relax easily, as compared with 34% of the suggestible women. Taking the sexes together, we find that of suggestible neurotics, 27% can relax easily, while of the non-suggestible neurotics, 47% can relax easily. Thus there is a difference of 53 points between the neurotics and the normals, and a difference of 20 points between the suggestible and the non-suggestible neurotics. Both differences are in the same direction, and consequently bear out the theory on which the argument was based. Altogether, of 25 items, only two fail to support our theory; item number 23 shows a negative difference (i.e. a difference not in the direction demanded by the theory) of 1 point, while item number 38 shows no difference at all. The remaining 23 items show differences in the expected direction. On the average the scores in column "Diff. s." average 8, as compared with the scores in column "Diff. n.", which average 38. This result is in accordance with our theory that suggestibility is correlated with neuroticism. If we like to assume that a linear relation obtains between degree of neuroticism and score on the neuroticism items, then we may say that the difference in neuroticism between the suggestible and the non-suggestible neurotics is about 20% of the difference between neurotics and normals. In other words, the non-suggestible neurotics are 20% less neurotic than the suggestible neurotics. This conclusion should be accepted with great reserve; too little is known about the linearity or otherwise of the relation between neuroticism and questionnaire score to feel much confidence in conclusions based on this premiss.

One further test may be made to show the essential identity of the quality which differentiates neurotics from normals with the quality which differentiates suggestible neurotics from non-suggestible neurotics. If this theory is correct, then not only should the differences in columns "Diff. n." and "Diff. s." be in the same direction, but in addition they should be *proportional*. An item which distinguishes particularly well between neurotics and normals should also discriminate particularly well between suggestible and non-suggestible neurotics. An item which does not distinguish particularly well between neurotics and normals should not distinguish particularly well between suggestible and non-suggestible neurotics.

Much importance attaches in our opinion to this proportionality criterion. It might be argued, for instance, that differences in questionnaire scores are not due to differences in neuroticism, but to differences in motivation, and that similarly differences in suggestibility scores are not due to anything else but a desire on the part of some patients to give as bad an impression as possible in order to "work their ticket". On this argument, the difference between normals and neurotics in questionnaire scores would be due to the fact that the normals want to give as good an impression as possible, while the neurotics want to give as bad an impression as possible. Similarly, the differences between suggestible and non-suggestible neurotics might be due to the same tendency, the suggestible ones wanting to give a bad impression of themselves, the non-suggestibles wanting to give a good impression. This argument is a very important one, as it is often advanced to explain data such as those reported in this book.

Now it is obvious that in the argument as it stands, there is an inconsistency. In comparing the non-suggestible neurotics with the normals, it is assumed that the normals want to give a good impression, while the non-suggestible neurotics want to give a bad impression. In comparing the non-suggestible neurotics with the suggestible ones, it is assumed that the non-suggestible neurotics want to give a good impression. Now clearly both propositions cannot be maintained at the same time, and consequently the argument as presented falls to the ground.

It is possible to revive the argument by making a slight change of stand. One of the two differences observed, it may be argued, is due to the factor of neuroticism, but the other difference is due to the desire to make a good impression. This argument is clearly much weaker psychologically than the original one, but it has to be answered none the less. It is here that the proportionality criterion appears useful.

If the differences in one of the two columns "Diff. n." and "Diff. s." are due to one factor, while those in the other column are due to an altogether different factor, then clearly there should be no correlation between them. If, however, as the writer maintains, differences in both columns are due to one and the same factor, then clearly there should be a significant correlation between them. In actual fact, the product-moment correlation between the two columns is $+ 0.56 \pm .14$, a value which strongly supports our own interpretation of the data. We may, therefore, conclude that our data give little support to the view that scores on questionnaires of the kind used are largely conditioned by the desire of the subject to make a good or a bad impression; while this view may have some validity under certain circumstances, it does not seem to apply to our work.

We may now briefly summarize the conclusions which seem to be indicated by the results reported in this appendix. In the first place, it would appear that the seeming incompatibility of the two main methods of factorial analysis does not prevent these methods from giving identical results when applied to the same matrices. In the second place, both methods agree in showing the presence of a general factor in the tables of intercorrelations of questionnaire-items analyzed. In the third place, this factor has been experimentally identified with "neuroticism". In the fourth place, it has been shown that suggestible neurotics and non-suggestible neurotics differ with respect to precisely the same factor as do neurotics as a whole and normals. In the fifth place, it has been shown that if we make certain assumptions regarding the linearity of the relation between neuroticism and questionnaire score, we are able to assign a numerical value to the difference in "neuroticism" between suggestible and non-suggestible neurotics. In the sixth place, we have shown that the results reported here cannot be accounted for on the basis of malingering, or any other intentional falsification of results on the part of our subjects. Taken together, these six findings give powerful support to the general position taken in the main body of the book.

# APPENDIX B

## Static Ataxia as an Index of Neuroticism

Static ataxia, or the "defective muscular co-ordination of the individual while attempting to maintain a fixed position of body or limbs" (Warren, 1933), has attracted the attention of both physiologists and psychologists. In particular, the body sway of subjects attempting to stand motionless in an erect position has been studied extensively. Failure to maintain equilibrium under those conditions is often referred to as "Romberg's sign"; originally, this sign was believed to be specific for *tabes dorsalis* (Romberg, 1853). In view of the fact that the body sway test of suggestibility makes use of an increase in static ataxia in order to measure the subject's primary suggestibility, it seemed necessary to investigate the relation between ataxia and neuroticism. The desirability of such a study became even more obvious when we found on several samples of neurotic men and women, both civilian and military, that correlations varying between + 0·4 and + 0·6 (with standard errors of about 0·06) emerged between static ataxia and body sway suggestibility. Consequently, a study is reported in this appendix of the ability of 900 male and 330 female neurotics to preserve their equilibrium under certain specified conditions. A brief review of the literature on static ataxia is also given.

Physiologists have been largely concerned with the influence of "defective vestibular activity" on body sway. They have shown that of the three portions of the vestibular labyrinth, the ampullae of the semi-circular canals and the utricular maculae play an important part in the maintenance of equilibrium; the sacculus would not appear to fulfil a similar function (Maxwell, 1923; McNally and Stuart, 1942). However, as Dusser de Barenne has pointed out in his discussion of the effects of labyrinthectomy, "the influence of the labyrinth on the motor mechanism becomes less and less as one ascends the vertebrate scale" (1934). The observations of Rademaker (1935), de No (1931), Spiegel (1944), and Birren (1945) lend support to this conclusion. A review of the literature on the physiology of the vestibular apparatus is given by Camis (1930), or more recently by André-Thomas (1940).

The variety of methods used for measuring body sway can be grouped into four broad categories; most modern practices were adumbrated in the earliest quantitative work on the subject by Crichton-Browne (1882), Hinsdale (1887), and Mitchell and Lewis (1886). Body sway may be measured:

(1) By means of an apparatus fixed to the head of the subject,
    (a) by recording sway graphically (Bullard, 1888; Hancock, 1894; Hinsdale, 1887; Lee, 1923; Miles, 1922; Rosenfeld, 1918; Wallin, 1912);
    (b) by summing total linear amount of movement (Brammer, 1925; Fearing, 1924, 1925; Miles, 1922, 1924).

(2) By attaching a rod or other fixture recording movement to the body of the subject (Eichkern, 1928; Skaggs, 1932, 1937; Skogland, 1942).

(3) By placing the subject upright on a mobile platform, thus recording movements occurring as his weight shifts forward or sideways (Moss, 1931, 1932; Omwake, 1932; Ricaldini, 1928).

(4) By attaching strings to the body at various levels and measuring their displacement in the direction or directions in which measurement is being carried out (Hull, 1933; Eysenck, 1943; Edwards, 1939, 1941, 1942).

Findings of different investigators are often contradictory, and difficult to compare because of different methods of measuring and recording. Also, the influence of such factors as position of the feet, distraction of attention, fatigue, diurnal variations, etc., has not always been equalized by research workers. In spite of these difficulties, certain definite conclusions have emerged with respect to (a) clinical, and (b) psychological correlates of static ataxia.

As regards the clinical findings, excessive body sway has been observed in *tabes dorsalis* (Edwards, 1942; Hinsdale, 1887; Mitchell and Lewis, 1886; Ricaldini, 1928; Romberg, 1853; Rosenfeld, 1918), chorea (Hinsdale, 1887), paralysis agitans (Edwards, 1942), and cerebro-arteriosclerosis (Edwards, 1942). It has also been reported that in Frederich's ataxia and in cerebellar ataxia no increase is observed in sway consequent upon closure of the eyes (Purves-Stewart, 1931). Findings in epilepsy are negative, no increased sway being observed (Skogland, 1942; Wallin, 1912).

Psychological findings include the following. There is considerable variation within groups of normal subjects (Brammer, 1925; Bullard, 1888; Eichkern, 1928; Fearing, 1924, 1925; Hancock, 1894; Hinsdale, 1887, 1890; Miles, 1922, 1924; Moss, 1931, 1932; Skogland, 1942), and also considerable individual fluctuation (Edwards, 1942; Eichkern, 1928; Fearing, 1924; Miles, 1922; Skogland, 1942). Position of the feet influences amount of body sway (Fearing, 1924; Skogland, 1942), as does vision (Brammer, 1925; Bullard, 1888; Edwards, 1942; Eichkern, 1928; Hancock, 1894; Hinsdale, 1887; Skogland, 1942) and attention (Fearing, 1925; Skaggs, 1932; Skogland, 1942). Sleeplessness, fatigue, alcohol, marihuana, and music all impair equilibrium (Husband, 1934; Lee, 1923; Miles, 1924; Moss, 1931, 1932; Wallace, 1944), whereas other factors such as sex, height, weight, race, smoking, and type or footwear show no marked effects (Edwards, 1942; Eichkern, 1928; Fearing, 1924; Hancock, 1894; Miles, 1922; Skaggs, 1937). Extreme youth and age, deafness, and blindness are accompanied by greater body sway (Edwards, 1942). Diurnal variations are observed (Moss, 1931; Omwake, 1932; but cf. Edwards, 1941), the early afternoon being apparently the period of greater stability. No significant relation is observed between body sway and flying ability (Brammer, 1925; Henmon, 1919); this result is probably due largely to preselection of testees.

One observer, who quotes results from over 1,400 subjects, gives the following order of body sway from greatest to least (Edwards, 1942): Huntingdon's chorea, paralysis agitans, cerebro-arteriosclerosis, senile psychosis, paresis, feeble-mindedness, extreme youth, blindness, extreme age, deafness. The writer concludes: "The accurate measurement of static ataxia has been found to be more indicative of organic and mental condition than most of the psychomotor tests. . . . Our knowledge of sway at various ages makes it possible to note symptoms of failure of general organic and nervous development and of impairment of motor co-ordination. . . . Ataxiametric measurements may also facilitate diagnosis of the extent of vestibular injury."

In our own study, we made use of the data collected in connection with our work on suggestibility. It will be remembered that before playing the body-sway record to our subjects, we had them stand quite still, with their eyes closed, for thirty seconds, and that a note was made of the maximum sway forward and backward from their original position. These two values added together give us a score of maximum total body sway (static ataxia) of the subject.

In Table 35 are shown the results of this test for 1,350 normal and neurotic subjects. Results are given separately for male and female neurotics; male and female normals are not separated as they showed no difference in average body sway. In the Table are given the numbers of subjects in each of the three groups who swayed 0 — 1, 1 — 2, . . . , and more than 6 inches.

TABLE THIRTY-FIVE

| Amount of Sway. | 0—1. | 1—2. | 2—3. | 3—4. | 4—6. | 6+. | |
|---|---|---|---|---|---|---|---|
| Normals . . | 98 | 22 | 0 | 0 | 0 | 0 | 120 |
| Male Neurotics . | 241 | 347 | 131 | 58 | 59 | 64 | 900 |
| Female Neurotics . | 162 | 103 | 38 | 12 | 2 | 13 | 330 |
| Total Number . . . . . . . . . | | | | | | | 1,350 |

In view of the abnormal distribution of scores, the chi square test of significance was used; according to this test, male neurotics sway significantly more than female neurotics or normals, and female neurotics sway more than do normals (P < ·01 in all cases). The difference between male and female neurotics is not evidence of any genuine sex difference, but is probably due to the different selection procedures of the male and the female services. The difference between neurotics and normals, on the other hand, is probably due to a definite and fundamental correlation between neuroticism and static ataxia.

This conclusion is borne out by another analysis. From the 1,230 neurotics, two groups were selected. On the one hand, 100 men and 50 women were chosen who had shown least amount of static ataxia; this group will be referred to as the *non-sway* group. On the other hand, 100 men and 50 women were selected who had shown maximum amount of ataxia; this group will be referred to as the *sway group*. For both these groups, certain clinical data were obtainable, and percentage incidence of these items is shown in Table 36. Also given in the Table is a measure of the significance of the differences, viz. Student's "t".

TABLE THIRTY-SIX

|  | Sway Group. | Non-Sway Group. | t. |
|---|---|---|---|
| Boarded out of army . . . | 60% | 46% | 2·5 |
| Abnormality in parents . . . | 45% | 35% | 1·8 |
| Satisfactory home . . . | 75% | 90% | 3·5 |
| Past physical health good . . | 52% | 78% | 4·5 |
| Abnormal before illness . . | 84% | 68% | 3·4 |
| Hysterical conversion . . . | 42% | 32% | 1·8 |
| Moderate or severe anxiety . . | 42% | 35% | 1·2 |

These results reinforce our previous conclusion that static ataxia and neuroticism are connected; they also show that there is little reason for assuming extraversion (hysteria) or introversion (dysthymia) to be specially connected with ataxia.

Tetrachoric correlations were calculated between static ataxia and body-sway suggestibility. For the neurotic men, $r_t = + 0·52$; for the neurotic women, $r_t = + 0·44$; for the normal group, $r_t = + 0·06$. In the main, the significant correlations in the neurotic groups would seem to be due to the presence of certain subjects in these two groups who show considerable sway both without and with suggestion; in the normal group, where there were none of these subjects, the correlation is insignificant.[1] This latter finding is important because it makes it impossible to use the difference between suggestion sway and non-suggestion sway as an index of suggestibility. If we were to use the difference between the two scores in this way, we would only succeed in giving the person who can stand quite still under non-suggestion conditions a higher suggestion score, and the person who cannot stand still under suggestion conditions a lower suggestion score, than they should rightly have. (For example, A and B both have a suggestion sway of 4 inches; A has a non-suggestion sway of 0 inches, B has a non-suggestion sway of 2 inches. The difference score would then be 4 for A, and 2 for

---

[1] In theoretical terms, the observed correlations are perhaps explicable by assuming that autosuggestion plays a part in static ataxia. This now seems probable on *a priori* grounds, but would, of course, require experimental verification.

T

B, punishing A for having stood still during the non-suggestion sway period.)

Various methods of scoring were tried to overcome this difficulty, including combination scores which took account of non-suggestion sway only when it was above the normal range. All these different methods of scoring, however, give results so similar that it was finally decided to retain the simple suggestion sway scores as our index of suggestibility

Psychogenetic history
level of development
& its history

---

Current clinical
status — cross
(a) symptoms ) below
(b) defenses ) inter
(c) integral
experience
The environment — (well)

therapy
implications

Total
Diagnoses

Past

Total Diagnoses

Present — some perfect future

Present

① behavior
② extreme psych
③ extreme
④ environment
⑤ extreme

future
① wo treat
② w treat
1
2
3

Past
① hunter
② ...
③ ...
④ demand

# BIBLIOGRAPHY

FOR THE CONVENIENCE OF THE READER, THE LIST OF REFERENCES HAS BEEN
COMBINED WITH THE AUTHOR INDEX, SO THAT AFTER EACH CITATION ARE GIVEN
IN ITALICS THE NUMBERS OF THE PAGES ON WHICH THE CITATION IN QUESTION
OCCURS. CARE HAS BEEN TAKEN TO ENSURE ACCURACY, BUT IN VIEW OF THE
CURTAILMENT OF LIBRARY FACILITIES DURING THE WAR IT HAS NOT BEEN POSSIBLE
TO RE-CHECK EVERY SINGLE REFERENCE. NO ATTEMPT HAS BEEN MADE TO
PROVIDE A COMPLETE BIBLIOGRAPHY OF THE FIELDS COVERED; ONLY REFERENCES
WHICH WERE CONSIDERED ESSENTIAL FOR THE ARGUMENT ARE INCLUDED.

ADICKES, G., *Charakter und Weltanschauung.* Berlin: 1907. *202.*
ADLER, H. M., and MOHR, G. J. Some considerations of the significance of
physical constitution in relation to mental disorder. *Amer. J. Psychiat.;*
1928, 7, 701-707. *84.*
ADRIAN, E. D., and YEALLAND, L. R. The treatment of some common war
neuroses. *Lancet,* June 9th, 1917. *111.*
AIKENS, H. A., THORNDIKE, E. L., and HUBBELL, E. Correlations among
perceptive and associative processes. *Psychol. Rev.,* 1902, 9, 374-382. *144.*
ALLERS, R., and SCHEMINSKY, F. Über Aktionsströme bei Muskeln bei motoris-
chen Vorstellungen. *Arch. f. d. ges. Physiol.,* 1926, 212, 169-182. *195.*
ALLESCH, G. J. Die aesthetische Erscheinungsweise der Farben. *Psychol.
Forsch.,* 1924, 6, 1-91. *207.*
ALLPORT, F. H. *Social Psychology.* Boston: Houghton Mifflin, 1924. *23.*
ALLPORT, G. W. A test for ascendance-submission. *J. abn. soc. Psychol.,*
1928, 23, 118-124. *13.*
—— *Personality: a psychological interpretation.* New York: Holt, 1937. *2, 15, 17,
22, 24, 165, 225.*
——, and VERNON, P. E. The field of personality. *Psychol. Bull.,* 1930, 27,
677-730. *23, 24.*
——, —— *Studies in expressive movements.* New York: Macmillan, 1933.
*15, 24, 146, 239.*
ANASTASI, A. Faculties versus factors: a reply to Professor Thurstone. *Psychol.
Bull.,* 1938, 35, 391-395. *17.*
——, and FOLEY, J. P. A survey of the literature on artistic behaviour in
the abnormal: III. Spontaneous productions. *Psychol. Mon.,* 1940,
237. *206.*
ANDRÉ-THOMAS, G. *Equilibre et équilibration.* Paris: Masson, 1940. *274.*
ANTHONY, S. Study of personality adjustment in school children as diagnosed
by a test of word-association. *Char. and Pers.,* 1943, 12, 15-31. *212.*
ARNETT, C. G., DAVIDSON, H. H., and LEWIN, H. N. Prestige as a factor in
attitude changes. *Sociol. Soc. Res.,* 1931, 16, 49-55. *168.*
ASCHNER, B. *Die Konstitution der Frau und ihre Beziehung zur Geburtshilfe and
Gynäkologie.* Munchen: 1924. *75.*
AVELING, F., and HARGREAVES, H. Suggestibility with and without prestige
in children. *Brit. J. Psychol.,* 1921, 11, 53-75. *164.*

BABCOCK, H. An experiment in the measurement of mental deterioration.
*Arch. of Psychol.,* 1930, 117. *126.*
—— *Time and the mind.* Cambridge, Mass.: Sci-Arts, 1941. *126.*
—— A neurosis? Or neurotic behaviour? *J. Psychol.,* 1944, 17, 61-74. *126.*
BABINSKI, J. F., and FROMENT, J. *Hysteria or pithiatism.* London: University of
London Press, 1918. *11, 161.*

BALKEN, E., and MASSERMAN, J. H. The language of phantasy: III. The language of the phantasies of patients with conversion hysteria, anxiety state, and obsessional-compulsive neurosis. *J. Psychol.*, 1940, 10, 75-86. *235*.
BARRY, H. A test for negativism and compliance. *J. abn. soc. Psychol.*, 1930, 25, 373-381. *168*.
——, MacKINNON, P. W., and MURRAY, H. A. Studies in personality: II. Hypnotizability as a personality trait and its typological relations. *Human Biol.*, 1931, 3, 1-36. *163*.
BARTLETT, M. R. Suggestibility in psychopathic individuals. *J. gen. Psychol.*, 1936, 14, 241-247. *164*.
—— The relation of suggestibility to other personality traits. *J. gen. Psychol.*, 1936, 15, 191-196. *164*.
BAUER, I. *Methoden der Konstitutionslehre.* Abderhaldens Handb. d. biol. Arbeitsmethoden, 1924. *75*.
BAUMGARTNER, M. The correlation of direct suggestibility with certain character tests. *J. appl. Psychol.*, 1931, 15, 1-15. *164*.
BAXTER, M. F. An experimental study of the differentiation of temperaments on a basis of rate and strength. *Amer. J. Psychol.*, 1927, 38, 59-96. *146*.
BEAN, R. B. The two European types. *Amer. J. Anat.*, 1923, 31, 359-371. *75*.
BECK, L. F. The relation of speed of reaction to intelligence. *Amer. J. Psychol.*, 1932, 44, 793-795. *145*.
BEEBE-CENTER, J. B. *Pleasantness and unpleasantness.* New York: Century, 1933. *208*.
——, and PRATT, C. C. A test of Birkhoff's aesthetic measure. *J. gen. Psychol.*, 1937, 17, 335-353. *208*.
BENDER, L. *Visual motor gestalt test and its clinical use.* New York: 1938. *237*.
BENEKE, F. W. *Die anatomischem Grundlagen der Konstitutions-anomalien des Menschen.* Marburg: 1878. *83*.
BERNHEIM, H. *De la suggestion, et de ses applications a la thérapeutique.* Paris: 1887. *162*.
BERNREUTER, R. G. The imbrication of tests of introversion-extraversion and neurotic tendency. *J. soc. Psychol.*, 1934, 5, 184-201. *52*.
BERNSTEIN, E. Quickness and intelligence. *Brit. J. Psychol. Mon. Suppl.*, 1924, 3. *144, 156*.
BERREMAN, J. V., and HILGARD, E. R. The effects of personal heterosuggestion and two forms of autosuggestion upon postural movement. *J. soc. Psychol.*, 1938, 7, 289-300. *195, 198*.
BETZ, B. Somatology of the schizophrenic patient. *Human Biol.*, 1942, 14, 21-47, 192-234. *74, 84, 85*.
BILLS, A. G. The influence of muscular tension on the efficiency of mental work. *Amer. J. Psychol.*, 1927, 38, 227-251. *195*.
BINET, A. La mésure en psychologique individuelle. *Rev. Phil.*, 1898, 46, 113-123. *13*.
—— Attention et adaptation. *L'Annee Psychol.*, 1900, 6, 248-404. *13*.
—— La suggestibilité. Paris: Schleicher, 1900. *167*.
—— Etude expérimentale de l'intelligence. Paris: 1903. *205*.
BINGHAM, W. V. A note on effects of introversion on dominant interests. *Brit. J. Psychol.*, 1925, 16, 354-362. *57*.
BIRD, C. *Social Psychology.* New York: Appleton and Cent., 1941. *165*.
BIRKHOFF, G. D. *Aesthetic measure.* Cambridge: Harvard Univ. Press, 1932. *208*.
BIRREN, J. E. Static equilibrium and vestibular function. *J. exp. Psychol.*, 1945, 35, 127-133. *273*.
BLEULER, E. *Textbook of psychiatry.* New York: Macmillan, 1924. *10, 162, 188*.
BLOCK, H. The influence of muscular exertion. *Arch. of Psychol.* 1936, 202. *195*.
BLOOR, C. *Temperament.* London: Methuen, 1928. *23*.

BOLDRINI, M., and MENGARELLI, C. *Comit. Ital. Stud. Prob. Popol. Atti Roma*, 1933, 195, 3-27. *202*.

BOWDEN, A., CALDWELL, F. and WEST, G. A study in prestige. *Amer. J. Sociol.*, 1934, 40, 193-204. *168*.

BOWLBY, J. *Personality and mental illness.* London: Kegan Paul, 1940. *14, 42, 250*.

BRAAT, J. P. Die experimentelle Psychologie und Kretschmers Konstitutionstypen. *Monatsschr. f. Psychiat. Neurol.*, 1937, 94, 273-297. *220*.

BRAHMACHARI, S. Moral attitudes in relation to upbringing, personal adjustment, and social opinion. *Thesis, Univ. of London*, 1937. *142*.

BRAMMER, G. The static equilibrium of airplane pilots. *J. comp. Psychol.*, 1925, 5, 345-364. *274*.

BRAUN, F. Untersuchungen über das persönliche Tempo. *Arch. f. d. ges. Psychol.*, 1927, 60, 317-360. *15, 145, 146*.

BRIGHOUSE, G. Variability in preferences for simple forms. *Psychol. Mon.*, 1939, 51, 231. *208*.

BRITT, S. H. Retroactive inhibition: a review of the literature. *Psychol. Bull.*, 1935, 32, 381-432. *157*.

—— *Social Psychology of modern life.* New York: Farrar and Rhinehart, 1941. *165*.

BROGDEN, H. G. A factor analysis of forty character tests. *Psychol. Mon.*, 1940, 234, 39-55. *40*.

BRONNER, A. F. *Comparative study of the intelligence of delinquent girls.* Teach. Coll. Contrib. Educ., 1914, 68. *158*.

BROWN, W. Individual and sex differences in suggestibility. *Univ. Calif. Publ. Psychol.*, 1916, 2, 291-430. *164*.

BROWN, W. M. A study of the "caution" factor and its importance in intelligence test performance. *Amer. J. Psychol.*, 1924, 35, 368-386. *148*.

BRUCE, A. N. *The basis of temperament.* Edinb. med. J., 1941, 48, 520-534. *41*.

BRUGSCH, T. *Allgemeine Prognostik, oder die Lehre von der ärtzlichen Beurteilung des gesunden und kranken Menschen.* Berlin: 1918. *75*.

BRUNNACCI, B., and DE SANCTIS, G. Sulla funzione secretoria della parotide nel l'uoma. *Arch. di Fisiol.*, 1914, 12, 441-454. *97*.

BULLARD, W. N., and BRACKETT, E. G. Observations on the steadiness of the hand and on static equilibrium. *Boston Med. Surg. J.*, 1888, 119, 595-603. *274*.

BULLEY, M. *Have you good taste?* London: Methuen, 1933. *210*.

BULLOUGH, C. The "perceptive" problem in the aesthetic appreciation of single colours. *Brit. J. Psychol.*, 1906, 2, 406-463. *205*.

—— Recent work in experimental aesthetics. *Brit. J. Psychol.*, 1921, 12, 76-99. *205*.

BURCHARD, M. L. Physique and psychosis. *Comp. Psychol. Mon.*, 1936, 13. *84*.

BURRI, C. The present status of the problem of individual differences in alternating activities. *Psychol. Bull.*, 1935, 32, 113-139. *156*.

BURT, C. General and specific factors underlying the primary emotions. *Rep. Brit. Ass.*, 69, 45, 1915. *40, 55*.

—— *Report on the consultative committee on psychological tests of educable capacity.* London: H. M. Stationery Office, 1924. *25*.

—— The analysis of temperament. *Brit. J. med. Psychol.*, 1937, 17, 158-188. *55, 86*.

—— The factorial analysis of emotional traits. *Char. and Person.*, 1939, 7, 238-254, 285-299. *205, 211*.

—— *The factors of the mind.* London: Univ. of London Press, 1940. *16, 17, 19, 31, 58*.

—— *The factorial study of physical types.* Man., 1944, 72, 82-86. *76, 92*.

BURTT, H. G. Measuring interest objectively. *Sch. and Soc.*, 1923, 17, 444-448. *158*.

BURTT, H. G. and FRY, O. G. Suggestions for measuring recklessness. *Person. J.* 1934, 13, 39-46. *147.*

CAMERON, D. E. Studies in depression. *J. ment. Sci.,* 1936, 82, 148-161. *107.*
CAMERON, H. C. *The nervous child.* Oxford: University Press, 1929. *162.*
CAMIS, M. *The physiology of the vestibular apparatus.* New York: 1930. *274.*
CAMPBELL, K. J. The relation of the types of physique to the types of mental diseases. *J. abn. soc. Psychol.,* 1932, 27, 147-151. *87.*
CAMPBELL, M. Individual differences in the speed of serial reactions of large muscle groups. *Psychol. Bull.,* 1930, 27, 639-640. *175.*
—— The "personal equation" in serial pursuit performance. *J. appl. Psychol.,* 1934, 18, 785-792. *175.*
CANTRIL, H. General and specific attitudes. *Psychol. Mon.,* 1932, 42. *15.*
CAROTHERS, F. E. Psychological examination of college students. *Arch. of Psychol.,* 1922, 46, 1-82. *146.*
CARPENTER, W. On the influence of suggestion in modifying and directing muscular movement independently of volition. *Notices, Proc. Roy. Inst.,* 1852. *193, 194.*
CARUS, C. G. *Symbolik der menschlichen Gestalt.* (Orig. 1853; Edit. 1925, Celle.) *83.*
CASON, H. An annoyance test, and some research problems. *J. abn. soc. Psychol.,* 1930, 25, 224-236. *70.*
—— The influence of tension and relaxation on the affectivities. *J. gen. Psychol.,* 1938, 18, 77-110. *195.*
CATTELL, R. B. Temperament tests: I. Temperament. II. Tests. *Brit. J. Psychol.,* 1933, 23, 308-329; 1934, 24, 20-49. *55, 146, 156.*
—— On the measurement of perseveration. *Brit. J. educ. Psychol.,* 1935, 5, 76-92. *156.*
—— *A Guide to mental testing.* Univ. of London Press: 1936. *149.*
—— The measurement of adult intelligence. *Psychol. Bull.,* 1943, 40, 153-193. *25.*
—— The description of personality: principles and findings in a factor analysis. *Amer. J. Psychol.,* 1945, 58, 69-90. *37.*
—— The primary trait clusters for describing personality. *Psychol. Bull.,* 1945, 42, 129-161. *37.*
—— The diagnosis of neuroticism: a re-interpretation of Eysenck's data. *J. nerv. ment. Dis.,* 1945. 102, 576-589.
——, and MALTENO, V. Contributions concerning mental inheritance: II. Of temperament. *J. genet. Psychol.,* 1940, 57, 31-47. *146.*
CHANDLER, G. R. *Beauty and human nature.* New York: Appleton Century, 1935. *207.*
CHANDLER, R. A. The sense of humor in children. *Cent. Mag.,* 1902, 959-960. *226.*
CHAO, W. H. Handwriting of Chinese mental patients. In: *Neuropsychiatry in China.* Ed. R. S. Lyman. Vetch-Peking: 1939. *235.*
CHAPMAN, J. C. Persistence, success, and speed in a mental task. *Ped. Sem.,* 1924, 31, 276-284. *158.*
CHEVREUL, M. G. *De la baguette divinatoire.* Paris: Mallet-Bachelier, 1954. *165.*
CHI, P. Statistical analysis of personality retings. *J. exp. Educ.,* 1937, 5, 229-245. *41.*
CHOJECKI, A. Contribution à l'étude de la suggestibilité. *Arch. de Psychol.,* 1911, 11, 182-186. *169.*
CIOCCO, A. The historical background of the modern study of constitution. *Bull. Inst. Hist. Med.,* 1936, 4, 23-38. *83.*
CLAPAREDE, E. La genèse de l'hypothèse. *Arch. de Psychol.,* 1934, 24, 1-154. *226.*

CLARK, J. R. The relation of speed, range, and level to scores on intelligence tests. *Thesis, Columbia University*, 1924. *146.*

CLARK, W. H. Two tests of perseverance. *J. educ. Psychol.*, 1935, 26, 604-610. *159.*

CLARKE, G. *Some character traits of delinquent and normal children in terms of perseveration.* Aust. Counc. educ. Res. Publ., 1934, 29. *156.*

CLEGG, J. L. The association of physique and mental condition. *J. ment. Sci.*, 1935, 81, 297-316. *87.*

CLITES, M. S. Certain somatic activities in relation to successful and unsuccessful problem solving: I. Inter-wink intervals during problem solving. *J. exp. Psychol.*, 1935, 18, 708-724. II. Skin resistance to an electric current in relation to successful and unsuccessful problem solving. *Ibid.*, 1936, 19, 106-115. III. Relation of action potentials and muscular movements and tensions to successful and unsuccessful problem solving. *Ibid.*, 1936, 19, 172-192. *194.*

COBB, I. B. *The glands of destiny.* London: Heinemann, 1927. *23.*

COHEN, J. I. Determinants of physique. *J. ment. Sci.*, 1938, 84, 495-512. *76.*

—— Physical types and their relation to psychotic types. *J. ment. Sci.*, 1940, 86, 602-623. *84.*

—— Physique, size, and proportion. *Brit. J. med. Psychol.*, 1941, 18, 323-337. *76.*

COHN, J. Experimentelle Untersuchungen über die Gefühlsbetonung der Farben, Helligkeiten und ihre Combinationen. *Phil. Stud.*, 1899, 10, 502-603. *207.*

COLLIER, R., and EMCH, M. Introversion-extraversion: the concepts and their clinical use. *Amer. J. Psychiat.*, 1938, 94, 1045-1075. *52.*

CONKLIN, E. S. Determination of normal extrovert-introvert interest differences. *Pedagog. Sem.*, 1927, 34, 28-37. *26, 56.*

CONNOLLY, C. J. *Physique in relation to psychosis.* Stud. Psychol. Psychiat. Cathol. Univ. Amer., 1939, 4, No. 5. *84.*

CORIAT, I. N. Humor and hypomania. *Psychiat. Quart.*, 1939, 13, 681-688. *225.*

COURTHIAL, A., STADT, V. D., and CLAPAREDE, E. Rapidité et qualité. *Arch. de Psychol.*, 1932, 23, 193-229. *146.*

CRACKNELL, S. H. *An investigation into some aspects of the development of character.* Thesis, Univ. of London, 1939. *40.*

CRICHTON-BROWNE, J. *The nervous system and education.* Quoted by Edwards, 1942. *274.*

CRICHTON-MILLER, H. Proc. Roy. Soc. Med., 1930, 23, 883. (Discussion). *42.*

CRUTCHER, R. An experimental study of persistence. *J. appl. Psychol.*, 1934, 18, 409-417. *159.*

CULPIN, M., and SMITH, M. *The nervous temperament.* Indust. Health Res. Brd. Rep., 61, 1930. *40.*

CURRAN, D. The differentiation of neuroses and manic-depressive psychoses. *J. Ment. Sci.*, 1937, 83, 156-174. *42.*

CUSHING, R. A perseverative tendency in pre-school children: a study of personality differences. *Arch. Psychol.*, 1929, 17, 108. *158.*

DALE, H. H. Chemical transmission of effects of nerve impulses. *Brit. med. J.*, 1934, 1, 835-841. *101.*

DAMBACH, K. Die Mehrfacharbeit und ihre typologische Bedeutung. *Ztsch. f. Psychol.*, 1929, Erg. Bd. 14. *220.*

DARLING, R. P. Autonomic action in relation to personality traits in children. *J. abn. soc. Psychol.*, 1940, 35, 246-260. *95.*

DARROCH, J. Variations in the score of a motor perseveration test. *Brit. J. Psychol.*, 1938, 28, 248-262. *157.*

DAVENPORT, C. B. *Body-build and its inheritance.* Washington: Carnegie Inst., 1923. *75.*
DAVIS, L., and HUSBAND, R. W. A study of hypnotic susceptibility in relation to personality traits. *J. abn. soc. Psychol.,* 1931, 26, 175-182. *162.*
DAVIS, R. C. An evaluation and test of Birkhoff's aesthetic measure and formula. *J. gen. Psychol.,* 1936, 15, 231-240. *208.*
DEARBORN, G. V. E. The determination of intellectual regression and progression. *Amer. J. Psychiat.,* 1927, 6, 725-741. *118.*
DEMBO, T. Der Arger als dynamisches Problem. *Psychol. Forsch.,* 1931, 15, 1-144. *128.*
DE NO, R. Ausgewählte Kapitel aus der vergleichenden Physiologie des Labyrinthes. *Ergeb. Physiol.,* 1931, 32, 73 et seq. *273.*
DENTON, E. R. Individual differences in fluctuation of attention. *Thesis, University of London,* 1943. *107.*
DERBY, G. S. J. Amer. med. Ass., 1921, 77, 1002. (Discussion). *97.*
DESŒUDRES, A. Couleur, forme, ou nombre? Recherches experimentales sur le choix suivant l'âge, le sexe et l'intelligence. *Arch. de Psychol.,* 1914, 14, 305-358. *220.*
DEWAR, H. A comparison of tests of artistic appreciation. *Brit. J. educ. Psychol.,* 1938, 8, 29-49. *210, 211.*
DIAMOND, B. L., and SCHMALE, H. I. The mosaic test: I. An evaluation of its clinical application. *Amer. J. Orthopsychiat.,* 1944, 14, 237-251. *236, 237.*
DORCUS, R. M. Color preference and color association. *Ped. Sem.,* 1926, 33, 432. *207.*
DOWD, C. E. A study of the consistency of rate of work. *Arch. of Psychol.,* 1926, 84, 1-33. *146.*
DOWNEY, J. E. *The will temperament and its testing.* Yonkers, N.Y.: World Book, 1923. *23, 205.*
DRAPER, G. *Human constitution.* Philadelphia: W. B. Saunders, 1924. *84.*
—— DUPERTUIS, C. W., and CAUGHEY, J. L. *Human constitution in clinical medicine.* London: Hoeher, 1944. *84.*
DUCKWORTH, W. L. H. "Anthropometry." *Encycl. Britt.,* 14th Ed. *77.*
DUKE ELDER, V. A. *Text-book of Ophthalmology.* London: 1938. *97.*
DUSSER DE BARENNE, J. G. *The labyrinthine and postural mechanisms. In: A handbook of experimental psychology,* C. Murchison, Ed. Worcester: Clark Univ. Press, 1934. *273.*
DVORÁK, M. *Idealismus und Naturalismus in der Gotischen Skulptur und Malerei.* München, 1918. *205.*

EASTMAN, M. *Sense of humor.* New York: C. Scribner's Sons, 1921. *227.*
EDWARDS, A. S. New apparatus for the measurement of bodily movement. *J. exp. Psychol.,* 1939, 15, 125-126. *274.*
—— Effects of the loss of one hundred hours of sleep. *Amer. J. Psychol.,* 1941, 54, 80-91. *274.*
—— Static ataxiameter for head and hips. *Amer. J. Psychol.,* 1941, 54, 576-577. *234.*
—— The measurement of static ataxia. *Amer. J. Psychol.,* 1942, 55, 171-188. *274.*
EGNER, F. Humor und Witz unter strukturpsychologischem Gesichtspunkt. *Arch. f. d. ges. Psychol.,* 1932, 84, 330-372. *225.*
EICHKERN, G. C., and SKAGGS, E. B. Some studies in body sway. *Mich. Acad. Sci., Arts, and Letters,* 1928, 10, 369-379. *274.*
ELJASCH, M. Neue Abstraktionsversuche bei vorschulpflichtigen Kindern. *Ztsch. f. Psychol.,* 1928, 105, 1-42. *220.*

Elste, R. Über die Anwendbarkeit eines Bildserientests zur Beurteilung psychischen Krankheitsgeschehens. *Ztsch. ges. Neurol. Psychiat.*, 1940, 112, 1. *225.*

Engel, P. Über die teilinhaltliche Beachtung von Farbe und Form. Untersuchungen an 800 Schulkindern. *Ztsch. f. pädag. Psychol.*, 1935, 36, 202-216, 241-258. *220.*

Enke, W. Experimentalpsychologische Studien zur Konstitutionsforschung. *Ztsch. f. d. ges. Neurol. Psychiat.*, 1928, 114, 770-794. *220.*

Eppinger, H. Vagotonia. New York: *Nerv. Ment. Dis. Mon.*, 20, 1917. *95.*

Estabrooks, G. H. Experimental studies in suggestion. *Ped. Sem. and J. genet. Psychol.*, 1929, 36, 120-139. *165.*

Evans, J. Taste and temperament. London: 1939. *205.*

Ewen, J. H. A handbook of psychiatry. Baltimore: Wood, 1934. *162.*

Eysenck, H. J. The validity of judgments as a function of the number of judges. *J. exp. Psychol.*, 1939, 25, 650-654. *210, 258.*

—— Primary mental abilities. *Brit. J. educ. Psychol.*, 1939, 9, 270-276. *25.*

—— Some factors in the appreciation of poetry, and their relation to temperamental qualities. *Char. and Person.*, 1940, 9, 160-167. *211.*

—— The general factor in aesthetic judgments. *Brit. J. Psychol.*, 1940, 31, 94-102. *208.*

—— 'Type'-factors in aesthetic judgments. *Brit. J. Psychol.*, 1941, 31, 262-270. *211, 219.*

—— Personality factors and preference judgments. *Nature*, 1941, 3751, 346. *208.*

—— Psychological aspects of colour measurement. *Nature*, 1941, 3735, 682-683. *208.*

—— A critical and experimental study of colour preferences. *Amer. J. Psychol.*, 1941, 54, 385-394. *207.*

—— The validity and reliability of group judgments. *J. exp. Psychol.* 1941, 29, 427-434. *210, 258.*

—— An experimental study of the improvement of mental and physical functions in the hypnotic state. *Brit. J. med. Psychol.*, 1941, 18, 304-316. *198.*

—— The empirical determination of an aesthetic formula. *Psychol. Rev.*, 1941, 48, 83-92. *208.*

—— Abnormal preference judgments as "complex" indicators. *Amer. J. Orthopsychiat.*, 1942, 12, 338-345. *205, 212.*

—— The experimental study of the "good gestalt"—a new approach. *Psychol. Rev.*, 1942, 49, 344-364. *206, 209, 211.*

—— The appreciation of humour—an experimental and theoretical study. *Brit. J. Psychol.*, 1942, 32, 295-309. *227, 229.*

—— Suggestibility and hypnosis—an experimental analysis. *Proc. Roy. Soc. Med.*, 1943, 36, 349-354. *178, 181.*

—— Neurosis and intelligence. *Lancet*, 1943, Sept. 18th, 362. *112, 118.*

—— Suggestibility and hysteria. *J. Neurol. Psychiat.*, 1943, 6, 22-31. *148, 165, 166, 168, 169, 178, 191, 273.*

—— Susceptibility to a visual Illusion, as related to primary and secondary suggestibility and other functions. *Brit. J. Psychol.*, 1943, 34, 32-36. *165.*

—— A study of human aversions and satisfactions, and their relation to age, sex, and temperament. *J. genet. Psychol.*, 1943, 62, 289-299. *203.*

—— An experimental analysis of five tests of "appreciation of humor". *Educ. and psychol. Measurement.*, 1943, 3, 191-214. *229.*

—— General social attitudes. *J. soc. Psychol.*, 1944, 19, 207-227. *15, 202.*

—— The effects of incentives on neurotics, and the variability of neurotics as compared with normals. *Brit. J. med. Psychol.*, 1944, 20, 100-103. *115, 120.*

EYSENCK, H. J.   States of high suggestibility and the neuroses. *Amer. J. Psychol.*, 1944, 57, 406-411. *178, 196.*
—— National differences in "sense of humor": three experimental and statistical studies. *Char. and Person.*, 1944, 13, 37-54. *229.*
—— Types of personality—a factorial study of 700 neurotics. *J. ment. Sci.*, 1944, 90, 851-861. *33, 39.*
—— Graphological analysis and psychiatry: an experimental study. *Brit. J. Psychol.*, 1945, 35, 70-81. *239, 240.*
—— A comparative study of four screening tests for neurotics. *Psychol. Bull.*, 1945, 42, 659-662. *252.*
——, and GILMOUR, J. S. L.   The psychology of philosophers—a factorial study. *Char. and Person.*, 1944, 12, 290-298. *16, 202.*
——, and FURNEAUX, W. D.   Primary and secondary suggestibility: an experimental and statistical study. *J. exp. Psychol.*, 1945, 35, 485-503. *166, 168, 171, 178, 196.*
——, and HALSTEAD, H.   The memory function: I. A factorial study of fifteen clinical tests. *Amer. J. Psychiat.*, 1945, 102, 174-179. *117.*
——, and HIMMELWEIT, H. T.   An experimental study of the reactions of neurotics to experiences of success and failure. *J. gen. Psychol.*, 1946. *132. 134.*
——, and REES, W. L.   States of heightened suggestibility: narcosis. *J. ment. Sci.*, 1945, 91, 301-310. *199.*
——, and YAP, P. M.   Parotid gland secretion in affective mental disorders. *J. ment. Sci.*, 1944, 90, 595-602. *96.*
EYSENCK, M. Davies.   The general factor in correlations between persons. *Brit. J. Psychol.*, 1939, 29, 404-421. *211.*
—— An experimental and statistical study of olfactory preferences. *J. exp. Psychol.*, 1944, 39, 246-252. *208, 211.*
—— An exploratory study of mental organization in senility. *J. Neurol., Neurosurg., and Psychiat.*, 1945, 8, 15-21. *113, 128, 149.*
—— A study of certain qualitative aspects of problem solving behaviour in senile dementia patients. *J. ment. Sci.*, 1945, 91, 337-345. *113,* 128.
—— The psychological aspects of ageing and senility. *J. ment. Sci.*, 1946, 92, 171-181. *113, 128.*


FARBER, M. L.   A critique and an investigation of Kretschmer's theory. *J. abn. soc. Psychol.*, 1938, 33, 398-404. *84.*
FARMER, E., and CHAMBERS, E. G.   *A psychological study of individual differences in accident rates.* London: Ind. Fat. Res. Brd., Rep. 38. H.M. Stationery Office, 1926. *145.*
FARNSWORTH, R., SEASHORE, R. H., and TINKER, M. A.   Speed in simple and serial actions as related to performance in certain 'intelligence' tests. *Ped. Sem. and J. genet. Psychol.*, 1927, 34, 537-551. *145, 146.*
FARR, C. B.   Bodily structure, personality, and reaction type. *Amer. J. Psychiat.*, 1928, 7, 231-244. *84.*
FEARING, F. S.   Factors influencing static equilibrium. An experimental study of the influence of height, weight and position of the feet on amount of sway, together with an analysis of the variability in the records of one reagent over a long period of time. *J. comp. Psychol.*, 1924, 4, 92-121. *274.*
—— Factors influencing static equilibrium. An experimental study of the effects of practice upon amount and direction of sway. *J. comp. Psychol.*, 1924, 4, 163-183. *274.*
—— Factors influencing static equilibrium. An experimental study of the effects of controlled and uncontrolled attention upon sway. *J. comp. Psychol.*, 1925, 5, 1-24. *274.*

FEARING, F. S. Experimental study of the Romberg sign. *J. nerv. ment. Dis.*, 1925, 61, 449-465. *234.*

FERGUSON, G. A. *The reliability of mental tests.* London: Univ. of London Press, 1941. *121.*

FERGUSON, L. W. An analysis of the generality of suggestibility to group opinion. *Char. and Person.*, 1944, 12, 237-244. *168.*

FERNALD, G. E. An achievement capacity test. *J. educ. Psychol.*, 1912, 3, 331-336. *158.*

FERREE, C. E., and RAND, G. Testing fitness for night flying: visual acuity. *Arch. Ophthalm.*, 1938, 20, 58-79. *99.*

——, ——, and LEWIS, E. F. Age as an important factor in the amount of light needed by the eye. *Arch. Ophthalm.*, 1935, 13, 212-226. *99.*

FILTER, R. O. An experimental study of character traits. *J. appl. Psychol.*, 1921, 5, 297-317. *146.*

—— A practical definition of character. *Psychol. Rev.*, 1922, 29, 319-324. *24.*

FISHER, R. A. *Statistical methods for research workers.* Edinburgh: Oliver and Boyd, 1932. *179.*

FISHER, V. E. *An introduction to abnormal psychology.* New York: Macmillan, 1937. *162.*

FISKE, P. W. A study of relationships to somatotype. *J. appl. Psychol.*, 1944, 28, 504-519. *87.*

FLANAGAN, J. C. *Factor analysis in the study of personality.* Stanford: University Press, 1935. *41, 55.*

FLUGEL, J. C. *Man, morals, and society.* London: Duckworth, 1945. *142.*

FOSTER, W. S. On the perseverative tendency. *Amer. J. Psychol.*, 1914, 25, 393-426. *154.*

FRANK, J. D. The influence of the level of performance in one task on the level of aspiration in another. *J. exp. Psychol.*, 1935, 18, 159-171. *133.*

—— Recent studies of the level of aspiration. *Psychol. Bull.*, 1941, 38, 218-225. *128.*

—— The contribution of topological and vector psychology to psychiatry. *Psychiat.*, 1942, 5, 15-22. *128.*

FREEMAN, G. L. Mental activity and the muscular processes. *Psychol. Rev.*, 1931, 38, 428-449. *195.*

—— The facilitative and inhibitory effect of muscular tension upon performance. *Amer. J. Psychol.*, 1933, 45, 17-52. *195.*

FREUD, S. *Wit and its relation to the unconscious.* London: 1916. *226.*

—— *General introduction to psychoanalysis.* New York: Liveright, 1920. *24, 52.*

FREYD, M. Introverts and extroverts. *Psychol. Rev.*, 1924, 5, 74-87. *52, 57.*

FRIEND, G. E. *The schoolboy: a study of his nutrition, physical development and health.* Cambridge: 1935. *77.*

FRISCHEISEN-KÖHLER, I. *Das persönliche Tempo.* Berlin: Thiehme, 1933. *145.*

—— The personal tempo and its inheritance. *Char. and Person.*, 1933, 1, 301-313. *146.*

FROLOV, Y. P. *Pavlov and his school.* London: Kegan Paul, 1937. *41.*

FURNEAUX, W. D. Tests of suggestibility and the prediction of hypnotic susceptibility. *J. Person.*, 1946. *171.*

FURUKAWA, T. A study of temperament by means of human blood groups. *Jap. J. Psychol.*, 1927, 4, 613-634. *57.*

GARNETT, J. C. M. General ability, cleverness and purpose. *Brit. J. Psychol.*, 1918, 9, 345-366. *55.*

GARRETT, H. E. A study of the relation of accuracy to speed. *Arch. of Psychol.*, 1922, 56. *148.*

GARRISON, K. C. An investigation of some simple speed activities. *J. appl. Psychol.*, 1929, 13, 167-172. *146.*

GARRISON, K. C. Further studies in various types of speed performances as related to mental ability. *J. genet. Psychol.*, 1929, 36, 344-349. *146.*

GARTH, T. R. Color preferences of 559 full-blooded Indians. *J. exp. Psychol.*, 1922, 5, 417-426. *207.*

GARVEY, C. R. Comparative body-build of manic-depressive and schizophrenic patients. *Psychol. Bull.*, 1930, 30, 567-568. *84.*

GATES, A. I. An experimental and statistical study of reading and reading tests. *J. educ. Psychol.*, 1921, 32, 303-314, 378-391, 445-464. *175, 176.*

——, and SCOTT, A. W. Characteristics and relations of motor speed and dexterity among young children. *J. genet. Psychol.*, 1931, 39, 423-453. *145, 146.*

GHISELLI, E. Changes in neuro-muscular tension accompanying the performance of a learning problem involving constant choice time. *J. exp. Psychol.*, 1936, 19, 91-99. *195.*

GIBB, C. A. Personality traits by factorial analysis. *Australasian J. Psychol.*, *Phil.*, 1942, 20, 1-15, 86-110. *41.*

GILBERT, L. W. (Ed.) *Kritische Aufsätze über die in München wieder erneuerten Versuche mit dem Schwefelkies-Pendeln und Wunschelruthen.* Halle: 1808. *194.*

GILLILAND, A. R., WITTMAN, P., and GOLDMAN, M. Patterns and scatter of mental abilities in various psychoses. *J. gen. Psychol.*, 1943, 29, 251-260. *118.*

GORDON, K. Group judgments in the field of lifted weights. *J. exp. Psychol.*, 1924, 7, 398-400. *209.*

GOULD, R. An experimental analysis of "level of aspiration". *Genet. Psychol. Mon.*, 1939, 21, 1-116. *133.*

—— Some sociological determinations of goal striving. *J. soc. Psychol.*, 1941, 13, 461-473. *141.*

GREENE, E. B. *Measurements of human behaviour.* New York: Odyssey Press, 1941. *60.*

GREGG, A., MILLER, M., and LINDER, E. *Laughter situations as an indication of responsiveness in young children. In: Some new techniques for studying social behaviour.* New York: R. S. Thomas, 1929. *225.*

GROSS, O. *Die zerebrale Sekundärfunktion.* Leipzig: Vogel, 1902. *20, 155.*

GRUHLE, H. W. Der Körperbau der Normalen. *Arch. f. Psychiat. Nervenkrankh*, 1926, 77, 1-31. *84.*

GUIDI, C. Récherches expérimentales sur la suggestibilité. *Arch. de Psychol.*, 1908, 8, 49-54. *169.*

GUILFORD, J. P. *Psychometric Methods.* New York: McGraw-Hill, 1936. *50, 58.*

—— Human abilities. *Psychol. Rev.*, 1940, 47, 367-394. *17.*

——, and BRALY, K. W. Extroversion and introversion. *Psychol. Bull.*, 1930, 27, 66-107. *57.*

——, —— An experimental test of McDougall's theory of extroversion-introversion. *J. abn. soc. Psychol.*, 1931, 25, 382-389. *106.*

——, and GUILFORD, R. B. An analysis of the factors in a typical test of introversion-extraversion. *J. abn. soc. Psychol.*, 1934, 28, 377-399. *38.*

—— —— Personality factors S, E, and M. *J. Psychol.*, 1936, 2, 109-127. *38, 203.*

—— —— Personality factors D, R, T, and A. *J. Abn. soc. Psychol.*, 1939, 34, 21-36. *38, 203.*

—— —— Personality factors N and GD. *J. abn. soc. Psychol.*, 1939, 34, 239-248. *38, 203.*

GUILLAUME, A. *Vagotonies, sympatheticotonies, neurotonies.* Paris: Masson et Cie., 1928. *95.*

GUTHRIE, E. R. *Personality in terms of associative learning.* In: Hunt, J. Mc. V. (Ed.), *Personality and the behaviour disorders.* New York: Ronald, 1944. *15.*

HAGGARD, E. G. A projective technique using comic strip characters. *Char. and Person.*, 1942, 10, 289-295. *225.*

HALL, W. S. Changes in the form of the body during the period of growth. *J. Anthrop. Inst.*, 1896, 25, 21-45. *77.*

HALSTEAD, H. An analysis of the Matrix (progressive matrices) test results on 700 neurotic (military) subjects and a comparison with the Shipley vocabulary test. *J. ment. Sci.*, 1943, 89, 202-215. *112.*

——, and CHASE, V. E. Review of a verbal intelligence scale as used on military neurotic patients. *Brit. J. med. Psychol.*, 1944, 20, 195-201. *112.*

HAMILTON, N. Perseveration and stability in school children. Thesis, Univ. of Sydney, 1940. (Quoted by Walker et al., 1943). *156.*

HANCOCK, J. A. Preliminary study of motor ability. *Ped. Sem.*, 1894, 3, 9-29. *274.*

HANSEN, C. F. Serial action as a basic measure of motor capacity. *Psychol. Mon.*, 1922, 31, 320-382. *145.*

HARGREAVES, H. L. The "faculty" of imagination. *Brit. J. Psychol. Mon. Supp.*, 1927, 10. *156.*

HARMAN, B. Testing night vision. *Brit. med. J.*, 1941, 1, 636-637. *97, 99.*

HARRIS, A., and SHAKOW, D. The clinical significance of numerical measures of scatter on the Stanford-Binet. *Psychol. Bull.*, 1937, 34, 134-150. *118.*

HARRISON, R., and DORCUS, R. M. Is rate of voluntary bodily movement unitary? *J. gen. Psychol.*, 1938, 18, 31-39. *146.*

—— Personal tempo and the interrelationships of voluntary and maximal rates of movement. *J. gen. Psychol.*, 1941, 24, 343-379. *146.*

HARROWER, M. Organization of higher mental processes. *Psychol. Forsch.*, 1932, 17, 56-120. *225.*

HARROWER-ERICKSON, M., and STEINER, E. *Large scale Rorschach techniques.* Springfield: C. C. Thomas, 1945. *213.*

HARSH, M., BEEBE-CENTER, J. G., and BEEBE-CENTER, R. Further evidence regarding preferential judgment of polygonal forms. *J. Psychol.*, 1939, 7, 343-350. *208.*

HART, H. H., JENKINS, R. L., AXELRAD, S., and SPERLING, P. I. Multiple factor analysis of traits of delinquent boys. *J. soc. Psychol.*, 1943, 17, 191-201. *41.*

HARTMANN, G. W. Precision and accuracy. *Arch. of Psychol.*, 1928, 100. *147.*

HARTSHORNE, H., and MAY, M. *Studies in deceit.* New York: Macmillan, 1928. *15, 258.*

——, ——, and MALLER, J. B. *Studies in service and self control.* New York: Macmillan, 1929. *15, 158.*

——, ——, and SHUTTLEWORTH, K. *Studies in the organization of character.* New York: Macmillan, 1930. *15.*

HAZLITT, V. Children's thinking. *Brit. J. Psychol.*, 1930, 20, 354-361. *220.*

HENCKEL, K. O. Körperbaustudien an Schizophrenen. *Ztsch. f. d. ges. Psychiat. und Neurol.*, 1924, 89, 82-106. *84.*

HENDERSON, D. K., and GILLESPIE, R. D. *A text-book of psychiatry.* Oxford: University Press, 1943. *1, 12, 41, 53.*

HENMON, V. A. C. Air service tests of aptitude for flying. *J. appl. Psychol.*, 1919, 3, 103-109. *275.*

HEYMANS, E., and WIERSMA, R. Beiträge zur speziellen Psychologie. *Ztsch. f. angew. Psychol.*, 1908, 1, 313-383. *13.*

HIMMELWEIT, H. T. A study of temperament of neurotic persons by means of level of aspiration tests. *Thesis, Univ. of London*, 1945. *137, 138, 139.*

—— Speed and accuracy of work as related to temperament. *Brit. J. Psychol.*, 1946, 36, 132-144. *150, 152.*

—— The intelligence vocabulary ratio as a measure of temperament. *J. Person.*, 1945, 14, 93-105. *124, 125.*

HIMMELWEIT, and EYSENCK, H. J. An experimental analysis of the mosaic projection test. *Brit. J. med. Psychol.*, 1945, *238*.

HINSDALE, G. The station of man, considered physiologically and clinically. *Amer. J. med. Sci.*, 1887, 93, 478-485. *274.*

—— Observations on station with reference to respiration. *N. Y. med. J.*, 1890, 51. *274.*

HIPPOCRATES. *On ancient medicine: the genuine works of Hippocrates.* New York: Wood. *75.*

HIRSCHLAFF, L. *Hypnotismus und Suggestionstherapie.* Leipzig: Barth, 1919. *162.*

HÜFFDING, H. *Humor als Lebensgefühl.* Leipzig: Teubner, 1918. *225.*

HOLLINGWORTH, H. L. *Psychology of functional neuroses.* New York: Appleton Century, 1920. *112, 118.*

—— *Abnormal psychology.* London: Methuen, 1931. *37, 112, 118, 126, 224.*

HOLT, E. B. *Animal drive and the learning process.* New York: Holt, 1931. *13.*

HOLZINGER, K. J. *Student manual of factor analysis.* Chicago: Dept. of Education, University of Chicago, 1937. *16.*

——, and HARMAN, H. H. *Factor analysis.* Chicago: University of Chicago, Press, 1941. *19.*

HOPPE, F. Erfolg und Misserfolg. *Psychol. Forsch.*, 1930, 14, 1-62. *128.*

HORST, L. Experimentell-psychologische Untersuchungen zu Kretschmers "Körperbau und Charakter". *Z. Neurol.*, 1924, 93-107. *84.*

HOSKINS, R. G. *The tides of life.* New York: Holt, 1933. *23.*

HOWARD, C. *Thesis, Univ. of London*, 1930. Quoted by Walker, K. F., et. al., 1943. *156.*

HOWELLS, T. H. An experimental study of persistence. *J. abn. soc. Psychol.*, 1933, 28, 14-29. *159.*

HOWIE, D. Aspects of personality in the classroom: a study of ratings on personal qualities for a group of schoolboys. *Brit. J. Psychol.*, 1945, 36, 15-28. *41, 55.*

HRDLIČKA, A. Art and literature in the mentally abnormal. *Amer. J. Insan.*, 1899, 55, 385-404. *206.*

HUANG, I. Abstraction of form and color in children as a function of the stimulus object. *J. genet. Psychol.*, 1945, 66, 59-62. *222.*

HÜBEL, W. Über psychische Geschwindigkeiten und ihre gegenseitigen Beziehungen. *Ztsch. f. Psychol.*, 1930, 35, 447-496. *145.*

HUDGINS, C. V. Conditioning and the voluntary control of the pupillary light reflex. *J. gen. Psychol.*, 1933, 8, 3-51. *198.*

HULL, C. L. *Hypnosis and suggestibility.* New York: Appleton Century, 1933. *165, 166, 178, 180, 196, 224, 274.*

HUNT, J. Erethitic and kolytic types. *J. abn. soc. Psychol.*, 1929, 23, 176-181. *57.*

HUNT, J. McV., and COFER, C. *Psychological deficit. In: Hunt, J. McV., Ed. Personality and the behaviour disorders.* New York: Ronald, 1944. *111.*

——, and GUILFORD, J. P. Fluctuation of an ambiguous figure in dementia praecox and in manic-depressive patients. *J. abn. soc. Psychol.*, 1933, 27, 443-452. *106.*

HUNT, W. A., WITTSON, C. L., and HARRIS, H. I. The screen test of military selection. *Psychol. Rev.*, 1944, 51, 37-46. *252.*

HUNSICKER, R. L. M. *A study of the relationship between rate and ability.* Col. Univ.: Teach. Coll. Contrib. Educ., 1925, 185. *146.*

HUSBAND, R. W. The effects of musical rhythms and pure rhythms on bodily sway. *J. gen. Psychol.*, 1934, 11, 328-335. *275.*

HUTER, C. *Illustriertes Handbuch.* Breslau, 1928. *87.*

HUXLEY, J. S. *Problems of relative growth.* London: 1932. *77.*

JACOB, C., and MOSER, K. Messungen zu Kretschmers Körperbaulehre. *Arch. f. Psychiat. und Nervenkrankh.*, 1923, 70, 93-108. *84.*

JACOBSON, E. Neuromuscular states during mental activities. *Amer. J. Physiol.*, 1929, 91, 567-608; 1930, 94, 22-34; 1930, 95, 694-702; 702-712; 1931, 96, 115-121, 122-125; 1931, 97, 200-209. *195.*
—— Action currents from muscular contractions during conscious processes. *Science*, 1927, 66, 403. *195.*
—— Electro-physiology of mental activities. *Amer. J. Psychol.*, 1932, 44, 677-694. *195.*
JACOBY, G. W. *Suggestion and psychotherapy.* New York: Scribner, 1912. *162.*
JAENSCH, E. R., et al. *Studien zur Psychologie menschlicher Typen.* Leipzig: Barth, 1930. *12, 109.*
JAENSCH, W. *Grundzüge einer Physiologie und Klinik der Psychophysischen Persönlichkeit.* Berlin: Springer, 1926. *12, 205.*
JAMES, W. *Principles of psychology.* New York: Holt, 1890. *194, 202.*
JANET, P. *L'Etat mental des hystériques.* Paris: Rueff, 1894. *11.*
—— *Les obsessions et la psychasthénie.* Paris; Alcan, 1903. *11, 37.*
—— *Major symptoms of hysteria.* New York: Macmillan, 1907. *161, 174.*
JASPER, H. H. Is perseveration a functional unit participating in all behaviour? *J. soc. Psychol.*, 1931, 2, 35-51. *156.*
JASTAK, J. *Psychometric patterns of state hospital patients.* Delaware St. med. J., 1937, 9, 7-10. Quoted by Hunt, J. McV., 1944. *112.*
JENSEN, B., and ROTTER, J. B. The validity of the multiple choice Rorschach test in officer candidate selection. *Psychol. Bull.*, 1945, 42, 182-185. *213.*
JONES, E. S. The influence of age and experience on correlations concerned with mental tests. New York: Warwick and York, 1917. *146.*
JONES, L. W. *Perseveration.* Proc. Britt. Ass., 1915, 698-699. *156.*
JONES, M., and MELHUISH, V. *Unpublished data,* 1945. *103.*
JONES, M., and STADIE, W. C. Choline esterase content of muscle of myasthenia gravis and of serum of four other groups of clinical conditions. *Quart. J. exp. Physiol.*, 1939, 29, 63-67. *101.*
——, and TOD, H. The inhibitory action of exercise upon choline esterase in vivo. *Biochem. J.*, 1935, 29, 2242-2245. *101.*
JUCKNAT, M. Leistung, Anspruchsniveau und Selbstbewusstsein. *Psychol. Forsch.*, 1937, 22, 89-179. *136, 141.*
JUNG, C. G. The psychology of dementia praecox. *Nerv. ment. dis. Mon.*, 1936, Ser. 3. (German ed. 1909). *11.*
—— *Psychological types.* New York: Harcourt, Brace, 1923. *11, 27, 52, 202.*

KADNER, S. *Rasse und Humor.* München: Lehman, 1939. *225.*
KAMBOUROPOULOU, P. Individual differences in the sense of humor. *Amer. J. Psychol.*, 1926, 37, 288-297. *225, 231.*
—— Individual differences in the sense of humor and their relation to temperamental differences. *Arch. of Psychol.*, 1930, 121. *225, 230, 231.*
KANNER, L., and SCHILDER, P. F. Movements in optic images and the optic imagination of movements. *J. nerv. ment. Dis.*, 1930, 72, 489. *195.*
KATZ, D. *Studien zur Kinderpsychologie.* Leipzig, 1913. *220.*
KEKCHEYEV, K. *Expediting visual adaptation to darkness.* Nature, 1943, 151, 617-618. *100, 101.*
——, DERZHAVIN, N., and PILIPCHUK, S. Problems of night vision. *War Med.*, 1943, 3, 171-173. *100, 101.*
KELLEY, T. *Crossroads in the mind of man.* Stanford: University Press, 1928. *156.*
—— *Essential traits of mental life.* Cambridge: Harvard Univ. Press, 1935. *17, 55.*
——, and KREY, A. C. *Tests and measurements in the social sciences.* New York: Scribner, 1934. *41.*
KEMPF, E. J. *The autonomic functions and the personality.* Washington: Nerv. ment. dis. Publ. Co., 1921. *57.*

KEMPF, E. J. Biological differentiae of energic constitutional types. *Med. Rec.*, N.Y. 1941, 154, 295-302. *13*.

KENDIG, I., and RICHMOND, W. V. *Psychological studies in dementia praecox.* Ann Arbor.: Edwards, 1940. *112*.

KENNEDY, M. Speed as a personality trait. *J. soc. Psychol.*, 1930, 1, 286-299. *145*.

KENT, G. H., and ROSANOFF, A. J. A study of association in insanity. *Amer. J. Insan.*, 1910, 67, 307-317. *212*.

KERR, M. The validity of the mosaic test. *J. Orthopsychiat.*, 1935, 9, 232-236. *237*.

KIBLER, M. Experimentalpsychologische Beiträge zur Typenforschung. *Ztsch. f. d. ges. Neurol. Psychiat.*, 1925, 98, 524-544. *220*.

KIMMINS, C. W. *The springs of laughter.* London: Methuen, 1932. *226*.

KIRSCHER, A. *De mundo subterraneo.* Roma, 1678. *194*.

KISSELEW, M. W. Der Körperbau und die besonderen Arten des Schizophrenieverlaufs. *Ztsch. f. d. ges. Neurol. Psychiat.*, 1931, 132, 18-56. *85*.

KLINCKOWSTROEM, C. *Bibliographie der Wünschelrute.* München, 1913. *193*.

KOLLE, K. Der Körperbau der Schizophrenen. *Arch. f. Psychiat. Nervenkrankh.*, 1925, 72, 40-88. *87*.

—— Körperbauuntersuchungen an Schizophrenen. *Ibid.*, 1925, 75, 21-61. *84*.

KRÄPELIN, E. *Psychiatrie.* Leipzig: Barth, 1899. *10, 160*.

KRANZ, H. *Lebensschicksale krimineller Zwillinge.* Berlin; 1936. *46*.

KRASNOGORSKI, N. I. Bedingte und unbedingte Reflexe im Kindesalter und ihre Bedeutung för die Klinik. *Ergeb. inn. Med. Kinderheilkunde*, 1931, 39, 613-730. *41*.

KRETSCHMER, E. *Physique and character.* New York: Harcourt and Brace, 1926. *10, 84, 202*.

—— *Textbook of medical psychology.* London: Oxford University Press, 1934. *14*.

KRÜGER, F., and SPEARMAN, C. Die Korrelation zwischen verschiedenen geistigen Leistungsfähigkeiten. *Ztsch. f. Psychol.*, 1906, 44, 50-114. *144*.

KUDER, G. F., and RICHARDSON, M. W. The theory and estimation of test reliability. *Psychometrika*, 1937, 2, 151-160. *121*.

KÜGELGEN, G. W. Eignungsprüfung für den Kaufmann oder Bureauangestellten. *Psychotech. Ztsch.*, 1932, 8, 70-84. *155*.

KÜNBERG, M. Über Abstraktionsfühigkeit und die Entstehung von Relationen beim vorschulpflichtigen Kinde. *Ztsch. f. angew. Psychol.*, 1920, 17, 270-294. *220*.

KUHLMAN, F. Experimental studies in mental deficiency: three cases of imbecility (Mongolian) and six cases of feeble-mindedness. *Amer. J. Psychol.*, 1904, 15, 391-402. *220*.

KÜHN, H. *Die Kunst der Primitiven.* München, 1923. *205*.

KULP, D. H. Prestige as measured by single experienced changes and their permanency. *J. educ. Res.*, 1934, 27, 663-672. *168*.

KÜLPE, O. Versuche über Abstraktion. *Ber. über d. I Kungr. f. exp. Psychol.*, Leipzig, 1904, 56. *220*.

LANDIS, C., and ROSS, J. Humor and its relation to other personality traits. *J. soc. Psychol.*, 1933, 4, 156-175. *225*.

LANGE, J. *Verbrechen als Schicksal: Studien an kriminellen Zwillingen.* Leipzig, 1929. *46*.

LANGFELDT, G. *The prognosis in schizophrenia and the factors influencing the course of the disease.* Copenhagen: Levin and Munksgaard, 1937. *85*.

LANIER, L. H. The interrelations of speed measurements. *J. exp. Psychol.*, 1934, 17, 371-399. *144, 145*.

LANKES, W. Perseveration. *Brit. J. Psychol.*, 1915, 7, 387-419. *156*.

LASHLEY, K. S. Reflex secretions of the human parotid gland. *J. exp. Psychol.*, 1916, 1, 461-493. *96, 97.*
—— The human salivary reflex and its use in psychology. *Psychol. Rev.*, 1914, 23, 446-464. *96, 97.*
LAUER, A. R. Personal 'tempo' or rhythm. *Proc. Ia. Acad. Sci.*, 1933, 40, 192-193. Quoted by Harrison, 1941. *146.*
LEBRUN, FATHER. *Lettres qui découvrent l'illusion de philosophes sur la baguette, et qui détruisent leur systèmes.* Paris, 1693. *194.*
LEE, M. A. M., and KLEITMAN, N. Studies in the physiology of sleep: II. Attempts to demonstrate functional changes in the nervous system during experimental insomnia. *Amer. J. Physiol.*, 1923, 67, 141-152. *274.*
LEMMON, W. The relation of reaction time to measures of intelligence, memory, and learning. *Arch. of Psychol.*, 1927, 94, 1-39. *145.*
LEWIN, K. *Dynamic theory of personality.* New York: McGraw-Hill, 1935. *26.*
——, DEMBO, T., FESTINGER, L., and SEARS, R. S. Level of aspiration. In: Hunt, J. McV., 1944. *128, 132, 136.*
LEWIS, A. Melancholia: a clinical survey of depressive states. *J. ment. Sci.*, 1934, 80, 277-378. *42.*
LEWITAN, C. Untersuchungen über das allgemeine psychomotorische Tempo. *Ztsch. f. Psychol.*, 1927, 101, 321-376. *145, 146.*
LINDBERG, B. J. *Experimental studies of colour and non-colour attitude in school children and adults.* Copenhagen: Levin and Munksgaard, 1938. *12, 220, 222, 223, 237.*
LINE, W., and KAPLAN, E. The existence, measurement and significance of a speed factor in the abilities of public school children. *J. exper. Educ.*, 1932, 1, 1-8. *146.*
——, and GRIFFIN, J. P. M. The objective determination of factors underlying mental health. *Amer. J. Psychiat.*, 1935, 91, 833-842. *40, 55.*
LISTER, A., and BISHOP, J. W. Night vision in the army: report of 10,333 tests. *Brit. med. J.*, 1943, 2, 325-327. *97, 99.*
LIVINGSTON, P. C. Examination of night visual capacity in relation to flying. *Brit. J. Surg.*, 1942, 29, 339-345. *98.*
——, and BOLTON, B. Night visual capacity of pathological cases. *Lancet*, 1943, 1, 263-264. *97, 98.*
LONGSTAFF, H. P., and PORTER, J. P. Speed and accuracy as factors in objective tests in general psychology. *J. appl. Psychol.*, 1928, 12, 636-642. *146, 147, 148.*
LOWENFELD, V. *The nature of creative activity.* London: 1939. *205.*
LOWENFELD, M. *Notes on the nature and use of the Mosaic test.* London: The Institute of Child Psychology, no date. *236.*
LOEWI, O. Ferrier lecture on problems connected with the principle of humoral transmission of nervous impulses. *Proc. Roy. Soc.*, 1935, 118, 299-316. *101.*
LUDOVICI, A. M. *The secret of laughter.* London: Constable, 1932. *226.*
LURIA, A. R. *The nature of human conflicts.* New York: Liveright, 1932. *24, 37.*
LÜTH, K. F. Über Vererbung und konstitutionelle Beziehungen der vorwiegenden Form—und Farbbeachtung. *Ztsch. f. menschl. Vererb.—und Konstitutionslehre*, 1935, 19, 61-81. *220.*
LUTZ, A. Teilinhaltliche Beachtung, Auffassungsumpfang und Persönlichkeitstypus. *Zeitsch. f. Psychol.*, 1929, Erg. Bd. 14. *220.*
LYTHGOE, G. J. Mechanisms of dark adaptation: critical resumé. *Brit. J. Ophthalm.*, 1940, 24, 21-43. *98.*

MAIER, N. R. F. A   talt theory of humour. *Brit. J. Psychol.*, 1932, 23, 69-79. *226.*

MAITRA, M. K., and HARRIS, L. J. Nutrition surveys: vitamin A deficiency among school children in London and Cambridge. *Lancet*, 1937, 2, 1009-1014. *97*.

MALAMUD, W., and GOTTLIEB, J. *Therapeutic results in psychoneurosis.* Quoted by Hunt, J. McV., 1944. *112, 118*.

MALLER, J. B. Studies in character and personality in German psychological literature. *Psychol. Bull.*, 1933, 30, 209-232. *23*.

—— General and specific factors in character. *J. soc. Psychol.*, 1934, 5 97-102. *40*.

MANSON, G. E. Personality differences in intelligence test performance. *J. appl. Psychol.*, 1925, 9, 230-235. *148*.

MARPLE, C. H. The comparative susceptibility of three age levels to the suggestion of group versus expert opinion. *J. soc. Psychol.*, 1933, 4, 176-186. *168*.

MARSTON, L. R. The emotions of young children. *Iowa Stud. Child Welf.*, 1925, 3. *57*.

MARUM, O. Character assessments from handwriting. *J. ment. Sci.*, 1945, 91, 22-42. *239, 241*.

MASLOW, A. H., and MITTELMAN, B. *Principles of abnormal psychology.* New York, 1941. *135*.

MASSERMAN, J. H. *Behaviour and neurosis.* Chicago: Univ. Press, 1943. *198*.

MATECKI, W., and SZPIDBAUM, H. Die Konstitution der schizophrenen Juden. *Ztsch. f. d. ges. Neurol. Psychiat.*, 1927, 109, 62-78. *84*.

MATEER, F. *The unstable child.* New York: Appleton, 1924. *118*.

MAUZ, F. *Die Prognostik der ergogensen Psychosen.* Leipzig: Thieme, 1930. *85*.

MAX, L. W. An experimental study of the motor theory of consciousness: I. Critique of earlier studies. *J. gen. Psychol.*, 1934, 11, 112-125. III. Action current responses in deaf during sleep, sensory, stimulation and dreams. *J. comp. Psychol.*, 1935, 19, 469-486. *194, 195*.

MAXWELL, S. S. *Labyrinth and equilibrium.* Philadelphia: Lippincott, 1923. *273*.

MAYER-GROOS, W. Über Spiel, Scherz, Ironie und Humor in der Schizophrenie. *Ztsch. f. d. ges. Neurol. Psychiat.*, 1921, 69, 332-353. *225*.

McCLOY, C. H. A factor analysis of personality traits to underlie character education. *J. educ. Psychol.*, 1936, 27, 375-387. *41, 55*.

McDOUGALL, W. *Suggestion.* Encyclop. Britt., 1911. *162*.

—— *Outline of psychology.* New York: Scribner's, 1923. *16, 23, 27*.

—— *Outline of abnormal psychology.* New York: Scribner's 1926. *11, 24, 37, 57, 106, 180*.

—— *Energies of men.* New York: Scribner's, 1933. *25, 106*.

McFARLAND, R. An experimental study of the relationship between speed and mental ability. *J. gen. Psychol.*, 1930, 3, 67-97. *145, 146*.

——, and HUDDLESON, J. H. Neurocirculatory reactions in the psychoneuroses studied by the Schneider method. *Amer. J. Psychiat.*, 1936, 93, 567 599. *103*.

MACKINNON, D. W. *The structure of personality.* In: Hunt, J. McV., 1944. *12, 15*.

McNALLY, W. J., and STUART, E. A. Physiology of the labyrinth reviewed in relation to seasickness and other forms of motion sickness. *War Med.*, 1942, 2, 643-771. *273*.

McNEILL, H. *Motor adaptation and accuracy.* Louvain: Editions de l'institut sup. de Phil., 1934. *147*.

MCTEER, W. Changes in grip tension following electric shock in mirror tracing. *J. exp. Psychol.*, 1933, 16, 735-742. *194*.

MENZIES, R. Further studies in conditioned vasomotor responses in human subjects. *J. ex. Psychol.*, 1941, 29, 457-482. *198*.

MESSER, A. L., HINCKLEY, G. R., and MOSIER, C. I. Suggestibility and neurotic symptoms in normal subjects. *J. gen. Psychol.*, 1938, 19, 391-399. *164.*

MEUMANN, E. *Vorlesungen zur Einführung in die experimentelle Pädagogik.* Berlin: Engelmann, 1913. *145.*

MEYERS, C. S., and VALENTINE, C. W. A study of the individual differences in attitude towards tones. *Brit. J. Psychol.*, 1914, 7, 68-100. *205.*

—— Individual differences in listening to music. *Brit. J. Psychol.*, 1922, 18, 52-71. *205.*

MICHEL, F., and WEBER, R. Körperbau und Charakter. *Arch. f. Psychiat.*, 1924, 71, 265. *84.*

MICHAELS, J. J., and SCHILLING, M. E. The correlation of the intelligence quotients of the Porteus Maze and Binet-Simon tests in 200 neuro-psychiatric patients. *Amer. J. Orthopsychiat.*, 1936, 6, 71-74. *112, 126.*

MILES, W. R. Static equilibrium as a useful test of motor control. *J. indust. Hygiene*, 1922, 3, 316-331. *274.*

—— Alcohol and human efficiency. *Carnegie Inst. Washington Publ.* No. 333, 1924. *274.*

MILLS, R. W. The relation of bodily habitus to visceral form, position, tonus, and motility. *Amer. J. Roentgen.*, 1917, 4, 155-169. *75.*

MITCHELL, S. W., and LEWIS, M. J. The tendon jerk, and muscle-jerk in disease, and especially in posterior sclerosis. *Amer. J. med. Sci.*, 1886, 92, 363. *274.*

MOLLENHOFF, F. Zur Frage der Beziehungen zwischen Körperbau und Psychose. *Arch. f. Psychiat.*, 1924, 71, 98. *84.*

MOORE, H. T. The comparative influence of majority and expert opinion. *Amer. J. Psychol.*, 1921, 32, 16-20. *168.*

MORGAN, J. B. *The psychology of abnormal people.* New York: Longmans, 1936. *162.*

MOSIER, C. I. A factor analysis of certain neurotic symptoms. *Psychometrika*, 1937, 2, 263-286. *39.*

MOSS, F. S. Further experimental work with the new wabblemeter. *S.A.E. Journal*, 1931, 29, 243-246. *274.*

—— New riding-comfort research instruments and wabblemeter applications. *S.A.E. Journal*, 1932, 30, 182-184. *274.*

MUDGE, E. L. Time and accuracy as related to mental tests. *J. educ. Psychol.*, 1921, 12, 159-161. *147.*

MÜLLER, F. *Aesthetisches und ausser-ästhetisches Urteilen des Kindes bei Betrachtungen von Bildwerken.* Berlin: 1912. *205.*

MÜLLER, G. E., and PILZECKER, A. Experimentelle Beiträge zur Lehre vom Gedächtnis. *Ztsch. f. Psychol.*, 1900, Eg. Bd. 1, 58 et seq. *154.*

MÜLLER-FREIENFELS, R. *Persönlichkeit und Weltanschauung.* Berlin Teubner, 1919. *202.*

MURPHY, G., and JENSEN, F. *Approaches to personality.* New York: Coward-McCamus, 1932. *27.*

——, MURPHY, L. B., and NEWCOMB, T. M. *Experimental social psychology.* New York: Harper, 1937. *165.*

MURRAY, H. A. *Explorations in personality.* New York: Oxford Univ. Press, 1938. *230.*

NACCARATI, S. The morphologic aspect of intelligence. *Arch. Psychol.*, 1921, N.Y., No. 45. *86.*

NELSON, J. F. *Personality and intelligence.* New York: Teach. Coll., 1931. *158.*

NEWMAN, H. H., FREEMAN, F. N., and HOLZINGER, K. J. *Twins: a study of heredity and environment.* Chicago: 1937. *46.*

NEYMAN, C. A., and KOHLSTEDT, K. D. A new diagnostic test for intro-version-extraversion. *J. abn. soc. Psychol.*, 23, 482-487. *27.*

NOTCUTT, B.  Perseveration and fluency.  *Brit. J. Psychol.*, 1943, 33, 200-208. *146, 156.*

NOYES, A. P.  *Modern Clinical psychiatry.*  New York: Saunders, 1939. *162.*

OATES, D. V.  Group factors in temperament qualities.  *Brit. J. Psychol.*, 1929, 20, 118-135. *40, 55.*

OESER, A. O.  Some experiments on the abstraction of form and colour. *Brit. J. Psychol.*, 1932, 22, 200-215, 287-323. *220.*

OLIVIER, H. G.  Der Körperbau der Schizophrenen.  *Ztsch. f. d. ges. Psychiat. Neurol.*, 1922, 80, 489-498. *84.*

OLSON, W. C.  The measurement of nervous habits in normal children. *Univ. Minn. Child Welf. Mon. Ser.*, No. 3, 1929. *15.*

OMWAKE, K. T.  Effects of varying periods of sleep on nervous stability. *J. appl. Psychol.*, 1932, 16, 623-632. *274.*

OMWAKE, L.  A study of sense of humor: its relation to sex, age, and personal characteristic.  *J. appl. Psychol.*, 1937, 21, 688-704. *225.*

OTIS, M.  A study of suggestibility of children.  *Arch. of Psychol.*, 1923, 70. *164.*

PATERSON, D. G.  *Physique and intellect.*  New York: Appleton Century, 1930. *87.*

PAVLOV, I. P.  *Conditioned reflexes and psychiatry.*  London: Lawrence and Wishart, 1941. *37, 41, 56.*

PEAK, H., and BORING, E. G.  The factor of speed in intelligence.  *J. exp. Psychol.*, 1926, 9, 71-94. *145.*

PEAR, T. H.  *Voice and personality.*  London: Chapman and Hall, 1931. *15.*

PEARL, R.  *Constitution and health.*  London: Kegan Paul, 1933. *74.*

PENDE, N.  *Konstitution und innere Sekretion.*  Budapest, 1924. *75.*

PENROSE, L. S.  Mental defect.  *J. ment. Sci.*, 1944, 90, 399-409. *73.*

PERRIN, F. A. C.  An experimental study of motor ability.  *J. exp. Psychol.*, 1921, 4, 24-56. *145.*

PERRY, R. C.  A group factor analysis of the adjustment questionnaire. *University of South Calif., Educ. Mon.*, 1934, 5. *41.*

PETERS, H. N.  The experimental study of aesthetic judgments.  *Psychol. Bull.*, 1942, 39, 273-305. *209.*

PETRIE, A.  The study of experimental methods of assessing personality. *Thesis, Univ. of London. 144, 149, 153, 191.*

—— Repression and suggestibility as related to neurotic syndrome.  *To appear.*

PILLSBURY, W. B.  Body form and success in studies.  *J. soc. Psychol.*, 1936, 7, 129-139. *92.*

—— Body form and introversion—extraversion.  *J. abn. soc. Psychol.*, 1939, 34, 400-401. *92.*

PINARD, J. W.  Tests of perseveration, I.  Their relation to character.  *Brit. J. Psychol.*, 1932, 23, 5-19. *156.*

PLATTNER, W.  *Körperbauuntersuchungen bei Schizophrenen.*  Arch. d. J. Klaus Stiftung, Zurich, 1932. *85.*

—— Das Körperbauspektrum.  *Ztsch. f. d. ges. Neurol. Psychiat.*, 1938, 160, 703-712. *87.*

PLATTNER-HEBERLEIN, F.  Persönlichkeit und Psychose asthenischer und pyknischer Schizophrener.  *Ztsch. f. d. ges. Neurol. Psychiat.*, 1932, 141, 277-320. *85.*

POPPINGA, O.  Die teilinhaltliche Beachtung von Form und Farbe bei Erwachsenen in ihrer Beziehung zur strukturpsychologischen Typenlehre. *Ztsch. f. Psychol.*, 1931, 121, 137-177. *220.*

PORTER, J. P.  A comparative study of some measures of persistence.  *Psychol. Bull.*, 1933, 30, 664. *159.*

PRIDEAUX, E.  Suggestion and suggestibility.  *Brit. J. Psychol.*, 1919, 10, 228-241. *165.*

PRINZHORN, H. *Bildnerei der Geisteskranken.* Berlin: Springer, 1923. *206.*
PURVES-STEWART, J. *The diagnosis of nervous disease.* New York: 1931. *275.*

RABIN, A. I. Test-score patterns in schizophrenia and non-psychotic states. *J. Psychol.*, 1941, 12, 91-100. *118.*
—— Differentiating psychometric patterns in schizophrenia and manic-depressive psychosis. *J. abn. soc. Psychol.*, 1942, 37, 270-272. *118.*
RADEMAKER, E. Réactions labyrinthiques. Paris: Masson et Cie., 1935. *273.*
RANGACHAR, F. Differences in perseveration among Jewish and English boys. *Brit. J. educ. Psychol.*, 1932, 2, 199-211. *156.*
RAPHAEL, T., FERGUSON, W. G., and SEARLE, O. M. Constitutional factors in schizophrenia. *Arch. Res. Neurol. Ment. Dis.*, 1928, 5, 100-132. *84.*
RAPPAPORT, D. *Emotion and memory.* Baltimore: Williams and Wilkins, 1942. *192.*
RAVEN, J. C. Standardization of progressive matrices, 1938. *Brit. J. med. Psychol.*, 19, 137-150. *112.*
—— Matrix tests. *Ment. Health*, 1940, 1, 10-18. *113.*
—— *The Mill Hill Vocabulary Test.* London: H. K. Lewis, 1944. *123.*
——, and WALSHAW, J. B. Vocabulary tests. *Brit. J. med. Psychol.*, 1944, 20, 185-194. *123.*
READ, H. *Education through Art.* London: Faber and Faber, 1943. *205.*
REAM, M. J. The tapping test as a measure of motility. *Psychol. Mon.*, 1922, 140, 293-319. *145.*
REBATEL, G. *Le rire dans la Démence Précoce.* Lyons: 1908. *225.*
REED, H. J. The influence of a change of conditions upon the amount recalled. *J. exp. Psychol.*, 1931, 14, 632-649. *195.*
REES, W. L. L. *Physical constitution in relation to effort syndrome, neurotic and psychotic types.* M.D. thesis, Univ. of Wales, 1943. *84, 92.*
—— Night visual capacity of neurotic soldiers' *J. Neurol., Neurosurg., Psychiat.*, 1945, 8, 34-39. *97.*
——, and EYSENCK, H. J. A factorial study of some morphological and psychological aspects of human constitution. *J. ment. Sci.*, 1945, 91, 8-21. *77, 95.*
REICHARD, S., and SHAFER, R. The clinical significance of scatter on the Bellevue scale. *Bull. Menn. Clin.*, 1943, 7, 93-98. *118.*
REITER, N. The relation of gross bodily movement to problem solving activity. *Psychol. Bull.*, 1933, 30, 572-573. *195.*
RETHLINGSHAFER, D. Relationship of tests of persistence to other measures of continuance of activities. *J. abn. soc. Psychol.*, 1942, 37, 71-82. *159.*
RÉVÉSZ, G. Abstraktionsversuche an niedrigen Affen. *Ber. über d. 9. Kongr. d. exp. Psychol.*, Jena, 1926, 209. *220.*
REXROAD, C. N. A factor analysis of student traits. *J. educ. Psychol.*, 1937, 28, 153-156. *41.*
REYBURN, H. A., and TAYLOR, J. Some aspects of personality. *Brit. J. Psychol.*, 1939, 30, 151-165. *41.*
REYMART, M. The personal equation in motor capacities. *Scand. Sci. Rev.*, 1923, 2, 177-222. *145.*
RICALDINI, M. A. Platforme mobile pour l'observation et l'enregistrement graphique du phénomène de Romberg et d'autres troubles de la statique. *Bull. et Mém. Soc. d'Hop. de Paris*, 1928, 52, 1138-1145. *274.*
RICHTER, C. P., and WADA, T. Method of measuring salivary secretions in human beings. *J. Lab. and clin. Med.*, 1924, 9, 271-273. *96.*
RICHTER, D., and LEE, M. Serum choline esterase and anxiety. *J. ment. Sci.*, 1942, 88, 428-434. *101.*
——, —— Serum choline esterase and depression. *J. ment. Sci.*, 1942, 88, 435-439. *102.*

RIEGL, A. *Stilfragen.* Berlin: 1893. *205.*
—— *Spätrömische Kunstindustrie.* München, 1927. *205.*
RITTER, E. *Die teilinhaltliche Beachtung von Form und Farbe bei Jugendlichen inihrer Beziehung zur strukturpsychologischen Typenlehre.* Thesis, Marburg, 1930. Quoted by Lindgren, 1938. *220.*
ROBACK, A. *The psychology of character.* New York: Harcourt, Brace, 1931. *22, 24.*
ROBERTS, F. Proc. Sev. Intern. Genet. Congr., 1939, 249. *43.*
ROE, A., and SHAKOV, D. Intelligence in mental disorder. *Ann. N. Y. Acad., Sci.,* 1942, 42, 361-490. *112, 118.*
ROGERSON, C. H. The differentiation of neuroses and psychoses, with special reference to states of depression and anxiety. *J. ment. Sci.,* 1940, 86, 632-644. *42.*
ROHDEN, F. Körperbauuntersuchungen an geistesschwachen und gesunden Verbrechern. *Arch. f. Psychiat. u. Nervenkrankh.,* 1926, 77, 151-163. *87.*
ROMBERG, M. H. *Manual of the nervous disorders of man.* London: Sydenham Trans., 1853. *273.*
RORSCHACH, H. *Psychodiagnostik.* Bern: Huber, 1942. *213, 224.*
ROSANOFF, A. *Manual of psychiatry.* London: Wiley, 1920. *162.*
ROSENFELD, M. Zur Methodik der Untersuchungen aud Gleichgewichtsstörungen. *Arch. Psychiat. Nervenkrankh.,* 1918, 59, 287-300. *274.*
ROSENTHAL, J. Typology in the light of the theory of conditioned reflexes. *Char. and Person.,* 1931, 1, 56-69. *41.*
ROSENZWEIG, S. The experimental study of repression. In: Murray, H., 1938. *162.*
——, and SARASON, S. An experimental study of the triadic hypothesis in relation to frustration, ego-defence, and hypnotic ability. *Char. and Person.,* 1942, 9, 1-19. *162, 163.*
ROSS, T. A. *The common neuroses.* London, 1937. *42.*
ROSTAN, L. *Cours elémentaire d'hygiène.* Paris: 1828. *83.*
ROTTER, J. B. Level of aspiration as a method of studying personality: I. A critical review of methodology. *Psychol. Rev.,* 1942, 49, 463-474. II. Development and evaluation of a controlled method. *J. exp. Psychol.,* 1942, 31, 410-421, III. Group validity studies. *Char. and Person.,* 1943, 11, 254-274. IV. The analysis of patterns of response. *J. soc. Psychol.,* 1945, 21, 159-177. *128, 141.*
ROUNDS, G. H. Is the latent time in the Achilles tendon reflex a criterion of speed in mental reactions? *Arch. of Psychol.,* 1928, 95, 1-91. *145.*
RYANS, D. G. The measurement of persistence: an historical review. *Psychol. Bull.,* 1939, 36, 715-739. *159.*
RYCROFT, B. W. Night vision in the army. *Brit. med. J.,* 1942, 2, 576-577. *97, 99.*

SACHS, W. *The vegetative nervous system.* London: Cassell and Co., 1936. *95.*
SALTER, A. *What is hypnosis?* New York: Smith, 1944. *197.*
SANFORD, R. N., ADKINS, M., KILLER, R. B., COBB, E. A., et al. *Physique, personality and scholarship.* Washington: Soc. Res. Child. Develop., Nat. Res. Counc., 1943. *87.*
SARTON, E. *Introduction to the history of science.* Baltimore: Williams and Wilkins, 1927. *49.*
SATOW, L. *Hypnotism and suggestion.* London, 1923. *162.*
SCHAFER, R., and RAPAPORT, D. The scatter in diagnostic intelligence testing. *Char. and Person.,* 1944, 12, 275-289. *118.*
SCHMIDT, B. Reflektorische Reaktion auf Form und Farbe und ihre typologische Bedeutung. *Ztsch. f. Psychol.,* 1936, 137, 245-310. *220.*
SCHOLL, R. Zur Theorie und Typology der teilinhaltlichen Beachtung von Form und Farbe. *Ztsch. Psychol.,* 1927, 101, 281-320. *11, 220, 237.*

SCHRIEDER, E. *Les types Humains.* 3 vols. Paris: Hermann, 1937. *83.*
SCHWERIN, O. Rasse und Körperbau bei 100 Schizophrenen aud Baden. *Allg. Ztsch. f. Psychiat.,* 1936, 105, 121-129. *84.*
SCOTT, W. Personal differences in suggestibility. *Psychol. Rev.,* 1910, 17, 147-154. *169.*
SEARS, P. S. Levels of aspiration of academically successful and unsuccessful children. *J. abn. soc. Psychol.,* 1940, 35, 498-536. *136, 141.*
—— Levels of aspiration in relation to some variables of personality: clinical studies. *J. soc. Psychol.,* 1941, 14, 311-336. *141.*
SEARS, R. N. Dynamic factors in the psychology of humor. *Thesis, Harvard Univ.,* 1934. Quoted by Murray, H., 1938. *230.*
SEASHORE, C. E. Measurements of illusions and hallucinations in normal life. *Stud. Yale Psychol. Lab.,* 1895, 2, 1-67. *169.*
SEASHORE, R. H. Individual differences in motor skills. *J. gen. Psychol.,*1930, 3, 38-66. *145.*
SEGERS, J. E. Recherches sur la perception universelle chez des enfants âgés de 3 à 12 ans et leur application à l'éducation. *J. de. Psychol.,* 1926, 23, 608-622. *220.*
SEMEONOFF, B. Further developments in a new approach to the testing of musical ability. *Brit. J. Psychol.,* 1940, 30, 650-654. *210.*
SENISE, T. Il riso in fisio-patologia. Napoli: *Bibl. d. Stud.,* 1941. *225.*
SHAFFER, L. F. *The psychology of adjustment.* New York: Houghton-Mifflin, 1936. *162.*
SHAW, F. A morphologic study of the functional psychoses. *State Hosp. Quart.,* 1925, 10, 413-421. *84.*
SHELDON, W. H. *The varieties of temperament.* New York: Harper, 1942. *87.*
—— *The varieties of human physique.* New York: Harper, 1940. *87.*
SHEVACH, B. J. Studies in perseveration: VII. Experimental results of tests for sensory perseveration. *J. Psychol.,* 1937, 3, 403-428. *156.*
SIOLI, F., and MEYER, A. Bemerkungen zu Kretschmers Buch "Körperbau und Charakter". *Ztsch. f. d. ges. Psychiat. Nervenkrankh.,* 1922, 80, 439-453. *84.*
SISK, T. K. The interrelations of speed in simple and complex processes. *G. Peabody Coll. Contrib. to Educ.,* 1926, 23, 1-48. *145.*
SKAGGS, E. B. Further studies of bodily sway. *Amer. J. Psychol.,* 1937, 49, 105-108. *274.*
——, SKAGGS, I. S., and JARDON, M. Attention and bodily sway. *Amer. J. Psychol.,* 1932, 44, 749-755. *274.*
SKOGLAND, J. E. A quantitative study of normal and pathological station in human subjects. *Med. Rec.,* 1942, 155, 15-22. *274.*
SLATER, E. The neurotic constitution. A statistical study of two thousand neurotic soldiers. *J. Neurol. Neurosurg. Psychiat.,* 1943, 6, 1-16. *2, 41, 46, 49, 51.*
——, and SLATER, P. A heuristic theory of neurosis. *Ibid.,* 1944, 7, 49-55. *37, 41, 45, 49, 56, 97.*
SLATER, P. Speed of work and intelligence. *Brit. J. Psychol.,* 1938, 29, 55-68. *145.*
—— Scores of different types of neurotics on tests of intelligence. *Brit. J. Psychol.,* 1945, 35, 40-41. *118.*
SMALL, M. H. The suggestibility of children. *Ped. Sem.,* 1896, 4, 176-220. *169.*
SMITH, B. The conversion of scores on Group Test 33 to intelligence quotients. *Occup. Psychol.,* 1940, 14, 184-197. *126.*
SMITH, H. Night blindness. *J. Amer. med. Ass.,* 1921, 77, 1001-1003. *97.*
SNOW, A. J. Tests for transportation pilots. *J. appl. Psychol.,* 1926, 10, 37-51. *148.*

SOROKIN, P. A., and BOLDYREFF, J. W. An experimental study of the influence of suggestion on the discrimination and the valuation of people. *Amer. J. Sociol.*, 1932, 37, 720-737. *168.*

SPEARMAN, C. *The abilities of man.* London: Macmillan, 1927. *12, 16, 25, 112, 156.*

—— *Creative mind.* New York: Appleton, 1931. *205.*

—— *Psychology through the ages.* London: Macmillan, 1938. *97.*

—— Thurstone's work reworked. *J. educ. Psychol.*, 1939, 30, 1-16. *25.*

SPIEGEL, E. G., and SOMMER, I. Vestibular mechanisms. In: Medical physics (O. Glasser, Ed.) *Yearbook Publ.*, 1944. *273.*

STAGNER, R. *Psychology of personality.* London: MacGraw-Hill, 1937. *26, 27.*

STAUFFACHER, J. C. The effect of induced muscular tension upon various phases of the learning process. *J. exp. Psychol.*, 1937, 21, 26-46. *194.*

STEPHENSON, W. Correlating persons instead of tests. *Char. and Person.*, 1935, 4, 17-24. *211.*

—— A new application of correlation to averages. *Brit. J. educ. Psychol.*, 1936, 6, 43-57. *208, 21.*

—— The inverted factor technique. *Brit. J. Psychol.*, 1936, 26, 344-361. *208, 211.*

STERN, W. *Über Psychologie der individuellen Differenzen.* Leipzig: Barth, 1900. *13.*

ST. GEORGE, M. V. Color preferences of college students with reference to chromatic pull, learning, and association. *Amer. J. Psychol.*, 1938, 51, 716-723. *207.*

STOCKARD, C. R. Human types and growth reactions. *Amer. J. Anat.*, 1923, 31, 261-269. *75.*

STRONGIN, E. I., and HINSIE, L. E. Parotid gland secretions in manic-depressive patients. *Amer. J. Psychiat.*, 1938, 94, 1459-1466. *96.*

—, —— A method for differentiating manic-depressive depressions from other depressions by means of parotid secretions. *Psychiat. Quart.*, 1939, 13, 697-704. *96.*

STROOP, J. R. Studies of interference in serial verbal reactions. *J. exp. Psychol.*, 1935, 18, 643-661. *155.*

STROUD, J. The role of muscle tension in stylus maze learning. *J. exp. Psychol.*, 1931, 14, 606-631. *195.*

STUDMAN, L. G. Studies in experimental psychiatry: V. W and F factors in relation to traits of personality. *J. ment. Sci.*, 1935, 81, 107-137. *41, 55, 146.*

STUMP, N. Sense of humor and its relationship to personality, scholastic aptitude, emotional maturity, height and weight. *J. gen. Psychol.*, 1939, 20, 25-32. *225.*

STUMPFL, F. *Die Ursprünge des Verbrechens, dargestellt am Lebenslauf von Zwillingen.* Leipzig, 1936. *46.*

STURT, M. A comparison of speed with accuracy in the learning process. *Brit. J. Psychol.*, 1921, 12, 289-300. *147.*

SUPER, R. The Bernreuter personality inventory: a review of research. *Psychol. Bull.*, 1942, 39, 94-125. *55.*

SUTHERLAND, J. D. The speed factor in intelligent reactions. *Brit. J. Psychol.*, 1934, 24, 276-294. *146.*

SYBEL, J. G. Biographische Nachrichten über . . . G. C. Beireis. *Asklä-pieion*, 1811, 810. *194.*

SYMONDS, C. P. The human response to flying stress; neurosis in flying personnel. *Brit. med. J.*, 1943, 2, 703-706. *46.*

SYMONDS, P. M. *Diagnosing personality and conduct.* New York: Appleton Century, 1931. *60.*

Symposium on Operationism, *Psychol. Rev.*, 1945, 52, 241-294. *22.*

TANSLEY, A. G. *The new psychology.* New York: Dodd, Mead, 1925. *57.*

TAYLOR, H. C., and RUSSELL, J. T. The relationship of validity coefficients to the practical effectiveness of tests of selection. *J. appl. Psychol.*, 1939, 23, 565-578. *214.*

TENDLER, A. D. The mental state of psychoneurotics. *Arch. of Psychol.*, 1923, 60. *112, 118.*

THOMSON, G. H. *The factorial analysis of human ability.* Boston: Houghton Mifflin, 1939. *17, 19, 31.*

THORNDIKE, E. L. Ideo-motor action. *Psychol. Rev.*, 1913, 20, 91-106. *194.*

—— *Educational psychology.* 3 vols. New York: Columbia University Press, 1913.

—— The relation between speed and accuracy in addition. *J. educ. Psychol.*, 1915, 5, 537-542. *147, 148.*

—— The measurement of intelligence. *Bur. of Publ., Teach. Coll., Columbia Univ.*, 1926. *26.*

THORNTON, G. R., and GUILFORD, J. P. A factor analysis of some tests purporting to measure persistence. *Psychol. Bull.*, 1938, 35, 708-709. *159.*

THORSON, A. The relation of tongue movements to internal speech. *J. exp. Psychol.*, 1925, 8, 1-32. *194.*

THURSTONE, L. L. *The vectors of mind.* Chicago: University of Chicago Press, 1935. *16, 19, 25, 31.*

—— Primary mental abilities. *Psychometrika Mon.*, 1938. *25.*

——, and THURSTONE, T. G. *Factorial studies of intelligence.* Chicago: University of Chicago Press, 1942. *25.*

TIFFIN, J. *Industrial psychology.* New York: Prentice Hall, 1943. *148, 214.*

TIPPETT, L. H. C. *The methods of statistics.* London: 1941. *124.*

TISCHNER, R. Zur Geschichte des ideomotorischen Prinzips. *Ztsch. f. Parapsychol.*, 1929, 4, 75-85, 155-161: *193.*

TOBIE, H. Die Entwicklung der teilinhaltlichen Beachtung von Farbe und Form in vorschulpflichtigem Kindesalter. *Ztsch. f. angew. Psychol.*, 1926, Beih. 38, 1-32. *220.*

TOD, H., and JONES, M. Study of choline esterase activity in nervous and mental disorders. *Quart. J. Med.*, 1937, 6, 1-3. *101, 102, 103.*

TRAVIS, L. E., and HUNTER, T. A. The relationship between 'intelligence' and reflex conduction rate. *J. exp. Psychol.*, 1928, 11, 342-354. *175.*

——, and YOUNG, C. W. The relations of electromyographically measured reflex times in the patellar and Achilles tendon reflexes to certain physical measurements and to intelligence. *J. gen. Psychol.*, 1930, 3, 374-400. *145.*

TRAWICK, M. Trait-consistency in personality: a differential investigation. *Arch. of Psychol.*, 1940, 248. *15.*

TROW, W. C. Trait consistency and speed of decision. *Sch. and Soc.*, 1925, 21, 538-542. *146.*

TUCKEY, C. L. *Treatment by hypnosis and suggestion.* London: Baillère, Tindall and Co., 1921. *162.*

UHRBROCK, R. S. An analysis of the Downey Will Temperament tests. *Columbia Univ. Teach. Coll. Contrib. Educ.*, 1928, 296. *146.*

VANELLI, A. *La constituzione somatica degli schizofrenici.* Schizofrenie, 1932, 1, 3-14. *85.*

VERNON, P. E. The American *v.* the German methods of approach to the study of temperament and personality. *Brit. J. Psychol.*, 1933, 24, 156-168. *23.*

—— A study of the norms and the validity of certain mental tests at a child guidance clinic. Brit. J. educ. Psychol., 1937, 7, 72-88, 115-137. *117.*

—— *The assessment of psychological qualities by verbal methods.* London: H. M. Stationery Off., 1938. *41, 52, 55, 60.*

VERWORN, M. Ideoplastische Kunst. Jena, 1914. *205.*

VIOLA, G. La costituzione individuale. Bologna: Cappeli, 1933. *75.*

VOLKELT, H. Fortschritte der experimentellen Kinderpsychologie. *Ber. uber d. 9 Kongr. f. exp. Psychol.*, Jena, 1926, 80. *220.*

WALKER, K. F., STAINES, R. G., and KENNA, J. C. Is there a general factor of perseveration? *Aust. J. Psychol. Phil.*, 1943, 19, 58-75. *156.*

——, ——, —— The influence of scoring methods upon score in motor perseveration. *Brit. J. Psychol.*, 1945, 35, 51-60. *157.*

WALLACE, G. B. *The marihuana problem in the City of New York.* Lancaster, Pa.: J. Cattell, 1944. *275.*

WALLIN, J. E. W. Experimental studies of mental defectives. *Educ. Psychol. Mon.*, 1912, 7. *274.*

—— A further note on scattering in the Binet scale. *J. appl. Psychol.*, 1927, 11, 143-154. *118.*

WALTON, W. E., GUILFORD, R. B., and GUILFORD, J. P. Color preferences of 1279 university students. *Amer. J. Psychol.*, 1933, 45, 322-328. *207.*

WANG, C. K. A. A scale for measuring persistence. *J. soc. Psychol.*, 1932, 3, 79-90. *70.*

WARREN, H. C. (Ed.) *Dictionary of psychology.* Boston: Houghton Mifflin, 1934. *23, 24, 273.*

——, and CARMICHAEL, L. *Elements of human psychology.* Boston: Houghton Mifflin, 1930. *23.*

WASHBURN, M. F., KEELER, K., NEW, K. B., and PASSHAL, F. M. Experiments in the relation of reaction time, cube fluctuation and mirror drawing to temperamental differences. *Amer. J. Psychol.*, 1929, 41, 112-117. *57.*

WATSON, J. B. *Behaviorism.* New York: People's Inst. Pub., 1924. *22, 23, 194.*

WEBB, E. Character and intelligence. *Brit. J. Psychol., Mon.*, 1, 3, 1915. *24, 40.*

WECHSLER, D. *The measurement of adult intelligence.* Baltimore: Williams and Wilkins, 1941. *122.*

WEISSENFELD, F. Körperbau und Charakter. *Ztsch. f. d. ges. Neurol. Psychiat.*, 1925, 96, 173. *84.*

WELLS, F. Relation between psychosis and physical type: a statistical study. *Amer. J. Psychol.*, 1938, 51, 136-145. *84.*

WELLS, F. L. *Mental tests in clinical practice.* Yonkers, N.Y.: World Book, 1927. *118.*

WENGER, M. A. The measurement of individual differences in autonomic balance. *Psychosom. Med.*, 1941, 3, 427-434. *95.*

—— The stability of measurement of autonomic balance. *Psychosom. Med.*, 1942, 4, 94-85. *95.*

—— A study of physiological factors: the autonomic nervous system and the skeletal musculature. *Human Biol.*, 1942, 14, 69-84. *95.*

WERTHAM, K., and GOLDEN, L. A differential-diagnosis method of interpreting mosaics and colored block designs. *Amer. J. Psychiat.*, 1941, 98, 124-131. *237.*

WERTHEIMER, F. I., and HESKETH, F. E. *The significance of the physical constitution in Mental disease.* Baltimore: Williams and Wilkins, 1926. *75, 84.*

WHEELER, D., and JORDAN, H. Change of individual opinion to accord with group opinion. *J. abn. soc. Psychol.*, 1929, 24, 203-206. *168.*

WHIPPLE, G. M. *Manual of mental and physical tests.* Baltimore: Warwick and York, 1915. *168.*

WHITE, R. S. Motor suggestion in children. *Child Develop.*, 1930, 1, 161-185. *163.*

WHITE, W. A. *Mechanisms of character formation.* New York: Macmillan, 1926. *57.*

WHITEHORN, J. C. In: Interrelationships of mind and body. Baltimore: *Ass. Res. Nerv. Ment. Dis.*, 1939. *102.*

——, LUNDHOLM, H., and GARDNER, G. E. Concerning the alleged correlation of intelligence with knee-jerk reflex time. *J. exp. Psychol.*, 1930, 13, 293-295. *145.*

WIERSMA, E. D. *Bodily build, physiological and psychological function.* Amsterdam, 1933. *86, 155.*

WILLIAMS, E. D., WINTER, L., and WOOD, J. M. Tests of literary appreciation. *Brit. J. educ. Psychol.*, 1938, 8, 265-284. *211.*

WILLMAN, J. M. An analysis of humor and laughter. *Amer. J. Psychol.*, 1940, 53, 70-85. *226.*

WILSON, D. J. An experimental investigation of Birkhoff's aesthetic measure. *J. abn. soc. Psychol.*, 1939, 34, 390-394. *208.*

WINSOR, A. L. The effect of mental effort on parotid secretion. *Amer. J. Psychol.*, 1931, 43, 434-446. *97.*

WISSLER, C. The correlation of mental and physical tests. *Psychol. Mon.*, 1901, 3, 1-62. *144, 145.*

WITTKOWER, E., and PILZ, W. Über affektive-somatische Veränderungen: Zur affektiven Beeinflussbarkeit der Speichelsekretion. *Klin. Wochenschr.*, 1932, 11, 717-718. *96.*

——, RODGER, F., SCOTT, G., and SEMEONOFF, B. Night blindness—a psychophysiological study. *Brit. med. J.*, 1941, 2 571, 607. *97.*

WITTSON, C. L., HUNT, W. A., and OLDER, H. J. The use of the multiple-choice Rorschach test in military screening. *J. Psychol.*, 1944, 17, 91-94. *213.*

WÖLFFLIN, H. *Kunstgeschichtliche Grundbegriffe.* München, 1915. *205.*

WORRINGER, A. *Abstraktion und Einfühlung.* München, 1906. *205.*

—— *Formprobleme der Gothik.* München, 1912. *205.*

WRENCH, G. T. *Grammar of life.* London: Heinemann, 1908. *226.*

WU, C. F. Personal tempo and speed in some rate tests. *J. Test.* (Cinese), 1934, 2, 85-94. Quoted by Harrison, 1941. *145, 146.*

WUNDT, W. *Grundfüge der physiologischen Psychologie.* 3 vols. Leipzig: Engelmann, 1903. *23.*

WYRSCH, J. Beitrag zu Kretschmers Lehre vom Körperbau und Charakter. *Ztsch. f. d. ges. Neurol. Psychiat,* 1924, 92, 526. *84.*


YELLOWLEES, H. Discussion. *Proc. Royal Soc. Med.*, 1930, 23, 887. *42.*

YOUNG, P. C. Suggestion as indirection. *J. abn. soc. Psychol.*, 1931, 26, 69-90. *167.*

YUDKIN, A. M. Nutrition as it affects eye. *M. Clin. North Amer.*, 1943, 27, 553-560. *98.*

YUDKIN, J. Critique of Bishop Harman's test for night vision. *Brit. med. J.*, 1943, 1, 633-635. *98.*

YULE, G. P. The resemblance of twins with regard to personal perseveration. *J. ment. Sci.*, 1935, 81, 489-501. *156.*


ZARTMANN, E. N., and CASON, H. The influence of an increase in muscular tension on mental efficiency. *J. exp. Psychol.*, 1934, 17, 671-679. *195.*

ZEIDLER, J. G. *Pantomysterium.* Halle, 1700. *194.*

ZILBOORG, G. *A history of medical psychology.* New York, 1941. *161, 193.*

ZILLIG, M. Experimentelle Untersuchungen über Umstellbarkeit. *Ztsch. f. Psychol.*, 1925, 95, 274-315. *155.*

# INDEX